THE ULTIMATE GUIDE TO
MARATHONS

BY DENNIS CRAYTHORN AND RICH HANNA

MP

MARATHON PUBLISHERS, INC.
SACRAMENTO, CALIFORNIA

THE ULTIMATE GUIDE TO MARATHONS © Copyright 1996 by Marathon Publishers, Inc.

ISBN 0-9655187-0-1

DESIGN AND PRODUCTION: Opus Productions Inc., 300 West Hastings Street, Vancouver British Columbia, Canada V6B 1K6

Distributed to the book trade by Independent Publishers Group (1-800-888-4741).

FRONT COVER PHOTO: New York City Marathon, Jack Gescheidt
BACK COVER PHOTO: St. George Marathon, Tim De Frisco

Printed in Canada

PREFACE

THE ULTIMATE GUIDE TO MARATHONS was conceived in a way that we suspect many other books are born. In October, 1995, we wanted a single resource that would give us the lowdown on marathons across the country — detailed course descriptions, race organization, amenities, course difficulty, and the like. We were shocked when we discovered that no such book existed, and the information that was available was often inaccurate or too general. After speaking to dozens of runners nationwide, expert and ordinary, we decided to undertake the massive effort of researching and writing this book.

We began by sending questionnaires to the race directors of more than 230 marathons throughout North America. We followed up this effort with reminder notices, postcards, and endless telephone calls. After all of our harassment, we received information on 190 marathons, quite a success rate. (Although there are 40 deadbeat race directors lurking out there, so runners beware!)

Concurrently, we funneled questionnaires to runners through the major running clubs in the United States. We asked them to provide us with their perspectives on the marathons they have completed. We scoured the Internet for marathon tidbits. Finally, everywhere we went we spoke to runners about marathons.

After gathering two filing cabinets of data, we compiled our tentative list of the top 100 destination marathons in North America. We then embarked on a series of excursions to visit as many of our top 100 marathon courses as possible. We made eleven separate trips covering more than half of the 50 U.S. states, plus parts of British Columbia, Ontario, Quebec, and New Brunswick. Of our top 100 marathons, we have personally toured or run 72 of them. After many adventures and encounters with highway patrol officers on both coasts and in two countries, we reshuffled our list based on our observations and conversations with fellow runners and pared the 190 races to 180. We completed the last of our trips in July, 1996 and finished the manuscript in September, 1996 — an incredible twelve months of whirlwind activity. Over this period, we have become walking marathon encyclopedias — to the vast amusement of our friends.

The product of our quest lies before you. We hope it provides you with the unbiased information you have been seeking about marathons throughout the continent. You no longer need to rely on the marketing information provided by race directors. In our book, flat and fast means flat and fast. Whether you have never run a marathon, are a long-run veteran seeking a new experience, or are an elite runner looking for some prize money, we hope THE ULTIMATE GUIDE TO MARATHONS becomes your marathon bible. Please keep your eye out for Marathon Publishers' future running guide titles and other books.

Dennis Craythorn
Rich Hanna
October, 1996

ACKNOWLEDGMENTS

We are indebted to many people for the completion of this book — especially Visa, Mastercard, and American Express. Slightly more seriously, our first thanks must go to our parents, Sheldon and Dorothy Craythorn, and Bob Hanna, who supported us from the beginning, both emotionally and financially. The Craythorns also supplied us with office space and innumerable brown bag lunches. We can never fully repay them, but we intend to try.

One thing we learned over the course of this project is that there are many people out there who talk a lot and then don't deliver when the time comes. Suzanne Rogers, our attorney and sounding board, was the one person we could rely upon without question. Without her guidance and tireless work on our behalf, we can honestly say that this book would never have been completed on time. Thanks also go to Suzanne's husband, Brian Plant, for keeping us sane during crunch times with his comic relief and witty perspective.

Of course, this book could not exist without significant financial support. Here, we are grateful for the participation of Andre Agassi and the folks at Agassi Enterprises — especially Perry Rogers and Marcia Ragan.

Brenda Dominguez and Suzanne Martinez provided critical writing assistance with the second part of the book. Several individuals reviewed portions of the manuscript, giving us very valuable comments and insights. We would particularly like to thank Alison Hanna, Laura Kulsik, Eric Wolfe, Margarita Altimirano, and Suzanne Martinez.

Thanks Tracy Reusch for handling many of our advertising chores and for keeping our phone bills so high. Dave Stringer provided feedback on many of our hair-brained marketing ideas.

Bjorn Gregersen took some wildly different elevation profiles and turned them into a uniform, attractive bunch that should help runners determine which courses are truly downhill.

Scores of race directors across North America provided us with information about their races. A few, however, went beyond the necessary. While it did not affect their ratings, we would like to thank them here: Bob Craver, Andrea Riha, Scott Schneider, Leopold Roberge, Mike Doyle, Peter Stasz, Les Smith, Roger Soler, Keith McClinsey, Captain Mal Granville, Carey Pinkowski, Frank Dobbs, and Lyle Clugg.

Nancy Hobbs, former race director of the Pikes Peak Marathon, provided the bulk of our information on that race. Thanks Nancy.

Special thanks also go to Tom Peterson for providing us with vast amounts of interesting, and in some cases eccentric, information on the Honolulu Marathon.

Hundreds of runners around the country gave us their perspectives on the marathons they have completed. Many of their comments have found their way into the book in some form. We are indebted to them all. Among those who provided especially detailed comments are: Cary Craig, Leonard T. Fisher, Steve Bainbridge, Paul Hargrave, Marilyn Arguelles, David Williams, Lou Peyton, Barbara Hildebrand, Leon Roby Blue, John Hunt, Carl Sakamoto, Will Aslin, Ruth Carter, Raouf Mallouh, Tony Milevsky, Jeff Bertram, Kathy Bell, Kathy Cook, Andre Tocco, Chris Morlan, David Greenberg, John Mason, Vic Lyons, John Brittain, and Jeff Hildebrandt. Thanks also Rodney Grossman for helping two non-surfers catch a few Internet waves.

In our long and extensive travels researching this book, a few people stand out in their assistance. Barry Duncan put us up, whipped up some excellent brats, poured us some mighty tasty brew from his personal tap, and showed us the sights of Milwaukee. Next time, Barry, we have to sample the custard. We are also grateful to the staff at the Hyatt Regency — Sacramento, especially Jennifer Block, Jeff Miller, Wendy Chynoweth, and Richard Hernandez.

We must thank our distributor, Independent Publishers Group, and its president, Curt Matthews, for believing in us and our company. We are grateful to the team at Opus Productions for producing this book in record time — especially Derik Murray, David Counsell, Joseph Llamzon, and Don Bull. Phillips Design came through with our ad designs on almost no notice thanks to Jill Chan and Lee Phillips.

Finally, thanks to all of the photographers and individuals who sent us the great shots used in the book.

TABLE OF CONTENTS

THE LEAD PACK
TOP 100 DESTINATION MARATHONS

THE MID PACK
80 LOCAL MARATHONS

APPENDIX
MARATHON RANKINGS AND COURSE PROFILES

INDEX

PHOTOGRAPHER CREDITS

MAUI SWEEPSTAKES

ABOUT THE AUTHORS

INTRODUCTION

HOW TO USE THIS BOOK

This book was written for runners who want to travel to a marathon, whether it be for a vacation or to try for a PR. It is divided into two main sections — our top 100 destination marathons and 80 other marathons. The Appendix contains a number of fun and useful rankings, and course profiles, arranged in alphabetical order, for many of our top 100 races.

THE LEAD PACK: TOP 100 DESTINATION MARATHONS

Organized chronologically, this section contains complete entries on our top 100 destination marathons. Each entry consists of information that will be useful to all types of runners.

HOW TO READ THE RATINGS

Beneath the title of each entry there is a series of ratings. The overall rating indicates our cumulative assessment of the race as a destination marathon, i.e., a marathon that a runner may want to travel to and perhaps build a vacation around. The top-ranked marathon, the Big Sur International Marathon, was assigned a score of 100, and every other marathon's score is a percentage of Big Sur's. The factors that make up the overall score are: course beauty, destination value of the location, race organization, and level of crowd support. The next four ratings (course beauty, course difficulty, appropriateness for first timers, and race organization) are based on a 10-point scale and are modified by pluses and minuses, just like school grades. Therefore, a score of 9- exceeds an 8+. The following legend applies to our scores for course beauty, appropriateness for first timers, and race organization:

10	**EXCEPTIONAL**
9	**VERY GOOD**
8	**GOOD**
7	**FAIR**
<6	**POOR**

For course difficulty, the following legend applies:

9-10	**EXTREMELY DIFFICULT**
7-8	**VERY DIFFICULT**
5-6	**MODERATELY DIFFICULT, ROLLING WITH SOME GOOD GRADES**
4	**AVERAGE DIFFICULTY, MOSTLY ROLLING**
3	**SLIGHTLY ROLLING**
2	**MOSTLY FLAT**
1	**PERFECTLY FLAT, FEW TURNS**

The **COURSE BEAUTY** rating scores just that. We tend to mark down courses that pass strip malls, urban blight, and industrial parks. We also tend to cast disfavor on monotonous scenery and never-ending brownness. So much for our biases. The **COURSE DIFFICULTY** rating considers the elevation changes along the route (i.e., hills), number of turns, running surface, altitude, and average weather conditions. The higher the score, the more difficult the course. A course difficulty rating of 3 indicates a relatively fast course, while an 8 denotes a very challenging route. You may use this rating as our equivalent of the relative quickness of the course. The **RACE ORGANIZATION** score consists of an overall evaluation of the race structure. It considers a wide range of factors, including professionalism of race personnel, amount and quality of race amenities (aid stations, pre/post-race activities, transportation, awards), volunteers, and general quality of the race. The **APPROPRIATENESS FOR FIRST TIMERS** is our attempt to help novice marathoners choose the right race for them. To us, the perfect first-timer marathon has a scenic course, excellent race organization, lots of aid stations, few hills, and huge crowds. We consider all of these factors in compiling this score. The **CROWDS** rating is based on a 5-point scale, with 5 indicating huge crowds, and 0 indicating you and your fellow runners.

WHAT'S IN A FULL ENTRY?

Following the ratings is a boxed section called **RACE DATA** containing useful information about the race. It tells you where to write or call to obtain an application; the dates of the 1997 and 1998 races; race start time; time course closes; number of runners in the most recent year; whether the course is certified and by whom (times run on certified courses may be used for entry into the Boston Marathon); course records for open and masters runners where available (many races do not maintain masters records); whether the race offers anything special to elite runners (e.g., free entry, expenses, transportation, lodging, prize money); entry fees (all amounts are in the local currency unless otherwise noted); age groups; average temperatures on race day (ranges indicate start time and noon); the number of aid stations on the course; and the location of split times.

The first narrative section consists of race **HIGHLIGHTS**. Here we try to capture the essence of the race; what makes this marathon special or not so special. Some races have interesting or noteworthy **RACE HISTORIES**. These histories follow the highlights section. The **COURSE DESCRIPTION** contains a detailed account of the course from a runner's perspective. It tells you what you see along the way and the location of major hills and terrain changes. **CROWDS/RUNNER SUPPORT** discusses the level of crowd support along the course and the locations of the greatest concentration of spectators. It also details the aid stations, medical assistance, and entertainment during the race. **RACE LOGISTICS** explains how to get to the race start and back. **ACTIVITIES** enumerates the pre and post-race activities offered by the event, including where to get your race packet, the pasta dinner, expo, victory party, awards ceremony, and any other activities. **AWARDS** lets you know about T-shirts, medals, age-group awards, prize money, and other relevant goodies. Races that have programs for elite runners contain an **ELITE RUNNER INFORMATION** section. It explains the race's criteria for elite status, what the race may offer you, and breaks down the prize money structure, including course record bonuses. A few races give **SPECIAL INFORMATION FOR FIRST TIMERS**. We also list some **ACCOMMODATIONS** convenient to the race site, including the host hotel, hotels offering discounts to marathon entrants, and in some cases other lodging options. All prices are in the local currency unless otherwise noted, i.e., amounts under Canadian races are given in Canadian dollars. **RELATED RACES/EVENTS** lists other races that run in conjunction with the marathon, such as a marathon relay, half marathon, 10K, 5K, and kids races. The **AREA ACTIVITIES** section gives you a general idea of the sights and things-to-do in the area. Not an exhaustive list, this section is intended only to help you decide whether to attend that particular marathon. You may still need to buy a relevant travel guide for that area should you want to linger before or after the race. Finally, most entries indicate a **LOCAL RUNNING STORE** should you require any last-minute items.

THE MID PACK:
180 LOCAL MARATHONS

These marathons did not make our top 100 destination marathons list, and in most cases are primarily local affairs. For these races, also organized chronologically, we indicate the contact information, 1997 and 1998 race dates (subject to change), and summarize the race. Most entries contain a brief course description, discuss race activities, and provide host hotel information.

APPENDIX:
RANKINGS AND COURSE PROFILES

Most of the rankings in this section are self evident, except perhaps for our **TOP 25 FASTEST MARATHONS** ranking. This ranking indicates what we believe to be the fastest races in North America. Similar rankings in other publications have used such things as course records, percentage of PRs, and the like. We believe such criteria are misleading at best. Instead, we try to consider the factors that affect a runner's performance at a given race. It is our firm belief that many variables determine whether a race is fast or slow. Our ranking considers three broad factors in descending order of importance: course difficulty, race organization, and crowd support. The most important ingredient is the course. Is it flat, rolling, or hilly? Where are the biggest hills, early or late? Are there many turns that could disrupt a runner's rhythm? What is the running surface? We personally toured 72 of the 100 courses considered under this ranking. For the other 28 races we relied upon detailed discussions with scores of runners who had completed the courses, and we reviewed course maps, elevation profiles, and other data. The second ingredient to producing a fast race is organization. The more support a runner has before, during and after a race the better his prospects for a fast time. Fewer hassles mean less energy spent worrying about details and logistics, and more energy reserved for running. The third ingredient is crowd support. Any runner can tell you that the extra lift provided by spectators can make the difference between pushing through the hurt and giving in to the struggle. The energy at Boston, New York, and LA contribute to faster times than would otherwise be run on those courses. We believe that the ranking of the fastest races based on our formula is the most accurate yet produced. There is always room for fine-tuning, however, and we welcome your comments.

A Note to Fellow Runners Many of you will undoubtedly disagree with some of our opinions, assessments, and various rankings. Reasonable people can differ. We have tried to be unbiased and thoughtful in our judgements, but we are human. Furthermore, races change constantly. We have made every conceivable effort to ensure the information in this book is as up-to-date and accurate as possible. However, there will be changes over the next two years. So, please, before making any plans or final decisions, contact the races themselves to get the latest information, especially race dates. We cannot be responsible for any inconvenience, loss, or other unhappiness you encounter. If you do have any suggestions, updates, or differing opinions, please let us know. Be as specific and constructive as you can; generic comments are of little use. For example, telling us we missed a huge hill toward the end of the race does us no good. But informing us that we missed a steep, half-mile hill at the 20-mile mark is very useful. Your comments will play a large role in improving the next edition of **The Ultimate Guide to Marathons**.

Direct all correspondence to:

The Ultimate Guide to Marathons
c/o Marathon Publishers, Inc.
P.O. Box 19027
Sacramento, CA 95819
USA

THE LEAD PACK

TOP 100 DESTINATION MARATHONS

CHARLOTTE OBSERVER MARATHON

OVERALL: 82.1

COURSE BEAUTY: 8

COURSE DIFFICULTY: 6+ (SEE APPENDIX)

APPROPRIATENESS FOR FIRST TIMERS: 8-

RACE ORGANIZATION: 9

CROWDS: 1+

RACE DATA

Contact: Marathon Administrator
Charlotte Observer Marathon
P.O. Box 30294
Charlotte, NC 28230
(704) 358-5425
Date: January 4, 1997
January 3, 1998
Start Time: 8:00 a.m.
Time Course Closes: 1:00 p.m.
Number of Participants: 957 in 1996
Certification: USATF
Course Records: Male: (open) 2:28:18
Female: (open) 3:20:03
Elite Athlete Programs: No
Cost: $15
Age groups/Divisions: <14, 15-19, 20-24, 25-29, 30-34, 35-39, 40-44,
45-49, 50-54, 55-59, 60-64, 65-69, 70-74, 75+
Temperature: 51°
Aid/Splits: 25 / every five miles

HIGHLIGHTS If you're the type of runner who has to run a PR each time out, then the Charlotte Observer Marathon, with its ever-present hills, probably isn't the race for you. If, however, you can pull yourself away from the PR chase, the Charlotte course offers a wonderful tour of some of the Queen City's most exclusive neighborhoods. Running under Charlotte's signature towering oak trees, the course takes you past the beautiful estate of golfer Arnold Palmer. You also run much of the same course used for the 1996 Olympic Marathon Trials, including the Providence Road pavement, between miles 23 and 24, where Trials winner Bob Kempainen made history by vomiting six times during a sub-five-minute mile.

COURSE DESCRIPTION The Charlotte Observer Marathon's hilly course runs on very smooth pavement through mostly residential and commercial areas of town. It's a challenging race. Although the first 10 miles produce a net drop of 150 feet, significant uphills keep you honest. The last 16 miles include more ups and downs than the stock market. Starting at Tryon and Stonewall Streets (the highest point on the course at 760 feet) in the heart of downtown, the course rises gently before turning left onto Morehead around the half-mile mark. After 1.5 miles, runners head through Myers Park West, one of Charlotte's most exclusive neighborhoods and usually teeming with spectators. The first significant incline occurs at mile 2.8 on Queens Road West. At mile 3.2, the course turns right on Selwyn Road, continues mostly downhill, and then goes sharply downhill from mile 4.8 to the turn onto Park Road at mile 4.9. With an already tough uphill from 4.9 to 5.5 miles, wind can also hinder you at this point as it is the barest part of the route. Another good uphill arises between miles 7.2 and 7.4 with a gradual descent from mile 7.6 to the turnaround at the 9.5-mile mark, possibly the race's fastest section. Tough and desolate, miles 10 to 11.9 roll with a net elevation rise of 40 feet. A nice downhill at 13.2 miles prefaces perhaps the most grueling climb on the course, 80 feet from mile 13.4 to 14.2. At 14.4 miles, the route begins to level off and is flat between miles 15 and 17 through high-traffic SouthPark (known for its shopping and upscale modern homes), providing a chance to recover from the preceding hills. Following a 30-foot drop from 18 to 18.3 miles, the road climbs 60 feet from 19.3 to 19.8 miles, turning left onto Randolph. Here, a brief downhill precedes a 3-mile incline before leveling off at the 21-mile mark. Relatively flat to mile 22.3, the race drops 50 feet between miles 22.8 and 23, followed by an easy rise to mile 23.5. Leveling off in Myers Park East, the route climbs from mile 24.1 to 24.4 as it approaches downtown. Then mostly rolling, the race climaxes with a .25-mile gradual uphill on 2nd Street to the finish.

CROWD/RUNNER SUPPORT Although Charlotte is better known for its beloved stock car racing, crowd support for the marathon increases every year. Scattered along the course, spectators mainly target Myer's Park West (2 to 3 miles), SouthPark (15 to 16 miles), Myer's Park East (23 to 24 miles), and the finish on 2nd Street. While open to traffic with one lane dedicated to runners, the roads allow supporters to maneuver easily around the route to cheer their favorite runners.

RACE LOGISTICS The start and finish areas lie near the downtown hotels, so transportation is not a concern. There is transportation to the finish for dropouts. Baggage deposit is available at the start line, with pickup at the finish.

ACTIVITIES The Charlotte Observer Marathon features a two-day Health, Fun & Fitness Expo beginning Friday from 11:00 a.m. to 9:00 p.m. at First Union Atrium in the 300 block of South Tryon Street. Packet pickup, late registration, running clinics and the Carb-Up Party (5:30 p.m.) take place here. Unofficial finish times are printed in the Sunday edition of the Charlotte Observer newspaper. Official results are mailed with the Race Review a month after the race.

AWARDS Every runner receives a T-shirt. However, a reduced entry fee is available for those who do not want a shirt. Each finisher is presented with a custom-designed medallion. Additionally, handsome finisher certificates are available for $1. The first three finishers in each age group receive recognition awards.

ACCOMMODATIONS The Westin Hotel, 222 East Third Street downtown (704-377-4441), serves as the race headquarters. Other hotels near the start/finish area include the Radisson Plaza Hotel, 101 South Tryon Street (704-377-0400); Charlotte Marriott City Center, 100 West Trade Street (704-333-9000); Holiday Inn — City Center, 230 North College Street (704-335-5400); and Adam's Mark Hotel, 555 South McDowell Street (704-372-4100).

RELATED EVENTS/RACES Race day features several other events for runners of all abilities. The Family Fun Run 1 Mile kicks off at 7:45 a.m. At 8:30 a.m., in one of the largest 10K runs on the East Coast, 4,500 runners attack an out-and-back course over the first 3 miles of the marathon route. For those wanting to sleep in, a 5K fitness walk starts at 9:00 a.m.

AREA ATTRACTIONS If you arrive a few days prior to the race, you can enjoy First Night Charlotte, an alcohol-free, civic arts festival in Uptown Charlotte with performance sites in lobbies, auditoriums, theaters, and church sanctuaries. Other entertainment options include cruising on Lake Norman, touring one of Charlotte's beautiful Victorian neighborhoods, or panning for gold at Reed Gold Mine where the first big gold lode was discovered.

LOCAL RUNNING STORES Run For Your Life, 1412 East Boulevard (704-358-0713) or 10618 Providence Road.

WALT DISNEY WORLD MARATHON

OVERALL: 94

COURSE BEAUTY: 9

COURSE DIFFICULTY: 3-

APPROPRIATENESS FOR FIRST TIMERS: 10

RACE ORGANIZATION: 10-

CROWDS: 2

R A C E   D A T A

Contact:	Walt Disney World Marathon
	P.O. Box 10,000
	Lake Buena Vista, FL 32830-1000
	(407) 939-7810
Date:	January 5, 1997
	January 11, 1998
Start Time:	6:30 a.m.
Time Course Closes:	1:30 p.m.
Number of Participants:	5,446 in 1996
Certification:	USATF
Course Records:	Male: (open) 2:11:50; (masters) 2:20:26
	Female: (open) 2:31:54; (masters) 2:49:44
Elite Athlete Programs:	No
Cost:	$50
Age groups/Divisions:	18-24, 25-29, 30-34, 35-39, 40-44, 45-49, 50-54,
	55-59, 60-64, 65+ (F), 65-69, 70+ (M)
Temperature:	35° - 65°
Aid/Splits:	16 / digital clocks every mile

HIGHLIGHTS Do you remember running through Walt Disney World as a child, rushing from the Pirates of the Caribbean to It's a Small World? Maybe you never got a chance to visit the home of Mickey Mouse, Goofy, Tinkerbell, and all their friends. Well, here's your opportunity to run as fast as you like through the Magic Kingdom and not be told to slow down by pesky parents. The Walt Disney World Marathon is blooming into a compelling, runner-friendly event with Disney's one-of-a-kind flair. Heeding runners' suggestions to improve the event, race organizers have worked out early kinks with the course and transportation. Now runners complete a fun, entertaining, and flat course, weaving through three theme parks in the 30,000-acre Disney World property. As you would expect, Disney puts on quite a spectacle, including light shows, a torrent of fireworks, lasers, music, and even snow flurries! The race offers a number of packages, including entry fee, two-nights accommodations, carbo-load party, and transportation from $169 to $573. Walt Disney World is a particularly great race for families. Leon Roby Blue of Searcy, Arkansas says, *"It is a good way to include the whole family in the marathon experience. Something for everyone."* This quality alone makes it one of the top destination marathons in the country.

COURSE DESCRIPTION The Disney Marathon begins near Epcot and winds through the Magic Kingdom, Disney-MGM Studios, Epcot, and Disney's new snow-themed water park, Blizzard Beach. The race also passes through several Disney resorts. Extremely flat, with a total elevation change of only 30 feet, the course runs mostly on asphalt, although the surface changes at several points. Many runners report that while flat, the course is not especially fast due to the large number of turns and tight spots. Disney characters mark the miles.

Mickey Mouse fires the starting gun just outside Epcot amid light figures of butterflies, dragonflies, dazzling spheres, and a storm of fireworks. Making it across the start line may take a while, not only because of the large number of runners, but more importantly because of a popular Disney tradition for runners to high-five Mickey and his friends. Running along Epcot Drive for just under 2 miles, you enter Epcot into Future World with lighted musical fountains. While passing eleven nations by dawn, you are greeted by frolicking lasers over World Showcase Lagoon. Runners exit Epcot at about 2.8 miles and return to Epcot Drive for the next 3 miles before merging onto World Drive toward the Magic Kingdom. At about 7.6 miles, runners veer left onto Floridian Way, passing the Polynesian Resort (just before the 9-mile mark) and the Grand Floridian Beach Resort. You enter the Magic Kingdom at mile 10 and stream through Caribbean Plaza, Frontierland, Liberty Square, and right through Cinderella Castle to Fantasyland. Then you jump to Tomorrowland, down Main Street, and by mile 11, it's all over as you exit the Magic Kingdom and head toward Blizzard Beach (just after mile 18) encountering snow flurries in Florida. Your next destination is Disney-MGM Studios where a gaggle of Disney stars greet you (mile 20.7). By mile 25, you're back at Epcot where you circle the Lagoon and finish in the parking lot with the Epcot sphere behind you.

CROWD/RUNNER SUPPORT Once known as one of the loneliest marathons because of thin crowds, the Walt Disney World Marathon has made significant strides in remedying this concern. Monorail takes spectators to several sites along the course, but most of the onlookers stay in Epcot and the other theme parks. In part to make up for smaller crowds, Disney packs in the entertainment along the course from Disney characters, to light presentations, to music. Steve Bainbridge of Fairbanks, Alaska calls the race *"A sensory overload! Nonstop entertainment."*

RACE LOGISTICS Runners take the monorail system or shuttle buses from their Disney Resort hotels to the start. The same transportation can return runners back to their hotels following the race. If you are staying outside the Disney complex, you must provide your own transportation.

ACTIVITIES On Friday and Saturday, visit the Health and Fitness Expo located at the Contemporary Resort Convention Center. On Saturday evening, devour mounds of pasta at the carbo-loading dinner, also at the Contemporary Resort. Following the race, you can reload at the generous food tables. The day after the marathon, complete results and finishers certificates are available at Epcot.

AWARDS Every entrant receives a long-sleeve T-shirt and an official race program. Marathoners who finish under seven hours are awarded heavy Mickey Mouse medallions and finishers' certificates. The top five finishers in each division earn additional awards. Disney no longer awards prize money or recruits elite athletes.

FIRST-TIMERS INFORMATION All of the excitement and thumping entertainment surrounding the race make it a good bet for first-time marathoners. There is nothing quite like that Disney magic to get you psyched up for your first 26.2 miles. In addition, the course is flat, if a bit twisty.

ACCOMMODATIONS Stay in one of the 16 distinctly Disney resorts since it will add significantly to your convenience on race day. Offering a number of race packages at all of its resorts, Disney includes two nights lodging, one race entry fee and carbo-load dinner, free transportation around Walt Disney World, and early theme park admission. Packages start at $169 for campsites at the Fort Wilderness Resort, and continue to: $240 at the All-Star Resorts; $293 for the Port Orleans and Dixie Landings Resorts; $382 at the headquarters Contemporary Resort (Tower) or $429 for the garden view; and $429 for the Wilderness Lodge and Polynesian Resort. For top-of-the-line accommodations, try the Grand Floridian Beach Resort at $573. For more information on resort packages call (407-939-7810) and reference Walt Disney World Marathon registration.

RELATED EVENTS / RACES Walt Disney presents the FamilyFun Run on Saturday morning beginning at 7:30 a.m. at Epcot. Open to the public ($15), the 5K runs through Epcot with a finish at the marathon finish line. Participants receive long-sleeve T-shirts. There are also shorter events for youngsters to earn their prized Mickey Mouse ears.

AREA ATTRACTIONS The big attraction in the area is the Walt Disney World complex itself, with its three theme parks, nighttime entertainment complex, three water parks, a zoological park, golf, tennis, and even an Indy Car track. In May 1997, a 200-acre, state-of-the-art sports complex opens that will include something for any sport fan. The complex will include the Atlanta Braves' new spring training facility, an 11-court tennis center, beach volleyball courts, a track and field stadium, basketball courts, and the Official All-Star Cafe, a sports-themed family restaurant owned by several sports celebrities. In all, the facility will accommodate some 32 sports.

LOCAL RUNNING STORE Track Shack, 1322 N. Mills Avenue (407- 898-1313).

HOUSTON MARATHON

OVERALL: 87.8

COURSE BEAUTY: 6+

COURSE DIFFICULTY: 2+

APPROPRIATENESS FOR FIRST TIMERS: 9+

RACE ORGANIZATION: 10+

CROWDS: 4+

RACE DATA

Contact:	Houston-Methodist Marathon
	720 North Post Oak Road, Ste. 335
	Houston, TX 77024
	(713) 957-3453
	http://www.chron.com/~marathon
Date:	January 12, 1997
	January 18, 1998
Start Time:	8:00 a.m.
Time Course Closes:	1:00 p.m.
Number of Participants:	6,147 in 1996
Certification:	USATF
Course Records:	Male: (open) 2:10:04
	Female: (open) 2:27:51
Elite Athlete Programs:	Yes
Cost:	$35/45
Age groups/Divisions:	<19, 20-24, 25-29, 30-34, 35-39, 40-44, 45-49, 50-54,
	55-59, 60-64, 65+ (F), 65-69, 70-74, 75+ (M)
Temperature:	45° - 50°
Aid/Splits:	24 / every mile from mile 2

HIGHLIGHTS Do you like hoopla, the noisy, uplifting, and often crazy entertainment along so many marathons routes today? Pioneering the hoopla phenomenon, the Houston Marathon does it better than most. With nearly every mile packed with some form of entertainment, the course loops through the city and its suburbs. A good place to try for a PR, the race offers excellent organization, superb runner support, ideal weather conditions, and substantial crowds.

RACE HISTORY A five-mile loop course marked by a parked station wagon debuted as the Houston Marathon in December 1972. Seventy-three runners endured that race and were treated to beef stew afterwards. Taking up sponsorship of the race in 1980, Tenneco Energy helped it blossom. In fact, in 1992, Houston was the site of the women's Olympic Marathon Trials. Houston also has been chosen as the site of the U.S. Corporate Athletics Association Marathon Championship. Tenneco ended its support of the race in 1996, ending one of the longest standing marathon partnerships. Over the years, Houston has witnessed some remarkable races, including perhaps the closest marathon finish in U.S. history: in 1984, a photo revealed that Charlie Spedding literally won by his foot.

COURSE DESCRIPTION The Houston Marathon's loop course starts and finishes downtown at the George R. Brown Convention Center. Passing through many of Houston's ethnically diverse neighborhoods, the race is completely closed to vehicular traffic. Houston sports a dual start, with men departing from LaBranch Street and women beginning on Crawford Street.

After the cannon-blast start, runners head for the Elysian Viaduct. At mile 1, which is on the viaduct, the course reaches one of its highest points at 85 feet. One of Houston's oldest neighborhoods, a Hispanic barrio in Houston's near north side, awaits runners on the down side of the viaduct and provides a fiesta atmosphere as runners pass mariachi bands and dancers. As the men and women merge at 2.5 miles, they head back into downtown, crossing the Main Street Bridge in front of the University of Houston's Downtown campus. After passing the 5-mile mark in the midst of downtown skyscrapers, runners continue south down Main Street toward its booming Asian office and retail centers. Mile 7 takes runners through a middle-class neighborhood where residents bring the kids out to view the race. Mile 8 brings the Herman Park Rose Garden and the Mecom Fountain. Between miles 8 and 9, enjoy the oak trees arching over Main Street as you run toward the beautiful Rice University Campus. Around 10.5 miles, runners enter trendy, fashionable West University Place, featuring some of Houston's finer homes. Soak in the encouragement here to fortify yourself for the Westpark Hump at the halfway point, a 35-foot climb over a quarter mile, and the following commercial sections of the course. Houston's well-known Galleria shopping area provides good crowd support and takes runners past the Transco Tower, the tallest building in the country that is outside a downtown area, and its sculptured "Water Wall." It's a tough time for runners as they again turn away from downtown at 15 miles. Between 15 and 20 miles, you pass through residential and commercial areas, Riverway, Tangelwood, and Church. At mile 18, you head toward downtown passing George Bush's church. Look for the former president as he's usually watching the runners as they continue downtown toward the finish. Miles 20 to 21.5 lead you through Memorial Park, the training ground for Houston's runners. Leaving the park, runners sense the finish, but must conquer the hills of Allen Parkway, actually two street underpasses that at 23.5 miles can be difficult for many marathoners. After making it through the Allen Parkway bumps, runners make one last pass through downtown. The last mile decorated with confetti streamers is a welcome sight, with the Convention Center finish within view.

CROWD/RUNNER SUPPORT The Houston Marathon provides unparalleled hoopla lining most of the marathon route. The entertainment consists of everything from belly dancers, bands, ballet, gymnastics, bagpipers, to cheerleaders. Complementing the hoopla are approximately 250,000 spectators at various sections of the course. Add on to that water stations and split times every mile, and you have outstanding runner support. Together with the other 6,500 runners, you shouldn't be too lonely out there. The Houston Marathon also supports the Run for a Reason program, where marathoners help raise money for any number of area charities.

RACE LOGISTICS The GRB Convention Center offers excellent indoor facilities for runners before and after the race.

ACTIVITIES Houston hosts a large, three-day Health and Fitness Expo at the GRB Convention Center, starting on Friday and running through race day. There, you can attend numerous seminars on running and fitness topics, pick up your race packet, or register late. There is no race-day registration or packet pickup. After the marathon, relax at the post-race party in the Convention Center.

AWARDS Each entrant receives a marathon T-shirt. Runners who finish under five hours also are awarded finisher T-shirts, glass mugs, and certificates. Trophies are given to the age-group winners, while top athletes compete for about $150,000 in prize money. The first local male and female finishers receive a trip to a top international marathon.

ELITE RUNNERS INFORMATION World-class runners could be offered lodging, travel, and expenses. Open winners receive $20,000, $15,000 for second, $8,000 for third, $6,000 for fourth, $4,000 for fifth, $2,000 for sixth, $1,500 for seventh, $1,000 for eighth, $500 for ninth, and $250 for tenth. The top three American runners also receive $5,000, $2,000, and $1,000 respectively. Masters prize money goes five deep, with $1,500 for first and $200 for fifth.

ACCOMMODATIONS The Hyatt Regency, 1200 Louisiana (800-233-1234), serves as the headquarters hotel for the Houston Marathon, offering runners special room rates. Also convenient are: the Four Seasons Hotel, 1300 Lamar Street (800-332-3442); the DoubleTree Hotel at Allen Center, 400 Dallas Street (800-231-6310); and The Lancaster, 701 Texas Avenue (800-368-5966). A little further out, try the Allen Park Inn, 2121 Allen Parkway (800-231-6310); Harvey Hotel, 2712 Southwest Freeway (713-523-8448); and Ramada Hotel-Galleria, 7787 Katy Freeway (713-681-5000).

RELATED RACES Houston also hosts the Downtown 5000, a 5K run or walk starting just after the marathon at the GRB Convention Center. The Downtown 5000 draws more than 1,500 runners and, as its name implies, tours the downtown area. There is no race-day registration.

AREA ATTRACTIONS While in Houston, you may want to catch a Houston Rockets basketball game at The Summit, 10 Greenway Plaza. Also, tour Space Center Houston for hands-on exhibits and a behind-the-scenes peek at the Johnson Space Center. Bone up on Texas' battle for independence at the San Jacinto Battleground State Historical Park. Houston boasts numerous museums, including the Houston Museum of Natural Science, and its Cockrell Butterfly Center, the Museum of Fine Arts, the Contemporary Arts Museum, and the Menil Collection.

LOCAL RUNNING STORES Fleet Feet Sports, 2408 Rice Blvd. (713-520-6353); Fleet Feet Sports, 6586 Woodway (713-465-0033); Runsport, 2183 Portsmouth (713-524-6662); Finish Line Sports, 13895 S.W. Freeway, Sugarland (713-242-7700); Runsport, 27602 I-45 North, Conroe (713-364-7723).

MARDI GRAS MARATHON

OVERALL: 88.8

COURSE BEAUTY: 9-

COURSE DIFFICULTY: 2+

APPROPRIATENESS FOR FIRST TIMERS: 8-

RACE ORGANIZATION: 9

CROWDS: 1+

RACE DATA

Contact: Chuck George
Nokia-Sugar Bowl Mardi Gras Marathon
New Orleans Track Club, Inc.
P.O. Box 52003
New Orleans, LA 70152-2003
(504) 482-6682 or (504) 468-1488
e-mail: NOTC@aol.com

Date: January 18, 1997
January 17, 1998

Start Time: 8:00 a.m.

Time Course Closes: 1:30 p.m.

Number of Participants: 400 in 1996

Certification: USATF

Course Records: Male: (open) 2:23:57
Female: (open) 2:55:03

Elite Athlete Programs: No

Cost: $25/30

Age groups/Divisions: <19, 20-24 (M), <24 (F), 25-29, 30-34, 35-39, 40-44,
45-49, 50-54, 55-59, 60+ (F), 60-64, 65-69, 70+ (M)

Temperature: 40° - 65°

Aid/Splits: 18 / miles 1, 5, 10K, 10, 13.1, 15 & 20

HIGHLIGHTS New Orleans pops like a firecracker — always explosive, fiery, flashy, illicit, and just this side of dangerous. Hence the appeal. The city's cultural melange provides much of the powder and the spark for the brilliant show, most notoriously exemplified by that brazen February rite known as Mardi Gras. Taking its name from the crazy festival, the Mardi Gras Marathon passes through the site of the festival's madness — the French Quarter — and many other New Orleans attractions: Bayou St. John, Lake Pontchartrain, and Esplanade Avenue. Despite the obvious allure, the Mardi Gras Marathon remains a small race of about 400 runners (the half attracts 1,000 runners), although it expects to grow in future runnings.

COURSE DESCRIPTION Mardi Gras' closed, loop course covers many of its roads twice, giving it an out-and-back quality. The race starts in Tad Gormley Stadium, site of the 1992 Olympic Track Trials and situated in 1,500-acre City Park. Heading to Marconi Drive, the course borders the park until just past the 2-mile mark where it does an about face returning past the stadium and down Roosevelt Mall. After a right turn on Stadium, the route passes through City Park alongside the Peristyle and Bandstand until hitting the Bayou St. John at mile 5.5. Lined with historic houses and mansions, Bayou St. John may be the highlight of the course. Tracing both sides of the Bayou from miles 5.5 to 6.7, runners reach historic Esplanade Avenue, entering the French

Quarter at mile 8.8. The French Quarter's narrow streets burst with beautiful homes and buildings hundreds of years old. In the French Quarter bowels, runners turn right on Royal Street, site of many beautiful homes, including Madame Lalaurie's "haunted house." At Jackson Square, home to musicians, artists, performers, and general crazies, the race follows St. Ann Street before turning on Chartres Street. Back on Esplanade at the 10-mile mark, the course exits the French Quarter at mile 10.3 and continues straight onto Roosevelt Mall (mile 13) and Marconi. Turning right on Harrison at mile 14.2, the course bisects City Park, and then continues up its east side on Wisner (mile 15). Upon reaching Robert E. Lee above the park, runners go into West End (miles 18 to 23), running at times along Lake Pontchartrain's shores on Lakeshore Drive and Breakwater Drive. Inside West End Park on the lake, several yacht construction and repair yards display their crafts on wooden pilings right off the road. With some yachts reaching almost 100 feet in length, the scene is spectacular. The Yacht Harbor also lies along this section. By mile 24, the course heads down Marconi along City Park to the finish at Tad Gormley Stadium.

CROWD/RUNNER SUPPORT Small but growing crowds linger at sections of the course. Numerous live musicians entertain runners in the French Quarter, and the turnaround on Breakwater Drive off Lake Pontchartrain is manned by a local college group which doesn't let you forget you made the turn. Runners are supported by 18 aid stations stocked with water, electrolyte replacement drink, petroleum jelly, hard candies, bananas, and bandages. Portable toilets also sit at several points along the course.

RACE LOGISTICS Race organizers provide bus transportation from the race headquarters hotel to Tad Gormley Stadium from 6:30 a.m. to 7:15 a.m. The race also gets you back to the hotel afterwards from 10:00 a.m. to 1:30 p.m. If you prefer to drive, park at the Stadium, on Victory Avenue, or Marconi Drive, but not on Roosevelt Mall.

ACTIVITIES Pick up your race packet or register at the headquarters hotel on Friday from 3:00 p.m. to 8:00 p.m. or at Tad Gormley Stadium on race morning. Refreshments, including Mardi Gras King Cakes and lots of beer, follow the marathon.

AWARDS Every Mardi Gras runner takes home a long-sleeve T-shirt, and each finisher receives a medallion, certificate, and results booklet. Age-group awards go 2 or 3 deep, and commemorative awards are given to the top three overall and the top masters runners.

ACCOMMODATIONS The Radisson Hotel, 1500 Canal Street (800-824-3359), serves as the official race hotel offering discount rates to Mardi Gras Marathon participants. Other possibilities include the Omni Royal Orleans, 621 St. Louis Street (504-529-5333); Monteleone, 214 Royal Street (504-523-3341); Windsor Court, 300 Gravier Street (504-523-6000); and Westin Canal Place, 100 Iberville Street (504-566-7006).

RELATED EVENTS/RACES Race organizers also offer a half marathon (1,000 runners) and 6K (700 runners).

AREA ATTRACTIONS Although best known for its spicy French Quarter, New Orleans does contain other points of interest. St. Charles Avenue boasts impeccable 19th-century homes, as does the Garden District. Get in your warm-up or warm-down run at Audubon Park, and return later to roam the excellent Audubon Zoo. The swamp curious should tour the Barataria Preserve along Lake Salvador.

LOCAL RUNNING STORE Phidippides, 6601 Veterans Blvd., Metairie (504-887-8900).

SAN DIEGO MARATHON

OVERALL: 88

COURSE BEAUTY: 8+

COURSE DIFFICULTY: 4

APPROPRIATENESS FOR FIRST TIMERS: 7+

RACE ORGANIZATION: 9+

CROWDS: 1

RACE DATA

Contact:	San Diego Marathon
	511 S. Cedros Avenue, Suite B
	Solana Beach, CA 92075
	(619) 792-2900
Date:	January 19, 1997
	January 18, 1998
Start Time:	7:30 a.m.
Time Course Closes:	Noon
Number of Participants:	2,000 in 1996
Certification:	USATF
Course Records:	Male: (open) 2:23:08
	Female: (open) 2:48:17
Elite Athlete Programs:	No
Cost:	$35/40/45
Age groups/Divisions:	<17, 18-24, 25-29, 30-34, 35-39, 40-44, 45-49,
	50-54, 55-59, 60-64, 65-69, 70-74, 75-79, 80+
Temperature:	45° - 72°
Aid/Splits:	26 / 5 points on course

HIGHLIGHTS The San Diego Marathon mixes all the ingredients that make Southern California famous — great weather, beaches, and beautiful scenery — into an appetizing race. The temperate January weather makes for excellent running conditions. The course takes in about 10 miles of the Pacific coastline. And, runners pass through the gorgeous Carlsbad flower fields. You won't, however, find one of the area's biggest headaches — traffic — since the race course is completely closed to vehicles. Known more for its larger half marathon, San Diego hopes to grow the full race into the premiere event. The race also makes a strong effort to attract runners of all abilities by offering early start times.

COURSE DESCRIPTION San Diego's modified out-and-back course circles the Plaza Camino Real shopping complex for just over a mile before making its way to the Pacific Ocean. Reaching water by 3.33 miles, runners go north on Carlsbad Blvd. for a brief detour, before turning around and heading south along the ocean (miles 3.66 to 7). Angling inland, the route moves through the Carlsbad flower fields (mile 10) on Palomar Airport Road. Rising near mile 11.5, the course climbs about 200 feet to mile 13, returning west on Palomar Airport Road through the flower fields. Back tracing the ocean near mile 16.5, runners reverse direction just after mile 18, heading north on Carlsbad Blvd. toward the start (miles 18 to 24). The route then retraces its way to the start/finish at Plaza Camino Real.

CROWD/RUNNER SUPPORT The race features entertainment — rock bands, bagpipers, Taiko drummers — at a number of locations on the route. Otherwise, crowd support is limited to a few areas. Organizers generously provide aid stations every mile of the course, with water, electrolyte replacement, petroleum jelly, and portable toilets generally available. Fruit provides a needed sugar boost at the final 6 stations.

RACE LOGISTICS Entrants staying at the official hotel can take advantage of shuttle service to the marathon start. Other runners need to provide their own transportation. You may park at Plaza Camino Real or in adjacent areas, but arrive early since access roads may be closed by 6:00 a.m. Entrants who intend to walk the marathon should start at 5:30 a.m. Others who expect to take longer than 4:30 to complete the race should begin at 6:15 a.m. However, if you start at 6:15 a.m. and run faster than 4:30, you will unfortunately be disqualified.

ACTIVITIES Pick up your race packet or register during the All About Fitness Expo at Plaza Camino Real on Friday, 2:00 p.m. to 7:00 p.m. or Saturday, 8:00 a.m. to 6:00 p.m. On Saturday, the expo features a number of running-related clinics. The Carbo Pasta Party with entertainment takes place at the headquarters hotel, Del Mar Hilton, on Saturday evening from 5:00 p.m. to 8:00 p.m. The post-race party features plenty of food, refreshments, live entertainment, and massages. The awards party at 5:00 p.m. at the official hotel features complimentary lavish hors d'oeuvres.

AWARDS All entrants get T-shirts, and medals are awarded to all finishers. The top three in each age group also receive awards.

ACCOMMODATIONS The Del Mar Hilton, 20 minutes south of Carlsbad (619-792-5200), is the official hotel. The Carlsbad Visitors Bureau (800-227-5722) can assist you with other hotel reservations in Carlsbad.

RELATED EVENTS/RACES On Saturday, the day before the marathon, there are a 5K Run/Walk and a Kids Marathon Mile for children 12 and under. A five-member marathon relay runs with the marathon. The first four team members each run 5-mile legs, and the last runner completes a 10K. Shuttle buses transport team members to the relay exchange points. The half marathon is the most well known of all the events, attracting a national-class field.

AREA ATTRACTIONS The San Diego area has a lot to offer visitors. You must visit the awesome San Diego Zoo in beautiful Balboa Park. Kids may also enjoy a day at Sea World and Wild Animal Park. Old Town provides that western/Mexican flair. Warm weather brings out the hoards to Mission Beach and La Jolla Shores. Great shopping can be had at Hortons Plaza. The 1998 Super Bowl will be held in San Diego the week following the marathon.

LOCAL RUNNING STORES Movin' Shoes, 3838 Mission Blvd., San Diego (619-488-2310); Fleet Feet, 161 S. Highway 101, Solana Beach (619-481-4148).

CAROLINA MARATHON

OVERALL: 74.8

COURSE BEAUTY: 8

COURSE DIFFICULTY: 5 (SEE APPENDIX)

APPROPRIATENESS FOR FIRST TIMERS: 7-

RACE ORGANIZATION: 8+

CROWDS: 1-

RACE DATA

Contact:	Larry Mattox
	Carolina Marathon Association
	P.O. Box 5092
	Columbia, SC 29250
	(803) 929-1996
Date:	February 8, 1997
	February 7, 1998
Start Time:	10:00 a.m.
Time Course Closes:	3:00 p.m.
Number of Participants:	264 in 1995
Certification:	USATF
Course Records:	Male: (open) 2:29:54; (masters) 2:40:36
	Female: (open) 2:43:42; (masters) 3:04:19
Elite Athlete Programs:	No
Cost:	$25/30
Age groups/Divisions:	<19, 20-24, 25-29, 30-34, 35-39, 40-44, 45-49,
	50-54, 55-59, 60-64, 65-69, 70+
Temperature:	46°
Aid/Splits:	12 / NA

HIGHLIGHTS The 1996 U.S. Women's Olympic Marathon Trials served as a coming-out party for both its host and winner. Virtual unknown Jenny Spangler shocked the pundits by surging to a strong victory over the pre-race favorites. The Trials also pulled the Carolina Marathon out of southern obscurity. Historically a small race, Carolina runs on a difficult course through Columbia's downtown, suburbs, Fort Jackson Army Base, and University of South Carolina campus. South Carolina's capital city, Columbia provides a hospitable setting for the now recognizable race.

COURSE DESCRIPTION Starting on Main Street near the South Carolina State House, the course circles downtown passing the landmark Hampton-Preston Mansion and Robert Mill House before returning to the State House near mile 2. Heading west, runners cross the Congaree River before mile 3 and pass through the residential communities of West Columbia and Cayce while dropping 150 feet to mile 6. Crossing back over the river near the 6-mile mark, the route contains two 100-foot hills between miles 5 and 8. After passing through the University of South Carolina, runners head through the quiet, shady neighborhoods of Shandon and Heathwood. At mile 11, runners descend 150 feet through Lake Katherine's residential community. Near mile 12, the course enters Fort Jackson (miles 12 to 19), one of the country's largest Army training centers. Gaining 170 feet over 2 miles, the route also contains several long downhill sections to mile 20. Exiting the fort after mile 19, runners head back toward downtown through suburban areas climbing 120 feet from mile 21 to mile 23. From here, runners head down Devine Street for a 1-mile straightaway on Main Street leading to the NationsBank Plaza finish.

CROWD/RUNNER SUPPORT Runners find the bulk of the crowd support downtown, at Five Points shopping center, and in Fort Jackson Army Base where the soldiers come out in force to cheer. Some spectators also scatter in the many residential communities along the route. The aid stations, located every 2 miles, offer water and electrolyte replacement drink.

RACE LOGISTICS Runners staying at the race headquarters hotel can walk to the starting line. Several other downtown hotels are within walking distance of the start. If you're staying further out, you will need to drive and park in the vicinity.

ACTIVITIES Browse the expo from noon to 9:30 p.m. and pick up your race packet from 4:00 p.m. to 9:30 p.m. on Friday at the race headquarters hotel. You can also retrieve your packet from 7:30 a.m. to 10:00 a.m. on race day, but there is no race-day registration. On Friday evening, the race holds a pasta party also at the official hotel. After the marathon, partake in the traditional luncheon starting at 1:00 p.m.; the awards ceremony begins at 2:30 p.m.

AWARDS Every entrant receives a marathon T-shirt, and finishers take home medals and certificates of completion. The top overall finishers receive small cash awards, while the top three division winners receive trophies.

ACCOMMODATIONS The official race hotel had not been determined at press time. The Adam's Mark, 1200 Hampton Street (803-771-7000), served as the race headquarters in the past. Other nearby hotels include: Comfort Inn Capital City, 2025 Main Street (803-252-6321); and Governor's House, 1301 Main Street (803-779-7790).

RELATED EVENTS/RACES The 1997 U.S. National Women's Marathon Championship begins prior to the open marathon at 9:00 a.m. Race day also features a 10K at 10:45 a.m. and events for the kids and walkers.

AREA ATTRACTIONS Columbia features one of the nation's best zoos, the Riverbanks Zoo and Garden. Visitors can also glimpse antebellum Columbia at the Robert Mills Historic House and the Hampton-Preston Mansion.

LOCAL RUNNING STORES Strictly Running, 736 Harden Street, Columbia (803-799-4786); The Extra Mile, 613 Harden Street, Columbia (803-799-8841); Cook's Personal Best, 205-H Columbia Avenue, Lexington, SC (803-356-8700).

LAS VEGAS INTERNATIONAL MARATHON

OVERALL: 80.7

COURSE BEAUTY: 6

COURSE DIFFICULTY: 2 (SEE APPENDIX)

APPROPRIATENESS FOR FIRST TIMERS: 8-

RACE ORGANIZATION: 9-

CROWDS: 1

RACE DATA

Contact: Las Vegas International Marathon
P.O. Box 81262
Las Vegas, NV 89180
(702) 876-3870
Date: February 9, 1997
February 8, 1998
Start Time: 7:30 a.m.
Time Course Closes: 12:30 p.m.
Number of Participants: 1,800 in 1996
Certification: USATF & AIMS
Course Records: Male: (open) 2:12:37; (masters) 2:16:53
Female: (open) 2:37:20; (masters) 2:44:30
Elite Athlete Programs: Yes
Cost: $40/50
Age groups/Divisions: 18-24, 25-29, 30-34, 35-39, 40-44, 45-49, 50-54,
55-59, 60-64, 65-69, 70+, Clydesdale
Temperature: 38° - 60°
Aid/Splits: 15 / every five miles

HIGHLIGHTS Known as the entertainment capital of the world, Las Vegas' fast-paced action occurs along "The Strip," a three-and-a-half block stretch that contains the lavish theme hotels not to mention their accompanying casinos, showgirls, nightclubs, and entertainers that make Vegas famous. However, once a year, the spotlight shifts to a lesser known strip — 26 miles of straight pavement just south of downtown — which features fast-paced action of a different variety. Nestled below the barren Las Vegas mountains, the rural point-to-point Las Vegas International Marathon (LVM) course lies in stark contrast to the neon-splashed 24-hour city located only a few miles from the finish. With a net downhill of 500 feet, Vegas offers excellent odds for a personal record. So, if you're looking for a fast winter marathon with a lot of glitz and glamour on the side, try your luck at Las Vegas.

RACE HISTORY The LVM was founded in 1967 by Hank Greenspun, publisher of the Las Vegas Sun newspaper. Heralded as the World Master's Marathon, the race drew 141 runners. Three years later, the newspaper dropped its sponsorship. The newly formed Las Vegas Track Club (LVTC) continued the race until 1982 when it, too, decided to end its involvement with the race. Up stepped LVTC member Al Boka who refused to let the race die and resolved to continue the race with the objective of transforming it into a much larger event. Today, the race draws nearly 1,800 marathoners and 3,500 half marathoners. Al is working to move the finish line to "The Strip" in the near future, making for a much more dramatic finale.

COURSE DESCRIPTION The race starts 3.5 miles south of Jean, NV on State Road 604 (elevation approximately 2,750 feet) and parallels I-15 to the finish at Vacation Village Hotel Casino. The course has very few turns and contains excellent asphalt pavement throughout. After traveling slightly uphill from the start to 6.3 miles, the course levels off until the first curve at mile 7. From mile 7 to 7.7, a gentle downhill occurs followed by a mild rise between miles 7.7 and 9.9. The course then runs flat for .1 miles, before ascending from mile 10 to 10.5. Runners face another short hill at the second curve on the course at mile 11. The slight hill continues to mile 11.25 (where you reach the maximum elevation of approximately 3,100 feet) then flattens out to the third curve and easy downgrade from 11.8 to 12.3. Between miles 12.3 and 12.6, runners encounter a slight incline, but the remainder of the race is almost entirely downhill until mile 22, losing nearly 770 feet in elevation. From 22 to 23.2, a slight upgrade ensues, and then the road levels off from there to the left turn and finish at Vacation Village.

CROWD/RUNNER SUPPORT Not surprisingly, few casino goers flee the slot machines and card tables to cheer the marathoners. In fact, as a rural, point-to-point course, the LVM is not particularly conducive to large crowds. Although the road is partially open and accessible to spectators after mile 16, most spectators assemble at the relay exchange points and at the finish where bleachers enhance the chance of spotting your favorite runner.

RACE LOGISTICS The race start in Jean, NV, is thirty minutes south of downtown. Free, mandatory bus transportation to the start is provided. Buses leave from the MGM Grand Hotel/Casino parking lot. Transportation back to the hotel is also provided. Specific details are provided in race packets.

ACTIVITIES The LVM features a three-day Health and Fitness Expo starting at noon on Thursday at Vacation Village, 6711 Las Vegas Blvd. South. Race packets are distributed here until 5:00 p.m. on Thursday, and from 10:00 a.m. to 5:00 p.m. on Friday and Saturday. The Pasta Party takes place at The Drink and Eat Too Night Club and Restaurant next to the MGM Grand. Food bags and beverages are available at the finish, and an awards ceremony begins at 11:00 a.m. at Vacation Village.

AWARDS Every marathoner receives a race T-shirt at the packet pickup. Medallions are awarded to all finishers, and result booklets are mailed to all participants. With Las Vegas being, well, Las Vegas, it's only fitting that the prize money structure is about as unique as they come. Money is not limited to the very top finishers. Sure, the top five open and masters runners are awarded from $3,000 to $400 and from $1,000 to $200, respectively, and are eligible for time incentive bonus money. Age groupers, usually excluded from the prize money fold, also compete for small purses for the top two places. Plaques are awarded to tenth place in some divisions. Although the plaques are presented at the awards ceremony, prize money winners should not plan on racing to the casinos to parlay their earnings into a huge jackpot — the checks are mailed within thirty days of the event.

ELITE RUNNERS INFORMATION Complimentary entries and limited, shared accommodations are given to sub 2:20 men, sub 2:45 women, sub 2:30 masters men, and sub 2:50 masters women. You may also receive partial reimbursement for transportation, meals, and rooms at the race director's discretion.

ACCOMMODATIONS Although there are more than 100,000 hotel rooms in Las Vegas, amazingly, they can fill, so book your reservation early. If you can stay on "The Strip" on Las Vegas Boulevard, do it! The various theme hotels are unparalleled, if you don't mind gaudy. You can choose between the medieval castle complete with knights, dragons and sorcerers offered by the Excaliber, $79/night (800-658-5000); the exciting MGM Grand Hotel and Theme Park, the world's largest hotel with 5,009 rooms, $129/night (800-288-1000); the glass pyramid and Nile River boat ride at the Luxor, $129/night (800-288-1000); the Mirage and its famous overflowing volcano, $199/night (800-627-6667); or you can stay near the finish line at Vacation Village (800-338-0608).

RELATED EVENTS/RACES The LVM features a half marathon run and race walk which takes place on the lightning fast second half of the marathon course, beginning at 7:00 a.m. On Saturday, a 5K "Breakfast Run" starts and finishes next to the MGM Grand Hotel.

AREA ATTRACTIONS The hotels alone offer so much entertainment for adults and children that you can easily do without a car. In fact, you may experience greater fatigue from hotel/casino activities than from the marathon. If it's culture you want, the Las Vegas Art Museum is one of the finest in the country. If you're interested in sights outside Las Vegas, visit Hoover Dam (30 minutes to the southeast), Lake Mead, the largest man-made lake in America (45 minutes north), or Laughlin, with its slower paced casinos and impressive views of the Colorado River (60 minutes south).

LOCAL RUNNING STORE The Running Store, 4350 E. Sunset Road, Henderson, NV (702-898-7866).

AUSTIN MARATHON

OVERALL: 84.7

COURSE BEAUTY: 7+

COURSE DIFFICULTY: 2 (SEE APPENDIX)

APPROPRIATENESS FOR FIRST TIMERS: 9+

RACE ORGANIZATION: 10

CROWDS: 2+

RACE DATA

Contact:	Lyle Clugg
	Motorola Austin Marathon
	P.O. Box 684587
	Austin, TX 78768-4587
	(512) 505-8304
Date:	February 16, 1997
	February 15, 1998
Start Time:	7:00 a.m.
Time Course Closes:	2:00 p.m.
Number of Participants:	1,433 in 1996
Certification:	USATF
Course Records:	Male: (open) 2:15:29; (masters) 2:18:07
Elite Athlete	Female: (open) 2:36:45; (masters) 2:41:01
Programs:	Yes
Cost:	$35/40
Age groups/Divisions:	<19, 20-24, 25-29, 30-34, 35-39, 40-44, 45-49, 50-54, 55-59, 60-64, 65-69, 70+, Clydesdales (males over 200 lbs., females over 150 lbs.) open and masters
Temperature:	43° - 65°
Aid/Splits:	25 / every mile, including expected finish time

HIGHLIGHTS "Six Sigma" is Motorola jargon for doing things with near-perfect quality. Well known for its superior products, Motorola hosts a "Six Sigma" marathon. The race organization's attention to detail is impressive, with aid stations, split and pace times, and portable toilets every mile; good transportation; a well-marked and patrolled course; an announcement of every runner's name as they cross the finish line; and excellent T-shirts (the 1995 version won Runner's World T-shirt of the year award). A fast course, the second half in particular becomes scenic as it runs through parkways near Town Lake. All of the amenities and the easy course make the race an excellent choice for first-time marathoners. The only wildcard is Texas weather. Race organizers moved the race from March to February to enhance the chances for cool weather, but there remains a real possibility for warm, humid conditions.

COURSE DESCRIPTION The course begins in northwest Austin and proceeds slightly downhill through a commercial/industrial district until mile 4. Much of this section is run in one lane along a busy thoroughfare toward downtown. It then winds through middle-class residential streets for another 4 miles, losing about 250 feet in elevation over these first 8 miles. Between miles 8 and 9, runners encounter the first hill of consequence, a 30-footer over 100 or so yards. Not particularly difficult, the hill should increase your heart rate a bit. The course runs along a scenic parkway for approximately 2 miles. Emerging from the trees, the skyline of Austin is a welcome sight at mile 10. The race then moves to an arty section of downtown before reaching the heart of its course, the parkways lining beautiful Town Lake, actually part of the Colorado River. You lose 150 feet between miles 9 and 12. Just after the halfway point, a fairly sharp downhill leads to a 50-foot incline over half a mile. The course then rolls somewhat (many runners won't even notice it) until another sharp downhill between miles 15 and 16. The rest of the course is slightly rolling with little net elevation change. At mile 25, however, a killer 25-foot hill awaits that leaves you ready for the finish line one mile away. The finish is a long stretch lined with onlookers next to Town Lake. Run entirely on well-maintained asphalt, much of the race shares the road with cars, but numerous cones leave runners well protected.

CROWD/RUNNER SUPPORT Enthusiastic crowds at the relay exchanges and the finish area spur you along with the help of a few bands. Scattered crowds pop up in the neighborhoods and along the major thoroughfares. Competing against each other for offering the best support, over 2,200 volunteers operate aid stations and provide other necessary assistance.

RACE LOGISTICS Race organizers provide bus service from the finish line to the start, from the start to the various relay exchanges, and from the relay exchanges to the finish line. Since buses are limited and service can take a little time, race officials urge runners to provide their own transportation if possible. The race also transports any clothes you may wish to have waiting for you at the finish. Though parking exists at both the start and finish areas, arrive early.

ACTIVITIES The marathon holds a two-day expo with about 30 exhibitors, ranging from running apparel to Amy's Ice Cream. On Saturday, a free fitness symposium addresses running-related topics. Pre-race activities culminate in the pasta dinner that features a nationally-known speaker. Tickets to the dinner (about $13) are in addition to the race entry fee, but you can hear the speaker for free. After the race, participants celebrate with a victory party featuring pizza, ice cream, other food and drink, live music, games for the kids, massage, and an awards ceremony.

AWARDS Every runner receives a great T-shirt and results booklet. All marathon finishers receive a medallion, finisher's T-shirt, and certificate. There are distinctive age-group awards five to ten deep. The last finisher across the line receives a trophy. About $40,000 in prize money is split among the top overall (ten deep), masters (ten deep), veterans (three deep), and wheelchair (three deep) athletes. Winners also win tickets from American Airlines.

ELITE RUNNERS INFORMATION The race offers special enticements to elite runners, men who have run under 2:20, and women who have sub 2:50 times. The race provides free hotel, complimentary entry, $50 in expenses, pasta dinner, and prize money. Prize money ranges from $3,000 for overall winners to $50 for tenth place.

ACCOMMODATIONS The headquarters for the 1997 event are the Marriott Courtyard, 9409 Stonelake Blvd. at the starting line (800-321-2211), and Residence Inn, same address (800-331-3131). Other convenient hotels that have offered deals to runners are: Hyatt Regency, 208 Barton Springs Road (512-477-1234), which is near the finish area; and Quality Inn, near the airport (512-452-4200). Otherwise, try the historic Driskill Hotel, 604 Brazos Street (512-474-5911); Radisson, near the finish line (512-478-9611); or La Quinta Capitol, 300 E. 11th Street (512-476-1166).

RELATED EVENTS/RACES For those who don't wish to run the entire marathon, there is a marathon relay (for both five- and two-member teams) and a four-mile fun walk near the marathon finish. The race provides excellent transportation between the relay exchange points and the finish line. The organizers also provide some transportation from the start to the various exchanges. Arrive early.

LOCAL RUNNING STORES Run-Tex, 919 W. 12th Street (512-472-3254) or 9607 Research Blvd., Gateway Market (512-343-1164).

For the long run.

Running. It's what you do.

We are committed and dedicated to serving you, the runner, for the long run.
We understand the essence of running and the importance of running.

Running. It's what WE do.

Brooks and **FLEET FEET**.

For the long run.

>BROOKS

You've Had This *Dream*

Even Before You Started

[*running*]

Walt Disney World. MARATHON

From the moment Mickey Mouse starts the race, you're heading for the most fun you've had in years. Plan now to be a part of The Walt Disney World Marathon, Sunday, January 5, 1997.

Spectacular things happen throughout the run. You're welcomed with dazzling fireworks, live music, kites and confetti. You glide right through Cinderella Castle. You discover Epcot, Blizzard Beach and Disney-MGM Studios.

Only one Marathon can make you feel this way. And you can double the fun by staying right in the middle of the magic at a Disney Resort hotel. Packages which include accommodations, race entry and carbo loading dinner start as low as $240 per person.

Don't miss a single magical mile. Be part of it all by calling your Travel Agent or the Walt Disney World Resort at 407-939-7810.

PRESENTED BY

HEALTHSOUTH

BLUE ANGEL MARATHON

OVERALL: 82.6

COURSE BEAUTY: 8

COURSE DIFFICULTY: 3+

APPROPRIATENESS FOR FIRST TIMERS: 7+

RACE ORGANIZATION: 9+

CROWDS: 1

RACE DATA

Contact: **Blue Angel Marathon**
190 Radford Blvd., Bldg. 632
MWR Dept., NAS
Pensacola, FL 32508-5217
(904) 452-2843
Date: **February 22, 1997**
February 28, 1998
Start Time: **7:00 a.m.**
Time Course Closes: **12:00 p.m.**
Number of Participants: **1,026 in 1995**
Certification: **USATF**
Course Records: **Male: (open) 2:22:45; (masters) 2:32:47**
Female: (open) 2:54:37; (masters) 3:15:56
Elite Athlete Programs: **No**
Cost: **$28/35**
Age groups/Divisions: **14-19, 20-24, 25-29, 30-34, 35-39, 40-44, 45-49,**
50-54, 55-59, 60-64, 65-69, 70-74, 75-79, 80+
Temperature: **55°**
Aid/Splits: **13 / miles 1, 5, 10, 15 & 20, digital clock at 13.1**

HIGHLIGHTS Heralded as the "Official Navy Marathon," the Blue Angel Marathon takes its name from the pride of the U.S. Navy — the Blue Angel Flight Demonstration Squadron based at Pensacola Naval Air Station. Open to both military and civilian entrants, this out-and-back course features a mostly flat and partially rolling journey through historic NAS and downtown Pensacola, along the waterfront of Pensacola Bay, and around two meticulously manicured golf courses. Shunning the traditional marathon start involving a speech and gun-firing by a local dignitary, BAM's send off includes a Blue Angel fly by and cannon blast.

COURSE DESCRIPTION The Blue Angel Marathon begins aboard Naval Air Station Pensacola, the "Cradle of Naval Aviation." Starting on the NAS waterfront, the course heads westward, wrapping around the National Cemetery in front of the National Museum of Naval Aviation prior to making a quick loop in front of the historic Light House. The Light House, constructed in 1858, is still in operation today. At the 4-mile mark, the course overlooks the impressive frontage of Ft. Barrancas and Barrancas Beach. Continuing on, the race leads runners off-base at the 6-mile marker. Winding down through Old Warrington Town, runners see magnificent homes surrounding Pensacola Country Club at the 11- and 12-mile markers. Runners are greeted by the sites in the historic City of Pensacola along with the fisheries, boats, parks, and businesses as they travel the route adjacent to the waterfront. At the 14-mile marker, runners turn left and journey up Palafox Street, the center of downtown Pensacola, continuing on to the highest point of the course at the

15-mile marker located at the top of Palafox Hill in beautiful Lee Square. Marathoners travel around Lee Square and down the hill with a left turn at the 17-mile mark, then onto Seville Square Historical District filled with beautiful old buildings, parks, gardens, stately homes with ginger-bread trim, and quaint shops. Now, runners head back to the waterfront at the 18-mile mark past the Vietnam "Wall South" Monument and Park overlooking Pensacola Bay and the numerous fishing and pleasure boats. Around the 22-mile mark, the course circles back through Old Warrington Town. Runners enter the Naval Air Station at the 24-mile mark with a run by beautiful A.C. Read Golf Course, completing the Blue Angel Marathon on the waterfront aboard NAS Pensacola.

CROWD/RUNNER SUPPORT The marathon is strongly supported by the community with many spectators gathering along the course to applaud the athletes. Added motivation comes in the form of keyboard players, bands, and high school cheerleaders on the route. Thirteen well-staffed aid stations keep you hydrated in the frequently humid race conditions.

RACE LOGISTICS Since the start and finish are located in the same place, your only transportation worry on race day involves getting to the start. Several hotels are located within two miles of the start. Barring an invasion or declaration of war, plenty of parking is available on the tarmac behind the gym.

ACTIVITIES A three-day Sports Expo and packet pickup kicks off on Thursday from 8:00 a.m. to 4:00 p.m. in Gym Bldg. 632 on NASP and continues on Friday from 8:00 a.m. to 9:00 p.m. Don't miss the spaghetti feed at the Mustin Beach Officer's Club Friday night from 6:00 p.m. to 8:00 p.m. On top of the carbo-loading, the evening includes door prizes, entertainment, and a video and slide show of the race course. The Sports Expo continues on race day from 5:00 a.m. to 3:00 p.m. with late packet pickup between 5:00 a.m. and 6:30 a.m. There is no race-day registration. After finishing the race, hasten your recovery with complimentary pasta, beverages, fruit, and cookies. Enjoy music as you wait for the awards ceremony in the finish area at 1:00 p.m. You must be present to receive an award.

AWARDS Every marathon entrant receives a commemorative long-sleeve T-shirt, race poster, Blue Angel Marathon mug, and other souvenirs. Complete race results and finisher certificates are mailed to all who complete the event within the 5-hour time limit. Overall male and female winners typically earn air fare to the Boston Marathon, running shoes, and a framed race poster. Masters winners receive running shoes, and the top five in each age group are awarded medals/rosettes.

ACCOMMODATIONS Hotels in the immediate vicinity include: Beachside Resort, 14 Via Deluna Pensacola Beach (800-232-2416); Best Western Pensacola Beach, 11 Via DeLuna Drive (904-934-3300); Best Western — Perdido Key, 13585 Perdido Key Drive (800-528-1234); Clarion Suites, 20 Via Deluna Pensacola Beach (800-874-5303); Comfort Inn, 3 New Warrington Road (800-554-3206); and Pensacola Grand, 200 E. Gregory Street (800-348-3336).

RELATED EVENTS/RACES If your racing plans don't call for an early season marathon, consider the Blue Angel 5K. The race runs entirely on the naval base and starts one hour after the marathon.

AREA ATTRACTIONS Located on Florida's Gulf Coast, Pensacola's year round temperate climate and white sand beaches beckon the winter vacationer. On NAS, don't miss the free Museum of Naval Aviation, with an IMAX theater and a virtual reality flight (for a fee). Historic Old Town provides a nice break from the omnipresent water recreation. If you need more excitement, head 50 miles west to the original Mardi Gras celebration in Mobile, AL.

COWTOWN MARATHON

OVERALL: 81.8

COURSE BEAUTY: 8-

COURSE DIFFICULTY: 4+

APPROPRIATENESS FOR FIRST TIMERS: 7

RACE ORGANIZATION: 9-

CROWDS: 2+

R A C E   D A T A

Contact:	Cowtown Marathon
	P.O. Box 9066
	Ft. Worth, TX 76147
	(817) 735-2033
Date:	February 22, 1997
	February 21, 1998
Start Time:	8:30 a.m.
Time Course Closes:	3:00 p.m.
Number of Participants:	671 in 1996
Certification:	USATF
Course Records:	Male: (open) 2:20:13
	Female: (open) 2:45:51
Elite Athlete Programs:	Yes
Cost:	$25/30
Age groups/Divisions:	18-21, 22-27, 28-33, 34-39, 40-44, 45-49, 50-54, 55-59, 60-69, 70-79, 80+, Big Person (200+ lbs.): open and masters (40+)
Temperature:	46° - 56°
Aid/Splits:	12 / every mile

HIGHLIGHTS Frank Shorter, when asked why he returns to Cowtown year after year, called it the biggest small race he knows, and while he specifically referred to the 10K race which routinely draws over 11,000 entrants, the description aptly fits the marathon as well. Cowtown offers a barrelful of country energy and charm. The historic Fort Worth Stockyards lends a decidedly Western flavor to the race. Appropriately, the Stockyard Coliseum's rodeo pit doubles as the race registration area! The large number of 10K runners only adds to the already festive and boisterous atmosphere. The course winds through residential areas, down the trail along the Trinity River, and finishes in the Stockyards. Faster runners will find a huge crowd waiting for them at the finish. Slower runners (over 4 hours) will have to be content with the race announcers reading their names.

COURSE DESCRIPTION Cowtown's marathon route literally winds through Fort Worth in a loop course that begins and ends in the Stockyards, a relic of Ft. Worth's cattle town past. Not particularly fast, the course twists and turns, challenging runners to find and maintain a rhythm. From the start, runners head through a commercial area to mile 3. Filing into one lane of a wide street, runners approach a 200-yard downhill followed by a slight 100-yard incline just after mile 2. Once you hit the 3-mile mark, the course moves into a nice residential area where it becomes slightly rolling. After mile 6, runners pass Rivercrest golf course and head 100 yards downhill into more neighborhoods for most of the next 12 miles. A 70-yard upgrade to mile

10 leads to the Hulen Bridge over the railroad yard and the Trinity River. After mile 18, the course follows the scenic Trinity Trail downward along the river. Miles 19 to 20 pass through grassy Trinity Park with its gnarled oak trees, then on to Fairington Field, followed by a commercial district (miles 20 to 21.5). Runners cross the busy Founders Bridge, traverse the Tandy parking lot, and head back down to the Trinity Trail from mile 23 to 25. Runners exit the trail after going under the North Side Drive overpass and head for the Stockyards finish on Exchange Avenue. The course is monitored by police officers, and cones protect runners from the passing traffic except on the closed Trinity Trail.

CROWD/RUNNER SUPPORT Cowtown is the big community event in Fort Worth. The Fort Worth Star-Telegram carries a special Cowtown supplement the day after the races with stories and complete results. Big crowds await you at the marathon finish if you can run 4 hours or so. Scattered along the course, crowds accompany high school cheerleaders at several points on the route. Volunteers read split times every mile. With any event that relies on volunteers, however, there can be a few minor bugs — like maybe the split timers show up and have the correct time, and maybe they don't. Just bring your own watch so it doesn't matter anyway.

RACE LOGISTICS The race provides bus transportation from the Radisson Plaza and Ramada downtown to the start at the Stockyards. Though difficult to find, shuttle buses back to the hotels wait down Mule Alley (across from the Coliseum) near the communications van. You can check in clothing and personal items before the race in the Coliseum. Even though you can find quite a bit of parking near the Stockyards, arrive early to avoid aggravation. Relay runners must provide their own transportation to the exchange points.

ACTIVITIES Register or pick up your race packet the week prior to the marathon at the Cowtown Marathon office, 3515 W. 7th Avenue in Fort Worth (817-735-2033) or at Luke's in the Dallas area. The evening before the marathon, the race hosts the Cowtown Symposium and Spaghetti Dinner. Regular guests include Bill Rodgers and Frank Shorter. Tickets are about $15. Following the race, relax at the festive post-race party with food and drink located in the old warehouses off Mule Alley. Get your picture taken with a bull, eat lunch at nearby restaurants or food stalls, or watch your fellow toilers coast down to the finish. The Awards Roundup follows at 4:00 p.m. at the finish line on Exchange.

AWARDS Every entrant receives a terrific, colorful T-shirt which is one of our personal favorites. All marathon finishers receive finisher's awards and personalized certificates. Trophies are awarded to age-group winners (up to seven deep). Overall winners earn trips to the next Boston or New York Marathon, in addition to trophies. The race offers a $1,000 cash bounty for new course records. If you are leaving town on Saturday, a results newspaper can be purchased from marathon officials and sent to you.

ELITE RUNNERS INFORMATION Cowtown recruits celebrity runners such as Bill Rodgers, Gwen Coogan, and Frank Shorter to run the 10K. Elites who want to run the marathon may be offered transportation, expenses, and free entry. Contact the race director for more details.

ACCOMMODATIONS The official race headquarters is the Radisson Plaza, 815 Main Street in downtown Fort Worth (817-870-2100), for about $65. Also try the Ramada Downtown, 1701 Commerce (817-335-7000); The Worthington Hotel, 200 Main Street (817-870-1000); or The Remington Hotel, 600 Commerce Street (817-332-6900).

RELATED EVENTS/RACES Three-person teams can enter the marathon relay and run legs of 10, 8 and 8.2 miles. Teams may be same-sex or coed. Over 115 teams participated in the 1996 version. The biggest draw is the 10K race, one of the largest in the country, which offers a fairly fast, loop course. The 10K begins one-half hour after the marathon start.

LOCAL RUNNING STORE Luke's, 1540 S. University Drive, Fort Worth (817-877-1448).

SMOKY MOUNTAIN MARATHON

OVERALL: 82.6

COURSE BEAUTY: 9-

COURSE DIFFICULTY: 5+

APPROPRIATENESS FOR FIRST TIMERS: 7

RACE ORGANIZATION: 9-

CROWDS: 0

RACE DATA

Contact:	Sherman Ames
	Smoky Mountain Marathon
	6401 Baum Drive
	Knoxville, TN 37919
	(423) 588-7465
Date:	February 22, 1997
	February 28, 1998
Start Time:	8:30 a.m.
Time Course Closes:	1:30 p.m.
Number of Participants:	258 in 1996
Certification:	USATF
Course Records:	Male: (open) 2:32:40
	Female: (open) 3:02:52
Elite Athlete Programs:	No
Cost:	$20/25
Age groups/Divisions:	<19, 20-24, 25-29, 30-34, 35-39, 40-44, 45-49,
	50+ (F), 50-54, 55-59, 60+ (M)
Temperature:	40° - 49°
Aid/Splits:	10 / miles 1, 5, 10, 13.5, 15 & 20

HIGHLIGHTS One of marathoning's best deals, the Smoky Mountain Marathon prides itself on offering down-home, East Tennessee hospitality to its nearly 300 runners. From the open house fireside gathering on Friday evening to the post-race soup gala, you should not need to step foot in your car, making for a hassle-free weekend. Smoky Mountain's moderately difficult course traces the Little River, providing an intimate glimpse of Southern Appalachia.

COURSE DESCRIPTION The marathon starts and finishes in the Townsend Village Center on the cusp of Great Smoky Mountains National Park. Most of the first 7.5 miles follow largely flat Highways 337 and 321. Crossing the Little River, the course rolls and winds through pine thickets and hardwood forests as it follows the river for the up and back from mile 8 to 17. Runners get a real taste of Appalachia here, with rustic mountain cabins, spectacular modern homes, small farm plots, and sheer rock facings which crop up to and sometimes over the road. Peeling away from the river after mile 17, the course challenges runners with hills between miles 18 and 22 on a patchy, gravel road. Weary runners receive a nice respite as the road improves and the terrain flattens from mile 23 to the finish.

CROWD/RUNNER SUPPORT A rural race, the Smoky Mountain Marathon attracts few crowds outside of family, friends, and race volunteers. To lift the spirits of tired runners, the race plans a special theme aid station near the 23-mile mark. Past themes, complete with costumes and props, have included Mardi Gras, Margaritaville, and Graceland.

RACE LOGISTICS With virtually no logistics, all race activities, the start, and finish are within a stone's throw of the headquarters hotel.

ACTIVITIES On Friday evening from 6:00 p.m. to 8:00 p.m., gather around the fire at the Valley View Lodge for complimentary soft drinks, beer, munchies, and camaraderie. Wander between the social and the $10 pasta dinner (from 6:00 p.m. to 7:30 p.m.). After the race, warm up with hot soup and good conversation at the post-race gala. The awards ceremony kicks off at 1:00 p.m.

AWARDS Every marathoner receives a long-sleeve, mock turtleneck shirt, commemorative hat, and gloves. Each finisher also reels in a medallion, finisher's certificate, finish-line photo, and a results booklet. All of this combined with the race activities give you an excellent bargain. The top three overall and Clydesdales, and the top masters and grandmasters, receive plaques. In 1996, overall winners received original sculptures. Age-group winners have received different awards over the years, ranging from coffee mugs, cloisonne pins, and plaques. There is also a drawing for Smoky Mountain crafts.

ACCOMMODATIONS For convenience, make every effort to stay at the race headquarters, the Best Western Valley View Lodge in Townsend (615-448-2237). Book early because the hotel does fill. Second choice is the Hampton Inn, 7824 E. Lamar Alexander Parkway, Townsend (615-448-9000).

RELATED EVENTS / RACES Some folks may prefer the Smoky Mountain 8K which starts at the same time as the marathon and goes to the 4-mile mark before returning to the start.

AREA ATTRACTIONS Most visitors like to explore Great Smoky Mountains National Park. Stop by the visitor's center in Cades Cove on Little River Road, 7 miles southwest of Townsend, to get information on the park. Dolly Parton fans may want to head to Dollywood (800-365-5996), an imaginary village in Pigeon Forge teeming with crafts people, rides, and country music, for a hefty price.

LOCAL RUNNING STORE The Runners Market, 2920 Sutherland Avenue, Knoxville (423-523-0330).

LOS ANGELES MARATHON

OVERALL: 92.6

COURSE BEAUTY: 6+

COURSE DIFFICULTY: 5-

APPROPRIATENESS FOR FIRST TIMERS: 9

RACE ORGANIZATION: 10+

CROWDS: 5+

RACE DATA

Contact: Los Angeles Marathon Office
Suite 100
11110 W. Ohio Avenue
Los Angeles, CA 90025
(310) 444-5544
Date: March 2, 1997
March 1, 1998
Start Time: 8:45 a.m.
Time Course Closes: 2:30 p.m.
Number of Participants: 19,227 in 1996
Certification: USATF
Course Records: Male: (open) 2:10:19
Female: (open) 2:26:23
Elite Athlete Programs: Yes
Cost: $40/50
Age groups/Divisions: <17, 18-24, 25-29, 30-34, 35-39, 40-44, 45-49,
50-54, 55-59, 60-64, 65-69, 70-74, 75-79, 80+
Temperature: 59°
Aid/Splits: 25 / every mile

HIGHLIGHTS The Los Angeles Marathon continues California's trend of leading the nation in innovation. LA was the first U.S. marathon to use the Real Time CHAMPIONCHIP, a personal digital timing device. Attached to each runner's shoe, the Chip serves as an individualized clock. The device provides accurate times for all runners since back-of-the-packers' clocks don't start ticking until they cross the starting line, cutting 20 minutes or more off their time as they wait to pass go. The Chip also cuts down on race fraud since checkpoints along the way ensure runners complete the entire course with no shortcuts.

If you like a large media event, and the entertainment capital of the world attracts you, try the LA Marathon. The third largest marathon in the country, LA enjoys tremendous community support. The first-rate organization translates into excellent aid stations, a completely closed course, and entertainment every mile. And if you're hungry, this course may pass more fast food joints than any other marathon in the country!

RACE HISTORY The LA Marathon grew out of the 1984 Olympic Games held in Los Angeles. Fresh from the success of the Games, the city wanted to institutionalize the marathon. In 1986, the inaugural LA Marathon became the largest first-time marathon in the world with 10,787 runners. Ten years later, participation had doubled, making it the world's fourth largest marathon. The race has added the financial muscle of American Honda Motor Company which should only enhance the event's high quality.

Perhaps the most memorable race in its eleven-year history occurred in 1994. Paul Pilkington of Roy, Utah, won the race under controversial and unusual circumstances. As the race rabbit, Paul was paid to lead the race through the halfway point to ensure a fast winning time. Race rabbit protocol suggests the rabbit should drop out after meeting the terms of the pace-setting agreement. However, on this particular day, Pilkington, feeling fresh, continued to lead the way out of the sight of trailing competitors. Luca Barzaghi of Italy crossed the finish line in 2:12:53 with his arms in the air celebrating what he thought was a major marathon victory only to learn that Pilkington had not dropped out but was the winner of the race, a new car, and a sizeable check.

COURSE DESCRIPTION Race organizers reversed the direction of the course in 1996 presumably to make it faster. Even with the new direction, the course challenges all runners. While PRs are possible here, the course is not especially fast. The LA Marathon offers an urban route, and like many urban courses, it is not particularly scenic, traveling through the major cultural centers of Los Angeles. The race starts on Figueroa in downtown LA. A nice, newly paved, wide street, Figueroa can accommodate the large number of runners. The course continues down Figueroa for about 2.5 miles, then turns right on Exposition at the University of Southern California (USC) campus, going through lower-income residential neighborhoods for the next several miles. Runners encounter the first hill on the course, a freeway overpass, at mile 6, then proceed gradually uphill for the next mile. Miles 7 through 8 gently roll. Runners turn right on Olympic Blvd. on their way through Koreatown (miles 8-10), where they encounter a series of short (50-yard) uphills and downhills, followed by two slightly longer upgrades to the 10-mile mark at Wilshire Blvd. After the turn onto Wilshire, a 200-yard descent precedes a quick uphill, followed by a long, gradual decline. This section is mostly commercial. At mile 12, the course moves into wealthy residential neighborhoods, containing a couple of short but good uphills. After mile 13, runners traverse N. Highland Avenue which features a palm-tree-lined median and Spanish-style homes. The course becomes more commercial one mile later as it reaches Melrose. As runners turn left on Vine Street, they face a long, gradual uphill until the left on W. Sunset Blvd. around mile 16. The course strolls down Hollywood Blvd. for nearly three miles, past tacky shops on rolling terrain into Sunset Blvd. Sunset contains a couple of long, tough hills at a tough time in the race — after 20 miles. At about mile 22, runners begin the descent into downtown and the finish near the Public Library.

As one would expect from a race of this caliber, the course is completely closed to traffic and is well monitored. Streets are in very good condition for the majority of the race. Quite visible, large mile markers stretch across the street. But beware — the banners don't necessarily mark the precise mile points. Look for the digital clocks.

CROWD/RUNNER SUPPORT The LA community strongly supports the marathon with more than one million spectators cheering your every step. Over 115 live bands and performers provide entertainment along the course, with eleven designated entertainment centers meant to be representative of LA's diversity — including rock, rap, and Latin music. Lining both sides of the marathon route, 3,700 community volunteers effectively staff the 25 aid stations. The community also gets involved by training local residents for the marathon through the Los Angeles Roadrunners Training Program and Students Run LA. Created in 1987 by teacher Harry Shabazian, Students Run LA is designed to train nearly 1,700 "at-risk" Angeleno students who wish to run the LA Marathon.

RACE LOGISTICS The start/finish area lies near the downtown hotels, so transportation is not a concern. Shuttle vans roam between miles 7 and 24 to return runners to the finish area should they not be able to complete the race. In addition, the LA Metro Rail system offers free rides on the Green, Red, and Blue Lines the day of the race, delivering runners and spectators to within 100 yards of the start/finish lines.

ACTIVITIES The LA Marathon features a huge, three-day Quality of Life Expo with over 400 exhibitors, seminars, demonstrations, and games. Runners pick up their race packets here. Held at the LA Convention Center, 100,000 people annually attend the expo. The race hosts a carbo-load dinner (about $10) the night before the marathon. The dinner, which draws 4,000 runners, family, and friends, features music and live entertainment and sells out each year. After runners pass through the finish chute, they are provided with water, electrolyte replacement, and lots of food. The race hosts the Family Reunion Festival, a day-long party offering arts and crafts booths, entertainment, massage, medical tent, food, and restaurant kiosks; the festival serves as the meeting place for runners, their family, and friends.

A W A R D S Every entrant receives a marathon T-shirt, poster, and stuffed goodie bag, all of which are obtained at the Quality of Life Expo. In addition, finishers earn an original medallion. Age-group winners earn plaques and other prizes.

F I R S T - T I M E R S   I N F O R M A T I O N The LA Marathon is perfect for first-timers — the course is not particularly difficult, aid stations exist every mile, performers entertain almost every step of the way, excellent crowds line the route, and thousands of fellow runners ensure you will never be lonely regardless of your pace. LA weather in March is variable, at times rather chilly and other times warm and humid. Plan accordingly.

E L I T E   R U N N E R S   I N F O R M A T I O N LA actively recruits between 50 and 100 elite runners and has been particularly successful in recruiting top Mexican athletes. The race offers excellent prize money, incentives for breaking course records, accommodations, transportation, expenses, and new Honda automobiles for overall winners. The amount of cash and prizes varies yearly. In 1996, the open cash prize pool totaled $67,000, with $15,000 (plus a Honda Accord EX V-6 Sedan) for first, $10,000 for second, $5,000 for third, $2,500 for fourth, and $1,000 for fifth. Contact race officials for the prize structure in 1997 and 1998.

A C C O M M O D A T I O N S The Biltmore Hotel serves as the official race headquarters (213-624-1011). Perhaps even more convenient is the Omni Los Angeles Hotel (800-THE-OMNI). Adjacent to the race starting line, the Omni offers reduced rates for marathon entrants, about $110. For cheaper accommodations, try the Hotel Figueroa (800-421-9092), situated about one mile from the start-finish areas and within blocks of the LA Convention Center. Rates are about $50 to $60 per night. Many other hotels are convenient to the start/finish lines. Contact the marathon office for a complete listing of hotels.

R E L A T E D   E V E N T S / R A C E S Within the marathon, corporate, law enforcement, and fire department teams compete against each other for top honors. Marathon organizers also host two other important events, The Los Angeles Marathon 5K and the Los Angeles Marathon Bike Tour. The 5K is held immediately following the marathon start and has its own pre-race and post-race activities and entertainment at the convention center. Celebrities, politicians and other VIPs often join in the 5K. LA is unique in offering a Marathon Bike Tour, a 21-mile ride that draws over 15,000 cyclists. Held before the marathon at 6:00 a.m., the tour features T-shirts, finisher medals, and a finish line festival.

A R E A   A T T R A C T I O N S A diverse city, LA offers a plethora of activities, including museums, Hollywood, Disneyland, and Venice Beach.

L O C A L   R U N N I N G   S T O R E S Frontrunners, 11640 San Vicente Blvd., Los Angeles (310-820-7585); Fleet Feet Sports, 1040 Hermosa Avenue, Hermosa Beach (310-798-1255); Phidippides Sports Center, 16545 Ventura Blvd., Encino (818-986-8686).

NAPA VALLEY MARATHON

OVERALL: 91.6

COURSE BEAUTY: 9+

COURSE DIFFICULTY: 3- (SEE APPENDIX)

APPROPRIATENESS FOR FIRST TIMERS: 9-

RACE ORGANIZATION: 9+

CROWDS: 1-

RACE DATA

Contact:	Sutter Home Napa Valley Marathon
	P.O. Box 4307
	Napa, CA 94558-0430
	(707) 255-2609
Date:	March 2, 1997
	March 1, 1998
Start Time:	7:00 a.m.
Time Course Closes:	12:30 p.m.
Number of Participants:	1,281 in 1996
Certification:	USATF
Course Records:	Male: (open) 2:16:20; (masters) 2:26:04
	Female: (open) 2:46:41; (masters) 2:54:46
Elite Athlete Programs:	Yes
Cost:	$45/50/60
Age groups/Divisions:	<19, 20-24, 25-29, 30-34, 35-39, 40-44,
	45-49, 50-54, 55-59, 60-69, 70+
Temperature:	40° - 70°
Aid/Splits:	12 / miles 1, 5, 10, 13.1 & 20

HIGHLIGHTS Low key and rural, the Napa Valley Marathon ("NVM") runs along the famed Silverado Trail through vineyards swept with pruned grape vines, emerald grasses, and golden mustard. Stir this incredible setting into Napa's world-class attractions, add a competent, runner-friendly race organization, and you've corked one of the top destination marathons in North America. A particularly fine choice for runners who appreciate serenity but don't like to be out there alone, NVM also seems to be blessed with near-perfect weather, raining only once in 18 years.

RACE HISTORY Designed as an intimate, rural marathon, the Napa Valley Marathon began in 1979 by the Silverado Striders, a Napa-based running club. The fact that the distance between Calistoga, at the northern end of the valley, and Napa, at the southern end, happened to be 26 miles seemed too coincidental to overlook.

A number of local companies with national reputations have acted as the race's primary sponsors. For the first dozen years, the Calistoga Mineral Water Company sponsored the race — NVM's start line is just 50 yards from the Calistoga plant. Sutter Home Winery took up sponsorship in 1993.

Throughout its first 10 years, the marathon remained a local secret, with 800 to 1,000 participants. However, in 1987 the race won notoriety when Dick Beardsley, the then second-fastest marathoner in America, used the course to make his comeback after a near career-ending leg injury. Intending to qualify for the 1988 U.S. Marathon Trials, he cruised to a course record of 2:16:20. The 1996 race was the first-ever RRCA California State Marathon Championship, and the

1997 race is the RRCA Western Regional Marathon Championship. Sutter Home Winery has installed a permanent trophy (a 7-liter bottle of Zinfandel) in its tasting room along Highway 29 south of Helena. Each year the male and female winners' names and times are etched into the bottle.

COURSE DESCRIPTION NVM's paved, gently rolling, point-to-point course, framed by wooded hills and picturesque vineyards, follows the Silverado Trail, a two-lane country road, for approximately 23 miles before turning into Napa's side streets on its way to the Vintage High School finish. The first 13 miles and the final 3 are completely closed to traffic, while cones protect the runners on the shoulder the middle 10 miles. At times, the road's camber makes finding a comfortable place to run difficult, particularly from mile 13 to 23.

The race starts just outside downtown Calistoga. About mile 1.25, runners hit a good, winding upgrade to 1.6, followed by a nice downhill to the 2-mile mark. The course then flattens briefly, going gently up from mile 2.2 to 2.75. This second hill is again followed by a good downhill. The final significant hill, the largest and steepest of the race, lies at 5.25 miles. As the course goes down following the rise, a particularly nice panorama of forested hills greets the runners. From there to the 21-mile mark, the course gently rolls, with some longer, gradual inclines and declines, but no major surprises. Runners pass some excellent wineries during this stretch, including Villa Mt. Eden at 12.7, Mumm at 13.5, Z-D Wines at 13.9, hilltop Silverado Vineyards just after 19, the low, stone buildings of Stag's Leap Wine Cellars at 21.5, followed closely by the ivy-covered Clos du Val. From 21 miles, the course flattens. Runners reach the 23-mile mark on a small bridge on Oak Knoll Avenue, just after the turnoff from the Silverado Trail, and pass Monticello Cellars at 24 miles. After the right turn on El Centro, the route becomes residential until the Vintage High School finish.

CROWD/RUNNER SUPPORT As you might expect, small numbers of spectators come out to cheer the runners, mostly family and friends who congregate at several major intersections on the Silverado Trail. NVM supports the runners well with 12 aid stations offering water, electrolyte replacement, sponges, medical supplies, and portable toilets. On the last half of the course, fruit is also available. The race will also put out your own special drinks at the aid stations you designate. The relatively short aid stations mean you will probably have to slow down to find and retrieve your bottle, but having your special brew may more than make up for the delay. The mile markers, located at ground level, may be a bit hard to spot if you're in a group.

RACE LOGISTICS The race provides free bus transportation to the start. Monitors direct you to the parking area at Vintage High School, with buses leaving between 5:15 a.m. and 5:30 a.m. sharp. With limited parking in Calistoga, it's best to use the bus. In addition, runners who park in Calistoga will have to find their own way back to the start, unless their handlers can meet them at the finish.

ACTIVITIES On Saturday, pick up your race packet at the Sports and Fitness Expo, held in the Napa Valley Marriott. The smallish expo also features guest speakers and panels, and NVM veterans discuss course strategy. Buy a raffle ticket for a chance to win some great Napa Valley prizes on Sunday with the proceeds benefitting local charities. Later that evening, hit the pasta feed (about $12). After the race, enjoy some delicious hot soup, bread, fruit, and drink. All registered runners are eligible for random drawing prizes, including wine. The drawing is held just prior to the awards ceremony.

AWARDS Every entrant receives a T-shirt, and each finisher earns a medal and a pat on the back for a job well done. Plaques are also awarded three deep in most age divisions. The top three overall winners receive prizes, including tasty Sutter Home wine. The top local finisher is also recognized.

ELITE RUNNER INFORMATION Lack of prize money means most big-name runners stay away from NVM, but fast runners may be offered complimentary entry and possibly free lodging. The 1997 race is the RRCA Western Regional Marathon Championship. Top prizes include a 5-liter etched bottle of Sutter Home Zinfandel and a set of luggage.

ACCOMMODATIONS The Napa Valley Marriott Hotel, 3425 Solano Avenue, Napa (707-253-7433), serves as the official race hotel, offering discounted rates to runners. Other possibilities in Napa include: Inn at Napa Valley, 1075 California Blvd. (707-253-9540); Best Western Inn, 100 Soscol Avenue (707-257-1930); John Muir Inn, 1998 Trower Avenue (707-257-7220); or Chablis Lodge, 3360 Solano Avenue (707-257-1944).

RELATED EVENTS/RACES NVM also sponsors the Three R's 5K Run, beginning and ending at the marathon finish line and staged by the Vintage High School English Department. Run proceeds help upgrade the school's computer lab.

AREA ATTRACTIONS The Napa Valley Mustard Festival, with food, drink, and tastings of hundreds of mustards, coincides with NVM. Of course, you must tour some of Napa's or nearby Sonoma's fabled wineries. Talk to locals to get tips on finding some lesser-known gems, or wander at will to make your own discoveries. After the marathon, pamper yourself with a spa and mud bath treatment in Calistoga. If the marathon didn't provide enough excitement, try a hot air balloon ride. Those who prefer more conventional locomotion can ride the Wine Train. Napa and Sonoma boast great restaurants and quaint shops. If by some freak of nature you get bored, San Francisco lies nearby.

LOCAL RUNNING STORE Fleet Feet, 507 4th Street, Santa Rosa.

CATALINA ISLAND MARATHON

OVERALL: 91.9

COURSE BEAUTY: 10-

COURSE DIFFICULTY: 9 (SEE APPENDIX)

APPROPRIATENESS FOR FIRST TIMERS: 4

RACE ORGANIZATION: 9+

CROWDS: 1-

R A C E   D A T A

Contact:	Catalina Island Marathon
	California Athletic Productions
	304 Stonecliffe Aisle, Irvine, CA 92715
	(714) 737-1495
Date:	March 15 or 22, 1997
	March 14 or 21, 1998
Start Time:	7:00 a.m.
Time Course Closes:	NA
Number of Participants:	600 in 1996
Certification:	None
Course Records:	Male: (open) 2:39:58
	Female: (open) 3:18:03
Elite Athlete Programs:	No
Cost:	$60/70
Age groups/Divisions:	15-18, 19-24, 25-29, 30-34, 35-39, 40-44, 45-49,
	50-54, 55-59, 60-64, 65-69, 70-74, 75+, Buffalo
	Division (men over 200 lbs. and women over 150 lbs.)
Temperature:	50° - 65°
Aid/Splits:	12 / none

HIGHLIGHTS Celebrating its 20th anniversary in 1997, the Catalina Island Marathon promises one of the most challenging and scenic runs of your life. A peaceful paradise 22 miles off the Los Angeles coast, Catalina Island features rugged mountain wilderness (complete with several hundred bison) encircled by 54 miles of pristine shoreline. Its breathtaking vistas soften the edges of a challenging, mostly dirt course that includes 3,700 feet of total climbing from the start in Two Harbors to the finish in Avalon. One of our top 20 marathon destinations, Catalina's temperate weather and unspoiled beauty make for a perfect race-weekend getaway.

COURSE DESCRIPTION Catalina's point-to-point course starts at sea level in Two Harbors on the west side of the island and ends at sea level in Avalon on the island's east side. In between, spectacular scenery and 3,700 feet of total climbing await you. Most runners finish about 20-25 minutes slower than their best road marathon time. From Two Harbors, the course starts flat but abruptly climbs 825 feet to the west summit around the 2.5- mile mark. Dropping and rolling until you veer left onto Empire Landing Road, the course reaches an elevation of 920 feet at Big Springs Reservoir 4 miles into the race. Although pretty rough, the road flows mostly downhill from there to the junction of Big Springs Road. After a right turn on Big Springs, you continue downhill to Little Harbor Road, hitting sea level at Little Harbor, 8.5 miles into the race. You then begin two climbs with a peak of 350 feet at 10.8 miles. At this point, you turn left onto Old Eagles Nest Trail — a now permanent detour made necessary by horrendous storms in 1995. Beginning with a downhill to an elevation of 260 feet, the trail has a series of three climbs with a peak of 700 feet. From that point, it drops down toward Eagles Nest Lodge where you turn left onto Middle Ranch Road at 500 feet. From Eagles Nest, you begin a long steady and gradual uphill through Middle Ranch — often the hottest section of the course. Middle Ranch stretches for about 5 miles rising from 500 feet to 1,000 feet. Here, the infamous "Pumphouse Hill" awaits with a 360-foot rise in less than a mile; you finally reach the top at about 19 miles. Continuing to climb up a picturesque ridge featuring spectacular views of Avalon and the harbor below, you finally veer right past the Wrigley Reservoir back onto a dirt road and again head uphill along Divide Road. This section of the course is a series of rolling hills with a peak at 1,560 feet. At 23 miles, you begin to drop (almost literally) into Avalon, going from 1,500 feet to 270 feet in 2 miles. You enter the final stretch of the course at 25 miles heading downhill on paved Avalon Canyon Road on your way to the finish near Front Street.

CROWD / RUNNER SUPPORT With no rental cars allowed on the island, spectators linger in the start and finish area. Encouragement is limited to aid station volunteers and Catalina's considerable wildlife population — most notably over 300 bison (descendants of 14 buffalo brought to the island in 1924 for a silent movie called "The Vanishing American").

RACE LOGISTICS Because the race is limited to 600 runners, your first consideration involves sending your registration early as the race generally fills by March 1. Next, participants must be on the island Friday night. Catalina-bound ferries leave regularly from the Los Angeles-area ports of Long Beach, San Pedro and Newport Beach, costing between $25 and $40 for the 60-70 minute ride. For reservations, call Catalina Cruises (Long Beach) (800-228-2546), Catalina Passenger Service (Newport Beach) (714-673-5245), or Catalina Express (Long Beach and San Pedro) (310-519-1212). If you stay in Avalon Friday night, you need to reserve a seat on the Avalon-to-Two Harbors Marathon Boat leaving at 5:00 a.m. race morning (request a reservation on your entry form). The race provides a truck to transport your personal gear back to Avalon on race morning. Additionally, if your family or friends would like to be with you in Two Harbors on Friday night, the race provides a bus leaving from the start at 7:30 a.m., arriving in Avalon by 9:00 a.m. in plenty of time to catch the finish. Catalina welcomes marathon walkers and allows them and slower runners to start at 6:30 a.m. The race provides portable toilets at five locations on the course.

ACTIVITIES Packet pickup occurs Friday night in Avalon at the Landing Bar and Grill from 4:00 p.m. to 9:00 p.m. and in Two Harbors from 4:00 p.m. to 7:00 p.m. and from 8:00 p.m. to 9:00 p.m. After finishing the race, enjoy food and beverages while you await the awards ceremony starting at 2:00 p.m. We recommend relaxing for the remainder of the afternoon as the day's exercise is not over. For an additional sum, celebrate your special achievement at the dinner buffet and dance at the famous Casino Ballroom from 6:00 p.m. to 11:00 p.m.

AWARDS Each marathon finisher receives a long-sleeve T-shirt, post-race refreshments, finisher medal, finisher pin, and special finisher memorabilia. Marathon results are available for pick up in Avalon the next day. The top three overall and Buffalo division winners receive plaques and merchandise awards. The top three finishers in each age group also receive awards, as do the first male and female Catalina residents and the second and third men and women in the Buffalo division.

ACCOMMODATIONS The marathon runs before the prime tourist season so accommodations are generally not hard to find. Marathon participants stay in either Avalon or Two Harbors. Avalon offers the Hermit Gulch Campground located just off Avalon Canyon Road one mile from Avalon, (310-510-8368). Avalon hotels include: Pavilion Lodge, 513 Crescent Avenue (310-510-7788); Catalina Canyon Hotel, 888 Country Club Drive (310-510-0325); Hotel Vista Del Mar, 417 Crescent Avenue (310-510-1452); and Hotel St. Lauren, Metropolis and Beacon (310-510-2299). If you'd rather awake in tiny Two Harbors on race morning, camp at the Little Fisherman Cove Campground, or on marathon weekend only, at the unimproved Buffalo Park behind the restaurant. The Banning Lodge (310-510-0303), a turn of the century hunting lodge, is available for those who care to stay indoors.

RELATED EVENTS/RACES Catalina offers non-marathoners the opportunity to race on beautiful shorter courses in Avalon. At 8:00 a.m., a challenging 10K treats runners to stunning views of Avalon and its bay. A flat and fast 5K gets going at 8:10 a.m., taking runners along the water's edge and through the town of Avalon. Leaving no one out, Catalina holds a 1/2-mile Kid's Run for those under age 7, and a 1-mile run for those ages 7-12, starting at 9:00 a.m.

AREA ATTRACTIONS Catalina offers visitors more than just her beauty. Excellent scuba diving exists at Avalon's Underwater Park off Casino Point. If you'd rather see marine life from a further distance, hop on a glass bottom boat tour of a nearby cove. Touring the elegant estates of the Wrigley family and Zane Grey, the western novelist, are other options.

LOCAL RUNNING STORE Runners High, 5463 E. Carson, Long Beach (310-496-4760).

MAUI MARATHON

OVERALL: 93.4

COURSE BEAUTY: 10-

COURSE DIFFICULTY: 4

APPROPRIATENESS FOR FIRST TIMERS: 7+

RACE ORGANIZATION: 9

CROWDS: 1

RACE DATA

Contact:	Bob Craver
	Valley Isle Road Runners Association
	P.O. Box 330099
	Kahului, HI 96733
	(808) 871-6441
Date:	March 23, 1997
	March 29, 1998
Start Time:	5:30 a.m.
Time Course Closes:	12:30 p.m.
Number of Participants:	920 in 1996
Certification:	USATF
Course Records:	Male: (open) 2:30:18
	Female: (open) 2:50:55
Elite Athlete Programs:	No
Cost:	$40/50
Age groups/Divisions:	18-24, 25-29, 30-34, 35-39, 40-44, 45-49,
	50-54, 55-59, 60-64, 65-69, 70+
Temperature:	68° - 82°
Aid/Splits:	15 / none

HIGHLIGHTS If your idea of a great marathon includes incredible scenery, a well-run race organization, small-race charm, and an unsurpassed vacation destination, then the Maui Marathon may be just your race! A well-kept secret for 26 years, the Maui Marathon word is starting to get out. The race grew from 574 runners in 1995 to 920 in 1996. For 1997, there is a 1,400 runner limit. Why the tremendous growth? In addition to the above, we know of no other race where you can watch humpback whales frolic offshore while you run, making the marathon's slogan, Run With The Whales, well suited. The race also hosts one of the best carbo-load parties in North America, held at sunset just off Kaanapali Beach with views of palm trees, the Pacific Ocean, and neighboring Lanai. The event boasts live Hawaiian music, hula dancers, entertainers, microbrewed beer, and a generous banquet spread. A great alternative to the Honolulu Marathon, Maui offers a lower-key event. Like Honolulu, there is a large Japanese contingent, approximately half of the field. One of the main sponsors of the race is Ryutaro Kamioka, the "Johnny Carson of Japan." He plugs the Maui Marathon nearly weekly on his television show and radio programs in Osaka, which contributes to the large Japanese showing.

RACE HISTORY The Maui Marathon has a surprisingly rich and long history. The oldest continuously held race in Hawaii, the event is one of the oldest in the United States, with 1997 marking the 27th running. Ironically, the Maui Marathon began on Oahu in the early 1940s and was known as the Hawaiian AAU Marathon. At that time, Hawaii's top runner was Norman

Tamanaha. In 1971, Mr. Tamanaha convinced the newly formed Valley Isle Road Runners to bring the race to Maui, and the Norman Tamanaha Marathon was run in Maui that same year. In 1974, the race officially became the Maui Marathon which consistently attracted about 600 runners in the late 1970s and early 1980s. Between 1985 and 1993, participation levels dropped following the national trend in marathon running. Beginning in 1995, the race obtained Japanese sponsorship from Ryutaro Kamioka and Runner's Inc., the premiere running publication of Japan. As part of the sponsorship agreement, 25% of contributed funds are donated to a local charity. Seeing hearty growth since 1994, the race expects to expand for the next several years.

COURSE DESCRIPTION The point-to-point course starts in Kahului at Kaahumanu Center (near the airport) and finishes in Kaanapali Resort at Whalers Village. The first 2 miles run on residential streets. The race then proceeds onto the shoulders of Highways 380 and 30 for the next 6 miles, covering the flat Central Valley sugar cane fields to Maalea fishing village. As you make the turn onto Honoapiilani Highway 30 after the 6-mile mark, there's a good chance you'll be pushed by a nice tailwind as you approach the rolling hills between miles 8.5 and 12.5. Sunrise over 10,023-foot dormant volcano Haleakala on your left and the rugged West Maui mountains on the right set the stage for inspired running. The next 4 miles hug the Pali (ocean cliffs) where humpback whales can be often seen playing in the waters below. The most difficult part of the course, this section includes moderate rolling hills between miles 10 and 12.5. Lacking large inclines, the hills come early enough so you should still be relatively fresh. If you are not concerned with time, whale searching can take your mind off the hills and the long road ahead. At mile 12.5, a welcomed, albeit short, break from the sun greets you in the form of a 100-meter tunnel. The tunnel signals the end of the hills and the beginning of a .25-mile downhill stretch prefacing the second half of the race. From this point to the finish, the course is flat and stays within 50 feet of sandy beaches and the Pacific Ocean, offering spectacular views of neighboring islands. At about mile 22, the course turns down Front Street into downtown Lahaina, a historic whaling town with many outstanding restaurants and shops. The final two miles are back onto the shoulder of Highway 30 and into Kaanapali Resort to the finish in Whalers Village. Well-marked, the course consists of asphalt in excellent condition as well as a not-too-steep camber of the shoulder. The one disadvantage with the course is that it cannot be closed to vehicle traffic (except for Front Street) since the highways are the only route to the airport and other destinations. The occasional passing tour bus can cause quite a gust in your face, but most traffic travels fairly slowly.

CROWD/RUNNER SUPPORT Excellent for supporters to follow the race, the course highways are open to traffic and provide sufficient space on the side of the road to pull over and root for your favorite runner. Providing plenty of support, the aid station volunteers do a great job dispensing fluids and aid. Manned by various community groups, the aid stations compete for the "best aid station award" as chosen by the runners. Crowds along the course are sparse except for the start, Front Street in Lahaina, and the finish area. Announcers read the names of finishers as they come down home stretch. If you're lucky, your name will also be read in Japanese!

RACE LOGISTICS Race organizers provide bus service from the Kaanapali Resort area to the start, with departures beginning around 3:30 a.m. (ouch!). Buses are limited and service can take a little time; so, race officials urge runners to provide their own transportation if possible. Since most visitors to Maui rent a car anyway, this is not a big deal. Also, if your friends and family want to watch your progress, a car is the only way to go. If you do take the bus, the race will transport any clothes you may wish to have waiting for you at the finish. Though there is a good deal of parking at both the start and finish areas, arrive early. Additionally, shuttle buses are provided to return runners to Kaahumanu Center after the awards ceremony.

ACTIVITIES The Maui Marathon holds a small Sports and Fitness Expo where you also can pick up your race packet, get a course briefing, and have your body kneaded. With an incredible view, party atmosphere, and great food, Maui's Carbo Load Party surpasses most in North America. Held at the Maui Marriott, oceanfront at the Makai Garden, the party includes live music, Hawaiian entertainment, and an all-you-can-eat buffet with a wide variety of food. Refreshingly, there is not the usual parade of celebrity runners to bore you. Instead, the festive atmosphere abounds partly because it is held two nights before the race so runners feel free to partake in the all-you-can-drink beer. Tickets are about $20. On the morning before the race, there is a short (2.6 miles) charity fun run around Kaanapali Resort. Completely noncompetitive, the run could serve as a nice day-before warm-up if you like to get up early. Otherwise, sleep in. All finishers are treated to a post-race massage, refreshments, and an awards ceremony.

AWARDS Every runner receives a nice Maui Marathon T-shirt, and all marathon finishers receive medallions. There are age-group awards three deep in all categories. Additionally, a drawing for prizes donated by local merchants occurs at the end of the awards ceremony.

ELITE RUNNERS INFORMATION Maui currently does not offer special remuneration for elite runners since organizers prefer to focus on mid- to back-of-the-pack participants. The race organizers are considering offering some type of incentive in 1998 or later, however. Among the possibilities are paid accommodations and bonus money for breaking an existing course record. Contact the race director for more information.

ACCOMMODATIONS By far the best area to stay for convenience is in Kaanapali Resort which boasts six beachfront hotels and four resort condominiums. The race headquarters hotel is the Maui Marriott (800-228-2180). A discount for Maui Marathon participants makes it a good deal, but book early. Other Kaanapali possibilities are the Hyatt Regency (808-661-1234); and Westin Maui (808-667-2525). For less luxurious digs, try the Aston Maui Park (808-669-6622) located further down the highway and off the beach, or Lahaina.

RELATED EVENTS/RACES Beginning in 1997, a 5K race will be held to coincide with the marathon. This could be a good way for family and friends to participate in race-day activities.

AREA ATTRACTIONS There is no shortage of activities on Maui, including lying on the beach, snorkeling, golfing, whale watching, shopping, hiking, and trips to neighboring islands. You will not get bored here, and if you do, see a psychiatrist.

Maui MARATHON
Run With The Whales
A KAMIOKA CHARITY

Sunday, March 23, 1997
Sunday, March 29, 1998 • Sunday, March 28, 1999

1998 and 1999 dates subject to change

"One of the ten most scenic marathons in America"
- Runners' World, February 1996

We welcome you to experience the Maui Marathon,
considered by many to be the most beautiful and challenging
international running event in the world.

Because the field is limited, we recommend
that you register in advance.

For information call Valley Isle Road Runners at (808) 871- 6441.

The Maui Marriott in Kaanapali Beach Resort is
our Headquarters Hotel. The Maui Marriott will
be the location of all race week events including
the Official Carbo-Load, Sports & Fitness Expo
and Race Packet Pick-Up. For reservation
information call 1-800-763-1333,
1-800-542-6821 (in Hawaii).

SHAMROCK SPORTSFEST MARATHON

OVERALL: 84.8

COURSE BEAUTY: 8+

COURSE DIFFICULTY: 2+

APPROPRIATENESS FOR FIRST TIMERS: 7+

RACE ORGANIZATION: 9

CROWDS: 1

RACE DATA

Contact: Jerry Bocrie
Shamrock Sportsfest, Inc.
2308 Maple Street
Virginia Beach, VA 23451
(757) 481-5090

Date: March 15, 1997
March 14, 1998

Start Time: 9:00 a.m.

Time Course Closes: 3:00 p.m.

Number of Participants: 1,700 in 1996

Certification: USATF

Course Records: Male: (open) 2:15:26
Female: (open) 2:38:47

Elite Athlete Programs: Yes

Cost: $20/25

Age groups/Divisions: <24, 25-29, 30-34, 35-39, 40-44, 45-49, (F) 50-59,
60+, (M) 50-54, 55-59, 60-64, 65-69, 70+

Temperature: 52°

Aid/Splits: 12 / mile 1 and every 5 miles

HIGHLIGHTS Providing intense excitement for runners crossing the finish line, the Shamrock Sportsfest Marathon — celebrating its 25th Anniversary in 1997 — uses one of the few indoor finishes in North America. Held in Virginia Beach, VA, Shamrock boasts an extremely flat course through this resort area, turning around in Fort Story. Marathon weekend includes a world-class 8K, a terrific expo, a rocking beach party Saturday night, and enough free beer to intoxicate the Irish army. Perhaps not coincidentally, Shamrock was recently named the National Military Marathon Championship.

COURSE DESCRIPTION Starting in front of the Virginia Beach Pavilion Convention Center on 19th Street, the Shamrock Sportsfest Marathon's out-and-back course heads straight toward the oceanfront. Just before reaching the beach (mile .75), the course turns right on Atlantic Avenue for 1 mile. Turning north, the route proceeds on the Rudee Loop with views of the Rudee Inlet and the beach's bungee jump. Miles 3 and 4 travel along the Virginia Beach Boardwalk past cafes and, in nice weather, springtime beach goers. Before the end of the board-walk, the course takes you back to Atlantic Avenue for 6 miles, providing great views of beautiful beach homes and bungalows, and then turns toward False Cape State Park. As you run through Fort Story army base (miles 10 to 18), look for the country's oldest lighthouse and its contemporary replacement. Exiting the base, runners retrace their steps to the Convention Center getting an opportunity to eyeball their competition.

CROWD/RUNNER SUPPORT Without a doubt, the finish before thousands of spectators inside the Convention Center provides the race's greatest excitement. The 12 aid stations along the course carry water and electrolyte replacement, and medical assistance is available near miles 13 and 16. A trolley collects the tired and injured.

RACE LOGISTICS Most area hotels lie within 10 blocks of the Convention Center, a perfect warm-up on race morning. If you insist on driving to the start, some free parking exists at the Convention Center. The Virginia Beach YMCA offers sitter service on race day from 7:00 a.m. to 1:00 p.m. with plenty of activities to keep kids out of trouble while you run the marathon.

ACTIVITIES A busy, compact race weekend in the Convention Center (on 19th Street) begins with the excellent Sports and Fitness Expo (where you also pick up your packet or register) on Friday from 2:00 p.m. to 10:00 p.m. Approximately 20,000 people plow through the expo making it one of the East Coast's largest. On Friday evening from 5:00 p.m. to 8:00 p.m., attend the all-you-can-eat Pasta Party, featuring plenty of free beer to assist in your carbo-loading efforts (about $15). If you didn't get enough to eat at the pasta dinner (or were too cheap to pay for it), crash the Hospitality Room for free fruit and more free beer, 5:00 p.m. to 10:00 p.m. The race typically sponsors a running clinic on Friday evening, too. You may pick up your race packet or register on race morning if you haven't already done so. After the race (which you may or may not have finished after all that free beer), treat yourself to a free massage, post-race goodies, and refreshments. You will need them to recuperate in time for the Post-Race Beach Music Party on Saturday night. The party offers food, entertainment, and plenty of beer.

AWARDS All runners receive race T-shirts; finishers are entitled to medals, parchment certificates, and professional results booklets. The top five runners in most age groups receive a custom cultured marble award, while the top five overall finishers earn tasteful etched marble awards. The top five overall runners also take home prize money of $1,000, $600, $400, $300, and $200. The top three masters runners take home $300, $200, and $100. Prize money recipients must be USATF members.

ELITE RUNNERS INFORMATION Elite runners may be offered travel expenses, free lodging, and complimentary entry. Interested runners should send their running resumes to Jerry Bocrie by February 14.

ACCOMMODATIONS The Shamrock Housing Bureau offers a lodging clearinghouse for Sportsfest participants complete with special rates. Simply indicate your top choices on your race application and the Bureau will take care of the rest. Closest to the Convention Center are the Radisson and the Quality Inn on 21st Street. Many of the other hotels sit near the beach.

RELATED EVENTS/RACES Parts of the Shamrock Sportsfest activities are the world-class 8K and Masters 8K (both with prize money), the 5K Walk, and the Children's Marathon (26.2 yards). Corporate teams also compete in the open 8K event. Several world records have been set on the 8K course in both the open and masters races.

AREA ATTRACTIONS The main attraction in Virginia Beach is, of course, the beach. Naval buffs may also want to explore the Virginia Marine Science Museum, and nearby Norfolk, the East Coast's largest U.S. Navy port. Learn about Colonial history at Williamsburg, about an hour drive north of Virginia Beach.

LOCAL RUNNING STORE Running Etc., 1707 Colley Avenue, Norfolk, VA (757-627-1500).

TRAIL BREAKER MARATHON

OVERALL: 78.2

COURSE BEAUTY: 8

COURSE DIFFICULTY: 5-

APPROPRIATENESS FOR FIRST TIMERS: 6

RACE ORGANIZATION: 8

CROWDS: 0

RACE DATA

Contact:	MDA/Trail Breaker Marathon
	2949 N. Mayfair Road, Suite 106
	Wauwatosa, WI 53222
	(414) 453-7600
Date:	April 5, 1997
	March 27, 1998
Start Time:	8:00 a.m.
Time Course Closes:	1:30 p.m.
Number of Participants:	680 in 1996
Certification:	None
Course Records:	Male: (open) 2:44:21
	Female: (open) 3:12:00
Elite Athlete Programs:	No
Cost:	$26
Age groups/Divisions:	20-29, 30-34, 35-39, 40-44, 45-49, 50-54, 55-59,
	60-64, 65-69, 70-74, 75+
Temperature:	40°
Aid/Splits:	7 / none

HIGHLIGHTS Held about 30 minutes outside Milwaukee, Trail Breaker Marathon follows a converted railroad bed for 17 miles while the middle seven miles cut through southeastern Wisconsin's glaciated hills on the famous Ice Age Trail. The one-of-a-kind turnaround point lies at the top of the 70-step observation tower on Lapham Peak. Snow often appears at this race, once forcing organizers to change the course when the tower became encrusted with ice. Many of the area's sizeable ultramarathon community run Trail Breaker as a training run while raising money for the race's beneficiary, the Muscular Dystrophy Association.

COURSE DESCRIPTION Trail Breaker's out-and-back course starts in Waukesha's Frame Park along the Fox River. After a brief stretch on cobblestones and city streets, the race goes on an asphalt path bordering the river to the Glacial Drumlin Trail. Runners follow the trail — a converted railroad bed of crushed limestone — for the next 6.5 miles, passing through hardwoods and under bridges. At mile 9.5, the course reaches the town of Wales, and by mile 10.3 runners hit the Ice Age Trail. The Ice Age Trail marks the edge of the glacier that covered much of Wisconsin 15,000 years ago. This rough trail leads to 1,233-foot Lapham Peak and its 60-foot observation tower at the halfway point. Formerly called Government Hill, the peak saw duty as a surveying vantage point, as a meteorological relay station between Pikes Peak and Chicago, and as a tuberculosis sanitarium. The hill provides great views of the Kettle Moraine Forest. After scaling the tower's 70 steps and trudging back down, runners head back the same route to Waukesha.

CROWD/RUNNER SUPPORT Trail Breaker doesn't attract large crowds, mostly runners' friends and family who tend to congregate near the start/finish and the halfway point. Handlers of runners can access the course at the aid stations and at Lapham Peak Tower (there is a $4 fee to enter the area).

RACE LOGISTICS Parking is available at the Schuetze Building and along the street. The heated indoor staging area provides showers for grimy runners.

ACTIVITIES After the marathon, enjoy hot food, beverages, and the cool sounds of a reggae band.

AWARDS Each marathon finisher who is early-registered receives a long-sleeve T-shirt that is customized with towers on the sleeve representing the number of Trail Breakers he or she has completed. Top open, master, and senior master runners, and the top three in each age group receive certificates.

ACCOMMODATIONS In Waukesha, try the: Country Inn, 2810 Golf Road (414-547-0201); Comfort Inn, 2111 E. Moreland Blvd. (414-547-7770); Fairfield Inn, 20150 W. Bluemound Road (414-785-0500); Motel 6, 20300 W. Bluemound Road (414-786-7337); Budgetel Inn, 20391 W. Bluemound Road (414-782-9100); Holiday Inn, 2417 W. Bluemound Road (414-786-0460); Super 8 Motel, 2501 Plaza Court (414-785-1590); Select Inn, 2510 Plaza Court (414-786-6015); or Hampton Inn, 575 Barney Street (414-796-1500).

RELATED EVENTS/RACES Trail Breaker makes everyone happy by having a few options. If you're not ready to tackle the Ice Age Trail and the Lapham Peak Tower, try the half marathon which starts at 9:30 a.m. The Fox River 5K Run/Walk goes along the Fox River and starts at 10:30 a.m. Finally, competitive race walkers can enter the judged, 5K race walk.

AREA ATTRACTIONS See Area Attractions under Lakefront Marathon.

LOCAL RUNNING STORE The Fast Foot, 2120 E. Moreland, Westbrook Shopping Center, Waukesha (414-547-9333).

BIG SUR INTERNATIONAL MARATHON

OVERALL: 100

COURSE BEAUTY: 10+

COURSE DIFFICULTY: 6+ (SEE APPENDIX)

APPROPRIATENESS FOR FIRST TIMERS: 7-

RACE ORGANIZATION: 10

CROWDS: 2

RACE DATA

Contact:	Joseph W. Sweeney III
	Big Sur International Marathon
	P.O. Box 222620
	Carmel, CA 93922-26200
	(408) 625-6226
Date:	April 27, 1997
	April 26, 1998
Start Time:	7:00 a.m.
Time Course Closes:	12:30 p.m.
Number of Participants:	3,000+ in 1996
Certification:	USATF
Course Records:	Male: (open) 2:16:39
	Female: (open) 2:41:34
Elite Athlete Programs:	Yes
Cost:	$60/70/75
Age groups/Divisions:	16-19, 20-24, 25-29, 30-34, 35-39, 40-44, 45-49, 50-54, 55-59, 60-64, 65-69, 70+, Active Military, Monterey County, Clydesdales (males over 195 lbs., females over 150 lbs.), Mozarctic, Professional
Temperature:	50° - 60°
Aid/Splits:	12 / every mile, including pace and projected finish time

HIGHLIGHTS Our Perfect 100 marathon, Big Sur has it all — a breathtaking course, first-rate race organization, exceptional entertainment, and an unbeatable location for a getaway vacation. Big Sur's only problem? Every race thereafter seems anticlimactic. An experience to savor, Big Sur should be sipped. The difficult course and the spectacular scenery make PRs unimportant. Instead, take it all in: the Robert Louis Stevenson Orchestra, Jonathan Lee on the piano, the Bixby Bridge, the jagged coastline, and especially running down famous Pacific Coast Scenic Highway 1. Many runners describe Big Sur in spiritual or mystical terms. After you run it, you may be speaking in tongues as well — if you can speak at all.

RACE HISTORY We do our best thinking on a run. Evidently, despite being a runner, Bill Burleigh does his best thinking in a car. While driving on Highway 1 from Carmel to his home in Big Sur, Bill noticed a road sign: "26 miles to Big Sur." Bill put twenty-six and point two (.2) together and founded one of the world's great marathons.

Debuting in 1986, Big Sur has become extremely popular lately. The race now quickly fills to its 3,000 runner capacity. Despite (possibly because of) the majesty of the surroundings, Big Sur organizers encourage humor and whimsy. One popular BSIM tradition, the naming contest started in 1988, asks runners to name everything from the 520-foot hill at mile 10 (Hurricane Point), the last hill at mile 25.5 (D minor Hill at D major Time), the 700-pound heifer mascot who gave birth near the course in 1989 (Tchaicowsky), a skeleton dressed in running clothes at mile 25.5 (DeComposer), and the slow-footed race founder (Bachward Burleigh). You may notice the classical music thread here, and for good reason; race organizers give extra points to classical connections.

COURSE DESCRIPTION BSIM runs along U.S. Highway 1 from Big Sur to Carmel, passing spectacular redwoods, incomparable coastline, and seaside ranches. Runners have the whole road to themselves. Although downhill (the race starts at 300 feet and ends at 25 feet), the course contains plenty of uphills, providing a serious challenge for all levels of runners.

BSIM starts at Pfeiffer Big Sur State Park and proceeds largely downhill the first 5 miles (a 200-foot drop). From mile 5 to Point Sur at mile 9, the course inclines 75 feet. Heading back down to the 10-mile mark just after Little Sur River Bridge, runners encounter a huge, roaring crowd, providing much needed encouragement for the 520-foot, 2-mile climb to Hurricane Point, the toughest part of the route. After scaling Hurricane Point, runners descend 285 feet to Bixby Bridge at the halfway point. Then it's down another 135 feet to Palo Colorado Canyon at 15 miles. Hopefully you've recovered enough to climb 80 feet to Rocky Point at 15.6 miles. The course slopes down 90 feet to the 19-mile point at Soberanes Point. Of course, this is Big Sur; so, you run up 90 feet to Yankee Point. Then, down you go 140 feet to Point Lobos at 24, and then down another 70 feet to San Jose Creek at 24.9. Here you encounter D minor Hill at D major Time, an 80-footer over a quarter mile. Finishing on a well-deserved one-mile downhill, you cross the finish line at the Crossroads Shopping Center in Carmel. Congratulations. You are now a proud member of the Hurricane Point Survivors Association.

CROWD/RUNNER SUPPORT The Big Sur course naturally limits spectators' access to the race. As a result, the vast majority of crowds lie at two points on the course: the 10-mile point and the finish. However, musical inspiration awaits each runner along various

parts of the route: the 26-piece Robert Louis Stevenson Orchestra performs at Hurricane Point; Jonathan Lee plays a concert piano at Bixby Bridge; the Wild Coast Brass Quintet entertains at Rocky Point (mile 15); and Youth Music Monterey inspires at mile 17. At Point Lobos, brace yourself for the 60-member choral group, I Cantori. Bagpipes, radio stations, and a few other surprises support you on the majestic course. Aid stations stock water, electrolyte replacement, sponges, medical aid, fruit, and have toilet facilities.

RACE LOGISTICS Race organizers provide shuttle bus service from Monterey to the start, and from the finish area to the start. Since the morning bus ride to the start travels the course in reverse, runners receive an excellent opportunity to check out the route. There is also transportation for your clothing and personal items to the finish.

ACTIVITIES The two-day Expo is held at race headquarters, the Monterey Conference Center. The good-sized expo contains all the usual goodies. On Saturday afternoon, race organizers offer a clinic on "How to Run the Big Sur Course." The clinic is presented by runners of all levels who have completed the Big Sur course. On Saturday night, attend the carbo meal for a pasta buffet, locally-grown artichokes, and live jazz (about $14). Reserve early since it sells out well ahead of time. After the race, relax to a classical music concert while receiving a well-deserved complimentary massage. You can shower up then celebrate at the post-race party with beer, fresh fruit juice, and a variety of foods and snacks. Awards ceremony follows.

AWARDS The entry fee for BSIM is one of the highest around and worth every penny. Each entrant receives a heavyweight, long-sleeve T-shirt, official results book, and race-day program. Finishers earn hand-crafted ceramic medals created by a local sculptor. Finishers also become members of the Hurricane Point Survivors Association, which entitles them to discounts on future BSIM entry fees. Unique age-division awards from three to seven deep, including merchandise awards, go to division winners. Other random awards are doled out on race day. There is also approximately $20,000 in prize money.

ELITE RUNNERS INFORMATION The top three finishers get reimbursed for transportation and lodging, and the top five receive prize money ($5,000 for first, $2,000 for second, $1,000 for third, $500 for fourth, and $350 for fifth). Overall winners also receive round trip airline tickets. If you do well, you can return as an invited elite runner and receive complimentary accommodations. Male runners who have run a recent 2:30, and females with a recent 2:40 could qualify as an elite athlete at BSIM. Non-invited elites receive free entry. A $2,000 bounty goes to the runner who sets a new course record.

ACCOMMODATIONS If you like to sleep in, try to stay in Big Sur with its 242 rooms and cabins and 431 campsites. For cabins call (800-424-4787). For more luxurious surroundings, try the award-winning Ventana Inn, starting at $195 (408-667-2331) or the Post Ranch Inn Resort, with rates beginning at $285 and a two-night minimum (800-527-2200). Monterey boasts a wider range of lodging but requires transportation to the bus-loading area. Call Monterey Travel (800-334-4433), and let them find you Monterey accommodations in your price range.

RELATED EVENTS/RACES For those of you who don't want to run the marathon, but would like to experience Big Sur, BSIM also offers 7, 10, and 21-mile walks that start in the middle of the marathon route, a marathon relay for 5-member teams, and a 5K that starts and ends at the marathon finish area. Most of the 5K race runs along the Pacific Ocean. Special entry forms are required for any of these events.

AREA ATTRACTIONS Big Sur has all the ingredients for a wonderful vacation. First and foremost is the coastline. You can also visit the Monterey Bay Aquarium, Cannery Row, Laguna Seca race track, shop in Carmel, golf at Pebble Beach or Spyglass, or just linger along 17-mile drive.

LOCAL RUNNING STORE The Treadmill, 111 The Crossroads, Carmel (408-624-4112).

LAKE COUNTY MARATHON

OVERALL: 84.3

COURSE BEAUTY: 7+

COURSE DIFFICULTY: 3

APPROPRIATENESS FOR FIRST TIMERS: 8-

RACE ORGANIZATION: 9

CROWDS: 1+

R A C E   D A T A

Contact:	Lake County Races
	P.O. Box 9
	Highland Park, IL 60035
	(847) 266-RACE
Date:	April 27, 1997
	April 26, 1998
Start Time:	8:15 a.m.
Time Course Closes:	1:45 p.m.
Number of Participants:	NA
Certification:	USATF
Course Records:	Male: (open) 2:16:55
	Female: (open) 2:50:36
Elite Athlete Programs:	NA
Cost:	$26.20/31.20
Age groups/Divisions:	<14, 15-19, 20-24, 25-29, 30-34, 35-39, 40-44, 45-49, 50-54, 55-59, 60-64, 65-69, 70-74, 75+
Temperature:	NA
Aid/Splits:	10 / miles 1, 3, 5, 10, 13.1, 20 & 22

HIGHLIGHTS From scary North Chicago to moneyed Highland Park, the Lake County Marathon shows a face of stark contrasts as it threads Lake Michigan's shore south from the Wisconsin/Illinois border toward Chicago. Offering a more exhaustive menu of races than the latest chain restaurant, Lake County attracts runners with its reasonably fast, point-to-point course and its something-for-everyone mentality.

COURSE DESCRIPTION Starting on Sheridan Road, a wide, unattractive stretch of asphalt, the Lake County Marathon cuts through strip malls, commercial districts, a warehouse area, and some low-income neighborhoods for most of the first 8 miles of the race. Cambered in some spots, the road contains some very gentle grades, but is mostly flat or downhill. Near mile 9, runners happily enter wooded Foss Park, marking a major change in the course's complexion. Miles 9 through 12 tour the Great Lakes Naval Base. Runners encounter Sousa Hill, the marathon's largest, at mile 10 on the base. Exiting the base is like bursting out of a 12-mile tunnel into the brilliant sunshine; it may take you a while to adjust. Now more rolling and winding, the course shows off Lake County's high society, passing estate after estate, mansion after mansion through the communities of Lake Bluff, Lake Forest, Highwood, and Highland Park to the finish. The merely large homes seem pedestrian, and thoughts of rundown North Chicago are a lifetime (and 4 miles) away.

CROWD / RUNNER SUPPORT You find most spectators scattered in the neighborhoods after exiting the Great Lakes Naval Base. Aid stations with water and electrolyte replacement and medical aid stations are located every 2.5 miles. Portable toilets sit at miles 3.5, 5, 6.2, 10, 13.1, 15, 20, and 23.5. Digital clocks show your progress at miles 1, 3, 5, 10, 13.1, 20, and 22.

RACE LOGISTICS We suggest you drive to Ravinia Park in Highland Park and take the free train to the start in Zion. The train departs Ravinia Park at 6:40 a.m. If you prefer, you can pick up the train at Clybourn Station in Chicago at 6:00 a.m. The train arrives in Zion at 7:15 a.m. If you must drive to the start, there is only one bus to take you back to Zion after the race. The bus leaves at 1:00 p.m. from the Western Gate of Ravinia Park in the parking lot. If you miss that bus, your only other alternative is to take the regularly scheduled (not free) METRA train at 3:21 p.m. from Ravinia Station. You may check your gear at the start for pickup after the race.

ACTIVITIES Race packet pickup and a Sports Expo are held on Friday from 3:00 p.m. to 8:00 p.m. and Saturday from 10:00 a.m. to 6:00 p.m. at the Sheraton North Shore. There is no race-day packet pickup or registration, but you may have your packet mailed to you for an extra charge. Hit the refreshments and snacks after the marathon.

AWARDS Every runner receives a Lake County Marathon T-shirt, and each finisher receives a memento. The top three runners in each age group and the top 10 overall are awarded prizes.

ACCOMMODATIONS The Sheraton North Shore Inn, 933 Skokie Blvd., Northbrook (800-535-9131), serves as the host hotel. Other hotels reasonably close to the marathon finish are: Hotel Moraine, 700 N. Sheridan, Highwood (847-433-5566); Residence Inn Deerfield, 530 Lake Cook Road, Deerfield (800-331-3131); Red Roof Inn Northbrook, 340 Waukegan Road (847-205-1755); Courtyard by Marriott, 1505 Lake Cook Road, Highland Park (800-321-2211); Hyatt Deerfield, 1750 Lake Cook Road (847-945-3400); and Embassy Suites Hotel, 1455 Lake Cook Road, Deerfield (847-945-4500).

RELATED EVENTS / RACES The Lake County Races offer six different races, including the marathon. The marathon, half marathon, 10K, and 5-person marathon relay share the same start time and location. The 3.5-mile Fun Run & Walk starts and finishes at Ravinia Park, while the Special Olympics Relay begins at the marathon's halfway point in Lake Bluff and finishes at Ravinia Park.

AREA ATTRACTIONS See the Chicago Marathon for area attractions.

LOCAL RUNNING STORES Vertel's, 2001 N. Clybourn Avenue (312-248-7400); Fleet Feet, 241-243 W. North Avenue (312-587-3338).

BOSTON MARATHON

OVERALL: 97

COURSE BEAUTY: 8

COURSE DIFFICULTY: 4 (SEE APPENDIX)

APPROPRIATENESS FOR FIRST TIMERS: NA

RACE ORGANIZATION: 10

CROWDS: 5+

RACE DATA

Contact:	Guy Morse
	Boston Athletic Assn.
	131 Clarendon
	Boston, MA 02116
	(617) 236-1652
Date:	April 21, 1997
	April 20, 1998
Start Time:	Noon
Time Course Closes:	Last Runner
Number of Participants:	9,416 in 1995
Certification:	USATF
Course Records:	Male: (open) 2:07:15
	Female: (open) 2:21:45
Elite Athlete Programs:	Yes
Cost:	$75
Age groups/Divisions:	18-34, 35-39, 40-44, 45-49, 50-54, 55-59, 60-64, 65-69, 70+
Temperature:	50° - 55°
Aid/Splits:	12 / every mile

HIGHLIGHTS The Mother of all Marathons, running's best friend, running's Mecca. Call it what you like, the 101-year-old Boston Marathon stands as the benchmark by which all other marathons are measured. Virtually all certified marathons in North America attest to Boston's preeminence in the sport by noting on their entry blank, "This is a Boston Qualifier." In addition to its age, part of the Boston mystique stems from the rigid qualification standards used to limit its field. If you're talented enough to qualify, expect to have an incredible running experience. One and a half million spectators frame the most famous course in the world: Hopkinton, Wellesley College, Heartbreak Hill, the Citgo sign, and Copley Square are all familiar landmarks of this landmark race.

RACE HISTORY Unchallenged as the world's oldest and most prestigious annual marathon, the Boston Marathon started on April 19, 1897 after Boston Athletic Association member and U.S. Olympic Team manager John Graham, so impressed with the spirit of the Olympic marathon, decided to stage one in the Boston area. Fifteen men participated in that first race, the second marathon ever held in the United States (New York held a marathon the previous year). Held on Patriot's Day, commemorating Paul Revere's famous ride marking the American Revolution, Boston remains a race of tradition and distinction for its participants, volunteers, and spectators. Starting with John J. McDermott's inaugural win, Boston lore includes Clarence DeMar's record seven victories, John Kelley's two victories and 58 finishes, Roberta Gibb and Kathy Switzers' barrier breaking efforts for women runners, Bill Rodger's record performances, and current stars Cosmas Ndeti and

Uta Pippig. While the world's elite marathoners dream of winning Boston, qualifying to run remains an aspiration of most other marathoners worldwide. After instituting qualifying times in the early 1970s, Boston has spurred many marathoners to times they never imagined possible. Whether an elite athlete, qualifier, spectator or volunteer, Boston represents the pinnacle of marathoning.

COURSE DESCRIPTION Starting on Main Street in the rural hamlet of Hopkinton, Boston's point-to-point course features a 450-foot elevation loss as it winds through seven towns before finishing near Copley Square in Boston's Back Bay. Following Route 135, the race heads downhill through Ashland past the impressive Ashland clock tower and the stirring waters of the Sudbury River between miles 4 and 5. Here, runners enter Framingham, passing the historic Framingham Train Depot at the 10K mark. Continuing mostly downhill, the route skirts tranquil Lake Cochituate at 9 miles and the Natick Town Green at 10.5 miles. The male runners always seem to quicken their step as they near the halfway point to the screaming sirens of Wellesley College. Once there, however, many don't seem to be in any hurry. Now on Route 16, runners climb 50 feet between miles 15 and 16 before crossing the Charles River into Newton Lower Falls. After turning right at the fire station onto Commonwealth Avenue, the route traverses the Newton Hills (the infamous Heartbreak Hill) rising 175 feet between miles 17 and 22, paying homage to the John Kelley Statue at 19.5 miles. The course then descends 200 feet over the last 4 miles to the finish. Bearing right at the Chestnut Hill Reservoir, the route makes its way onto Beacon Street continuing mostly downhill past the landmark Citgo sign at the 25-mile mark in Kenmore Square. Here, the course rejoins Commonwealth Avenue turning right onto Hereford Street, then left onto Boylston Street to the finish line.

CROWD/RUNNER SUPPORT The largest single-day sporting event in New England, the Boston Marathon's crowd support is unparalleled, attracting more than 1.5 million spectators. Held on a holiday, the race draws onlookers over 10 deep at several points. Generations of families come out to cheer the runners, with kids holding out orange slices or water, dreaming of the day when they will take part in the spectacle. Several thousand volunteers help coordinate the start, finish and course logistics. If you miss one of the aid stations located every 2 miles, don't worry, unofficial neighborhood aid stations saturate the entire course. Additionally, American Red Cross aid stations occur every mile to assist anyone requiring medical attention. If it's media not medical attention you want, you have a very good chance of being captured in print or television by the approximately 1,100 media personnel representing more than 300 media outlets from around the world who cover the Boston Marathon each year.

RACE LOGISTICS Part of Boston's attraction comes from its unique qualification standards. The following qualifying times must be run between January 1 of the previous year and February 1 of the year you would like to run Boston:

AGE GROUP	18-34	35-39	40-44	45-49	50-54	55-59	60-64	65-69	70+
MEN	3:10	3:15	3:20	3:25	3:30	3:35	3:40	3:45	3:50
WOMEN	3:40	3:45	3:50	3:55	4:00	4:05	4:10	4:15	4:20

In 1997, the race instituted a 15,000 runner limit. If the limit is reached prior to February 1, you are out of luck. All U.S. residents must have a valid USATF number. Foreign athletes must be registered with their country's federation. On race morning, shuttle bus transportation to the start is provided to runners from South Street and State Park.

ACTIVITIES Race packets may be picked up at the race headquarters hotel during the extraordinary, 2-day Sports and Fitness Expo all day on Saturday and Sunday. You may do more gawking than eating at the celebrity-laden Boston Marathon Pasta Party on Sunday night. After the race, enjoy the awards ceremony and the Post-Race Dance Party, including dinner, live music and entertainment.

AWARDS Each entrant receives a long-sleeve T-shirt and an official full-color Race Program. Runners finishing under 7 hours receive pewter medallions and certificates of completion. An official Results Booklet which chronicles the race and lists all official finishers is mailed after the event. Elite athletes compete for a portion of the $600,000 prize purse — largest in the sport. Division winners also receive special awards.

ELITE RUNNERS INFORMATION The B.A.A. recruits elite runners from every part of the globe, specifically men with sub-2:15 credentials and women under 2:35, though elite status may not always be this straightforward. The race covers travel, lodging and food expenses for elites. Prize money for open men and women extends 15 places with the winner receiving $100,000 and 15th place netting $1,500. Masters men and women compete for prize money extending 5 places with $12,000 earmarked for the winner and $1,000 for 5th place. In addition, bonuses are awarded for course records and world best performances.

ACCOMMODATIONS Hotels abound in the Boston Metropolitan area. In addition to the race headquarters hotel, the Copley Plaza Hotel (617-267-5300), your lodging options include: Four Seasons Hotel, 200 Boylston Street (617-338-4400); Ritz Carlton Hotel, 15 Arlington Street (617-536-5700); Sheraton Boston, 39 Dalton Street (617-236-2000); Westin, 10 Huntington Avenue (617-262-9600); and Marriott Copley, 110 Huntington Avenue (617-236-5800).

AREA ATTRACTIONS Not only the site of marathoning's most historic race, Boston rates as one of the country's best walking cities. You can visit some of the city's historic landmarks along the two-and-a-half mile red-painted line of the Freedom Trail through downtown Boston. Explore the Boston Massacre site, Paul Revere's House, and Bunker Hill Monument. Before catching a Boston Red Sox game at Fenway Park, the oldest major league ballpark, spend some time milling about the book stores and cafes of Harvard Square in nearby Cambridge. Shop on trendy Newbury Street near the marathon finish.

LOCAL RUNNING STORES Bill Rodgers Running Center, 353 N. Market Place (617-723-5612); Marathon Sports, 1654 Massachusetts Avenue (617-354-4161).

RUNNING FIT TRAIL MARATHON

OVERALL: 77.2

COURSE BEAUTY: 9-

COURSE DIFFICULTY: 8

APPROPRIATENESS FOR FIRST TIMERS: 3+

RACE ORGANIZATION: 8-

CROWDS: 0

RACE DATA

Contact:	Randy Step
	Running Fit
	123 E. Liberty
	Ann Arbor, MI 48104
	(313) 769-5016
Date:	April 27, 1997
	April 26, 1998
Start Time:	8:00 a.m.
Time Course Closes:	2:00 p.m.
Number of Participants:	158 in 1996
Certification:	None
Course Records:	Male: (open) 2:52:59; (masters) 3:03:21
	Female: (open) 3:44:00; (masters) 3:51:00
Elite Athlete Programs:	No
Cost:	$15/20
Age groups/Divisions:	<19, 20-24, 25-29, 30-34, 35-39, 40-44, 45-49,
	50-54, 55-59, 60-64, 65-69, 70+
Temperature:	50° - 60°
Aid/Splits:	10 / none

HIGHLIGHTS Up in Michigan there is a trail marathon run among the thin, bare trees, through swamps, and over rocky trails. Affectionately called The Beast, the Potawatomi Trail has claimed more than a few runners. The race director's motto is "No Wimps" because he doesn't want to hear any whining about skinned knees, bruised shins, and muddy countenances. Expect them. Despite the seemingly harsh attitude (meant in jest), the warm campfires at the aid stations and the camaraderie among the runners mark the true spirit of the race.

COURSE DESCRIPTION Characterized by constant hills, muddy trails, and elevations ranging from 300 feet to 1,200 feet, Running Fit's double loop course begins along Silver Lake in the Pinckney Recreation Area just 20 miles north of Ann Arbor, Michigan. Quickly funneling onto the narrow, rocky and hilly Potawatomi Trail, runners huff and puff past dense woods, through occasional swamplands, and over several bridges. Sixteen lakes, fields of wildflowers, and budding trees help runners cope with the unrelenting hills. Race organizers ring a bell signaling the last lap — if you're doing the full marathon, the bell tolls for you.

CROWD/RUNNER SUPPORT Five aid stations dot the loop providing almost everything you may require: water, electrolyte replacement drink, GU, bananas, cookies, petroleum jelly, first aid (always a few falls) and cozy campfires. Usually in full party mode, aid station volunteers provide the bulk of your external encouragement along the course. At the halfway point and the finish, runners' families are often on hand picnicking along Silver Lake.

RACE LOGISTICS In keeping with the spirit of the race, you must find your own way to the start. Runners considering the race are clearly resourceful enough to handle this detail. The roving time limit requires you to maintain at least a 6-hour pace at each of the aid stations, or you will be forced to withdraw from the race.

ACTIVITIES Register or pick up your packet at Running Fit on Saturday from 10:00 a.m. to 4:00 p.m. You may also take care of this on race morning near the start from 7:00 a.m. to 7:50 a.m. One of the race highlights is the legendary Saturday evening race meeting and campfire held at 7:30 p.m. at Crooked Lake Campsite on Silver Hill Road. Hear lies and stories about the race at this irreverent gathering, which also features storytelling and trivia contests. The raging bonfire should encourage you to new heights of exaggeration. Campers at Crooked Lake can enjoy the pizza loading party delivered to your campsite. Perhaps the most popular post-race activity involves a visit to the chiropractor.

AWARDS The entry fee does not include a T-shirt. If you would like a shirt, you must pay an extra $8 to $25 depending on the type of shirt desired. Marathon finishers receive commemorative awards, as do the top five runners in each age group. Men under 3:00 and women under 3:30 receive a pair of Brooks running shoes.

ACCOMMODATIONS The official accommodation is the Crooked Lake Campground in the Pinckney Recreation Area. If you prefer a roof, try the Best Western in Howell, 1500 Pinckney Road, off I-96 exit 137 (517-548-2900).

RELATED EVENTS/RACES Runners who prefer a single scoop of mud can enter the half marathon, which is one loop of the course. There is also a 5-Mile Trail Run that includes a patch near the start worse than any terrain on the marathon route.

AREA ATTRACTIONS Many of the participants enjoy a weekend of camping built around the marathon. If that seems just a bit too rustic for your tastes, head to Ann Arbor, the Berkeley of the Midwest. Home to the huge University of Michigan, Ann Arbor is an eclectic college town filled with restaurants, bars, and crunchy people.

LOCAL RUNNING STORES Running Fit, 123 E. Liberty, Ann Arbor (313-769-5016); Tortoise & The Hare, 213 E. Liberty (313-769-9510).

AVENUE OF THE GIANTS MARATHON

OVERALL: 91.6

COURSE BEAUTY: 10

COURSE DIFFICULTY: 3- (SEE APPENDIX)

APPROPRIATENESS FOR FIRST TIMERS: 9

RACE ORGANIZATION: 9-

CROWDS: 0+

RACE DATA

Contact: Avenue of the Giants
281 Hidden Valley Road
Bayside, CA 95524
(707) 443-1226
Date: May 4, 1997
May 3, 1998
Start Time: 9:00 a.m.
Time Course Closes: 2:00 p.m.
Number of Participants: 466 in 1996
Certification: USATF
Course Records: Male: (open) 2:17:43
Female: (open) 2:45:40
Elite Athlete Programs: No
Cost: $40/45/50
Age groups/Divisions: <19, 20-29, 30-34, 35-39, 40-44, 45-49, 50-54,
55-59, 60-64 65-69, 70-74, 75-79, 80+
Temperature: 45° - 70°
Aid/Splits: 9 / miles 1, 5, 15 & 20

HIGHLIGHTS Few marathons match the natural beauty contained in northwestern California's Avenue of the Giants Marathon. Staged in Humboldt Redwoods State Park, Avenue's gently undulating route weaves along the South Eel River Valley through a canopy of prehistoric Giant Redwoods that in some places barely allows enough sunlight to nourish the luscious ferns and wild iris growing below. In its heyday 20 years ago, Avenue reigned as one of California's most popular marathons filling its 2,000 runner limit in days. While participation has waned recently due to other excellent races coming along, the race remains a quality event through one of earth's most remarkable environments.

COURSE DESCRIPTION Avenue of the Giants runs on the same L-shaped course as autumn's Humboldt Redwoods Marathon, except Avenue completes the Bull Creek leg first and the Avenue of the Giants leg second, while Humboldt does the reverse. See Humboldt Redwoods Marathon for more detail.

CROWD/RUNNER SUPPORT If your performance hinges on the support of boisterous spectators, the almost eerie quiet of Avenue may not be for you. Your greatest support, in addition to the aid station volunteers every 2.5 to 3 miles, comes from the "ambassadors from another time," as John Steinbeck referred to the mammoth redwoods. These goodwill ambassadors provide a protective canopy for most of the route, effectively insulating you from wind and direct sunlight.

RACE LOGISTICS Unless camping nearby, you'll probably need to drive to the start since lodging is scarce in the immediate vicinity. If you are traveling north on Hwy. 101, take the Founder's Tree exit, while southbound travelers should take the second Redcrest exit. The race's staging area lies on the north side of the Dyerville Bridge and overlooks the convergence of the south and main forks of the Eel River. Parking is located on the Eel River flats adjacent to the staging area. You can avoid the congestion by arriving early.

ACTIVITIES Containing none of the pomp and circumstance that you find at many other marathons, Avenue's principal attraction is its spectacular course. The American Legion Hall in Fortuna serves as the race registration site on Saturday from 2:00 p.m. to 5:00 p.m. Avenue allows race-day registration from 7:30 a.m. to 9:00 a.m. Since few restaurants exist around the area, three separate pasta feeds are available Saturday night from 4:00 p.m. to 7:00 p.m. Choose between the American Legion Halls in either Fortuna or Weott and South Fork High School in Miranda. After the race, enjoy refreshments while waiting for the awards ceremony at 1:00 p.m.

AWARDS All participants receive race T-shirts, and finishers receive medals. Overall and age-group winners receive plaques. A results booklet is mailed to each participant a few months following the event.

ACCOMMODATIONS Avenue does not have an official race hotel, but several hotels exist in nearby small towns. In Weott (about 2 miles away), try the Sequoia Motel, 151 Weott Heights Road (707-946-2276). For other accommodations, see the entry for Humboldt Redwoods Marathon.

RELATED EVENTS/RACES You don't have to be a marathoner to enjoy a gorgeous run through the redwoods. Avenue offers a related 10K which starts at 9:10 a.m. heading south on an out-and-back course along the redwood-lined Avenue of the Giants.

AREA ATTRACTIONS Although your kids will go nuts over some of the touristy attractions like the Drive-thru Tree near Leggett, the best way to appreciate the majestic redwoods involves escaping to the less crowded trails. Rockefeller Forest (which you pass in the first half of the marathon) contains a grove with the largest redwoods in the world. If you have some time, obtain a hiking guide and explore the dramatic sea cliffs and rugged wilderness along the nearby Lost Coast, so named because no coastal highway exists along its 31 miles. (For other options, see Humboldt Redwoods Marathon.)

LOCAL RUNNING STORE The Jogg'n Shoppe, 1090 G Street, Arcata (707-822-3136).

LINCOLN MARATHON

OVERALL: 77.7

COURSE BEAUTY: 7

COURSE DIFFICULTY: 4 (SEE APPENDIX)

APPROPRIATENESS FOR FIRST TIMERS: 7

RACE ORGANIZATION: 10-

CROWDS: 2-

RACE DATA

Contact:	Nancy Sutton
	Lincoln/All Sport Marathon
	5309 S. 62nd Street
	Lincoln, NE 68516
	(402) 423-4519
Date:	May 4, 1997
	May 3, 1998
Start Time:	7:00 a.m.
Time Course Closes:	12:00 p.m.
Number of Participants:	1,246 in 1996
Certification:	USATF
Course Records:	Male: (open) 2:20:09; (masters) 2:29:11
	Female: (open) 2:42:45; (masters) 2:56:58
Elite Athlete Programs:	No
Cost:	$25/30/40
Age groups/Divisions:	12-19, 20-24, 25-29, 30-34, 35-39, 40-44, 45-49,
	50-54, 55-59, 60-64, 65-69, 70-74, 75-79, 80+
Temperature:	45° - 60°
Aid/Splits:	12 / every mile, 10K & 13.1

HIGHLIGHTS Although possessing the classic runner build, President Abraham Lincoln probably wasn't the slave to mileage like President Clinton. Nonetheless, his memory enjoys an interesting connection with the world of marathons. The Marine Corps Marathon runs past the Lincoln Memorial. Maryland's Northern Central Trail Marathon travels along a former railroad bed traced by the train that carried "Honest Abe's" body back to Illinois after his assassination. And, Nebraska's Lincoln Marathon is held in the city bearing his name. One score and zero years ago, the Lincoln Marathon offered runners a not-so-glorious tour of area cornfields. Since the recent renovation of the city's downtown, the race offers runners more than a run through "amber waves of grain." Instead, the route takes runners on a citywide tour passing many area landmarks including the breathtaking Capitol Building — the "Tower of the Plains." As a testament to Lincoln's stellar race organization, the Army National Guard has chosen Lincoln for twelve straight years as its marathon trials to decide its World Military Games marathon team.

COURSE DESCRIPTION Runners assemble in front of Memorial Stadium, home of the National Champion Cornhusker football team, on the University of Nebraska campus. The National Guard Band plays marching music to rouse the runners for a peak performance. After two blocks, the race turns south on 16th Street for 2 miles. At the 1-mile mark, runners see the Nebraska State Capitol Building, a jewel among state capitols. Turning left on South Street, runners follow historic Lincoln Sheridan Blvd. for 2 miles past many of the finest old homes in the city, climbing about 100 feet between miles 2 and 3. At the 5-mile mark, runners turn at 48th and Calvert, the highest point on the course. Traveling through College View, a community of small shops and student hangouts, runners are greeted by the students of Union College. After a gradual downhill to 10K, runners veer onto a paved bike path, following it for 2.5 miles. At 20th Street, runners exit the trail making their way north to the Country Club of Lincoln. This uphill stretch past the Country Club may be one of the toughest in the first half of the race. Coming down the other side of the hill, runners enter Van Dorn Park, a pleasant neighborhood of tree-lined streets. Proceeding down 10th Street, the City of Lincoln approaches as runners pass the County-City Building and the "Big Red N" over the football stadium looms ahead. Half marathoners peel away, finishing on Ed Weir Track, while marathoners circle the baseball stadium, cruise through the University campus, and return to 16th Street heading toward the Capitol building. At the Capitol, runners turn onto flat Capitol Parkway (which becomes Normal Blvd.) as they head toward Holmes Lake Park. The beautiful lily pads of the Sunken Gardens lie at 27th and Capitol Parkway. Winding its way past the Children's Zoo, the course then proceeds along the Ager Memorial Jr. Golf Course and Antelope Park. At about 17.5 miles, runners return to a bike path for a half mile and begin a 100-foot climb into Holmes Lake Park, the city's most beautiful park. Ducks and geese fill the water, and bands and giant balloons encourage runners. The climb up the dam to the park and the climb up 70th from Holmes Park to Van Dorn may be the two toughest stretches in the race. Looping around Holmes Park (19-20), the course returns down Normal Blvd./Capitol Parkway on a gradual downgrade, giving runners a chance to view their compatriots going in the opposite direction. The marathon finishes on Ed Weir Track on the UN-L campus.

CROWD / RUNNER SUPPORT Although nothing like a Nebraska Cornhusker football game, Lincoln attracts several thousand spectators along its citywide route. Most of the onlookers collect around the start/finish, where they can see the half marathon finish and cheer the marathoners embarking on the second half of the race, and in the residential areas. Twelve aid stations throughout the course carry ice, water and electrolyte replacement in cups with lids and straws, and orange slices after halfway. Particularly noteworthy, Lincoln General Hospital operates an imaginative and uplifting aid station near mile 9. Shag wagons roam the course to scoop up pooped-out runners.

RACE LOGISTICS If you're staying at the Ramada or at a neighboring hotel, you'll experience few hassles on race day as the start/finish is a short walk away. If you cannot complete the marathon in 5 hours or less, the race offers the option of starting at 5:30 a.m.

ACTIVITIES The Runner's Expo and Packet Pickup take place on Saturday from 10:00 a.m. to 7:00 p.m. at the race headquarters in the Ramada Hotel & Convention Center, 141 N. 9th Street. All participants over 50 years old are invited to attend the Harry Crockett over-50 Club's annual luncheon held at 11:30 a.m. at Spaghetti Works, 228 N. 12th Street. Runners, their families and volunteers are invited to enjoy a free spaghetti dinner at the Pastathon from 4:00 p.m. to 7:00 p.m. at the UN-L Fieldhouse. After your marathon, relax with a massage, enjoy food and beverages, and call your friends long distance for free to brag about your accomplishment. A post-race party kicks off at 12:00 p.m. followed by the awards ceremony and door prizes at 1:30 p.m.

AWARDS Whether it's effective budget management, excellent sponsorship, or both, you get more than what you pay for at Lincoln. Each participant receives a race T-shirt, finisher's medal, free night-before pasta party, pre- and post-race booklet, and finisher's photograph. Every woman finisher receives a rose. Faster runners compete for modest prize money with the following breakdown: $500-first, $250-second, $125-third, $100-fourth, $75-fifth, and $50-sixth through tenth. Masters prize money extends two deep, $125 and $75, respectively. Course record bonuses, $500 for open and $125 for masters, are also offered. Plaques are presented to the first three to eight men and women in each age division, depending on the number of runners. Runners breaking certain age-graded time standards receive an athletic bag.

ACCOMMODATIONS The Ramada Hotel, 141 N. 9th Street (402-475-4011), serves as the race headquarters offering special marathon rates. Other hotels featuring special marathon rates include: Cornhusker Hotel, 333 S. 13th Street (800-793-7474); Days Inn, 2920 NW 12th Street (402-475-3616); Motel 6, 3001 NW 12th Street (402-475-3211); and Town House Mini-Suite, 18th Street (402-475-3000).

RELATED EVENTS/RACES Race weekend gets going with the KFRX Mayor's Children Run on Saturday at 8:30 a.m. Kids in eighth grade or younger participate in a one-mile run around the Nebraska State Capitol. Additionally, Lincoln offers a half marathon which runs on the first half of the marathon course and starts along with the longer race.

AREA ATTRACTIONS After running by the architectural wonder in the marathon, you'll likely want to see the interior of Lincoln's impressive State Capitol Building. Free tours are available every hour. Afterward, roam the botanical gardens in Antelope Park or visit the Sunken Gardens at 27th and D Streets.

LOCAL RUNNING STORE Athlete's Foot, 1213 O Street, Lincoln (402-474-4557).

PITTSBURGH MARATHON

OVERALL: 87.7

COURSE BEAUTY: 7

COURSE DIFFICULTY: 3+ (SEE APPENDIX)

APPROPRIATENESS FOR FIRST TIMERS: 9+

RACE ORGANIZATION: 10

CROWDS: 4

RACE DATA

Contact: Larry Grollman
City of Pittsburgh Marathon, Inc.
3434 Fifth Avenue, First Floor
Pittsburgh, PA 15213
(412) 647-7866
http://www.upmc.edu/pghmarathon

Date: May 4, 1997
May 3, 1998

Start Time: 8:30 a.m.

Time Course Closes: 2:30 p.m.

Number of Participants: 2,340 in 1996

Certification: USATF

Course Records: Male: (open) 2:12:02; (masters) 2:20:30
Female: (open) 2:36:12; (masters) 2:54:11

Elite Athlete Programs: Yes

Cost: $27/37

Age groups/Divisions: <19, 20-24, 25-29, 30-34, 35-39, 40-44, 45-49,
50-54, 55-59, 60-64, 65-69, 70+

Temperature: 50° - 63°

Aid/Splits: 20 / every 2 miles

HIGHLIGHTS Charles Dickens once referred to Pittsburgh as "hell with the lid off" because its billowy smokestacks produced a perpetual dusk. Dickens would not recognize Pittsburgh today, and the City of Pittsburgh Marathon showcases much of the city to prove it. Starting in shiny downtown with its numerous architectural landmarks, the race crosses the Allegheny, Monongahela, and Ohio Rivers before the striking finish at the three rivers' nexus. On the way, runners encounter Pittsburgh's diversity, from the Golden Triangle, to working-class Lawrenceville, to well-to-do Shadyside. Community support of the marathon has grown tremendously, so that now, with marathon organizers' assistance, each community holds a unique, marathon-day festival to commemorate the race and support the runners. As our fastest spring marathon, the Pittsburgh Marathon also appeals to runners looking to improve their time. In 1997, many of the country's elite runners will aim to improve their times as Pittsburgh hosts the USA Track and Field Men's National Marathon Championship.

RACE HISTORY The brainchild of Larry Kuzmanko, the Pittsburgh Marathon started in 1985 with about 1,800 runners. Over the years, the primary sponsorship has changed from USX, to Giant Eagle food stores, to the current University of Pittsburgh Medical Center. In 1988, the marathon served as the U.S. Women's Olympic Marathon Trials won by Margaret Groos in 2:29:50. The City of Pittsburgh took over the event in 1990, and its mayor, Tom Murphy, regularly participates.

COURSE DESCRIPTION The Pittsburgh Marathon's near loop course crosses the city's famous three rivers cutting through 12 distinct and diverse neighborhoods. The convenient new layout, revised in 1996, places the start and finish within a half mile of each other. The race starts in front of the City-County Building in the midst of downtown's gleaming high rises. The course, completely closed to traffic, heads along Grant Street (passing the well-known USX tower), then onto Liberty Avenue for the first mile. A slight upgrade faces the runners at mile 2 as they pass through the Strip District, an historic waterfront area of fresh produce, vegetables, and seafood. Running into the working-class community of Lawrenceville, the course passes the neighborhood's tribute to WWI, the Doughboy statue, before returning to the Strip District for miles 3 and 4. The runners cross the Allegheny River by way of the 16th Street Bridge, passing the fabled Heinz Factory at mile 5. Upon turning off the bridge, runners go through the flat North Side for miles 6 and 7, passing the famous Mexican War streets. A slight downgrade greets runners as they prepare to leave the North Side. Runners encounter a spectacular view of the Golden Triangle as they cross the Ohio River via the West End Bridge. As they turn off the bridge, runners have a slight downgrade for .25 miles until mile 8 on Carson Street. On this street, runners go through Pittsburgh's South Side for miles 8 to 11, passing historic Station Square at mile 9. They encounter boisterous spectators at the array of antique shops, bookstores, coffee houses, neighborhood bars, and restaurants along Carson Street between miles 10 and 11. Leaving the South Side, runners cross the last of the city's three rivers, the Monongahela, by way of the Birmingham Bridge. At the end of the bridge, runners face their one significant hill, climbing about 200 feet over .75 miles along Forbes Avenue leading to Oakland. At the top of the climb, they find a flat stretch for miles 12 to 13 as they pass the University of Pittsburgh Medical Center and the university. The runners travel on relatively flat Fifth Avenue entering unique Shadyside with its huge Victorian mansions, art galleries, and upscale restaurants and shops. The course passes by Mellon Park turning onto Penn Avenue. Relatively flat from miles 15 to 19, the course travels through the neighborhoods of Point Breeze, historic Homewood/Brushton, and East Liberty. Facing some slight rolling hills, runners pass through Highland Park from miles 19 to 22. At mile 22, runners receive an overwhelming greeting from the citizens of Bloomfield, who traditionally have a weekend-long series of events culminating with the race. The large, predominantly Italian, community fills the streets to encourage runners on their final stretch. The course returns to Lawrenceville and the Strip District for miles 23 to 25 with a gradual downgrade. At mile 25, runners enter the Golden Triangle via Penn Avenue, passing historic Heinz Hall and the Benedum Center. The turn onto Liberty Avenue leads to the finish at scenic Point State Park at the confluence of Pittsburgh's three rivers.

CROWD/RUNNER SUPPORT Enjoying the warm support of the city's residents, the Pittsburgh Marathon traditionally draws between 100,000 to 200,000 spectators around the course. Prior to 1996, a few of the neighborhoods the course bisects would schedule a festival to coincide with marathon race day. Marathon organizers have since developed a matching funds program to assist all twelve communities in hosting a race-day festival to showcase their individual neighborhood and to support the runners. In another nice touch, the Pittsburgh Post-Gazette includes all race registrants in the race-day newspaper. Many spectators attend the race with the list in hand and look for the names of the approaching runners to yell their encouragement. Pittsburgh also boasts some of the top medical assistance of any race, with approximately 800 to 900 medical volunteers. Medical personnel staff all 20 aid stations.

RACE LOGISTICS The start and finish lie within a ten-minute walk of all major downtown hotels. Runners staying outside of downtown can find plenty of convenient parking in the area. Marathoners can shower at the Downtown YMCA for a $4 fee.

ACTIVITIES On Friday and Saturday of marathon weekend, a Marathon and Fitness Expo is held in conjunction with packet pickup and late registration at the PPG Wintergarden on Stanwix Street between Third and Fourth Avenue, a five-minute walk from the Westin William Penn

Hotel, the headquarters hotel. Although you may retrieve your packet on race morning, there is no race-day registration. The race hosts a pasta party the evening before the marathon for about $10. After the marathon, attend the post-race party at the Westin William Penn Hotel, starting at 1:00 p.m. The awards ceremony begins at 2:00 p.m.

A W A R D S Every runner receives a marathon T-shirt, and finishers receive medallions and official results certificates (sent in mid-July). All registrants also receive souvenir program/results booklets in August. The top three runners in each age group are sent award plaques. Elite runners compete for approximately $100,000 in prize money.

E L I T E   R U N N E R S   I N F O R M A T I O N The City of Pittsburgh Marathon recruits elite runners (men under 2:18 and women under 2:41). Depending on their credentials, elites may be offered transportation, lodging, meal expenses, and free entry. The top 10 overall winners earn the following prize money: $10,000, $7,000, $4,000, $3,000, $2,000, $1,500, $1,250, $1,000, $750, and $500. The top five masters runners earn: $2,000, $1,250, $750, $500, and $200. The top five Pennsylvania residents earn: $1,000, $500, $250, $150, and $100. The top three Pittsburgh residents receive: $1,000, $500, and $250. The race also offers a number of incentive bonuses, including a $3,000 bounty for times under the previous course's record (2:10:24 for males and 2:29:50 for females), and $1,500 for the first man under 2:14 and first woman under 2:34. The first male or female U.S. citizen who finishes in the top 10 receives an additional $2,000. For the 1997 U.S. Men's Marathon Championship, prize money (U.S. men only) extends to tenth place — from $15,000 to $1,000. The top three American men under 2:14 receive $500 time incentive bonuses.

A C C O M M O D A T I O N S The Westin William Penn Hotel, 530 William Penn Place (800-228-3000), serves as the headquarters hotel. Other downtown hotels that offer discounts to runners include the DoubleTree Hotel (800-367-8478) for $95; Ramada Hotel at $75 (800-225-5858); and Downtown Marriott Hotel at $100 (800-228-9290). Within a ten-minute drive of downtown are Sheraton Station Square for $99 (800-255-7488); Greentree Marriott for $70 (800-525-5902); and Holiday Inn Select in University Center for $95 (800-864-8287).

R E L A T E D   E V E N T S / R A C E S Marathon week kicks off with the Children's Marathon held on the weekend prior to the marathon. Events include a 6.2 yard Diaper Derby for tots aged 1 to 2; a Tot Trot (26.2 yards) for kids 3 to 6; and a Fun Run/Walk for children 7 to 12. All children's events require preregistration. On marathon day, the race holds the City of Pittsburgh 10K which attracts 2,000 runners annually. Teams of four runners can run the marathon relay, starting with the full marathoners, with 9.1, 5.1, 7.6, and 4.4-mile legs. Teams can participate in one of several divisions, Corporate, Neighborhood Groups, Running Clubs, College, or High School. Team members must provide their own transportation to the relay exchange points.

A R E A   A T T R A C T I O N S While in Pittsburgh, catch a Pittsburgh Pirates baseball game at Three Rivers Stadium. Regular attractions include the view from Mount Washington up the Duquesne Incline; the Andy Warhol Museum; the Carnegie art museum and natural history collection; the hands-on Carnegie Science Center; the Children's Museum; the Pittsburgh Zoo; Station Square; and the National Aviary.

L O C A L   R U N N I N G   S T O R E Athlete's Foot in Shadyside, 800 S. Aiken Avenue, Pittsburgh (412-621-2997).

CLEVELAND MARATHON

OVERALL: 91

COURSE BEAUTY: 8-

COURSE DIFFICULTY: 3-

APPROPRIATENESS FOR FIRST TIMERS: 9

RACE ORGANIZATION: 10

CROWDS: 3-

RACE DATA

Contact: Revco-Cleveland Marathon
P.O. Box 550
Twinsburg, OH 44087
(800) GO-REVCO
(216) 487-1402
Date: May 4, 1997
May 3, 1998
Start Time: 8:00 a.m.
Time Course Closes: 1:30 p.m.
Number of Participants: 1,031 in 1996
Certification: USATF
Course Records: Male: (open) 2:11:59; (masters) 2:19:21
Female: (open) 2:32:14; (masters) 2:49:23
Elite Athlete Programs: Yes
Cost: $20/25
Age groups/Divisions: <14, 15-19, 20-24, 25-29, 30-34, 35-39, 40-44,
45-49, 50-54, 55-59, 60-64, 65-69, 70+
Temperature: 50° - 73°
Aid/Splits: 15 / every mile

HIGHLIGHTS When the Cuyahoga River caught fire in the 1970s, Cleveland residents realized something had to be done to clean up their city. An all-out revitalization effort ensued that has transformed Cleveland from the butt of all jokes to a pleasant place to live and a vibrant tourist destination. The Revco-Cleveland Marathon takes runners past many of the city's new showpieces such as Jacobs Field and The Flats, all the while surrounding runners with expert race organization. RCM offers 15 aid stations, pre- and post-race massages, and one of the richest prize purses in North America. Our seventh-rated fastest marathon, Cleveland should appeal to those runners seeking good times.

COURSE DESCRIPTION The Cleveland Marathon's out-and-back course begins at the Cleveland State University campus at E. 18th and Euclid Avenue, first making a loop to the northeast, returning downtown, and then heading west paralleling the shore of Lake Erie. About six blocks into the race, on Euclid Avenue, runners pass Playhouse Square, the second largest theater district in the United States. After rounding the corner toward Superior Avenue, runners pass Public Square (mile .75), site of the modern BP America Building, Soldiers & Sailors Monument, and the U.S. Courthouse. Just beyond lie the Cleveland Public Library and the Federal Reserve Bank. Runners turn left on E. 45th and then left on St. Claire Avenue (mile 3) to begin the trek back to the heart of downtown. At mile 4.75 near the Galleria, crane your neck to the north up E. 9th Street to catch a glimpse of The Rock 'n' Roll Hall of Fame and the Great Lakes Science

Museum. Runners hit the other side of Public Square near mile 5, going left on Ontario with the distinctive spires of the Terminal Tower (mile 5.25) and the Landmark Tower (mile 5.4) coming into view. At mile 5.5, the course goes by Jacobs Field, home of the Cleveland Indians, and the Cavaliers' Gund Arena. Runners cross the Hope Memorial Bridge, an early 1900s span overlooking the Cuyahoga River and the industrial flats, at mile 6 and enter the West Side Market (mile 6.9), a beautiful farmers market with Old World charm. By mile 8 on Detroit Avenue, the course turns residential with some views of Lake Erie. Lakewood, an eclectic middle-class neighborhood, lies near mile 10, and gracious Rocky River near 14. Runners turn around at mile 15.5, retracing their steps on Lake and Detroit Avenues (miles 15.5 to 24). As you return downtown via the Veterans Memorial Bridge, look down at The Flats entertainment area (mile 24.25) bordering the Cuyahoga River. Once over the bridge's hump, you have practically a straight shot for the final 1.2 miles through the city to the finish at Cleveland State University.

CROWD/RUNNER SUPPORT The largest crowds gather downtown and in the westside neighborhoods of Lakewood and Rocky River. One happy consequence of Cleveland's former status as a constant punch line is that its residents go out of their way to project a positive image of their city to guests. Many residents hold marathon parties, where friends and neighbors congregate to spur on the runners and celebrate their own good judgment for not entering the race. While many a church delegation has forced a marathon to change its starting time to accommodate its flock, one Cleveland church actually changed its hours so that members could participate as volunteers! Including the church delegation, Cleveland's plentiful volunteers man the 15 aid stations well stocked with water, electrolyte replacement, sponges, petroleum jelly, and bandages.

RACE LOGISTICS Several of the downtown hotels are within walking distance of the start. Runners staying at other hotels will have to drive; parking is available near the start and in CSU lots. The race maintains a secured area for your sweats in the gymnasium at the CSU Physical Education Building, 2451 Euclid Avenue.

ACTIVITIES Stop by the CSU Physical Education Building for race packet pickup, late registration, and the runners expo. Hours are Friday, noon to 8:00 p.m., Saturday 10:00 a.m. to 6:00 p.m., and race day at 6:30 a.m. to 8:00 a.m. Work out your pre-race jitters with a free massage. To supply your carbo-load needs, the race coordinates Restaurants for Runners, where a number of area restaurants offer special deals to Revco participants. After the marathon, shower in the CSU gym, and then refresh those glycogen stores with the post-race food and beverages.

AWARDS Every marathon entrant bags a T-shirt and results booklet. If you make it through the 26.2 miles under the cutoff, you also receive a custom medallion, personalized certificate, and results postcard (within two days). The top three finishers in each age group receive awards, and the fastest overall and masters runners compete for approximately $115,000 in prize money.

ELITE RUNNERS INFORMATION Cleveland does recruit elite runners, men under 2:13 (sometimes under 2:15) and women under 2:40. Depending on your resume, you could be offered travel, lodging, expenses, and entry. Regardless, you will have a shot at the $115,000 prize purse. The top seven overall rake in $15,000 (plus $10,000 for a course record), $10,000, $7,500, $5,000, $3,000, $2,000, and $1,000. The first Ohioan receives $1,000. The first three masters runners earn $1,000, $750, and $500, and the top Ohioan masters runner receives $250. Note that you may not win two awards; simply take the highest amount.

ACCOMMODATIONS Remember to book your hotel early to get the special rates because many out-of-towners come for the large Revco Cleveland 10K race. The Marriott Society Center ($100), about .75-miles from the race start, 127 Public Square (800-228-9290), serves as the official host hotel. Other downtown hotels with special deals for Revco runners include: Comfort Inn Downtown ($65), 1800 Euclid Avenue, 1 block from the start (800-221-2222); Holiday Inn Lakeside City Center ($75), 1111 Lakeside Avenue, 1 mile from the start (216-241-5100); Omni International Hotel ($90), 2065 E. 96th Street, 3 miles from the start (800-THE OMNI); Radisson Plaza Suite Hotel Cleveland ($100), 1701 E. 12th Street, .4 miles from the start (800-333-3333); Ritz-Carlton Hotel Cleveland ($150), 1515 W. Third Street, .75-miles from the start (800-241-3333); Sheraton Cleveland City Centre Hotel ($85), 777 St. Clair Avenue, 2 miles from the start (800-321-1090); and Wyndham Cleveland Hotel at Playhouse Square ($105), 1260 Euclid Avenue, 2 blocks from the start (800-WYNDHAM).

RELATED EVENTS/RACES Gobs of runners enter the fast Revco Cleveland 10K. Run mostly in downtown Cleveland, the 10K attracts top runners from around the world, and about 5,700 others. In the 1996 race, Joseph Kimani of Kenya set a road 10K World Record (27:20), which fell soon thereafter.

AREA ATTRACTIONS Music fans should take note of the new Rock and Roll Hall of Fame, 1 T Plaza. The respected Cleveland Museum of Art, 11150 East Blvd., also may catch your interest. If not, watch the Indians play in awesome Jacobs Field, or catch the Cavaliers at Gund Arena. For nighttime entertainment, head to The Flats, the restored warehouse district on the banks of the Cuyahoga River now bursting with nightclubs, bars, restaurants, and shops.

LOCAL RUNNING STORE Fasttrack, 138 The Arcade, 401 Euclid Avenue, Cleveland (216-621-1414).

VANCOUVER INTERNATIONAL MARATHON

OVERALL: 92.4

COURSE BEAUTY: 8

COURSE DIFFICULTY: 5- (SEE APPENDIX)

APPROPRIATENESS FOR FIRST TIMERS: 8+

RACE ORGANIZATION: 10-

CROWDS: 3

R A C E   D A T A

Contact:	Vancouver International Marathon Society
	P.O. Box 3213, Vancouver, B.C., Canada, V6B 3X8
	(604) 872-2928
	e-mail: VIM@MINDLINK.BC.CA
	http://www.wolfifs.com/wolf/
Date:	May 4, 1997
	May 3, 1998
Start Time:	7:00 a.m.
Time Course Closes:	12:00 p.m.
Number of Participants:	2,300 in 1996
Certification:	B.C. Athletics & AIMS
Course Records:	Male: (open) 2:17:24
	Female: (open) 2:43:16
Elite Athlete Programs:	Yes
Cost:	US$38/42/60/75
Age groups/Divisions:	<19, 20-29, 30-34, 35-39, 40-44, 45-49, 50-54,
	55-59, 60-64, 65+
Temperature:	44° - 65°
Aid/Splits:	13 / miles 1 & 13.1

HIGHLIGHTS Spectacularly located, Vancouver seduces visitors with seafaring charm, natural beauty, and a risqué air. The Vancouver International Marathon, our highest-rated Canadian race, captures all this and more, wafting through nearly every conceivable section of the Vancouver area by girdling the Burrard Inlet and False Creek. By way of three bridges, runners drift through high-rise buildings, beachfront, urban forest, commercial districts, Indian land, industrial yards, bawdy locales, and Chinatown. Like many West Coast marathons, VIM attracts a large number of Japanese runners lending an international complexion to the race.

COURSE DESCRIPTION Vancouver's partially closed course starts on Pacific Blvd. sandwiched between B.C. Stadium, Plaza of Nations, and General Motors Place, home of the NBA's Vancouver Grizzlies. The largely flat first 3 miles circumnavigate False Creek, traveling through mostly commercial South Vancouver, including the futuristic ball of Science World and bustling West 2nd Avenue. Runners cross the Burrard Street Bridge at 5K, rising just over 100 feet to the apex at 3.8 miles where the high-rise apartment buildings of downtown appear. Down the other side, and by mile 4.5, runners follow the shoreline of beautiful Beach Avenue until Stanley Park (5.9 to 12). World famous Stanley Park — an amazing urban wilderness — offers the most scenic stretch of running, with mountain and harbor views, including the sails of Canada Place, while maintaining the feel of running through a forest. The course turns rolling here, with a 200-foot incline from about mile 10.7 to 11.7. Runners exit the park on Lion's Gate Bridge, running against traffic in a fairly narrow lane. Once up the bridge, nice views lie to the right and ahead. Runners then take a quick trip through West Vancouver (12.5 to 14.1) and its large Park Royal Shopping Mall before suddenly entering the greenery of the Squamish Indian area (14.1 to 14.5). Welch Street turns slightly more commercial and has a very slight downward pitch, becoming mostly flat on 1st Street (14.6 to 16). After a right turn on Marine, runners have a gradual incline up 3rd Street leading to an easy downgrade on Forbes (16.1 to 16.9). From mile 16.9 to 17.6, runners pass the shops and restaurants on Esplanade Street with the Lonsdale Quay to the right. A popular hangout, this mostly flat stretch has a slight upgrade after Lonsdale. You then hit a tough patch on the course, flat and ugly with an embankment to your left and a railroad yard to your right. This section mercifully ends around 18.6 miles, but you now face perhaps the most challenging part of the race, a 200-foot incline up the Second Narrows Bridge (19 to 19.8). Vancouver's skyline rises to your right, hills and eastern Burrard Inlet to your left. Then it's a nice downhill from mile 19.8 to 20.8 where you come to residential, slightly rolling, potholed Wall Street (20.8 to 22.1). From rolling Wall to flat Powell, lonely runners may find a date for the evening along the sidewalks (22.1 to 23.2). After a bump at mile 24.1, runners enter downtown near 25 and, after a short loop through Chinatown, finish at B.C. Place Stadium.

CROWD/RUNNER SUPPORT Thirteen aid stations carrying water and electrolyte replacement drinks support the runners along the course. About 40,000 spectators dot the route, with the most dense concentrations at the start/finish area and Stanley Park. Starting in 1997, runners will enjoy on-course entertainment at several points during the race.

RACE LOGISTICS B.C. Place lies near 20 or more downtown hotels, so most visitors will not require transportation to the start/finish area. If you need to drive to the start, plenty of pay parking exists at B.C. Place Stadium and nearby streets. The race does not provide shuttle bus service, so plan ahead to ensure you are not scrambling on race morning.

ACTIVITIES Pick up your race packet at the City Square Shopping Centre, 12th Avenue and Cambie Street, on Friday or Saturday before the race. There is no race-day registration or packet pickup. You can also stop by the Lifestyle and Fitness Expo. On Saturday morning, eat with the VIPs at the Celebrity Breakfast (US $8). The traditional carbo-load dinner starts at 4:00 p.m. Saturday afternoon, for US $10. Both meals happen at the Holiday Inn Downtown. After the marathon, head to the awards ceremony and post-race social.

AWARDS Each marathon finisher receives a T-shirt, medal and certificate. The top three age-group winners receive trophies. VIM offers $7,000 in prize money, and Canadian runners are eligible for travel awards.

ELITE RUNNERS INFORMATION On a case-by-case basis, VIM offers transportation, lodging, meal allowances, and/or entry fee waivers to top marathoners. Prize money goes to the top three finishers, with $2,000 for first, $1,000 for second, and $500 for third. Top Canadian and B.C. finishers may also earn awards to overseas sister events.

ACCOMMODATIONS The Holiday Inn Downtown, 1110 Howe Street (604-684-2151), serves as the headquarters hotel. The Hyatt Regency is also convenient at 655 Burrard Street (604-683-1234). Otherwise, call the Vancouver Housing Bureau (800-224-0659) for help in finding the right accommodations for your budget and taste.

RELATED EVENTS/RACES For those souls not ready to tackle the marathon, Vancouver offers a half marathon and a 5K walk. About 2,000 runners participate in the half marathon, which starts with the marathon

AREA ATTRACTIONS Call Tourism Vancouver (604-682-2000) for information on what's going on in Vancouver around marathon time. Cosmopolitan Vancouver offers many sights and activities, including Stanley Park, Chinatown, Gastown, and Robsonstrasse for shopping.

LOCAL RUNNING STORES Forerunners, 3504 W. Fourth Avenue (604-732-4535); Running Room, #001 City Square, 555 W. 12th Avenue (604-879-9721).

WALTER CHILDS
MEMORIAL RACE OF CHAMPIONS

OVERALL: 72.8

COURSE BEAUTY: 8

COURSE DIFFICULTY: 5-

APPROPRIATENESS FOR FIRST TIMERS: 6+

RACE ORGANIZATION: 8

CROWDS: 0

RACE DATA

Contact:	Peter Stasz
	c/o Fast Feet
	231 Elm Street
	West Springfield, MA 01089
	(413) 734-0955
Date:	May 4, 1997
	May 3, 1998
Start Time:	8:00 a.m.
Time Course Closes:	NA
Number of Participants:	139 in 1996
Certification:	USATF
Course Records:	Male: (open) 2:29:48
	Female: (open) 3:03:00
Elite Athlete Programs:	No
Cost:	$15/20
Age groups/Divisions:	NA
Temperature:	60° - 80°
Aid/Splits:	12 / mile 13.1

HIGHLIGHTS One of the United States' most historic marathons, the Race of Champions blasted out of the blocks with two wins by Boston Marathon great John Kelley in 1963 and 1964. Recently renamed in honor of a long-time Massachusetts race promoter, the race assumed notoriety in 1967 as the "Holyoke Massacre." Designated as the trials to select the U.S. Pan American Games marathon team and the U.S. National Marathon Championships, the 1:00 p.m. race featured 90° temperatures that claimed over half the field. Even with the elite group of U.S. runners, the ultimate survivor struggled in at 2:40:04. Now run on a pleasant new (since 1991) course, the ROC continues as a small, rural race through Holyoke in eastern Massachusetts. Runners with a keen sense of running's past may want to share in ROC's history.

COURSE DESCRIPTION Starting at Mt. Tom Ski Area, the race proceeds immediately uphill for several hundred yards, then drops sharply at .5 miles down the beautiful wooded hill. At mile 1, runners cut to Whiting Reservoir which they circle 2 2/3 times on a mostly flat dirt road (about 10 miles). Climbing a moderate hill while leaving the scenic reservoir, runners detour briefly on a rough road before reaching the country homes on Southampton Street. After a moderate .33-mile rise, the course rolls downhill to the halfway point on Rock Valley Road. A short, gentle incline to 13.7 miles precedes the dirt road from 14 until 15. Turning right on residential Pomeroy Street, runners face another dirt/gravel road from mile 16 to 16.5. Beginning to circumscribe Mt. Tom, the course is mostly flat on East Street and unshaded Northampton Street. Near mile 24, the route ascends gently then becomes rather steep after turning onto the ski area access road for the last half mile.

CROWD/RUNNER SUPPORT There are no crowds to speak of in this rural race other than the volunteers at the aid stations every two miles. The stations carry water and electrolyte replacement drink.

RACE LOGISTICS You will need to drive to the start; plenty of parking exists in the ski area parking lot. After the race, rather than hobbling up the steep hill on stiff legs, take the shuttle bus the three-quarters mile back to the start.

ACTIVITIES Enjoy the post-race chicken feast at the Mt. Tom Ski Area as you swap race heroics with fellow runners and family. Other refreshments are also provided.

AWARDS The first 100 entries receive T-shirts. Overall and masters winners receive merchandise prizes.

ACCOMMODATIONS The Holiday Inn Holidome, 245 Whiting Farms Road, Holyoke (413-534-3311), serves as the headquarters hotel. Other hotels include: Susse Chalet, 1515 Northampton Street, Holyoke (413-536-1980); Mt. Tom Motor Court, Rt. 5N, Holyoke (413-534-3429); Riviera Motel, 671 Northampton Street, Holyoke (413-536-3377); and Holiday Inn Springfield, 711 Dwight Street, Springfield (413-781-0900).

AREA ATTRACTIONS The primary tourist attraction in Springfield is the Basketball Hall of Fame. Boston lies about 100 miles east of Springfield.

LOCAL RUNNING STORE Fast Feet, 231 Elm Street, West Springfield (413-734-0955).

LAKE GENEVA MARATHON

OVERALL: 83.2

COURSE BEAUTY: 9

COURSE DIFFICULTY: 7

APPROPRIATENESS FOR FIRST TIMERS: 5+

RACE ORGANIZATION: 8

CROWDS: 0

RACE DATA

Contact:	Frank Dobbs
	Lake Geneva Marathon
	P.O. Box 1134
	Lake Geneva, WI 53147
	(414) 248-4323
Date:	May 10, 1997
	May 9, 1998
Start Time:	8:00 a.m.
Time Course Closes:	1:00 p.m.
Number of Participants:	150 in 1996
Certification:	USATF
Course Records:	Male: (open) 2:33:36
	Female: (open) 2:56:14
Elite Athlete Programs:	No
Cost:	$25/30
Age groups/Divisions:	<17, 18-24, 25-29, 30-34, 35-39, 40-44, 45-49, 50-54, 55-59, 60-69, 70+
Temperature:	55° - 70°
Aid/Splits:	9 / none

HIGHLIGHTS A getaway for wealthy Chicagoans, gorgeous Lake Geneva sparkles sapphire blue like its Swiss Alps cousins. Taking advantage of this spectacular setting in southeastern Wisconsin's glaciated hills, race director Frank Dobbs holds the tough, charming Lake Geneva Marathon that has runners returning year after year. The marathon traces the lake, heads into the surrounding farm country, passes through some spectacular neighborhoods, and finishes on an ancient Indian path. The last lake in the United States to have full mail service by boat, Lake Geneva makes a wonderful destination for a relaxing weekend or week along its serene shores.

COURSE DESCRIPTION Lake Geneva's loop course, open to local traffic, starts in downtown Lake Geneva on the lakefront bridge at the sound of a stern-wheel boat whistle. The course warms you up almost immediately with a steep, 400-yard hill through Lake Geneva's residential area. By mile 1.2, runners head downhill to the lakefront for a spectacular view of Lake Geneva. Once runners reach the lake at 1.4, they face another good hill to 1.9. Rolling away from the lake, the course then heads toward the surrounding farm country (miles 4 to 14). At mile 2.8, the course starts downhill to 3.2 where it becomes flat until 3.6. Facing a slight upgrade to the 4-mile mark, runners then encounter slight rollers until 8.5 miles. The course passes through the tiny town of Zenda near mile 7. Perhaps the fastest mile on the course occurs from mile 8.5 to 9.5, a perfectly flat stretch leading to a good climb from 9.5 to 9.8. The course returns to slightly rolling until a down and up from 14.2 to 14.5 and 14.5 to 14.7. Runners sharply descend through a residential neighborhood to the lakefront at Fontana and the finish line for 25K runners. A beautiful, inspirational view greets runners here, which is good because the most difficult and scenic part of the race lies ahead. As the course winds along the lakefront, a tough uphill occurs from mile 16 to 16.3, followed by a welcomed downhill (16.3 to 16.8) that may rest searing lungs for the second difficult climb from 16.8 to 17.1. Runners roll past the beautiful George Williams College Golf Course before the course turns residential through the Village of Williams Bay. The route passes Yerkes Observatory at mile 18.5 and soon thereafter travels along the lakeshore for a brief spell. Facing another uphill from 20 to 20.4, runners take a short jaunt along the highway from 21.6 to 23, mostly a slight incline or rolling. At mile 23.7, the course drops into a gorgeous, wooded area with pastures and palatial homes. This section includes some challenging rolling hills. After another steep downhill from 24.9 to 25.1 into another neighborhood, the course picks up an ancient Indian trail for the dash to the finish line at Library Park on the lake.

CROWD / RUNNER SUPPORT Spectator turnout for most resort community marathons is light, and Lake Geneva is no exception. The miles are marked on the pavement; bring your watch since there are no split timers.

RACE LOGISTICS There is plenty of parking near the start/finish in Lake Geneva. The loop marathon course means that transportation is not a concern. Runners completing the 25K can opt to enjoy the beautiful trip from their finish at Fontana to Lake Geneva aboard a stern-wheel boat. On windy days, however, seasick prone runners may want to stick with the school bus.

ACTIVITIES On Friday evening, you can pick up your race packet or register late at the pasta dinner at Celebration on Wells Restaurant, 422 Wells Street, Lake Geneva. You may also retrieve your packet or register early race morning in Library Park. After the race, hang out in Library Park for the Jaycees brats and beer party, and enjoy the spectacular view of Lake Geneva. Following the awards ceremony, prizes donated by area merchants are presented in a raffle drawing. You can shower at the YMCA Health Club at 203 Wells Street.

AWARDS Every marathon and 25K entrant receives a Lake Geneva sweatshirt. The top three age-group finishers take home pottery awards, and the overall winners are awarded large pieces of pottery, merchandise, and paintings.

ACCOMMODATIONS There are plenty of lodging options in Lake Geneva from luxurious resorts to more modest motels. Among the resorts are: The Abbey in Fontana (414-275-6811); The Geneva Inn, N2009 State Road 120, on the marathon course (800-441-5881); and the Grand Geneva Resort and Spa (800-558-3417). Other options include: Budget Host Hotel, 1060 Wells Street, Lake Geneva (800-264-5678); Elizabethian Inn, 463 Wrigley Drive, Lake Geneva (414-248-9131); Harbor View Motel, 76 Johnson Street, Williams Bay (414-245-5036); Alpine Motel, 682 Wells Street, Lake Geneva (414-248-4264); Pederson Victorian Bed & Breakfast, 1782 Hwy. 120 North, Lake Geneva (414-248-9110); Roses — A B&B, 429 S. Lake Shore Drive (414-248-4344); Strawberry Hill B&B, 1071 Jenkins Drive, Fontana (414-275-5998); and The Watersedge of Lake Geneva, W4232 West End Road, Lake Geneva (414-245-9845).

RELATED EVENTS / RACES Runners not quite ready for the grueling marathon can opt for the popular 25K which avoids the nastiest hills on the course. Runners in the 25K get the added treat of riding the stern-wheel boat back to the start/finish area. Alternatively, friends and family can join in the 5K run/walk which begins just after the marathon/25K start. The 5K finishes in Library Park.

AREA ATTRACTIONS While Lake Geneva is a place to relax and enjoy the beautiful lake, you may want to take one of the many boat tours, have a leisurely round of golf at one of the six area courses, take a horseback or carriage ride, or go hiking.

LOCAL RUNNING STORE Geneva Sports, 270 Broad Street, Lake Geneva (414-248-1521).

FOREST CITY MARATHON

OVERALL: 77.5

COURSE BEAUTY: 8+

COURSE DIFFICULTY: 3+

APPROPRIATENESS FOR FIRST TIMERS: 7+

RACE ORGANIZATION: 9-

CROWDS: 1

R A C E   D A T A

Contact:	Price Waterhouse Forest City Marathon
	Thames Valley Children's Center
	779 Baseline Road E.
	London, Ontario, Canada, N6C 5Y6
	(519) 685-8675
Date:	May 11, 1997
	May 10, 1998
Start Time:	8:00 a.m.
Time Course Closes:	1:00 p.m.
Number of Participants:	415 in 1996
Certification:	Unknown
Course Records:	Male: (open) 2:26; (masters) 2:34
	Female: (open) 2:58; (masters) 2:59
Elite Athlete Programs:	No
Cost:	$30/35
Age groups/Divisions:	<19, 20-24, 25-29, 30-34, 35-39, 40-44, 45-49,
	50-54, 55-59, 60-64, 65+
Temperature:	38° - 68°
Aid/Splits:	14 / mile 1, clock at 13.1

HIGHLIGHTS Considered a microcosm of Canada, London, Ontario attracts great attention from product test marketers. Like mid-America, if something sells in London, it generally sells well throughout Canada. One of the city's own products, the Forest City Marathon, fits snugly in this category. With its attractive course through the Forest City (so named because of its 50,000 trees), quality race organization, and worthy cause (Thames Valley Children's Center for kids with physical disabilities), it's no wonder that the race field has nearly doubled in only five years. Not surprising given the city's test market status, every Forest City entrant receives a marathon opinion survey. One respondent quipped, *"To improve the race, you would have to pay me money to come and run in it. Oh, wait, maybe dancing girls, yeah, belly dancing girls."* With or without the dancing girls, the Forest City Marathon should continue to grow along with its reputation.

COURSE DESCRIPTION The Forest City Marathon's modified out-and-back course starts outside J.W. Little Memorial Stadium, home of the powerful University of Western Ontario Mustangs football team. The race winds through the paved streets of the university campus for the first 1.9 miles and proceeds through one of London's most exclusive neighborhoods. Runners face a gradual 300-yard hill in mile 1, followed by a quarter-mile downgrade. From 3.75 to 5, the course travels through Old London North, home to many turn-of-the-century "old wealth" houses. The course tours the flat north section of London until mile 10, before returning to the university for 1.5 miles. After a short 1.5-mile jaunt on London's bike path system, the course becomes a true out-and-back through downtown streets before reentering the bike path at the Terry Fox Parkway (mile 14). For the next 4 miles, runners trace the picturesque Thames River through Greenway Park and Springbank Park, a combined 150-acre green space surrounding Storybook Gardens, home to Slippery the Seal and his friends. Runners turn around at mile 18, retracing their steps along the Thames to the university campus. The race finishes on the track inside Little Memorial Stadium before a good, enthusiastic crowd.

CROWD/RUNNER SUPPORT Although scattered about the course, most spectators position themselves near University Drive, where the marathon and 10K courses converge; of course, the stadium finish draws a nice crowd as well. The volunteers managing the frequent aid stations provide tremendous encouragement along the route. More motivation comes from fellow runners, especially as you pass each other on the out-and-back second half of the race. If you're concerned about splits, signs are posted every 2K.

RACE LOGISTICS Runners need to drive to the start at the University of Western Ontario. Park on the right at the bottom of the short hill on Huron Drive. You will see the stadium and start/finish areas to your left. Runners may change or shower at the university's Thames Hall.

ACTIVITIES Register or pick up your race packet at the Runners' Expo at Station Park Inn, 242 Pall Mall, on Saturday from 10:00 a.m. to 6:00 p.m. If you miss Saturday's registration, race-day registration lasts until one hour before the start. Following your race, join the many children of the Thames Valley Children's Center for the festive post-race celebration complete with food, drink, live entertainment, and perhaps most important, a free massage. An awards ceremony and prize drawing begin at 12:30 p.m.

AWARDS All marathoners receive T-shirts, and each marathon finisher receives a commemorative medal and ticket for the prize drawing held during the awards ceremony. The top three overall men and women receive $350, $175, and $100, respectively. Masters prize money for men and women extends three places, $200, $100, and $75, respectively. Age-group winners earn running shoes, while 2nd and 3rd place finishers receive other merchandise prizes. If that's not enough, medals are awarded to the top three in all categories.

ACCOMMODATIONS The Station Park Inn, 242 Pall Mall (519-642-4444), serves as the official race headquarters and offers a special marathon rate of about $80. Otherwise, try: Delta London Armouries, 325 Dundas Street (800-268-1133 or 519-679-6111); Radisson Hotel — London Centre, 300 King Street (519-439-1661); or Lamplighter Inn, 591 Wellington Road (519-681-7151).

RELATED EVENTS/RACES Forest City offers a marathon team event for up to six-member teams. Each member runs the marathon, and the four fastest age/gender-graded times are aggregated for the final results. The team event involves no additional cost but team members must preregister and submit all entries together. For those preferring shorter distances, a 10K loop through residential streets commences at 9:00 a.m., followed by a 2K winding through the university campus, starting at 9:15 a.m.

AREA ATTRACTIONS While not quite the attraction as its overseas counterpart, this London does offer some fun activities without the jet lag. Fool yourself and take a city tour on an authentic red, double-decker bus. Stop in at Storybook Gardens, a children's attraction, or Labatts, an adult's attraction and one of Canada's best breweries.

LOCAL RUNNING STORE London's Runners' Choice, 207 Dundas Street, London (519-672-5928).

NATIONAL CAPITAL MARATHON

OVERALL: 88.1

COURSE BEAUTY: 9

COURSE DIFFICULTY: 4-

APPROPRIATENESS FOR FIRST TIMERS: 9+

RACE ORGANIZATION: 9+

CROWDS: 2-

RACE DATA

Contact: National Capital Marathon
P.O. Box/TP426 Station A
Ottawa, Ontario, Canada, K1N 8V5
(613) 234-2221
Date: May 11, 1997
May 10, 1998
Start Time: 8:30 a.m.
Time Course Closes: 1:30 p.m.
Number of Participants: 982 in 1996
Certification: Athletics Canada
Course Records: Male: (open) 2:26:02; (masters) 2:30:39
Female: (open) 2:52:03; (masters) 3:11:09
Elite Athlete Programs: Yes
Cost: $45
Age groups/Divisions: <19, 20-24, 25-29, 30-34, 35-39, 40-44, 45-49,
50-54, 55-59, 60-64, 65-69, 70+
Temperature: 60°
Aid/Splits: 16 / every 5K

HIGHLIGHTS Unless you run on your toes, you'll be "heel-toeing through the tulips" in Canada's capital city of Ottawa during the National Capital Marathon. The haven of the Dutch royal family during World War II, Ottawa was rewarded with 100,000 tulip bulbs in 1945 and 20,000 replenishments every year thereafter. On top of the thousands of colorful tulips, majestic parliament buildings, scenic parkways, and pristine neighborhoods characterize the two-loop course. Held on Mother's Day, NCM celebrates by presenting every woman finisher with a rose.

COURSE DESCRIPTION Starting near Ottawa's Confederation Park and RMOC Plaza, NCM's sparkling course wastes no time in passing some of the city's greatest landmarks. The route glides past the historic Lord Elgin Hotel and the architecturally impressive National Gallery of Canada before crossing the Alexandra Bridge into Hull, Quebec at the 1-mile mark. Colorful flags line the road while you pass the striking architecture of the Canadian Museum of Civilization, located on the left around 1.3 miles. A short hill at 1.4 is followed by a flat to slightly uphill stretch to 2 miles. Crossing over the raging waters of the Ottawa River via the Portage Bridge, runners engage the impressive sight of the British-inspired Parliament Buildings to the left. Gradual ups and downs follow as the course parallels the river before hitting Island Park, a handsome residential area, around 5 miles. A short rise and fall occur around the 6-mile mark as the route soon connects with a pleasant, tree-lined bike path leading to the flat expanses of the Central Experimental Farm at 8.5 miles. From here, the course travels around boat-swollen Dows Lake and continues for 3.5 miles on a flat path along the picturesque Rideau Canal before returning to the start of the second loop.

CROWD/RUNNER SUPPORT NCM attracts some 10,000 spectators throughout the course with most gathering around the start/finish area in downtown Ottawa. Participants from the other races and scores of aid station volunteers provide excellent encouragement for your effort.

RACE LOGISTICS You'll find NCM hassle-free on race morning if you stay at the official race hotel or one of several downtown hotels within walking distance of the start/finish. If you're driving to the race, parking is plentiful. Also, the race provides a sweats check at the start.

ACTIVITIES The pre-race check-in and race expo at RMOC Plaza, located between Laurier Street W and Lisgar Street at the Rideau Canal, takes place on Saturday 9:00 a.m. to 4:00 p.m. and Sunday 7:00 a.m. to 8:00 a.m. After the race, unless you're extremely thirsty, enjoy some solid refreshments before heading to the beer tent (sorry, not free). A Sports Active Expo is held for sponsors and merchants to exhibit and sell their products. An awards ceremony, live music and dance show round out the day's festivities.

AWARDS Every runner receives a T-shirt, while finishers receive medallions and certificates. The top three overall competitors receive prize money, $1,500, $750, and $500, respectively. Age-group awards extend three deep, with winners generally receiving merchandise. All female finishers receive roses for Mother's Day. The morning after the race, see your name published in the Ottawa Sun. Results are also mailed to marathon participants.

ELITE RUNNER INFORMATION Previous winners and elite runners, at the discretion of the race director, may receive some expense money and accommodations.

ACCOMMODATIONS The Radisson Hotel, 100 Kent Street (800-333-3333), serves as the official race hotel offering a special marathon rate. Other nearby hotels include: Lord Elgin, 100 Elgin Street (613-235-3333); Journey's End Hotel, 290 Rideau Street (613-789-7511); Chateau Laurier, 1 Rideau Street (613-241-1414); Capital Hill Motel & Suites, 88 Albert Street (613-235-1413); Parkway Motor Hotel, 475 Rideau (613-232-3781); Days Inn Roxborough-Ottawa City Center, 123 Metcalfe Street (613-237-9300); Aristocrat Apartment Hotel, 131 Cooper Street (613-232-9471); and Chateau Cartier, Aylmer, Quebec (800-807-1088).

RELATED EVENTS/RACES NCM sees to it that everyone has a chance to exercise by hosting several events over the weekend. Saturday evening brings an 8K in-line-skate race starting at 6:00 p.m. and a 10K run at 6:30 p.m. Point to point, both courses travel from the Central Experimental Farm to RMOC Plaza, site of the marathon finish. Race day includes an in-line-skate marathon that takes skaters on the same course that runners later follow. A half marathon starts with the marathon at 8:30 a.m. Finally, a 6K and 2K run/walk leaves at 8:45 a.m. taking participants on Queen Elizabeth Driveway along the Rideau Canal.

AREA ATTRACTIONS North America's largest tulip display has turned into one of Ottawa's largest celebrations, the Spring Tulip Festival. Don't miss the festivities which include live music, street dancing, hot air balloon rides, craft fairs, boat rides, and fireworks. Other must sees are the collection of fine art at the National Gallery of Canada and the re-creation of a rain forest at the National Museum of Civilization.

LOCAL RUNNING STORES Running Room, 121 Bank Street (613-233-5165); Running Room, 911 Bank Street (613-233-5617); Sports 4, 149 Bank Street (613-234-6562).

CAPITAL CITY MARATHON

OVERALL: 83.7

COURSE BEAUTY: 8+

COURSE DIFFICULTY: 4 (SEE APPENDIX)

APPROPRIATENESS FOR FIRST TIMERS: 9-

RACE ORGANIZATION: 9

CROWDS: 2-

RACE DATA

Contact: Capital City Marathon
P.O. Box 1681
Olympia, WA 98507
(360) 786-1786
Date: May 18, 1997
May 17, 1998
Start Time: 7:30 a.m.
Time Course Closes: 1:00 p.m.
Number of Participants: 640 in 1995
Certification: USATF
Course Records: Male: (open) 2:28:43; (masters) 2:38:32
Female: (open) 2:43:18; (masters) 3:00:45
Elite Athlete Programs: No
Cost: $35/50
Age groups/Divisions: <19, 20-24, 25-29, 30-34, 35-39, 40-44, 45-49,
50-54, 55-59, 60-64, 65-69, 70+
Temperature: 52° - 65°
Aid/Splits: 12 / mile 13.1

HIGHLIGHTS There seems to be a special bond between runners and beer, so what better place for a marathon in the Pacific Northwest than Olympia, home of Olympia Brewery? The Capital City Marathon's course provides views of beautiful Capitol Lake, Budd Inlet, the State Capitol building, and on clear days, Mt. Rainier and the Olympic Mountains. Well-organized, Capital City hosts several shorter events that should keep the whole family busy. Afterward, head to the Olympia Brewery to celebrate your achievement in true runners' style.

COURSE DESCRIPTION Passing through primarily rural and residential areas, Capital City's loop course starts near the State Capitol building. After a gentle 100-yard downgrade followed by an easy rise to 5th Street, runners reach the most scenic stretch of the route on Deschutes Parkway along beautiful Capitol Lake and its Canadian geese residents, with wooded hills to their right. A little after mile 2, runners reach the most significant upgrade on the course, 170 feet over 2 miles. During this span, the route parallels Interstate-5, separated by a high sound barrier until the right on Capitol Blvd. at mile 3.1. Turning commercial near 3.9, the course quickly jaunts over Interstate-5. At mile 4.3, runners turn on Littlerock Road, going very slightly uphill through a rural community. The course hits Airindustrial Way at the 6-mile mark, passing the small rural airport at 7.4 miles. Back on Capitol Blvd. at 7.6, the course heads back toward downtown, passing the Olympia Brewery at 9.9 miles, followed by a good, 100-yard uphill. The route then becomes chiefly residential, rolling slightly by mile 11. Runners face a tough, 70-foot climb from mile 13 to 13.5 on Boulevard Road. More noticeably rolling, the course goes mostly through rural subdivisions and residential neighborhoods until it reaches Capitol Way near mile 25. From there, it's a nice downhill finish through downtown Olympia to Sylvester Park.

CROWD / RUNNER SUPPORT Runners find the best crowd support during the last two miles of the marathon. Although particularly light on the Littlerock Road-Airindustrial Way-Capitol Blvd. loop, support does scatter along the rest of the course. Over 600 volunteers help the runners, with most at the 12 aid stations. Portable toilets are located every five miles on the course, and a medical aid station sits at mile 22.

RACE LOGISTICS The race does not provide transportation to the start, but if you are staying at the race headquarters hotel, this is no problem since it lies only a short walk from the start. Clothing storage is available; look for the marked vehicle.

ACTIVITIES On Saturday afternoon, register, pick up your race number, and browse trade exhibits at Sylvester Park. You may register on race morning in the park. You can also tour the marathon course for no charge in a 20-person van. Tours start at noon on Saturday. The Ramada Inn hosts a pasta dinner from 6:00 p.m. to 8:00 p.m. Saturday evening. After the marathon, savor food, refreshments, music, and the awards ceremony in Sylvester Park. Massage is available for a suggested $10 donation on a first-come, first-served basis.

AWARDS Finishers earn long-sleeve T-shirts and commemorative medals. Age-division awards range from three to ten deep. Age-group winners receive special awards, while others receive medals. Awards are also presented to the top overall, masters, international, and inspirational runners.

ACCOMMODATIONS The Ramada Inn — Governor House, 621 Capitol Way (800-356-5335), serves as the headquarters hotel. The Ramada is four-and-a-half blocks from the start. Also within walking distance of the start are: Best Western Aladdin Motel, 900 Capitol Way S (800-528-1234); Golden Gavel, 909 Capitol Way S (360-352-8533); and Golden Carriage, 1211 Quince Street SE (360-943-4710). Other possibilities include: Quality Inn, 2300 Evergreen Park Drive SW (800-562-5635); Comfort Inn, 4700 Park Center Avenue NE (360-456-6300); Capital Inn, 120 College Street SE (360-493-1991); Tyee Motel, 500 Tyee Drive SW (360-352-0511); and Best Western Tumwater Inn, 5188 Capitol Blvd. S (360-956-1235).

RELATED EVENTS / RACES Capital City hosts a number of related events on marathon race day. The Capital City Half Marathon (8:00 a.m.) and the D.A.R.E. Kid's Run (8:20 a.m.), a one-mile run for children 6 to 13, start at 5th and Columbia Streets. The Capital City Five Miler (8:15 a.m.) begins at the marathon start.

AREA ATTRACTIONS Make sure to tour the Olympia Brewery if you are a beer drinker. You can also wander through the State Capitol building and its surrounding grounds. Within a couple of hours of Olympia are Olympic National Park, Mt. Rainier National Park, and Seattle.

LOCAL RUNNING STORE Rainbow Sports NW, 2410 W. Harrison (206-943-9984).

Sugarloaf Marathon

Overall: 75.9

Course Beauty: 9-

Course Difficulty: 5-

Appropriateness for First Timers: 7-

Race Organization: 7+

Crowds: 0

R A C E   D A T A

Contact:	Chip and Nancy Carey
	Sugarloaf Marathon
	RR 1, Box 5000
	Kingfield, ME 04947
	(207) 237-6903
Date:	May 18, 1997
	May 17, 1998
Start Time:	7:00 a.m.
Time Course Closes:	12:00 p.m.
Number of Participants:	200 in 1996
Certification:	USATF
Course Records:	Male: (open) 2:18:38
	Female: (open) 2:50:19
Elite Athlete Programs:	No
Cost:	$25
Age groups/Divisions:	<29, 30-34, 35-39, 40-49, 50-59, 60+
Temperature:	40° - 70°
Aid/Splits:	10 / none

HIGHLIGHTS More accustomed to seeing visitors slide down winter slopes, Sugarloaf calls runners to its hills each May for the Sugarloaf Marathon and 15K. The pretty course, lined with king pine trees, rolls along Maine Scenic Highway, Route 27 through the mountains of western Maine falling 590 feet. The last part of the marathon chases the Carrabasset River into Kingfield. The area offers golf, white water rafting, hiking, and mountain biking for your post-marathon recreation.

COURSE DESCRIPTION Sugarloaf Marathon starts about 3 miles north of Stratton, Maine (elevation 1,170 feet), under towering, ramrod-straight king pine trees. Mostly flat, the race carves through beautiful hills and woods going through Stratton from miles 2.8 to 4.3. Runners hit a short incline at mile 3.4 then gently roll until a good hill from 4.8 to 5. Waving, except for a moderate rise from 6.2 to 6.5, the course climbs steadily from mile 8 to 10.1, and then falls just as sharply to 11. Passing the Sugarloaf USA ski area at 11.1, the route ascends gently from 11 to 12.8, becoming steeper toward the apex as it now begins its journey with the Carrabasset River. Rolling mostly downhill, the course flattens briefly from 16.2 to 17.6 and rises slightly from 21.9 to 22.1. Runners reach the outskirts of Kingfield near mile 25 and finish in its heart (elevation 580 feet).

CROWD/RUNNER SUPPORT There are few spectators along this rural course, except for the aid stations every 2.5 miles or so that offer water and electrolyte replacement.

RACE LOGISTICS For a $5 fee, marathon runners can park at the finish line and take the race shuttle to the start. The bus leaves at 5:30 a.m., and seats must be reserved in advance. Runners with handlers can be dropped off at the start, and then handlers can follow their progress down the highway. There is no shuttle from the finish back to the start after the race. Shower and changing facilities are available near the finish at Kingfield Elementary School on Route 142.

ACTIVITIES The race does not accept late registration so you must register prior to the deadline. On Saturday evening, you can attend the pasta dinner with details to be announced at a later date. A post-race barbeque is set up for all to enjoy with hot dogs and burgers available for purchase while sipping on complimentary beverages. Massage is also available, and an awards ceremony follows the race.

AWARDS Every finisher receives a long-sleeve T-shirt and a finisher's certificate. Coffee mugs go to the top 25 overall runners. The top three in each age group receive awards.

ACCOMMODATIONS The Sugarloaf Inn at the ski resort (800-THE-LOAF) serves as the headquarters hotel ($80). Other possibilities include: Valley Motel at Sugarloaf, Kingfield (207-235-2730); Herbert Hotel, Kingfield (207-265-2000); Inn on Winters Hill, Kingfield (207-265-5421); Lumberjack Lodge, Kingfield (207-237-2141); Judsons Sugarloaf Motel, Kingfield (207-235-2641); Stratton Motel (207-246-4171); Stratton Plaza Hotel (207-246-2000); and Mountain View Lodge, Stratton (207-246-2033).

RELATED EVENTS/RACES You can also choose to run the very fast Sugarloaf 15K, which drops 300 feet. The Sugarloaf Cup is awarded to the two-person team with the combined highest finish, one in the marathon and one in the 15K. Teams may be same sex or coed. Club teams also compete for the marathon team title, determined by the team's top four runners.

Coeur d'Alene Marathon

Overall: 82.4

Course Beauty: 9

Course Difficulty: 4-

Appropriateness for First Timers: 7

Race Organization: 8

Crowds: 1-

RACE DATA

Contact:	Coeur d'Alene Marathon
	P.O. Box 2393
	Coeur d'Alene, ID 83816
	(208) 773-5992
Date:	May 25, 1997
	May 24, 1998
Start Time:	7:00 a.m.
Time Course Closes:	12:00 p.m.
Number of Participants:	400 in 1996
Certification:	USATF
Course Records:	Male: (open) 2:28:43
	Female: (open) 2:55:21
Elite Athlete Programs:	No
Cost:	$25/35
Age groups/Divisions:	<19, 20-24, 25-29, 30-34, 35-39, 40-44, 45-49, 50-54, 55-59, 60-64, 65-69, 70+
Temperature:	60° - 70°
Aid/Splits:	13 / every 5 miles

HIGHLIGHTS You won't see the reputedly world's largest floating boardwalk or the world's only floating golf green (both Coeur d'Alene attractions) during this old-fashioned marathon, but you will discover why the popularity of this northern Idaho resort town is soaring. As Idaho's premier running event, the Coeur d'Alene Marathon offers a wonderful tour of the area, including thick evergreen forests, deep blue lakes, beautiful golf courses, and a fashionable city center along the lakefront.

COURSE DESCRIPTION At an average elevation of 2,300 feet, Coeur d'Alene's loop course starts and finishes at North Idaho College in the heart of downtown. The race travels through evergreen-covered countryside, open fields, past three lakes, two golf courses, through several rural subdivisions and the city center and park. Although basically flat, the course contains one significant hill at the 9-mile point.

CROWD/RUNNER SUPPORT For a city of only 60,000, Coeur d'Alene attracts an impressive 6,000 spectators throughout the course. Volunteers at 13 aid stations provide additional encouragement. Although race temperatures are normally ideal, organizers make sure you properly warm up by placing clothing drop boxes at each mile. Portable toilets are located at miles 5, 6.5, 11.25, 16, and 21.

RACE LOGISTICS Coeur d'Alene starts and finishes within walking distance of downtown lodging. Plenty of parking is available for those arriving by car on race morning.

ACTIVITIES Race packet pickup and Mini-Trade Fair take place on Saturday from 9:00 a.m. to 6:00 p.m. at Inland Northwest Membership Student Union Building, North Idaho College. A deluxe shuttle bus takes course-conscious runners through the route from 1:00 p.m. to 5:00 p.m. leaving from the campus gymnasium. Catch an early bus if you want to hit the $6 all-you-can-eat carbo dinner from 5:00 p.m. to 7:00 p.m. at Trinity Church, 812 N. 5th Street. After the race, enjoy food, beverages and war stories while you wait for the awards ceremony which starts at 12:15 p.m.

AWARDS All entrants receive T-shirts, and finishers receive medals and gold-embossed certificates. Overall winners and division winners receive trophies.

ACCOMMODATIONS The Riverbend Inn in Post Falls, Idaho, 4105 W. Riverbend Avenue (208-773-3583), serves as the official race hotel and offers special marathon rates. Other nearby hotels include the four-star Coeur d'Alene Resort, downtown on Sherman Street (208-765-4000); Holiday Inn, 414 W. Appleway Avenue (208-765-3200); and Days Inn, 2200 Northwest Blvd. (208-667-8668).

RELATED EVENTS / RACES Coeur d'Alene holds a half marathon which starts concurrently with the marathon. The 13.1-mile loop follows the full marathon for over 5 miles, changes course, and then rejoins the marathon from the 19-mile marker to the finish. Race organizers encourage marathon walkers by providing an early start time of 5:00 a.m.

AREA ATTRACTIONS Before or after the race, visit the four-star Coeur d'Alene Resort, walk along the endless floating boardwalk, or treat yourself to a memorable round of golf on the beautiful resort course. For a stunning view of Lake Coeur d'Alene, hike 2 miles up Tubbs Hill. If you prefer a closer lake view, rent a canoe or take a popular boat cruise.

LOCAL RUNNING STORE Sport Town, 131 Parkade Plaza, Spokane, WA (509-838-4232).

MADISON MARATHON

OVERALL: 85.4

COURSE BEAUTY: 9-

COURSE DIFFICULTY: 4

APPROPRIATENESS FOR FIRST TIMERS: 9

RACE ORGANIZATION: 9

CROWDS: 2

R A C E   D A T A

Contact:	Madison Marathon, Inc.
	449 State Street
	P.O. Box 5088
	Madison, WI 53705-0088
	(608) 256-9922
Date:	May 25, 1997
	May 24, 1998
Start Time:	7:30 a.m.
Time Course Closes:	2:00 p.m.
Number of Participants:	1,387 in 1996
Certification:	USATF
Course Records:	Male: (open) 2:38:29; (masters) 2:41:32
	Female: (open) 2:57:46; (masters) 3:26:56
Elite Athlete Programs:	No
Cost:	$35/40
Age groups/Divisions:	<19, 20-24, 25-29, 30-34, 35-39, 40-44, 45-49,
	50-54, 55-59, 60-64, 65-69, 70+
Temperature:	53° - 64°
Aid/Splits:	23 / NA

HIGHLIGHTS Hip Madison, Wisconsin, home of the large and respected University of Wisconsin and the State Capitol, exudes an eclectic manner unusual for a city of this size. Pinched between two lakes, Madison offers a picturesque and vibrant setting for the youthful Madison Marathon. The marathon makes full use of Madison's resources, taking in the Capitol, the university, Lake Mendota, Lake Monona, and area parks. The marathon organizers try hard to put on a runner-friendly event, with 23 aid stations, five separate races, and a scenic course.

COURSE DESCRIPTION The Madison Marathon's course begins in Capitol Square, near the State Capitol building. A quick downhill leads runners to Johnson Street, past coffee houses and bookstores. With some very gentle slopes, the course goes down mostly residential Fordem and Sherman Avenues. At mile 3.4, runners reach Warner Park, leaving it behind by mile 4.9. From mile 5.3 to 5.5, runners climb the first hill of the race, a moderate incline past Warner Park Beach. The course hits Lake Mendota at 5.5 miles, passing through Maple Bluff's beautiful lakefront homes tucked into heavy woods, including the Governor's Mansion at 7.25, until mile 7.7. Turning onto Sherman Avenue, the course becomes slightly rolling at mile 8. Gorham Street contains two good, .2-mile hills, one just after 9 miles and the other at mile 10. From mile 11 to 16, the course winds through the University of Wisconsin campus and surrounding area. At mile 17.3, the course enters a very scenic stretch along Lake Monona, traveling on a narrow wooded road that contains some gradual rollers. Primarily downhill or flat on Monroe, runners face a short hill near the Arboretum entrance and challenge the final hill on the course near the 20-mile mark inside the Arboretum. Runners tour the scenic Arboretum from 20 to 22 and then head toward downtown until turning south just before mile 25. The final 2.2 miles of the race are run mainly along the lakeshore, finishing in Olin Park.

CROWD / RUNNER SUPPORT Although scattered throughout the course, most spectators gather at the start and finish and the relay exchange points. Each of the 23 aid stations generously offers water, electrolyte replacement, energy bar samples, Vaseline, and sunscreen. Medical assistance is available at six locations on the course, and portable toilets are located at the relay exchange points and at a few selected places later in the race.

RACE LOGISTICS You have a couple of options for getting to the start on race morning. First, you may park at the Dane County Expo Center (near the finish) for $3 and take the free shuttle bus to the start. Second, you can hunt for a parking place near Capitol Square. If you park downtown, you must find your own way back after the race. Be aware that there is no parking at Olin Park (the finish). The race will transport your sweats from the start to the finish area. Walkers and slower runners may take advantage of the special 6:00 a.m. starting time. After 12:30 p.m., those still on the course will have to move to the sidewalk, but course services will remain available until 2:00 p.m.

ACTIVITIES All day Friday and Saturday, pick up your race packet at the Dane County Expo Center. The Health and Fitness Expo in conjunction with packet pickup includes clinics on training for and running the Madison Marathon. During the day Saturday, you can take a bus tour of the marathon course for $5. On Saturday evening, the race holds a Pasta Dinner at the Expo Center (about $8). A variety of door prizes will be awarded during dinner. You may register on race morning at Capitol Square. After the marathon, get kneaded for free by massage therapists. Once you can walk again, gather up some food among the many food stalls to replenish some energy, and then enjoy the finish line festival, with live music and more substantial food for purchase. then enjoy the finish line festival, with live music and more substantial food for purchase.

AWARDS All marathon finishers receive T-shirts and medals. The overall male and female winners, and the top three in each age group receive plaques.

ACCOMMODATIONS The Sheraton Inn, 706 John Nolan Drive (near the finish), is the official race hotel. Others with special marathon rates include: Comfort Inn, Hampton Inn, Holiday Inn, and Ramada Limited, all east off I-90 and East Washington Avenue; Howard Johnson on U.W. campus; Best Western University Avenue near campus; Madison Concourse, one block off Capitol Square; University Inn, corner of State and Frances Street; and Radisson Inn, 517 Grand Canyon Drive. To obtain the special marathon rates at any of these hotels you must book through MMI's official travel agency, Wannago Travel (800-493-5979).

RELATED EVENTS / RACES Three to five-person teams can enter the marathon relay, running legs from 4 to 7 miles. Any one team member may run up to three consecutive legs. Buses transport team members to the relay exchange zones and then to the finish. The half marathon starts in Capitol Square and ends on U.W.'s campus. Both the marathon relay and the half marathon start with the marathon. Other runners may consider the 10K Road Race or the 5K Run/Walk. Both start at 8:15 a.m. at Capitol Square and finish in Olin Park.

AREA ATTRACTIONS Two institutions mark Madison life, state government and the university, and both are worth a visit. The State Capitol building is topped by the only granite dome in the United States. Places of interest on the campus include the Olbrich Botanical Gardens at 3330 Atwood Avenue; and Memorial Union Terrace overlooking Lake Mendota, 800 Langdon Street. The Madison Art Center exhibits contemporary art at 211 State Street. On Saturday mornings, check out the Farmer's Market on Capitol Square.

LOCAL RUNNING STORE Movin' Shoes, 604 S. Park Street (608-251-0125).

VERMONT CITY MARATHON

OVERALL: 92.2

COURSE BEAUTY: 9

COURSE DIFFICULTY: 4+

APPROPRIATENESS FOR FIRST TIMERS: 10-

RACE ORGANIZATION: 9+

CROWDS: 2+

RACE DATA

Contact: Andrea Riha
Key Bank Vermont City Marathon
P.O. Box 152
Burlington, VT 05402
(800) 880-8149 e-mail: Andreatr@aol.com

Date: May 25, 1997
May 24, 1998

Start Time: 8:05 a.m.

Time Course Closes: 1:00 p.m.

Number of Participants: 2,000 in 1996

Certification: USATF

Course Records: Male: (open) 2:18:03; (masters) 2:26:32
Female: (open) 2:38:32; (masters) 2:47:28

Elite Athlete Programs: Yes

Cost: $30/40/45

Age groups/Divisions: 16-29, 30-34, 35-39, 40-44, 45-49, 50-54, 55-59,
60-69, 70+

Temperature: 49° - 71°

Aid/Splits: 15 / none

HIGHLIGHTS Personal recommendations often lead to our greatest experiences — the corner Italian restaurant, that foreign film treasure from Mexico, and the Vermont City Marathon. The success of VCM is owed mainly to contented runners passing the word to their friends. Word of mouth has created a 20% increase in participants each year. Not surprisingly, Vermont City boasts one of the highest repeat runner rates in North America. What's its secret? For starters, location. Burlington radiates beauty with the Adirondack Mountains reflecting off gorgeous Lake Champlain. The marathon skirts the shoreline for several miles, providing spectacular views. Also, very few cities embrace a marathon quite like Burlington. As the city's largest annual event, VCM sports an incredible 1,200 volunteers for 4,000 runners, a number that translates into superb organization and happy participants.

RACE HISTORY Most people agree that autumn is the nicest time of year in New England. No mystery then why most marathon race directors in the area hold their race during this time. The trees radiate color, the weather usually cooperates, and Boston is long gone. Not deterred by Boston, VCM organizers believed that an alternative to Boston was just what the New England spring racing schedule needed. Therefore, in 1989, the VCM was born, its name reflecting that it is a city course rather than a dirt mountain road.

COURSE DESCRIPTION The marathon starts in Battery Park, the site of famous artillery exchanges in the Revolutionary War, and finishes at Waterfront Park on the shore of Lake Champlain. Run entirely within the city of Burlington, the course travels through the Downtown Marketplace, the surrounding Hill Section, and the Old and New North Ends. Beginning with a 3.3-mile loop around the downtown area, a gentle incline greets the runners between .8 and 1.3 miles. At 1.5, runners proceed down a sharp, short decline after a right turn on Beach Street. From here, the course returns to the downtown area and Church Street with a gradual hill from 2.5 to 2.9 miles. Upon leaving town, the route continues to a divided 6.6-mile, out-and-back section on the closed Northern Connector Highway (Beltline). Although still early in the race, this is a difficult section due to the severe camber of the road, absence of crowd support, and lack of protection from the elements. Moderate inclines and declines occur from 6 to 6.5 and from 9 to 9.5 miles. Returning downtown, the course heads south for a 6.6-mile loop through mostly residential Burlington, Oakledge Park and along the waterfront with the picturesque Adirondacks in the background. Runners are welcomed back to downtown by hundreds of spectators, the Taiko drummer corps, and a challenging hill between mile 16 and 16.5 which takes the runners conveniently past the Radisson Hotel. The race proceeds slightly downhill on North Avenue from 16.5 to 21.5 with a short, steep down and up from 17 to 17.5 and a sharp .125-mile downhill at mile 18. The final 4.7 miles trace the mostly flat to slightly downhill bike trail paralleling Lake Champlain to the finish in Waterfront Park. Overall, the course drops 100 feet.

CROWD / RUNNER SUPPORT For a town of Burlington's size (40,000), the marathon attracts an impressive crowd of 10,000 spectators. Most of the bystanders take advantage of the spectator friendly course layout by hovering near Battery Park, which the race passes several times. Fifteen excellent aid stations are located throughout the course along with

several musical groups providing entertainment along the way, most notably the Taiko drummers at the foot of the course's toughest climb.

RACE LOGISTICS The start and finish are close to each other and to the race hotel, so transportation is not a concern. We recommend staying at the Radisson due to its proximity to the start/finish and to capture more of the race flavor. If you arrive by car, ample free parking is available.

ACTIVITIES VCM hosts a two-day Sports & Wellness Expo and packet pickup beginning on Friday from 4:00 p.m. to 8:00 p.m. and Saturday from 10:00 a.m. to 6:00 p.m. VCM also offers various seminars throughout the day on Saturday. Try not to miss the "Mile by Mile Preview," an excellent slide show and discussion of the course. Runners, family, and friends are invited to enjoy an all-you-can-eat pasta party for a modest price, featuring a special guest speaker. The party always sells out, so purchase your tickets early. If you miss the pasta party, don't worry; nearby Church Street is loaded with great restaurants to meet your carbo-loading needs. After the race, runners are treated to complimentary food, drinks, massages and live music. The awards ceremony is held in Waterfront Park at 1:00 p.m.

AWARDS Every marathon runner receives a T-shirt and hospitality booklet, and finishers are presented with uniquely Vermont medallions, certificates by professional calligraphers, and results booklets. Division awards of Vermont pottery extend three deep, and prize money is awarded to top open and masters runners. Additionally, the first Vermont resident to cross the finish line receives a cash prize.

ELITE RUNNERS INFORMATION VCM has a modest budget to recruit elite runners (men under 2:20 and women under 2:55). Transportation, hotel accommodations, free entry and expenses are provided. Open prize money is offered to sixth place with the overall winner receiving $1,300, $650 for second, $325 for third, $200 for fourth, and $100 for fifth and sixth. Masters prize money extends to third place with $300 for the winner, $200 for second, and $100 for third.

ACCOMMODATIONS Try to stay at the Radisson Hotel Burlington which functions as VCM headquarters. The scenery from the upper lakeview rooms will make you loathe to leave. The Radisson is located at 60 Battery Street (800-333-3333). Other hotels offering special marathon rates include the Sheraton Burlington Hotel and Conference Center, 870 Williston Road (800-677-6576); and the Holiday Inn, 1068 Williston Road, South Burlington (800-799-6363).

RELATED EVENTS/RACES Runners not ready to tackle the marathon may consider the marathon relay, run simultaneously on the same course. The unique, 5-leg relay consists of 3.3, 6.6, 6.6, 4.1 and 5.6-mile legs, with teams consisting of 2 to 5 members with each member running at least one complete leg. Any one member may run up to four legs, in any order. In 1996, 550 teams entered the marathon relay, competing for the most creative team name, and in the corporate and open challenge.

AREA ATTRACTIONS Art loving runners will want to check out the Festival of Fine Art which coincides with race weekend. Over 25 Vermont artists open their studios to the public. Maps are available from Art's Alive (802-864-1557). History buffs may want to tour Revolutionary War hero Ethan Allen's homestead. For great lake views, take a scenic ride on Lake Champlain aboard the Ethan Allen, a 500-passenger, triple-deck cruise ship. Or, spend a few hours strolling along Church Street with its trendy shops, nice restaurants, and street entertainers.

LOCAL RUNNING STORES Ski Rack, 85 Main Street, Burlington (802-863-5668); Sportshoe Center, Dorset Square, South Burlington (802-862-5666).

MED-CITY MARATHON

OVERALL: 73.7

COURSE BEAUTY: 8

COURSE DIFFICULTY: 4

APPROPRIATENESS FOR FIRST TIMERS: 7+

RACE ORGANIZATION: 8+

CROWDS: 1-

RACE DATA

Contact:	Med-City Marathon
	1417 14th Avenue NE
	Rochester, MN 55906
	(507) 282-1411
Date:	May 25, 1997
	May 24, 1998
Start Time:	8:00 a.m.
Time Course Closes:	2:00 p.m.
Number of Participants:	435 in 1996
Certification:	USATF
Course Records:	New Course in 1997
Elite Athlete Programs:	No
Cost:	$20/25
Age groups/Divisions:	<29, 30-39, 40-49, 50-59, 60+
Temperature:	45° - 65°
Aid/Splits:	11 / mile 13.1

HIGHLIGHTS Attracting thousands of ailing people from all parts of the globe, the renowned Mayo Clinic medical facility has long been Rochester, Minnesota's claim to fame. Thanks to the newly established Med-City Marathon, however, the collective health of Rochester's visitors is improving (though many folks question the mental health of marathoners). The race features a scenic tour of Rochester's pleasant mix of bike paths and rural and urban streets. And, of course, you won't get away without passing a few medical facilities before the finish. In fact, "Pass the Mayo, do you have the Mustard?" has become the race's slogan.

COURSE DESCRIPTION Providing a pleasant citywide tour, Med-City's course starts in Soldiers Memorial Field. Heading north for a 2-mile downtown loop, runners pay their respects to Methodist Hospital and the Mayo Clinic before returning to the attractive upper-class neighborhood surrounding Memorial Parkway. Around 3 miles, the route joins one of the course's many bike paths for 1 mile, then cuts quickly through a residential area before rejoining the bike path near 5.2 miles. At mile 6, the route turns right entering the beautiful wooded confines of Mayowood Road. Although mostly flat to rolling on Mayowood Road, a steeper upgrade occurs around 8 miles as the route slowly makes its way toward Lake George. Back on the bike path at 10.4 miles, the course passes Lake George at 11 miles continuing toward Soldiers Memorial Field and downtown. Runners pass the Mayo Building and Slatterly Park before hitting McQuillan Field at 17 miles. To take your mind off the route's most unattractive section (the commercial section between 17.5 miles and 19.25 miles), listen for music along the street. Be alert for a short but challenging hill cresting at the 20-mile mark on 30th Street. After a one-mile stretch through middle-class, residential Pinewood Road, the route rejoins the bike path as runners pass each other going opposite directions. Returning downtown, the course passes the Mayo Park and Civic Center just after 25 miles and finishes adjacent to the flag pole in Soldiers Memorial Field.

CROWD/RUNNER SUPPORT Although scattered throughout the course, most spectators congregate near the aid stations and the start/finish area in Soldiers Memorial Field. Corporate-sponsored aid stations compete for the best aid station award voted on by the runners.

RACE LOGISTICS The race is limited to 750 marathoners, so enter early. If you're staying at the Kahler Hotel, a complimentary shuttle service takes you to and from the start/finish. Otherwise, you need to drive to the start, where plenty of parking is available. Shuttle buses take relay runners to the exchange zones.

ACTIVITIES Pick up your race packet at Heritage Hall in the Kahler Hotel, 20 Southwest Second Avenue (800-533-1655), Friday night from 6:00 p.m. to 10:00 p.m. or Saturday from 9:00 a.m. to 8:00 p.m. There is no race-day registration or packet pickup. For an extra $5, your packet can be mailed to you. On Saturday from 10:00 a.m. to 7:00 p.m., attend the Health and Fitness Expo appropriately sponsored by the Mayo Clinic Sports Medicine Center. Also at the Kahler Hotel, a pasta buffet takes place Saturday evening from 3:00 p.m. to 8:00 p.m. After the race, replenish yourself with refreshments while awaiting the awards ceremony starting at noon. To honor all involved with the race, a post-race party complete with music and cash bar runs from 5:00 p.m. to 9:00 p.m. at the Kahler Hotel penthouse.

AWARDS Every finisher receives a T-shirt and medallion. The first overall male and female and division winners earn plaques, and 2nd and 3rd place runners receive medals. The big winner at the event is the official charity; in its first year, the race raised $8,000 for Special Olympics Minnesota.

ACCOMMODATIONS In addition to the Kahler, the following hotels offer special rates and late checkout for the marathon: Clinic View Inn and Suites, 101 E. Center Street (507-289-8646); and Holiday Inn Downtown, 220 S. Broadway (507-288-3231).

RELATED EVENTS/RACES If you want to participate in the Med-City experience but don't want to run 26.2 miles, consider joining a relay team. Choose between a two and four-person relay, both of which start with the marathon at 8:00 a.m. Kids can keep occupied with an all-comers track meet held from 9:00 a.m. to 11:00 a.m.

AREA ATTRACTIONS If you have time, visit the Mayowood Mansion and Plummer House and Gardens. Antique shopping or picnicking at Silver Lake are other options.

GOVERNOR'S CUP
"GHOST TOWN" MARATHON
OVERALL: 74.8

COURSE BEAUTY: 8

COURSE DIFFICULTY: 6

APPROPRIATENESS FOR FIRST TIMERS: 5

RACE ORGANIZATION: 8

CROWDS: 1-

RACE DATA

Contact:	Governor's Cup
	P.O. Box 451
	Helena, MT 59624
	(406) 444-8261
Date:	June 7, 1997
	June 6, 1998
Start Time:	7:00 a.m.
Time Course Closes:	Noon
Number of Participants:	180 in 1996
Certification:	USATF
Course Records:	Male: (open) 2:20:35; (masters) 2:34:42
	Female: (open) 2:53:29; (masters) 3:12:44
Elite Athlete Programs	No
Cost:	$25/27
Age groups/Divisions:	<19, 20-29, 30-39, 40-49, 50-59, 60-69, 70+
Temperature:	30° - 75°
Aid/Splits:	10 / none

HIGHLIGHTS A potluck of races, the Governor's Cup offers an event to suit everyone's interest and condition. Originally conceived to migrate from town to town in Montana, the Governor's Cup sits firmly entrenched in Helena's prairie soil. The challenging marathon — part dirt wagon trails, part asphalt — starts in the ghost town of Marysville and finishes in downtown Helena. With plenty of big sky all around, the open Ghost Town Marathon course loses 1,243 feet despite a 350-foot elevation gain in the final three miles.

COURSE DESCRIPTION Set in a broad valley framed by forested mountains, the Ghost Town Marathon starts in Marysville, Montana, at an elevation of 5,400 feet. Located in Montana's old gold mining country, this ghost town with its weather-worn buildings, was named after the first resident white woman, Mrs. Mary Ralston. The first 6 miles go generally downhill along the original horse and buggy trail. After reaching Lincoln Road, runners detour on a 1.4-mile loop (still a dirt road) beginning at the Silver City Bar. Once done, the course hits pavement for the first time on Birdseye Road leading to Helena. Miles 8 through 12 contain some tough uphill climbs, followed by a generally descending course. At about mile 18, the course ducks into the Montana National Guard and Fort Harrison complexes. Runners hit a 1-mile dirt stretch near the old Kessler Brewery around the 23-mile mark, and then hit Helena. Gaining about 300 feet over the final 3.5 miles, runners reach the finish line on Park Avenue in downtown Helena, elevation 4,157 feet.

CROWD / RUNNER SUPPORT You wouldn't expect a lot of spectators at the "Ghost Town" Marathon, and you're not disappointed. Except at the relay exchange points and the aid stations, spectators outside of Helena are definitely ghost-like. The finish line, however, is a different story, with thousands of race fans cheering on the participants. The aid stations, located approximately every 3 miles, carry water and minor first-aid supplies.

RACE LOGISTICS Since cars are not allowed on the course, park in the garage at Park Avenue and 6th in downtown Helena and catch the race bus just above the parking garage. The marathon buses leave at 5:45 a.m. It can be chilly in Marysville so make sure to take some warm-up clothing to the start. The race will return the clothing to you in the finish area.

ACTIVITIES If you preregister, your race number and T-shirt will be mailed to you. If you register late, or you need to register in person, go to the race headquarters at the Visitor and Commerce Center on Sixth Avenue and Cruse in downtown Helena to retrieve your race number. On race morning, you can pick up your race number, but you may not register. On Friday evening at the Cathedral of St. Helena, attend the Carboload Spaghetti Feed. The awards ceremony starts around noon, and refreshments are also available. Plans for other events have not been finalized.

AWARDS Each entrant receives their choice of a short-sleeve or long-sleeve T-shirt, polo shirt, or sweatshirt. The top three places in each age group receive medals, and the top male and female overall and masters finishers receive specially crafted awards.

ACCOMMODATIONS Perhaps most convenient to race-day activities is the Park Plaza (406-443-2200). Other hotels in Helena include: Holiday Inn Express (406-449-4000); Shilo Inn (406-442-0320); Comfort Inn (406-443-1000); Days Inn (406-442-3280); Motel 6 (406-442-9990); Colonial Inn (406-443-2100); Super 8 (406-443-2450); Budget Inn Express (406-443-1770); Appleton B&B (406-449-7492); and Sanders B&B (406-442-3309).

RELATED EVENTS / RACES The Governor's Cup consists of a series of events, including: a four-person marathon relay, 20K Race, 10K Race, 5K Race, and 400-meter Special Olympian Run. Nearly 7,000 runners participate in the Governor's Cup races, with most entering the nationally-known 5K Race.

AREA ATTRACTIONS Among the activities to consider in Helena are the Gates of the Mountains boat tour, a visit to the Historical Society Museum, a train tour of Helena's historical sights, a State Capitol building tour, and a stroll through the Downtown Walking Mall.

STEAMBOAT MARATHON

OVERALL: 84.2

COURSE BEAUTY: 9+

COURSE DIFFICULTY: 5+ (SEE APPENDIX)

APPROPRIATENESS FOR FIRST TIMERS: 6

RACE ORGANIZATION: 8

CROWDS: 0

RACE DATA

Contact:	Janet Nichols
	Steamboat Springs Chamber Resort Association
	P.O. Box 774408, Steamboat Springs, CO 80477
	(970) 879-0882
	e-mail: info@steamboat-chamber.com
	http://www.steamboat-chamber.com
Date:	June 8, 1997
	June 7, 1998
Start Time:	7:30 a.m.
Time Course Closes:	1:00 p.m.
Number of Participants:	479 in 1996
Certification:	USATF
Course Records:	Male: (open) 2:23:59
	Female: (open) 2:54:59
Elite Athlete Programs:	Yes
Cost:	$30/40
Age groups/Divisions:	<19, 20-29, 30-39, 40-49, 50-59, 60+
Temperature:	35° - 74°
Aid/Splits:	8 / every 2 miles

HIGHLIGHTS Famous as a winter playground, Steamboat Springs equally entices in the summer when the Steamboat Marathon runs. Green mountains. Waving aspen. Rustling rivers. Pure air. All make Steamboat one of the most compelling marathons on the continent. You won't find hoopla here. You won't find throngs of screaming spectators. And, you won't find air, at least a lot of it. Steamboat starts in tiny Hahns Peak Village, elevation 8,128 feet and ends in downtown Steamboat Springs, elevation 6,728 feet, making it a challenge for lowlanders even though most of the course runs downstream. You will find exhilarating nature which soothes your searing lungs. After the marathon, enjoy hot springs, fishing, horseback rides, air balloon flights, river rafting, and golf.

RACE HISTORY Steamboat began in 1982 as an art benefit with 106 runners. The rustic setting sometimes can make for some interesting races. While the llamas along the course usually behave themselves, we can't always say the same about the cows. In 1984, a cattle drive swept right through the course significantly delaying the race. Runners who did not want to run with the bulls had to wait for the cowpokes to clear the way. There haven't been any serious cattle incidents since, but you never know.

COURSE DESCRIPTION Wonderfully scenic, high altitude, moderately difficult, and point-to-point, the Steamboat course loses 1,400 feet from start to finish. The course begins in Hahns Peak Village, passes alpine ranches, Sleeping Giant mountain, and the Elk River on its way to downtown Steamboat Springs. Despite the significant elevation loss, several hills, made even more difficult by the thin air, tax runners. The open course runs on a narrow, country road, so beware the hurried fisherman on his way to the daily catch.

From the start, the setting treats runners to sweeping mountain vistas and meadows as they head down a gradual decline for the first half mile. Runners soon warm up on a modest incline between mile .6 and 1.2 that steepens near the crest, and then head sharply downhill past ranch land to the 2-mile mark. The next .75 miles roll slightly downhill. Then you face the first real hill on the course, a moderate, 1-mile incline, followed by an acute, sweeping downhill to the 10K point. This hill screams, fully testing your quadriceps muscles. You get a chance to recuperate over the next several miles: mostly flat from mile 6.2 to 6.8, slight upward slant from mile 6.8 to 7, and then gently down to mile 8.7. From 8.7 to 11.4, the course rolls slightly until you hit another moderate climb from mile 11.4 to 12.2. The Sleeping Giant mountain reclines to your right, and the Elk River tumbles down below. The next 10 miles roll easily down the mountain, until a short but abrupt climb at mile 22.5. A downhill to the turn onto Highway 40 leads toward downtown Steamboat at 24.5. A short, easy rise to 24.7 precedes a downward slope until a slight incline from mile 26 to the Courthouse lawn finish.

CROWD/RUNNER SUPPORT A small mountain resort, Steamboat doesn't attract many spectators to its marathon course but compensates with its scenery.

RACE LOGISTICS The extremely narrow road up Hahns Peak and the scarce parking once there make the free shuttle service extremely attractive. Shuttles leave from the parking lot at 8th and Oak Streets in downtown Steamboat between 6:00 a.m. and 6:15 a.m. There are also shuttle buses from the Sheraton to 8th and Oak. The race transports any personal belongings from the start to the finish area.

ACTIVITIES Pick up your race packet on Friday or Saturday on race weekend at Inside Edge Sports in Central Park Plaza. You can attend the pasta dinner the night before the marathon. The dinner features a guest speaker and all the food you can eat (about $12). After the race, soak in the famous Steamboat Springs Hot Springs. Immediate race results are generally handed out at the finish line. The awards ceremony and random drawing are held in the finish area at noon.

AWARDS All entrants receive T-shirts, and finishers also corral finisher's medals. Steamboat offers approximately $2,500 in prize money, plus age-group awards for the top finishers in each category.

FIRST-TIMERS INFORMATION A challenging race for the novice marathoner, Steamboat's altitude, sparse crowds, relatively few aid stations, and pounding course make it less than ideal for the beginner. On the other hand, the beauty of the area doesn't hurt. If you are a first-timer training for Steamboat, we suggest you try to include some downhill training to accustom your quads to the pounding of running sharp downhills and some altitude training. While you could complete the race without these, you will be in better shape afterwards with them.

ELITE RUNNERS INFORMATION Steamboat offers inducements to elite runners. The criteria vary, so you need to contact Janet Nichols to see if you qualify for elite status. Men with sub 2:30 times and women with sub 2:50 times will likely qualify. For those who are awarded elite status, the race offers lodging, expenses, free entry, and prize money (about $2,500) for the top three in the marathon, half marathon and 10K races. And, of course, a great weekend in Steamboat Springs.

ACCOMMODATIONS Call Steamboat Central Reservations (800-922-2722) to arrange your accommodations in Steamboat. They can take care of just about any lodging requirement to fit most budgets.

RELATED EVENTS/RACES In addition to the marathon, three other events for friends and family kick off on Sunday. The half marathon starts at the marathon midpoint (elevation 6,990 feet) and ends in downtown Steamboat. A 10K run and fitness walk over rolling hills begins at 8:00 a.m. Starting and finishing at the courthouse in downtown Steamboat Springs, the 10K attracts many celebrity runners. Finally, the race holds a free, half-mile fun run for children starting at 11:15 a.m. at the courthouse.

AREA ATTRACTIONS Steamboat during the summer hosts one festival after another, beginning with the Yampa River Festival the week following the marathon. Contact the Chamber Resort Association for a list of the current calendar of events.

LOCAL RUNNING STORE Inside Edge Sports, Central Park Plaza, Steamboat Springs (970-879-1250).

Manitoba Marathon

OVERALL: 78

COURSE BEAUTY: 7+

COURSE DIFFICULTY: 4

APPROPRIATENESS FOR FIRST TIMERS: 7

RACE ORGANIZATION: 9-

CROWDS: 1+

RACE DATA

Contact:	Shirley Lumb
	Manitoba Marathon Foundation
	200 Main Street
	Winnipeg, Manitoba, Canada R3C 4M2
	(204) 925-5751
Date:	June 15, 1997
	June 14, 1998
Start Time:	7:00 a.m.
Time Course Closes:	12:30 p.m.
Number of Participants:	450 in 1995
Certification:	MRA, Athletics Manitoba
Course Records:	Male: (open) 2:13:53; (masters) 2:24:27
	Female: (open) 2:38:08; (masters) 2:45:30
Elite Athlete Programs:	Yes
Cost:	$33/43 Adults, $18/23 Youth
Age Groups/Divisions:	16-19, 20-24, 25-29, 30-34, 35-39, 40-44, 45-49,
	50-54, 55-59, 60-64, 65+
Temperature:	75°
Aid/Splits:	25 / mile 1

HIGHLIGHTS If you're looking for a way to gather fitness, family, friendship and fun on Father's Day, consider the Manitoba Marathon in Winnipeg. Offering all this and more, the MM fundraises for local charitable projects. Everyone has an opportunity to participate as this event features four races in addition to the marathon — bringing together over 6,500 runners in all. What better way to spend Dad's Day than to pay tribute to health and posterity?

COURSE DESCRIPTION You'll appreciate the enthusiasm of the Winnipeg community as you make your way from the start at the University of Manitoba through the flat, loop course. Winnipeg residents typically come out to praise participants and happily shower them with water. The marathon course takes you down many main arteries of the city. Traveling down Wellington Crescent, you pass many stately old homes through beautiful Assiniboine Park (a shady respite from the summer sun) and the Legislative Buildings as you wind your way to the finish line at University Stadium. If you hate hills, be thankful, for they are virtually nonexistent on this course: the maximum elevation variance is barely over 10 feet with most of the course at 770 feet.

CROWD/RUNNER SUPPORT Since the Manitoba Marathon has a long history in the Winnipeg community, the marathon has become a very popular event for spectators, participants and volunteers alike. Watch at the intersections for course marshals and their antique cars. Water, medical staff, sponges, portable toilets and lubrication are part of what to expect at each station. Splits are provided only at the first-mile mark so bring your watch if you're tracking your pace. Runners worried about completing the entire distance will be interested in Manitoba's "exit with dignity" program, allowing runners to drop out at any point, turn in their tags, and catch a complimentary bus back to the finish area. A certificate attesting to the distance completed is then mailed to the participant.

RACE LOGISTICS Transportation is not provided to the start/finish so plan ahead! For those with cars, there is plenty of parking within a short walk of the start.

ACTIVITIES Race kits may be picked up at the race headquarters hotel during the two-and-a-half weeks prior to race day. There is no race-day registration or packet pickup. Join runners and volunteers at the Pasta Fest held Friday night. As a marathon participant, you're entitled to free admission to the dinner, held from 5:30 p.m. to 8:00 p.m. at the Winnipeg Convention Centre. If you didn't get enough to eat at the Pasta Fest, you have a second opportunity to fill up at the Carbo Brunch held Saturday morning at the International Inn. Listen to well-known running gurus share their expertise and experiences with you as you make your way through your meal. Tickets are available at the race headquarters. After you exit the finish chute, the pancake breakfast at University Stadium awaits you and your family. Here, you have an opportunity to share your race-day stories and compare times with other competitors. What's more, at an affordable price, you can treat everyone to a Father's Day feast!

AWARDS The Manitoba Marathon salutes top finishers with $10,000 in total prize money. The top Manitoban male and female finishers are recognized, and the Rick McLennan Memorial Trophy is awarded to the first Manitoban breaking a three-hour finish for the first time. Medals are mailed to all 1st, 2nd, and 3rd place finishers in each age group.

ELITE RUNNERS INFORMATION Ten thousand dollars in prize money is divided between the top three overall and the first masters finishers as follows: 1st — $2,500; 2nd — $1,200; 3rd — $800; and masters — $500. The race also offers course record bonus money.

ACCOMMODATIONS The official hotel is the International Inn (204-786-4801), adjacent to the International Air Terminal. Or, if you prefer less expensive accommodations about 100 yards from the start line, try the University of Manitoba, St. Andrews College (204-474-8895). Don't delay setting up reservations — this event attracts thousands of runners and space fills quite quickly.

RELATED EVENTS / RACES If you're with those who wish to participate in less laborious activities, guide your guests to the Marathon Relay (team of 5 over 26.2 miles), the Super Run (2.6 miles), the Half Marathon (13.1 miles) or the 10K Walk. All of these events are featured on race day, and friends or family members can register at the headquarters if they've missed the preregistration deadline.

AREA ATTRACTIONS In Winnipeg, check out Forks Market located downtown on the banks of the Red and Assiniboine Rivers, featuring river walks, a children's museum, restaurants, and craft shops. Get a taste of life in central Canada's fur trading past at Ft. Garry, reachable by riverboat, double decker bus, or car. Perhaps spend an afternoon at Assiniboine Park and Zoo, located on the marathon course. Other Winnipeg staples include the Winnipeg Art Gallery, Captain Kennedy House, Leo Maude Sculpture Gardens, Oak Hammock Marsh, and the Winnipeg Mint.

LOCAL RUNNING STORE Running Room, 2091 Portage Avenue (204-832-7031).

MARATHON DE TAOS

OVERALL: 75.5

COURSE BEAUTY: 8-

COURSE DIFFICULTY: 8- (SEE APPENDIX)

APPROPRIATENESS FOR FIRST TIMERS: 4+

RACE ORGANIZATION: 8-

CROWDS: 0+

RACE DATA

Contact:	Marathon de Taos
	c/o Bruce Gomez
	P.O. Box 2245
	Taos, NM 87571
	(505) 776-1860
Date:	June 15, 1997
	June 14, 1998
Start Time:	6:00 a.m.
Time Course Closes:	NA
Number of Participants:	50 in 1996
Certification:	USATF
Course Records:	Male: (open) 2:34:17
	Female: (open) 3:27:09
Elite Athlete Programs:	No
Cost:	$25/30
Age Groups/Divisions:	18-29, 30-39, 40-49, 50-59, 60+
Temperature:	50° - 80°
Aid/Splits:	17 / none

HIGHLIGHTS A magnet for artists from Georgia O'Keeffe to R.C. Gorman, Taos perches high in the mountains. Its adobe buildings, boundless horizons, and crystalline air rouse the creativity of those inclined to stark beauty. Despite being held for fifteen years, Taos attracts only 250 people to its five races. For the most part, runners lag behind artists in discovering this lofty retreat; most high-altitude seekers seem to congregate in Albuquerque to the south or Boulder to the north. Its remote, mountain location is certainly a prime explanation, although skiers have been shushing down its slopes for years. The challenging marathon, which reaches 7,200 feet, includes a debilitating hill at 12.5 miles.

COURSE DESCRIPTION Starting outside Taos center at 6,950 feet, the marathon goes north on Taos Pueblo Road on a gentle decline for 200 yards with the mountains ahead of you. After 1 mile, runners make a sharp left through pastures and grassy fields. Turning onto Hwy. 64, runners face a gentle incline from mile 1.7 to 4.6 past the commercial outskirts of Taos with fields on the left and the mountains toward the right. A moderate uphill hits from mile 5.3 to 5.9, followed by a gradual decline from 5.9 to 6.3 characterized by high desert scrub brush. Mostly flat from mile 6.3 to 9.7, the course takes a steep, curving plunge from 9.7 to 11.4, losing 600 feet. Passing through an adobe residential area, the course flattens briefly allowing runners to recover their legs before embarking on the difficult ascent to Arroyo Seco. The climb begins at mile 12.5 and is mercifully over by 13.2, but in that .75 miles runners have climbed 600 feet to an elevation of 7,100 feet. After several curves, the route flattens briefly before gradually ascending about 100 feet from mile 13.8 to 16. Rolling to 19, the town and surrounding mountains soon come into view as you begin the easy descent into Taos. A gentle incline at mile 24.8 precedes the journey through residential and commercial areas of Taos leading to the finish in Kit Carson Park.

CROWD/RUNNER SUPPORT Minimal crowds come out for the marathon, mostly race volunteers, friends and family of runners, and some residents in the neighborhoods along the course. The aid stations, located every 3 miles to mile 12, then every mile thereafter, carry water, electrolyte replacement, and energy bars. Runners can catch their own splits from the miles marked on the ground.

RACE LOGISTICS A small town, Taos is not difficult to get around, if a bit crowded near the town center. You need to find your own way to the start, located about a half mile from the town center. The start and finish are within walking distance of each other.

ACTIVITIES Saturday evening, the race expects to hold a pasta/pizza party at an undetermined location. There is no race-day registration. A post-race massage is available for a donation. You also have a chance to win one of the many random merchandise prizes.

AWARDS All runners get to wear home Taos Marathon T-shirts. Overall and age-group winners receive special prizes.

ACCOMMODATIONS Possible accommodations in Taos include: Best Western Kachina Lodge (505-758-2275); Holiday Inn Don Fernando de Taos, 1005 Paseo Del Pueblo (505-758-4444); Quality Inn, 1043 Paseo Del Pueblo (505-758-2200); Rancho Ramada Inn de Taos, 615 Paseo Del Pueblo (505-758-2900); Taos Civic Plaza, 121 Civic Plaza Drive (505-758-5792); Taos Inn, 125 Paseo Del Pueblo (505-758-2233); and El Pueblo Lodge, 412 Paseo Del Pueblo (505-758-8700).

RELATED EVENTS/RACES The Taos extended family of races includes several events for so few runners. A Marathon Relay for 5-member teams runs concurrently with the marathon (4 legs of 5 miles each, and one leg of 6.2 miles). At 7:00 a.m., a half marathon, 5K Run, and 5K Walk begin at the marathon start.

AREA ATTRACTIONS Made for browsing, Taos boasts numerous art galleries and curio shops. Also, stop by the still active Taos Pueblo.

GRANDMA'S MARATHON

OVERALL: 88.1

COURSE BEAUTY: 9-

COURSE DIFFICULTY: 3-

APPROPRIATENESS FOR FIRST TIMERS: 9+

RACE ORGANIZATION: 10

CROWDS: 2-

R A C E   D A T A

Contact:	Scott Keenan
	Grandma's Marathon
	P.O. Box 16234
	Duluth, MN 55816
	(218) 727-0947
Date:	June 21, 1997
	June 20, 1998
Start Time:	7:30 a.m.
Time Course Closes:	1:30 p.m.
Number of Participants:	6,528 in 1995
Certification:	USATF
Course Records:	Male: (open) 2:09:37
	Female: (open) 2:29:36
Elite Athlete Programs:	Yes
Cost:	$25/30/35
Age groups/Divisions:	12-18, 19-34, 35-39, 40-44, 45-49, 50-54, 55-59,
	60-64, 65-69, 70+, Grandmother
Temperature:	50° - 65°
Aid/Splits:	15 / miles 5, 6.2, 10, 13.1, 15, 20, 25 & 26

HIGHLIGHTS What's this? A race for all the blue-haired, little old ladies of the world? Not quite. You don't have to be a grandma to run, but if you are, you can vie for the top Grandma award. Grandma's has earned a reputation as fast, exceptionally well organized, and a celebration. The race has attained cult-like status among marathon runners, possibly because of the odd name and Duluth location. The community really gets behind the race making Grandma's a BIG DEAL. And, event organizers have plenty of other activities to keep the family occupied. Kids love the Aerial Lift Bridge, reputedly one of only two left in the world. Straight and scenic in many places, the course rolls along the shores of Lake Superior. Few races match Grandma's in overall excellence for the runners and their families.

RACE HISTORY Sadly, Grandma's is not named for that rocking chair planted, sweater-making, bespectacled woman we all remember so fondly. Rather, the race gets its name from its original sponsor, Duluth-based Grandma's Saloon and Deli. Ironically, rumor has it that the original Grandma's is located in a former brothel. The race, not the brothel, was started by a group of Duluth runners in 1977 and had 150 entrants. Since then, Grandma's has grown into one of the top races in the country, with more than 6,000 runners. Because of its popularity, organizers limit entries at 7,000.

COURSE DESCRIPTION Grandma's runs on a point-to-point course beginning in Two Harbors, MN and ending in Duluth's Canal Park. The completely closed course follows

Old Highway 61 along the shore of Lake Superior, the largest freshwater lake in the world, rolling lazily most of the way with newly resurfaced asphalt. The rural start turns more residential around mile 2. On the right are heavy woods. The first real hill on the course hits from mile 5.3 to 5.6, then it's an easy downhill. The course soon loses its residential quality and by mile 9.5 you are running right next to Lake Superior. Houses still pop up, and by mile 12, you pass some envy-worthy homes. The course continues to roll until mile 22, location of infamous Lemon Drop Hill which is actually two short hills to mile 22.4. Though not particularly difficult, Lemon Drop Hill could hit tired runners hard. Luckily, the thick crowds push you up the hill, and as you veer onto Superior Street, downtown Duluth emerges. Entering downtown after mile 24, you run on cobblestones and bricked streets. Just after 25, you make the turn toward the harbor, trudge up an overpass, wind through renovated Canal Park, and finish within a stone's throw of the Aerial Lift Bridge.

C R O W D / R U N N E R   S U P P O R T   The Duluth community looks forward to the Grandma's celebration every year. An old train runs parallel to the marathon course to help spectators follow the race. Onlookers are mostly scattered, though, until roughly the 19-mile mark as runners approach downtown. Then the crowds become quite sizeable growing thicker and thicker as you near Canal Park. While every race claims it has great volunteers, Grandma's truly does. The 15 aid stations are very ably handled. Water, electrolyte replacement, sponges, and ice are all available at the stations, located at 3, 5, 7, 9, 11, 13, 15, 17, 19, 20, 21, 22, 23, 24, and 25 miles.

RACE LOGISTICS The race provides bus transportation to the start at Two Harbors. Buses leave from a number of area hotels and the Duluth Convention Center from 5:15 a.m. to 6:00 a.m. You could provide your own means to the start, but parking is not extensive. The race gladly transports your belongings to the finish.

ACTIVITIES Grandma's hosts a number of events and activities on marathon weekend. On Thursday, the two-day Health and Fitness Expo kicks off at the Duluth Entertainment Convention Center (DECC), where you can also pick up your race packet. On Friday, attend the free presentations by noted running experts. Also on Friday, kids can compete in the Whipper Snapper Races. During the day, take a bus tour of the marathon course. Buses leave from the Radisson Hotel at noon, 2:00 p.m., and 4:00 p.m. Friday evening, make sure you join in the all-you-can-eat Michelina's spaghetti dinner at DECC, possibly the lengthiest in the country, from 11:00 a.m. to 9:00 p.m. Afterward, get jazzed-up by the live entertainment at DECC or under the Big Top in Canal Park. Following the marathon, relax at one of the most festive post-race parties around, with live entertainment, a beer tent, and awards ceremony. All in all, Grandma's has just about the best pre- and post-race activities in the country.

AWARDS All marathon finishers receive T-shirts and medallions. The top three runners in most age groups win special awards, including the top local runner and grandmother. There is also over $50,000 in prize money up for grabs.

ELITE RUNNERS INFORMATION Speedsters can negotiate with the race director for elite status. Elites may be offered entry, transportation, food expenses, and possibly lodging, depending on just how speedy you are. Prize money goes to the top eight runners: $6,000 for first, $4,500 for second, $3,500 for third, $3,000 for fourth, $2,000 for fifth, $1,500 for sixth, $1,000 for seventh, and $500 for eighth. Masters runners earn $1,000 for first, $700 for second, and $300 for third. There are a number of incentive bonuses for men who run under 2:20 and women under 2:40. The incentive bonuses range from $500 for men with sub 2:20s and women with sub 2:40s to $10,000 for men under 2:09 and women under 2:29.

ACCOMMODATIONS The key to finding the right place to stay in Duluth is to start early. No kidding. It you procrastinate you may find yourself pitching a tent. It's probably easiest to first call the Duluth Conventions & Visitors Bureau (800-4-DULUTH) since they act as Grandma's lodging clearinghouse. Most convenient are brand new The Inn on Lake Superior (218-726-1111); Radisson (218-727-8981); Holiday Inn (218-722-1202); Park Inn International (218-727-8821); and Comfort Suites (218-727-1378), all near the finish area. Other good bets are Fitger's Inn (800-726-2982); and the Best Western — Edgewater (800-777-7925).

RELATED EVENTS/RACES In addition to the Whipper Snapper Races, Grandma's offers two other top-flight races: the William A. Irvin 5K and the Garry Bjorklund Half Marathon. Perfect for friends and family, the 5K is held Friday evening in an extremely festive atmosphere. On Saturday morning, the popular half marathon starts at the marathon halfway point. The half has become one of the most popular in the Midwest, reaching its 2,800 limit months in advance.

AREA ATTRACTIONS Make sure you wander through Canal Park, Duluth's restored harbor area. While Grandma's activities will keep you quite busy, you may be able to catch a Duluth Dukes baseball game. The Dukes are part of the independent International League.

LOCAL RUNNING STORE Austin-Jarrow Sports, 123 W. Superior Street (218-722-1185).

MAYOR'S MIDNIGHT SUN MARATHON

OVERALL: 88.8

COURSE BEAUTY: 9

COURSE DIFFICULTY: 5-

APPROPRIATENESS FOR FIRST TIMERS: 9+

RACE ORGANIZATION: 9-

CROWDS: 1-

RACE DATA

Contact:	John McCleary
	Anchorage Parks & Recreation
	P.O. Box 196650
	Anchorage, AK 99519-6650
	(907) 343-4474
Date:	June 21, 1997
	June 20, 1998
Start Time:	8:00 a.m.
Time Course Closes:	4:00 p.m.
Number of Participants:	1,800 in 1996
Certification:	USATF
Course Records:	Male: (open) 2:24:48
	Female: (open) 2:50:29
Elite Athlete Programs:	No
Cost:	$23/25
Age groups/Divisions:	10-14, 15-19, 20-24, 25-29, 30-34, 35-39, 40-44,
	45-49, 50-54, 55-59, 60-64, 65-69, 70+
Temperature:	55° - 70°
Aid/Splits	10 / none

HIGHLIGHTS Alaska, the last frontier, is quickly becoming the first frontier for many marathoners. The main lodestone, Mayor's Midnight Sun Marathon, pulls in the runners with its trademark Alaskan scenery, including the majestic Chugach Mountain Range and historic Cook Inlet. Enjoyed predominantly by locals until 1994, MMS's popularity changed when the Leukemia Society's Team in Training, a national fundraising and first-time marathoner training program, added the race to its marathon agenda. The largest Team in Training destination in the country, MMS's field has mushroomed from a long-standing few hundred runners to over 1,800 in 1996. With TNT's involvement, MMS boasts the largest percentage of first-time marathoners of any marathon in North America. What better place for a marathon adventure than the adventure capital of the world?

RACE HISTORY Named to commemorate the summer solstice and honor the area's two mayors, the Mayors' Midnight Sun Marathon began in 1974 with 71 entries and 36 finishers. Realizing a politician's normal penchant for ego boosting, race organizers smartly named the race Mayors' Marathon to gain support for services, permits, and police patrol from the city and borough of Anchorage. The name soon changed to Mayors' Midnight Sun Marathon, and upon unification of city services, the apostrophe moved to reflect a singular mayor.

COURSE DESCRIPTION Mayor's Midnight Sun Marathon's attractive, point-to-point course navigates through Anchorage from the striking Chugach Mountains to the historic Cook Inlet. It runs on a variety of surfaces, from paved bike trail, to road, to gravel road, to wooded trail, and back to bike trail and road. Including an uphill gain of 500 feet and downhill loss of 600 feet, the course boasts the possibility of spotting porcupines, moose, bears and other wildlife. Starting at Bartlett High School in east Anchorage (elevation 220 feet), the course travels northeast paralleling wooded Glenn Highway for 4 mostly flat miles on a paved bike path. After crossing the highway at mile 4, the course continues southwest on Arctic Valley Access Road for 3 miles of rolling hills before turning southeast on flat Arctic Valley Road passing the military guard-house and Ship Creek. With the grand Chugach Mountains on the left, the course heads northeast on a dirt/gravel roadway and intersects the historic Oilwell Tank Trail at mile 9. The next 6 miles provide a shaded, meandering trail through an urban forest marked with several short but steep uphills and one long, gradual uphill from the half-marathon point to mile 14 (the highest point on the course at 500 feet). An enthusiastic aid station and a quick glimpse of downtown Anchorage greet the runners at 15 miles as the course turns right and heads downhill to Tudor Road, one of Anchorage's main thoroughfares. Jaunting briefly through a residential neighborhood on Checkmate Street, runners then return to another scenic bike path leading toward Westchester Lagoon (elevation 15 feet) at mile 25. On a clear day, a glance to the right reveals magnificent Mt. McKinley which provides inspiration for the challenging 400-yard hill awaiting at mile 25.5. Another short pass through a residential area precedes the finish on the West High School track.

CROWD/RUNNER SUPPORT Although a smattering of spectators position themselves along the course, the rural nature of the race limits most of the support to the start and finish areas. The spectacular and peaceful scenery, however, more than makes up for the small number of spectators. Well-manned aid stations are found every 2-3 miles. Keep your eyes peeled between 18 and 19 miles for a generous, unofficial aid station on Checkmate Street. Last year, family members handed popsicles to marathon competitors, and other residents cooled runners with garden hoses.

RACE LOGISTICS Since hotels are not located near the start/finish, you need to arrange transportation to the race. Fortunately, the race provides transportation from a number of hotels throughout Anchorage. Buses also transport runners from the finish back to their hotels. In addition, an equipment shuttle truck transports belongings to the finish.

ACTIVITIES With the exception of a course tour, provided by local runners the day before the event, and loud, upbeat music played at the starting area, MMS has no pre-race activities. This should be of little concern as you will find plenty to do with your time, perhaps taking in one of the many solstice celebrations found city wide. Awards ceremonies occur directly upon the conclusion of each event.

AWARDS Sweatshirts and medallions are awarded to marathon finishers. Overall and age-group winners are awarded plaques or trophies. A special award, known as the Visitor's Cup, is presented to the best performance by an out-of-state female and male. The Anchorage Daily News newspaper publishes race results the following day. Official race results are mailed 4 to 6 weeks after the event.

ACCOMMODATIONS There is no official race hotel for the marathon. Some hotels in the area involved with the marathon transportation system include: Regal Alaskan Hotel, 4800 Spenard Road (907-243-2300); Best Western Barratt Inn, 4616 Spenard Road (907-243-3131); Super 8 Motel, 3501 Minnesota Drive (907-276-8884); Comfort Inn, 111 W. Ship Creek Avenue (907-277-6887); Days Inn, 321 E. Fifth Avenue (907-276-7226); and Inlet Tower, 1200 L Street (907-276-0110).

RELATED EVENTS/RACES In addition to the marathon, MMS features other events. A marathon walk takes place on the same marathon course and begins one hour before the run. One hour after the marathon start, a half marathon and 5.6 miler start and finish at West High School, finish site for the marathon. Assuring that there is something for everyone, race organizers have added a 1.6-mile youth run for kids ages 8 to 13. The course loops around Westchester Lagoon with the start/finish at West High School.

AREA ATTRACTIONS Anchorage and the surrounding area offer plenty to see and do. If the marathon does not fulfill your physical activity quota, Kincaid Park, the Tony Knowles Coastal Trail and Chugach National Forest, all within arms length of Anchorage, offer excellent hiking, climbing, fishing, kayaking, and mountain biking. More sedate entertainment takes the form of sightseeing while cruising south on the Seward Highway. Keep your eyes peeled for whales at Beluga Point and Dall sheep on the steep cliffs near Windy Point. Also along the highway is the Alyeska Ski Resort and its 60-passenger tram which provides a panorama of the Girdwood area. Twenty minutes further south sits Portage Glacier, the state's most popular tourist attraction. Take a walk along Portage Lake for a close-up look at countless, floating icebergs, or get to the glacier itself aboard a tour boat. Back in Anchorage, a must-see is the Museum of History and Art which depicts 10,000 years of Alaskan history. Finally, celebrate your marathon finish at one of the scores of solstice parties happening around town.

LOCAL RUNNING STORE Skinny Raven Sports, 800 J Street, Anchorage (907-274-7222).

CALGARY MIRACLE MARATHON

OVERALL: 88.4

COURSE BEAUTY: 8

COURSE DIFFICULTY: 3

APPROPRIATENESS FOR FIRST TIMERS: 8

RACE ORGANIZATION: 9+

CROWDS: 1+

R A C E   D A T A

Contact:	Heather McRae
	Stampede Run-Off
	P.O. Box 296, Station M
	Calgary, Alberta
	Canada T2P 2H9
	(403) 244-42KM
Date:	July 6, 1997
	July 5, 1998
Start Time:	7:00 a.m.
Time Course Closes:	12:30 p.m.
Number of Participants:	752 in 1995
Certification:	Athletics Alberta
Course Records:	Male: (open) 2:23:49
	Female: (open) 2:45:59
Elite Athletes Programs:	Yes
Cost:	$45/55/65
Age Groups/Divisions:	18-29, 30-34, 35-39, 40-44, 45-49, 50-54, 55-59, 60-64, 65+
Temperature:	50° - 57°
Aid/Splits:	14 / every mile and every 5K; projected finish times at 15K and 30K

HIGHLIGHTS Lovers of things Western will want to consider the Calgary Miracle Marathon. Held during the world-famous Calgary Exhibition and Stampede, the marathon assumes much of its cowboy flavor — the Carbo Chow Down, Post Race Whoop Up, and white cowboy hats for the winners. Mostly flat, the marathon takes in the wonderful Calgary Zoo, the Bow River, residential communities, and Canada Olympic Park.

RACE HISTORY The Calgary Miracle Marathon carries through a long tradition in Calgary, site of the 1988 Winter Olympics. In 1963, the nascent Calgary Miracle Marathon — then-named the Alberta and Western Canada Marathon Championship — hosted a meager nineteen participants. Its fate was forever changed, however, in the following year when Calgary hosted the Canadian Marathon Championship and the trials for the Tokyo Olympics. The Calgary Miracle Marathon joined the Stampede 10K and the Mayor's Fun Run/Walk in 1989 to become the Stampede Run-Off. To date, the event has raised over $140,000 for the Alberta Children's Hospital Foundation.

COURSE DESCRIPTION Calgary's relatively flat, out-and-back course runs through the scenic Bow River Valley; the only changes in elevation occur at roadway overpasses and underpasses. The race starts in downtown Calgary in the thriving Eau Claire district. Heading east through Chinatown, the course crosses the Bow River and continues east to loop through the Calgary

Zoo at 2.5 miles. Runners go up a short rise (about 50 feet) to cross Memorial Drive and swing through Bridgeland, Calgary's Italian district. At 5 miles, the course heads west on Memorial Drive, paralleling the tree-lined Bow River, and takes a short loop through the West Hillhurst community at 7.5 miles. Crossing over the Crowchild Trail near 8.5 miles, runners loop through Parkdale, a quiet, shady community, before passing under the TransCanada Highway and through the community of Montgomery from 11.75 to 13 miles. At the halfway point, the course crosses the Bow River into Bowness, heading down the main avenue through this former suburb. The race loops past the old Bowness High School and then takes in the western section of the community near mile 17 just below Canada Olympic Park. With the ski jumps of the 1988 Winter Olympics looming overhead near 18.5 miles, runners turn for home on a straight, flat stretch along the Bow River to the recently-restored Louise Bridge, the one-mile-to-go-point. An underpass draws runners onto the river pathway until returning to city streets for the finish at Eau Claire Plaza in front of the commemorative sandstone Olympic Pillars.

CROWD/RUNNER SUPPORT Most spectators congregate near the bridge at 10K, in the neighborhoods, and at the finish in the popular Eau Claire area.

ACTIVITIES The Calgary Miracle Marathon holds the Runners' Fitness Fair the two days preceding the race at the Eau Claire YMCA. There, you have an opportunity to visit health and fitness-related exhibits, purchase merchandise, pick up your race package, or register late. Complimentary course tours are available on Saturday at 9:00 a.m., noon and 3:00 p.m. Another event you shouldn't miss is the all-you-can-eat Carbo Chow Down ($13), a buffet held Saturday evening in the fresh air of the Fiesta Fun Zone, just yards from the Eau Claire YMCA. All finishers can gather at the Stampede Breakfast for a monumental pancake spread, a part of Calgary's great Stampede tradition. Additional tickets are available at the breakfast for $3. The Whoop Up starts at 2:30 p.m. in the Fiesta Fun Zone. All race participants, volunteers and their guests are invited to sample fresh pastas, sauces and beer.

AWARDS In the finish area, the first overall finishers are honored. In keeping with its Western theme, marathon winners are crowned with a white cowboy hat! Prize draws are held, including the drawing for a trip to Vancouver. Each runner receives a T-shirt, and all finishers are awarded medals at the finish line. Certificates for all finishers, as well as age-group medals, trophies, and more draw prizes are presented at the Post Race Whoop Up. Trophies are awarded to the fastest Overall, First-Time Marathoners, Masters Overall (40-49), Masters B (45-49), and Seniors (50-59).

ELITE RUNNERS INFORMATION Complimentary entry and some expense coverage are available for those with PRs faster than the course record. Fastest overall runners receive $500 for first place, $250 for second and $175 for third. A $500 bonus is handed out to the first runner to break an existing course record.

ACCOMMODATIONS The Delta Bow Valley Hotel, 209th Avenue S.E. (800-268-1133 in Canada) and (800-877-1133 in the U.S.), offers special rates to marathoners. Book early since rooms fill quickly during Stampede week. Limited low-cost accommodation is available at the Southern Alberta Institute of Technology. Call Linda (403-284-8012) to book a room. You can also contact the Calgary Convention & Visitors' Bureau (800-661-1678) for more information regarding accommodations.

RELATED EVENTS/RACES If you have family or friends who aren't prepared for 26.2 miles, the flat Stampede 10K and the Mayor's Fun Run/Walk (3K) are options.

AREA ATTRACTIONS You'll have no problem finding activities at the Calgary Exhibition & Stampede. Food, entertainment, rodeos, and chuckwagon races are among the possibilities. If you seek the outdoors, Calgary lies one hour away from the majestic Canadian Rockies.

LOCAL RUNNING STORES The Tech Shop, 2415 Fourth Street, SW (403-228-3782); Calgary Running Room, 321-A 10th Street, NW (403-270-7317); Gord's Running Store, 123 14th Street, NW (403-270-8606)

GRANDFATHER MOUNTAIN MARATHON

OVERALL: 76.6

COURSE BEAUTY: 8-

COURSE DIFFICULTY: 7

APPROPRIATENESS FOR FIRST TIMERS: 5

RACE ORGANIZATION: 8-

CROWDS: 1

RACE DATA

Contact:	Grandfather Mountain Marathon
	c/o Harry Williams
	460 Deerfield Forest Parkway
	Boone, NC 28607
	(704) 265-3479
Date:	July 12, 1997
	July 11, 1998
Start Time:	7:00 a.m.
Time Course Closes:	12:00 p.m.
Number of Participants:	268 in 1996
Certification:	None
Course Records:	Male: (open) 2:34:51
	Female: (open) 3:09:57
Elite Athlete Programs:	No
Cost:	$20/25
Age Groups/Divisions:	<19, 20-24, 25-29, 30-34, 35-39, 40-44, 45-49,
	50-54, 55-59, 60+
Temperature:	50° - 60°
Aid/Splits:	11 / none

HIGHLIGHTS Kilts, bagpipes, and log throwing may seem mismatched with marathons and out of place in North Carolina, but at the Grandfather Mountain Marathon they come together in a boisterous mix of athletics and pageantry. Starting in Boone, NC, the race (celebrating its 30th anniversary in 1997) winds through the scenic Blue Ridge Mountains before culminating in MacRae Meadows to the shrill sound of bagpipes and 15,000 cheering spectators attending the world's second largest Scottish Highland Games.

COURSE DESCRIPTION Grandfather Mountain's point-to-point course starts in Kidd Brewer Stadium on the Appalachian State University campus in Boone. After dashing through the campus, the course enters the country including a section of the Blue Ridge Parkway. Winding through Blue Ridge Mountain forests, the mostly paved course (the course contains 3 miles of gravel) climbs from 3,333 feet to 4,279 feet. After two flat miles, runners roll through the mountains before twisting and turning uphill for the last 4 miles to the finish at MacRae Meadows.

CROWD/RUNNER SUPPORT As a runner, you're probably accustomed to delayed gratification. Keep this in mind as you trudge up and down the lonely Grandfather Mountain course anticipating the finish line scene amidst the Highland Games. Volunteers at 11 aid stations provide water and encouragement along the way. If you need something other than water during the race, be sure to make your own arrangements.

RACE LOGISTICS Located 80 miles west of Winston-Salem, Boone is a 2-hour drive from both the Charlotte Airport and the Piedmont Triad International Airport in Greensboro. Family and friends are encouraged to attend the 6:00 a.m. meeting on Saturday morning for special instructions about accessing the course and parking permits. Finish-line parking (for a fee) may be an adventure because of the Highland Games, so car pooling is highly recommended. The race director provides a bus to transport your gear from the start to the finish. If you need to return to the start, the same bus leaves after 1:00 p.m.

ACTIVITIES Packet pickup takes place Friday from 1:00 p.m. to 4:00 p.m. at Kidd Brewer Stadium at Appalachian State University. A pre-race Spaghetti Feast and Marathon Clinic, called "Enduring the Mountain," runs from 6:00 p.m. to 7:30 p.m. Race-day registration extends from 6:00 a.m. to 6:50 a.m. at which time all runners must report to the starting line for last minute instructions. Following the race, enjoy food, beverages, and Highland Games music and entertainment while waiting for the race results and awards scheduled for 12:15 p.m. under the marathon tent.

AWARDS All finishers receive T-shirts, while the top three male and female finishers receive special awards presented by both the GMM committee and the Highland Games. Age-group awards extend three places.

ACCOMMODATIONS Although Boone, Linville and neighboring towns offer many lodging options, July is high-tourist season so make early reservations. Possibilities near the start in Boone include: Cabana Motel, 782 Blowing Rock Road (704-264-2487); Elk Motel, 321 Blowing Rock Road (704-264-6191); Elliott Inn, 358 E. King Street (704-264-9002); High Country Inn, 1785 Hwy. 105 (704-264-1000); Perkins Park Inn, 1905 E. King Street (704-264 3638); and Red Carpet Inn, 862 Blowing Rock Road (704-264-2457). Accommodations near the finish include: Linville Resorts Inc., 175 Linville Hwy. (704-733-9241); Prixie Motel, Linville (704-733-2597); Linville Falls Motel, Linville Falls (704-765-2658); and Park View Motor Lodge, Linville Falls (704-765-4787).

AREA ATTRACTIONS If you have some time, there are many entertainment options in the area. After enjoying the kilts, bagpipes and unique athletic competitions of the Scottish Highland Games, stroll through some of the many antique and arts and crafts shops scattered about the area. If you're not afraid of heights, enjoy the view below as you walk across The Mile High Bridge over Linville Gorge. Nature lovers also should catch the beautiful Linville Falls.

SAN FRANCISCO MARATHON

OVERALL: 95.1

COURSE BEAUTY: 10-

COURSE DIFFICULTY: 5+ (SEE APPENDIX)

APPROPRIATENESS FOR FIRST TIMERS: 9+

RACE ORGANIZATION: 9-

CROWDS: 3-

RACE DATA

Contact: San Francisco Marathon c/o Pacific Association
P.O. Box 77148
San Francisco, CA 94107
(916) 983-4622
(800) 722-3466 in California

Date: July 13, 1997
July 12, 1998 (tentative)

Start Time: 8:00 a.m.

Time Course Closes: 1:00 p.m.

Number of Participants: 3,000 in 1996

Certification: USATF

Course Records: Male: (open) 2:17:34
Female: (open) 2:40:32

Elite Athlete Programs: No

Cost: $35/45/55

Age groups/Divisions: <18, 19-24, 25-29, 30-34, 35-39, 40-44, 45-49,
50-54, 55-59, 60-64, 65-69, 70+

Temperature: 50° - 60°

Aid/Splits: 11 / every mile

HIGHLIGHTS Held in one of the world's great cities and starting on earth's most famous span, the San Francisco Marathon should be the top destination marathon in North America. Yet it attracts only about 3,000 runners. The main reasons for this are lack of a big-time sponsor and organizational malaise. Despite these hurdles, the San Francisco Marathon sports an exciting and spectacular course over the Golden Gate Bridge, through the Presidio, Marina District, Fisherman's Wharf, North Beach, Chinatown, Financial District, Haight-Ashbury, Golden Gate Park, and Sunset District — the ultimate tour of San Francisco! While challenging, the course avoids many of the city's most egregious hills.

COURSE DESCRIPTION San Francisco's beautiful, point-to-point course begins on the Marin County side of the Golden Gate Bridge. With only two of the bridge's six lanes dedicated to the runners, anticipate a crowded and slow first mile. On a clear morning, the bridge offers incomparable views of San Francisco's skyline ahead and Alcatraz to the left. Upon crossing the bay, the course drops 225 feet in 2.25 miles, going through the scenic Presidio, a 200-year-old former military base. Runners then enter the Marina District, passing the Palace of Fine Arts, the Exploratorium, and the red-brick buildings of Ghirardelli Square. The course climbs approximately 50 feet between mile 4 and 5 and drops 50 feet from mile 5 to 6. At mile 6, you head up Columbus Street, the heart of North Beach, home to many of the city's great Italian restaurants, rising another 50 feet to mile 7. Telegraph Hill and Coit Tower sit to your left. Heading straight into bustling, vibrant Chinatown, the course falls 50 feet once again to mile 8. The route then quickly touches the Financial District before proceeding down the Embarcadero, temporary home to the large ships docking in the harbor. Around mile 11, the course goes past the warehouses and cheap clothing outlets of the Mission District. At the half marathon point, runners hit the toughest part of the course — a 200-foot climb in just over a mile. Coming in stages, the climb begins on Guerrero and ends on Haight Street. Here, runners pass sidewalk cafes and bargain shopping in the world's hippie capital. You then start downhill into gorgeous Golden Gate Park, one of San Francisco's true wonders. The downhill trek through the park reaches land's end at the Great Highway near 18.5 miles. After a short jaunt along the ocean just before the 19-mile mark, the course begins to climb about 100 feet to 20 miles at Sunset Boulevard. The race then leaves the park to go up and back for 3 miles on Sunset, giving you a nice, flat break before completing the climb through Golden Gate Park (another 100 feet) to the finish inside Kezar Stadium, former home of the San Francisco 49ers.

CROWD/RUNNER SUPPORT Perhaps the most important way a large sponsor could contribute to the race lies in promotion. Unlike other big-city marathons that hang banners throughout the city to promote the race and energize residents, the San Francisco Marathon is like an orphan on race day. In fact, you'd never know there was a marathon unless you happened to stumble right on top of it. Despite the limited promotion, city dwellers, with and without homes, and tourists provide pockets of support along the course, particularly in the Marina District, along Columbus, in Chinatown, and in Haight-Ashbury.

RACE LOGISTICS The fantastic Golden Gate Bridge start means that all runners must use the race-provided transportation. No cars or spectators are allowed at or near the starting line. Buses leave from the race headquarters hotel and from Kezar Stadium in Golden Gate Park at 6:00 a.m. The race provides shuttle service from the finish back to the race hotel.

ACTIVITIES On Friday and Saturday of race weekend you can attend the Sports and Fitness Expo held with packet pickup and late registration at the race headquarters hotel. You may not register on race day. Also, San Francisco is one of the handful of races that require USATF membership to enter the marathon ($15). The pasta dinner dishes out on Saturday evening. After the race, relax with refreshments and snacks in Kezar Stadium.

AWARDS Every entrant gets to wear home a San Francisco Marathon T-shirt, and finishers also get to drape a nice medal around their neck. Age-group awards (generally engraved marble paperweights) go three deep in each division with special awards going to the overall winners.

ACCOMMODATIONS The San Francisco Marriott at 4th and Mission Street (415-896-1600) serves as the headquarters hotel. Other convenient hotels include the Grand Hyatt San Francisco on Union Square (415-398-1234); Hyatt Regency San Francisco, 5 Embarcadero Center (415-788-1234); Ramada Limited Downtown, 240 7th Street (415-861-6469); Ramada Inn at Union Square, 345 Taylor Street (415-673-2332); Best Western Carriage Inn, 140 7th Street (415-552-8600); Best Western Canterbury Hotel, 750 Sutter Street (415-474-6464); Days Inn Downtown, 895 Geary Street (415-441-8220); Holiday Inn, 1500 Van Ness Avenue (415-441-4000); and Donatello Hotel on Post (415-441-7100).

RELATED EVENTS/RACES Your non-marathoning family and friends can join in the San Francisco 5K which starts in Kezar Stadium and winds through Golden Gate Park. San Francisco 5K runners may register on race day, and a USATF card is not required.

AREA ATTRACTIONS One of the world's great destination cities, San Francisco beckons with its incredible setting, colorful neighborhoods, eccentric population, world-class dining, and activities to suit any taste. Don't miss Golden Gate Park, loaded with interesting things to do and see, such as the Japanese Tea Gardens, a romantic picnic, or an outdoor performance. After making the Fisherman's Wharf circuit, make sure you check out some of San Francisco's myriad neighborhoods — exclusive Nob Hill, the beautiful Marina District, Italian North Beach, frenzied Chinatown, Japantown, wacky Haight-Ashbury, or industrial/arty SOMA (south of Market). For a cross-cultural experience, or culture shock depending on your point-of-view, stroll the Castro District, center of San Francisco's infamous gay community. If you need a break, head across the Golden Gate Bridge to artistic Sausalito. If you really need a break, trek up gorgeous Mt. Tamalpais (about 20 minutes north of SF), hit the beach at Santa Cruz (about 90 minutes south of SF), hike at Point Reyes National Seashore (about 45 minutes north), or head to the wine region of Sonoma and Napa Valleys (about 45 minutes north). A visitor could literally spend weeks in the area and not come close to exhausting the possibilities.

LOCAL RUNNING STORES Fleet Feet Sports, 2086 Chestnut Street (415-921-7188); Fleet Feet Sports, 2308 Market Street (415-255-1064); Hoy's Sports, 1632 Haight Street (415-252-5370); On The Run, 751 Irving Street (415-655-5311).

LEADVILLE MOSQUITO MARATHON

OVERALL: 82.3

COURSE BEAUTY: 9

COURSE DIFFICULTY: 10+ (SEE APPENDIX)

APPROPRIATENESS FOR FIRST TIMERS: 1

RACE ORGANIZATION: 8-

CROWDS: 0

RACE DATA

Contact: Jay Jones
Leadville Mosquito Marathon
500 E. 7th Street
Leadville, CO 80461
(719) 486-2202

Date: July 19, 1997
July 18, 1998

Start Time: 7:00 a.m.

Time Course Closes: 4:00 p.m.

Number of Participants: 130 in 1996

Certification: None

Course Records: Male: (open) 4:02:08
Female: (open) 5:15:56

Elite Athlete Programs: No

Cost: $35/45

Age groups/Divisions: <29, 30-39, 40-49, 50+

Temperature: 20° - 60°

Aid/Splits 3 / none

HIGHLIGHTS This mosquito bites! Actually, mosquitoes are the least of your concerns at the Leadville Mosquito Marathon, named for a recurring obstacle on the course — Mosquito Pass. Quite simply the toughest marathon in North America, Mosquito runs above 11,000 feet for 80% of the race. Heap onto that between 5,500 and 6,500 feet of climbing in paper-thin air. Did we mention the fixed-rope drop over the snow cornice near mile 15? Or, the fact that race organizers require toting a map? Obviously not for the novice, Leadville appeals to those runners seeking an extreme experience to challenge their minds and bodies. Leadville also attracts ultramarathoners wanting a tune up for longer trail runs, including the Leadville 100 miler at the end of August.

COURSE DESCRIPTION Race organizers alter the Mosquito Marathon course yearly, depending on snow conditions and their whim. Be assured that the race will run on a variety of surfaces, including Jeep roads, rocky single-track trails, paved roads, and cross country with no trail. During one half-mile section of ridge called "hands-on saddle," runners with shaky balance could spend as many as two hours negotiating the irregular large rocks. Expect at least 2 to 4 miles of snow, possibly including the fixed-rope drop over the snow cornice. The race starts in Leadville at 10,150 feet, the lowest point on the loop course. The elevation profile depicts the 1996 course which contained about 800 fewer feet of vertical climbing than usual. Even with fewer uphills, the course included a 2,000-foot climb (from 11,500 feet to 13,500 feet) in 2 miles, and two 1,000-foot ascents in less than 2 miles. About 70% of the race takes place above timber-line. In these higher elevations, you must be prepared for whipping winds, snow, cold, rain, and sun, possibly all in the same race.

CROWD / RUNNER SUPPORT Crowds here are a misnomer. Your support consists of your handlers and the race volunteers. The race sets up three aid stations, at approximately miles 8, 13, and 18.7, where water, food, medical aid, and phones are available. You must pack your own food and water to get you from one aid station to the next. Consider wearing some type of ankle protection against the rocks, and you should also consider leg protection for the snow. A hat and windbreaker will also be beneficial for the upper elevations.

RACE LOGISTICS Unlike most marathons, getting to the start at 6th and Harrison in Leadville is the least of your concerns. You must sign in on race morning even if you already have your bib number so they know you are out on the course. Pre-race orientation starts at 6:45 a.m., and the race begins at 7:00 a.m. The race has two cutoff times, which means you must reach the designated points by a certain time, or you will be forced to withdraw from the race. The cutoff time for reaching aid station #1 at 8 miles is 9:30 a.m. and for aid station #2 at 13 miles is 11:30 a.m. It is possible that an injured runner will ask you to turn around or go ahead to summon help from the nearest aid station. This is simply the nature of these mountain races.

ACTIVITIES You can pick up your packet or register at Club Lead, 500 E. 7th Street in Leadville on Friday from 6:00 p.m. to 8:00 p.m. You may register on race day at Hard Rock Park near the start from 5:45 a.m. to 6:45 a.m. as long as the total 300 runner limit (for both races) has not been reached. Nurse your aching body at the post-race picnic; the awards ceremony starts at 3:00 p.m. with the chance to win many random prizes.

AWARDS Every early-registered runner receives a race shirt, as do the first 25 entrants who missed the postmark cutoff date. The top three in each age group receive ribbons with the age-group winners also receiving merchandise prizes, such as trail running shoes, clothing, and ski passes. The top finishers in each age division receive rosette ribbons.

ACCOMMODATIONS Leadville offers a number of lodging choices: Wood Haven Manor, 807 Spruce Street (800-748-2570); Grand West Village Resort (800-691-3999); Leadville Country Inn (719-486-2354); The Delaware Hotel (800-748-2004); Mountain Hideaway (800-933-3715); Timberline Motel (800-352-1876); The Apple Blossom Inn (719-486-2141); Twin Lakes Nordic Inn (719-486-1830); and Club Lead with simple rooms and bunks (719-486-2202). Others are given on the entry brochure.

RELATED EVENTS / RACES Runners still on this side of sanity may want to test the mountain waters with about 100 other borderline cases by first trying the 15 Mile Short Race. The short race contains about 3,000 feet of climbing on dirt roads past Lake Isabelle to the summit of Mosquito Pass at 13,200 feet and back to Leadville. The top men finish in about 2:20 and the top women in about 2:45.

AREA ATTRACTIONS The Leadville area contains outstanding recreational activities, including mountain biking, white water rafting, hiking, and trail running. Visitors also can head to nearby Vail (35 miles) and Aspen (60 miles).

LOCAL RUNNING STORE Bill's Sport Shop, 3rd and Harrison, Leadville (719-486-0739).

University of Okoboji Marathon

Overall: 75.9

Course Beauty: 9
Course Difficulty: 5-
Appropriateness for First Timers: 6
Race Organization: 7-
Crowds: 0

R A C E   D A T A

Contact: University of Okoboji Marathon
Box 7933
Spencer, IA 51301 - 7933
(712) 338-2424
Date: July 19, 1997
July 18, 1998
Start Time: 6:00 a.m.
Time Course Closes: 11:00 a.m.
Number of Participants: 110 in 1996
Certification: None
Course Records: Male: (open) 2:23:07
Female: (open) 2:57:43
Elite Athlete Programs: No
Cost: $15/20
Age groups/Divisions: <19, 20-29, 30-39, 40-49, 50-59, 60-69, 70+
Temperature: 73°
Aid/Splits: 8 / miles 1, 2 & 3

HIGHLIGHTS Most people have never heard of Okoboji, nor know that it houses a famous university which hosts a marathon every year. Okoboji lies in the beautiful Iowa Great Lakes area and features West Lake Okoboji, heralded by National Geographic as one of the most beautiful blue water lakes in the world. The lake serves as the centerpiece of the University of Okoboji Marathon which takes runners in and out of the surrounding resort areas. With its beautiful course, small field, and low-key race management (remember it's a vacation resort), Okoboji harkens back to the days when running a marathon was a novel endeavor. The marathon is but one of many festivities tied into homecoming weekend at the University of Okoboji — the most famous nonexistent university in the world.

RACE HISTORY The story of the University of Okoboji Marathon is directly connected to the founding of the University of Okoboji by a group of lakes-area residents and sports enthusiasts. "We were always playing tennis, or softball, or something," says one of the founders, Herman Richter, "and we used to kid each other, 'What's going on at Camp Okoboji tomorrow?'" The group began talking about their private club so much that they printed their own University of Okoboji T-shirts which became an instant hit with local residents and Okoboji's large tourist population. The usual university souvenirs (bumper stickers, pennants, sweatshirts) followed for this nonexistent school that offers only two courses of study — recreation and running. The university quickly evolved into a fundraising organization which sponsors several events each year including the marathon. The race has grown from forty runners in its inaugural year in 1978 to its current average of just over one hundred. And don't worry, the marathon, unlike the university, really does exist.

COURSE DESCRIPTION The Okoboji Marathon begins at Pikes Point State Park on the upper northeast side of West Okoboji Lake. In a clockwise manner, the course circles the lake and runs through resort areas passing million-dollar homes on oak tree-lined roads. After completing one loop of the lake, the course retraces the first 5.5 miles and ends on the waterfront at Arnold's Park at the lake's southeast end. Lake Okoboji lies at approximately 1,400 feet so elevation is not a concern. Held on a smooth, asphalt road, the race contains only two noticeable inclines near the 2-mile mark (100 yards) and 10-mile mark (200 yards).

CROWD / RUNNER SUPPORT Most of the race spectators concentrate at the start in Pikes Point State Park and at the finish in Arnold's Park. In addition to family and friends of the marathoners, the spectator base is enhanced by the other events that directly follow the marathon. Since the race course is not closed to traffic, spectators can easily follow their favorite runner throughout the event. With the exception of a handful of early bird fishermen, don't expect to experience overwhelming crowd support through the resort areas until later in the morning.

RACE LOGISTICS Shuttle buses are provided from the finish line to the starting area. In addition, runners who park at the starting line may catch a shuttle bus back to the start after completing the race. The race will transport warm-up clothing from the start to the finish.

ACTIVITIES Again, this is a no frills race which offers none of the pomp and circumstance that many other races provide. Take advantage of the peaceful setting that Okoboji offers to relax and center yourself for race day. Runner's packets can be picked up at the Three Sons Clothing Store in Milford on the Friday before the race from 10:00 a.m. to 8:00 p.m. Packets may also be picked up on race day at the start in Pikes Point State Park. Race-day registration is available until 15 minutes prior to the start. After finishing, relax at the waterfront while you enjoy music, food and drinks. An awards ceremony gets under way at 11:00 a.m.

AWARDS Race T-shirts displaying the coveted U of O emblem are presented to each participant. Overall winners and top division finishers receive special awards.

ACCOMMODATIONS Virtually all of the lakeshore cabins, inns and motels provide excellent accommodations and easy access to the start and finish areas. Some worth noting include: Beaches Resort, 15109 215th Avenue, Spirit Lake (712-336-2230); Crescent Beach Lodge, 1620 Lakeshore Drive, Wahpeton (712-337-3351); and Crow's Nest Resort, 304 Lake Drive, Arnold's Park (712-332-2221). Camping is available at the White Oaks Campground, 1508 4th Street, West Okoboji (712-332-5114).

RELATED EVENTS / RACES Okoboji hosts a festival of races on marathon day including a half marathon, 10K run and triathlon. Be advised that the 10K and half marathon start at separate locations.

AREA ATTRACTIONS If you have not used all of your energy in the marathon, there are plenty of things to do around the lakes. Swimming, fishing, golfing, and boat cruising are some considerations. Strolling through the many area antique shops and Indian museums or exploring the amusement park are other options. If you're a scuba diver, bring your gear. Homecoming weekend features a contest held for divers to search the bottoms of the lakes for the most unusual items in several different categories. Better yet, just plain relaxing may be the ticket, and there are few better places for it than Okoboji and its peaceful surroundings.

LOCAL RUNNING STORE The Three Sons, Financial District, Milford (712-338-2424).

DESERET NEWS MARATHON

OVERALL: 90.7

COURSE BEAUTY: 9

COURSE DIFFICULTY: 7 (SEE APPENDIX)

APPROPRIATENESS FOR FIRST TIMERS: 7-

RACE ORGANIZATION: 9-

CROWDS: 3+

R A C E   D A T A

Contact:	Deseret News Marathon
	Salt Lake County Recreation
	2001 S. State Street, #S-4900
	Salt Lake City, UT 84190
	(801) 468-2560
Date:	July 24, 1997
	July 24, 1998
Start Time:	5:00 a.m.
Time Course Closes:	11:00 a.m.
Number of Participants:	650 in 1995
Certification:	USATF
Course Records:	Male: (open) 2:16:57
	Female: (open) 2:45:35
Elite Athlete Programs:	Yes
Cost:	$20/25
Age groups/Divisions:	<11, 12-14, 15-18, 19-24, 25-29, 30-34, 35-39,
	40-44, 45-49, 50-54, 55-59, 60-64, 65-69, 70+
	Clydesdale (M) 200+ lbs., (F) 140+ lbs.
Temperature:	50° - 75°
Aid/Splits:	17 / every mile

HIGHLIGHTS When Brigham Young descended the Wasatch Mountains on July 24, 1847, he looked out over the Salt Lake Valley below and exclaimed, "This is the place!" for his Mormon settlers. When you run the Deseret News Marathon and lope down Emigrant Trail, you may very well agree. With spectacular scenery, the end of July is perhaps the best time to visit Salt Lake City outside of ski season. Part of the Days of '47 festivities, the DNM helps celebrate the state holiday commemorating those Mormon settlers. The challenging marathon course retraces the steps of these first pioneers down into the valley. Faster runners finish in front of 200,000 screaming onlookers waiting for the start of the Days of '47 Parade, one of the largest in the country. After the race, join in the Founder's Day festivities.

RACE HISTORY Conceiving the idea of a Salt Lake City marathon, runner/newspaperman Bill Smart convinced his paper, the Deseret News, to sponsor the event. More than a quarter century later, DN still sponsors the race, though many changes have occurred. Altering the course several times, organizers finally hit on the current historic route that takes advantage of the area's rich past. In 1984, organizers added a 10K race which has become one of the finest road races in the country, attracting the nation's top runners. The 10K's success has overshadowed the marathon for many years, but that may change in the near future as race organizers work to make the marathon the marquee event of the Founder's Day races once again.

COURSE DESCRIPTION The Deseret News Marathon starts in the beautiful Wasatch Mountains and follows the very path that the original pioneer settlers took in 1847. Runners battle altitude and several tough climbs on this challenging course. Entirely closed to traffic, the race begins at the entrance to Washington Park, elevation 5,880 feet. The first 1.5 miles are a gradual to steep downhill. Runners then have a quick uphill, followed by a .3-mile downhill. At 1.9 miles, you begin a long, arduous 377-foot climb to the turnaround at the 6-mile mark. Watch your fellow runners go by as you retrace your steps to just past 8 miles, make a sweeping right turn, and climb another 3 miles to the course's zenith, 6,227-foot Little Mountain Summit. A 3-mile downhill through a peaceful residential area rewards your previous hard work. The course then flattens around mile 14, but quickly goes downhill again as you run alongside a creek, past the Santa Fe Inn at 17 miles and the This Is The Place Monument just after mile 18. This area offers a nice, panoramic view of the city and the surrounding mountains. After a right turn on Foothill Blvd., runners face a slight upgrade for a half mile, and then it's a down slope to 13th East at 21.5. Here, runners traverse an older residential neighborhood, going up a very slight grade to mile 21.9, then it's a steep down and up before the left turn on South Temple toward downtown. You have a good downhill on South Temple as you pass the Governor's Mansion and wind through downtown, enjoying the roar of the spectators if you make it there under 3:45. You're still on a slight down slope until the left turn on 9th South around 25.5, and the last .75 miles are slightly uphill to the finish at Liberty Park, elevation 4,265 feet.

CROWD/RUNNER SUPPORT The early morning and remote start mean crowds are limited for most of the race. Runners who can make it to Main Street under 3:45, however, are greeted by the huge crowd — about 200,000 strong — waiting for the start of the Days of '47 Parade. Seventeen aid stations along the course carry water, electrolyte replacement drink and sponges. To avoid dehydrating as the summer day wears on, make sure to take advantage of every station.

RACE LOGISTICS With no parking at the marathon starting line, runners must take shuttle buses to the start. Buses leave between 3:00 a.m. and 3:30 a.m. from the Delta Center downtown and the University of Utah football stadium. Shuttles return runners from the finish to the University of Utah following the race.

ACTIVITIES Enjoy live music, a sports expo, and the parade while you wait for the awards ceremony following the race. There is also a special area for children near the finish.

AWARDS Marathon entrants receive a T-shirt and free transportation to the race start. Finishers earn a finisher's medallion. The top three runners in each age and special division receive medals. Overall winners earn $1,000 for first, $500 for second, and $250 for third.

ELITE RUNNERS INFORMATION DNM does recruit elite marathoners, but no criteria have been established. The race could offer transportation expenses, hotel accommodations, entry and prize money, depending on your credentials. Contact Scott Kerr for more information (801-468-2560).

ACCOMMODATIONS University Park Hotel, 480 Wakara (801-581-1000), serves as the sponsoring accommodations. Otherwise, try the Little America Hotel, 500 South Main Street (801-363-6781); Shilo Inn, 206 SW Temple Street (801-521-9500); or Holiday Inn Hotel, 999 South Main Street (801-359-8600).

RELATED EVENTS/RACES The well-known Deseret News 10K starts at the marathon 20-mile mark at 6:15 a.m. The 10K, which attracts over 2,500 runners, is generally recognized as one of the fastest in the country.

AREA ATTRACTIONS Numerous events are held in conjunction with Founder's Day, including the parade, rodeo, art show, and fireworks display.

LOCAL RUNNING STORES inSoles, 1356 S. Foothill Drive, Salt Lake City (801-582-1919); Fleetfoot, 50 S. Main Street, Salt Lake City (801-532-7008).

KILAUEA VOLCANO MARATHON

OVERALL: 86.4

COURSE BEAUTY: 9+

COURSE DIFFICULTY: 9-

APPROPRIATENESS FOR FIRST TIMERS: 4

RACE ORGANIZATION: 8

CROWDS: 0

RACE DATA

Contact:	Basil and Luanne Takeda
	Kilauea Volcano Marathon & Wilderness Runs
	HCR 2 Box 9595
	Keaau, HI 96749
	(808) 982-7783
Date:	July 26, 1997
	July 25, 1998
Start Time:	6:00 a.m.
Time Course Closes:	NA
Number of Participants:	151 in 1996
Certification:	USATF
Course Records:	Male: (open) 2:56:18
	Female: (open) 3:33:41
Elite Athlete Programs:	No
Cost:	$35/40
Age Groups/Divisions:	<19, 20-29, 30-39, 40-49, 50-59, 60+
Temperature:	50° - 90°
Aid/Splits:	8 / none

HIGHLIGHTS A race worthy of our rugged pioneer ancestors, the Kilauea Volcano Marathon runs on some of the most virgin soil on earth created by the world's most active volcano. Possibly North America's toughest certified marathon, only the hardy and adventurous should brave the sharp lava fields, the wafting sulfur, and the hilly, uneven terrain brimming the Kilauea caldera. Started in 1983 as a way to whisk park rangers into shape, the race now raises money for the Volcano Art Center which supports area artists. With this connection, you can be assured of beautiful T-shirts and original awards in addition to the incredible memories of running on top of earth's most billowiest fire pit.

COURSE DESCRIPTION The marathon's loop course starts at the Kilauea Military Camp flagpole (elevation 4,000 feet) and heads west on a relatively calm and scenic paved road. You proceed past Hawaiian Volcanoes Observatory on the Kilauea Crater rim and take the right fork to the Ka'u Desert Trail, a 7.1-mile stretch dropping 1,018 feet over rugged lava and uneven terrain. When you're not hopping rocks, you may be running in deep black sands. Runners pick up the Mauna Iki Trail for 6.3 miles over sharp lava fields and newer lava flows. Don't stray here as there are unstable lava tubes and bottomless pit craters. The course turns left on Hilina Pali Road, 4 miles of curvy paved road that climbs 220 feet. At the 17-mile mark, the route descends 170 feet on Chain of Craters Road; be alert for cars but rest up for the brutal uphill which approaches. Get plenty of fluids at the Mauna Ulu parking lot aid station before proceeding up the

Escape Road, a 700-foot climb over 4 miles. The Escape Road is a four-wheel drive road used when lava flows interrupt traffic on Chain of Craters Road. Wild pigs, a National Park pest, have been seen here eating blackberries and ohela berries. Emerging at the incredible Thurston Lava Tube near mile 23, the course finishes on narrow trails through ohia-fern forests and blooming yellow gingers. The race merges with the ten-mile Crater Rim Trail Run course at Waldron's Ledge, which overlooks Kilauea Crater. Runners proceed on Crater Rim Trail behind the Volcano House, past the Visitor Center and the Art Center toward the Steaming Bluffs Trail. Although less than a mile to the finish, one cannot help but take in the spectacular view overlooking Steaming Bluff, enhanced by puffs of steam. The race finishes at the Kilauea Military Camp Theater.

C R O W D / R U N N E R   S U P P O R T   Over 375 volunteers support the runners along the course. Aid stations, stocked with water, electrolyte replacement drink, and energy bars, lie approximately every 3 miles. Sorry, gas masks not available.

R A C E   L O G I S T I C S   Unless you are staying in Hawaiian Volcanoes National Park, you will need to drive to the start. We suggest you reserve your rental car far in advance because they can be completely booked. Head to the KMC Back Gate off Highway 11 (milepost 30); Marines will show you where to park. You must have your shoes scrubbed before starting the race to avoid introducing foreign weeds into the sensitive environment, so arrive a little early. You may check your personal belongings near the T-shirt area.

A C T I V I T I E S   Race weekend starts with the Carbo Load Dinner on Friday evening from 5:00 p.m. to 7:00 p.m. at the Kilauea Military Camp Dining Room (about $11). Runners who find their bravery dwindling can take advantage of the no-host cocktails. You may register or pick up your race number at the dinner or at the pre-race check-in starting at 5:00 a.m. on race morning. After the race, nurse your psyche with fresh Hawaiian-grown fruit, refreshments, massage, and Hawaiian entertainment. The awards ceremony starts at 10:30 a.m.

A W A R D S   Entrants who don't finish get to take home memories and possibly some scrapes and bruises from their trek through the lava fields. Finishers receive the distinctive Makoa finisher T-shirt. Special prizes designed by Volcano Art Center artists are awarded to the top three overall, military, and age-group winners. In all, over 200 prizes go to winners and random award recipients.

A C C O M M O D A T I O N S   The Hilo Hawaiian Hotel, 71 Banyan Drive (808-935-9361) serves as the official headquarters hotel for the Kilauea Wilderness Runs. A limited number of dormitory rooms are available at the Kilauea Military Camp (808-438-6707). The Volcano House (808-967-7321) is located in Hawaii Volcanoes National Park. Other accommodations include: Kilauea Lodge in Volcano Village (808-967-7366); Hale Ohia Cottages (800-455-3803); Kilauea Volcano Kabins (800-626-3876 or 808-967-7773); Carson's Volcano Cottage (800-845-LAVA); Country Goose B&B and Vacation Rentals (800-238-7101); and My Island B&B at Volcano (808-967-7216).

R E L A T E D   E V E N T S / R A C E S   The Kilauea Volcano Wilderness Runs, which attract 900 runners total, comprise a menu of races: the challenging 5-Mile Kilauea Caldera Run & Walk which goes down into the caldera and back out; the popular 10-Mile Rim Run which circles Kilauea Caldera; and the marathon.

A R E A   A T T R A C T I O N S   Brimming with attractions, the diverse Big Island boasts Hawaii Volcanoes National Park, with the massive Mauna Loa and Mauna Kea Volcanos, and Kilauea. Be sure to explore the amazing Thurston Lava Tube lined with beautiful ferns. See the artwork supported by the marathon at the Volcano Art Center. Beaches ring the island, including Black Sand Beach formed by worn lava.

L O C A L   R U N N I N G   S T O R E S   Action Sports Hawaii, Kopiko Plaza, Kailua-Kona; B & L Bike & Sports, 75-5699 Kopiko Plaza, Kailua-Kona.

PAAVO NURMI MARATHON

OVERALL: 78.8

COURSE BEAUTY: 8-

COURSE DIFFICULTY: 6+

APPROPRIATENESS FOR FIRST TIMERS: 5+

RACE ORGANIZATION: 9-

CROWDS: 1

RACE DATA

Contact:	Ricky Alvey
	Hurley Area Chamber of Commerce
	207 Silver Street
	Hurley, WI 54534
	(715) 561-4334
Date:	August 9, 1997
	August 8, 1998
Start Time:	7:30 a.m.
Time Course Closes:	1:30 p.m.
Number of Participants:	288 in 1995
Certification:	USATF
Course Records:	Male: (open) 2:19:10
	Female: (open) 2:47:49
Elite Athlete Programs:	No
Cost:	$25/30
Age groups/Divisions:	M: <15, 16-21, 22-29, 30-34, 35-39, 40-49, 50-59, 60+
	F: <17, 18-22, 23-29, 30-39, 40-49, 50+
Temperature:	75°
Aid/Splits:	13 / miles 5, 10, 13, 15 & 20

HIGHLIGHTS Affectionately known by locals as "The Paavo," the Paavo Nurmi Marathon (named for the Finnish distance runner who won nine Olympic gold medals during the 1920s) ranks as Wisconsin's oldest and most notorious marathon. Steeped in tradition, from its opening ceremonies — complete with an Olympic torch relay and lighting ceremony — to its delicious post-race Mojakka (Finnish-style beef stew), The Paavo relishes in such intense community support that individual miles along the course bear the names of longtime race supporters. Runners enjoy the rural hills and historic towns on the peaceful course through Iron County in northern Wisconsin. While awarding no gold medals, The Paavo's coveted T-shirts adorn runners like badges of honor for completing the grueling course, often in sweltering conditions.

COURSE DESCRIPTION The point-to-point course over rural, wooded roads travels through several small logging and mining communities. Starting in the little town of Upson on Hwy. 77, the course loops around town before turning right on Hwy. 122 at .4 miles. Substantial rolling hills take you over Alder Creek at 1.6 miles. With a right turn onto County Road E at 2.1 miles, the road improves, rolling past a cemetery on the left before returning to Hwy. 77 on the way to the town of Ironbelt. Gently climbing from Ironbelt to 9.5 miles, you descend into the town of Pence at the 10-mile point. The route continues down to 10.6 miles with subsequent ups and downs to another iron town, Montreal, at 11.5 miles. From mile 11.5 to 12.4, the course contains a nice downhill past quaint roadside homes. At 12.6 miles, the route detours from Hwy. 77

through the town of Gile (miles 12.6 to 13.9). A short climb greets runners as they exit Gile, returning to Hwy. 77. The course remains mostly flat once on the highway from Gile at the 14-mile point until 15.4 miles and the right turn onto County Road C. After a .1-mile steep uphill, County Road C rolls across the Gile Flowage, a scenic pond flowing with birds, at 18.2 miles. Another steep uphill awaits from 19.9 to 20 miles. You'll probably be ready to shoot the smiley face leering at you from the side of the road at mile 20.3 (at least someone is smiling at this point!). At 20.5, you endure more steep rollers until a left turn at 21.4 miles onto Hwy. 51. Refreshingly flat until a slight grade from mile 23.8 to 24.1 and another from mile 25.4 to 25.8, Hwy. 51 descends into charming downtown Hurley and the Silver Street finish line in front of John Wiita Insurance.

CROWD/RUNNER SUPPORT The entire community anticipates this Iron County rite of summer, supporting The Paavo as race sponsor, volunteer, or cheerleader. Spectators are most visible in the small towns along the race route and at the finish line in downtown Hurley. The volunteers at the 13 aid stations, which lie every 3 miles to 18 then every mile, provide even more support and encouragement.

RACE LOGISTICS Buses to the start in Upson depart at 6:30 a.m. from the Hurley Holiday Inn on Hwy. 51 N, and the Citgo Station (corner of Hwy. 51 and Silver Street). If you have your own special drink, mark the bottles with your bib number and your desired aid station, drop it off at the Chamber of Commerce by 9:00 p.m. Friday night, and the race will distribute them to the aid stations of your choice.

ACTIVITIES The Hurley Chamber of Commerce, 207 Silver Street, serves as the registration and pre-race packet pickup site. You may want to hit the all-you-can-eat Paavo Spaghetti Feed from 4:00 p.m. to 7:00 p.m. at the Iron County Senior Center. Signaling the start of race weekend, the torch relay and lighting ceremony take place in the parking lot of Tom's North Pride Foods. Be sure to speed your marathon recovery by replenishing lost calories with The Paavo's patented Mojakka and easing tight muscles with a post-race massage. At 12:30 p.m., the traditional Paavo party begins in Riccelli Park. Stick around for the music while downing a cold beer and bratwurst sold by the Hurley Volunteer Fire Department. Finally, if you didn't win an award in the race, your luck may change in the prize drawing held at 2:30 p.m. after the awards ceremony.

AWARDS Every finisher receives a coveted race T-shirt. The top 10 overall males and top five overall females receive an award plus free entry to next year's race. The top age-group finishers receive trophies, with second and third place receiving medals.

ACCOMMODATIONS No hotel officially hosts the marathon. However, hotels near the finish include: Holiday Inn, Hwy. 51 and Silver Street (715-561-3030); Hobo's Inn, near downtown Hurley (715-561-4684); and Silver Street Motel, on Silver Street (715-561-4684).

RELATED EVENTS/RACES Share the pain with your friends in the increasingly popular 5-person and 2-person marathon relays. Each team must provide its own transportation to each relay station. The day after the marathoners have their fun, it's time for them to root on the shorter distance specialists in the annual Kiwanis Interstate 5K and 10K Walk/Runs. The races, which wind through the streets of Hurley and Ironwood, start at 9:00 a.m. in front of the Michigan Travel Information Center on U.S. 2 in Ironwood.

AREA ATTRACTIONS The marathon coincides with the annual Iron County Heritage Festival which features arts and crafts fairs, ethnic cuisine, a parade, history tours, concerts, and dances. While you're in Iron County, visit the Plummer Mine headface located off Hwy. 77 between Pence and Iron Belt; Copper Peak, the only ski flying hill in the Western Hemisphere, offering a breathtaking view of the Gogebic range; or the "Pines and Mines" Mountain Bike Trail with over 200 miles of mapped and marked trails.

LOCAL RUNNING STORES Trek & Trail, Ironwood (906-932-5858); Dunham's Sporting Goods, Ironwood (906-932-0990).

MARATHON BY THE SEA

OVERALL: 84.7

COURSE BEAUTY: 7+

COURSE DIFFICULTY: 5- (SEE APPENDIX)

APPROPRIATENESS FOR FIRST TIMERS: 8

RACE ORGANIZATION: 9+

CROWDS: 2-

RACE DATA

Contact:	Mike Doyle
	Marathon By The Sea
	c/o Canada Games Aquatic Center
	50 Union Street
	Saint John, New Brunswick, Canada E2L 1A1
Date:	August 17, 1997
	August 16, 1998
Start Time:	8:00 a.m.
Time Course Closes:	2:00 p.m.
Number of Participants:	310 in 1995
Certification:	Run NB
Course Records:	Male: (open) 2:38:24; (masters) 2:45:46
	Female: (open) 3:14:36; (masters) 3:38:04
Elite Athlete Programs:	No
Cost:	$30
Age groups/Divisions:	<19, 20-29, 30-34, 35-39, 40-44, 45-49, 50-54,
	55-59, 60-64, 65-69, 70+
Temperature:	49° - 62°
Aid/Splits:	12 / none

HIGHLIGHTS No other marathon in North America offers more bang for the buck than Marathon By The Sea, and if you're American, the bang resounds even louder with the favorable exchange rate. On top of the usual race amenities, this urban/rural marathon features free pre-race massage, free oceanfront pasta dinner, free post-race BBQ with musical entertainment, free day care, and use of the impressive Canada Games Aquatic Center complete with water slide and hot tub. All of this takes place during the Festival by the Sea Celebration, a ten-day performing arts extravaganza ranked among the top 100 in North America.

RACE HISTORY What happens when you grow tired of traveling long distances to find a fun, vacation-like marathon? Most people appease themselves with shorter races. A few energetic souls like Mike Doyle simply create a marathon in their own backyards. The first Festival by the Sea Marathon, under the stewardship of Doyle, took place in 1995 and attracted 275 participants. So successful was the first race that it was awarded the 1996 Canadian National Masters Championship. With the event solidly in place, the question now is whether Doyle can shed his race director duties long enough to run his own marathon, now called Marathon By The Sea.

COURSE DESCRIPTION Marathon By The Sea's diverse, loop course incorporates many parts of downtown Saint John before exiting west through older, attractive residential neighborhoods, industrial areas and forest, all preceding the return to the city center finish. After the start alongside the Canada Games Aquatic Center, a quick left turn reveals a short stint through a warehouse district and an immediate .75-mile hill which becomes relatively steep for the last 200 yards. From 1 to 2.3 miles, the course rolls through a downtown residential district on a notably cambered street. After another short hill at 2.3, the course goes flat to downhill through a commercial area to 4.1 miles. A short grade followed by a .25-mile hill leads to a quick downhill to the Harbour Bridge at 4.9 miles. From the bridge, the course continues mostly uphill to another residential area at 5.8 miles and then to the tree-lined neighborhood of West Saint John after mile 7. By the 8-mile mark, the course flattens to 9.8 where a mild 300-yard hill greets runners. Continuing through a light industrial/motel district after the 10-mile mark, the route goes slightly downhill along a wooded highway to the U-turn at mile 16. The course returns gradually uphill to mile 19 where it enters Hwy. 1 heading back toward downtown Saint John. Miles 19 to 22.3 are predominately downhill after which runners face a challenging climb from 23.4 to 24 miles. After sharply descending, the course goes up over the Harbour Bridge at mile 25, providing a welcome view of downtown Saint John and the finish line.

CROWD/RUNNER SUPPORT Scattered throughout the course, most spectators concentrate around the start/finish and Harbour Bridge areas. Twelve aid stations along the course provide additional support for the runners. As the race matures, crowd support will undoubtedly blossom.

RACE LOGISTICS Since the start/finish line is conveniently located within walking or jogging distance from area hotels, race morning involves little transportation hassle. To ease race-morning stress further, the race provides day care for your children. The kids can glide down a cool water slide in the Aquatic Center or participate in a plethora of fun activities.

ACTIVITIES Race packet pickup occurs at the Aquatic Center, 50 Union Street, Friday from 4:00 p.m. to 8:00 p.m., Saturday from 10:00 a.m. to 6:00 p.m., and race day from 6:00 a.m. to 7:30 a.m. Race-day registration is available. The race offers free course tours on Saturday between 10:00 a.m. and 4:00 p.m. On Saturday night, eat at the free outdoor pasta party overlooking the harbor. Cries of sore muscles on the starting line fall on deaf ears as the race provides free, pre-race massages. Massages are available after the race as well, and an awards ceremony takes place as soon as results are available. To round out race weekend, attend the post-race BBQ, with music, at the Aquatic Center.

AWARDS Every runner receives the following goodies: T-shirt, finisher's medallion (inscribed on site), race certificate, and a 4 x 6-inch finish-line photograph. The top three open and masters runners receive special awards as do the top three finishers in each age group.

ACCOMMODATIONS Hotels located close to the finish line include: Delta Brunswick Hotel, 39 King Street (800-268-1133 from Canada) and (800-877-1133 from USA); and Saint John Hilton, One Market Square (800-561-8282). Keddy's Fort Howe Hotel, Main and Portland Streets (800-561-7666), lies less than one-half mile from the start/finish as does the Howard Johnson Hotel, 400 Main Street, Chesley Drive (800-475-4656).

RELATED EVENTS/RACES Race day includes a half marathon and four-person marathon relay which run concurrently with the marathon. The marathon relay consists of four 6.55-mile legs, with the race providing transportation to and from the relay exchange points.

AREA ATTRACTIONS Canada's oldest incorporated city, Saint John houses one of the world's most phenomenal ecosystems. Take time to see the highest and wildest tides in the world at the Bay of Fundy, or check out the Reversing Falls from Falls View Park. Don't miss visiting the boutiques, cafes and historic buildings that dot downtown Saint John. While in the area, wander over to the New Brunswick Museum at Market Square where a full-sized right whale and mastodon welcome you, and a geological trail hike through time awaits inside. The Festival by the Sea performing arts celebration continues throughout the weekend with hundreds of entertainers singing and dancing in local parks and commercial venues.

LOCAL RUNNING STORE Green Lee Shoe Ltd., 59 Bently Street, Saint John.

PIKES PEAK MARATHON

OVERALL: 85.4

COURSE BEAUTY: 9

COURSE DIFFICULTY: 10

APPROPRIATENESS FOR FIRST TIMERS: 3

RACE ORGANIZATION: 9-

CROWDS: 0

RACE DATA

Contact:	Pikes Peak Marathon
	P.O. Box 38235
	Colorado Springs, CO 80937
	(719) 473-2625
Date:	August 17, 1997
	August 16, 1998
Start Time:	7:00 a.m.
Time Course Closes:	5:00 p.m.
Number of Participants:	800 limit, filled by late May
Certification:	None
Course Records:	Male: (open) 3:16:39; (masters) 3:56:18
	Female: (open) 4:15:18; (masters) 4:26:59
Elite Athlete Programs:	No
Cost:	$35/40/45
Age groups/Divisions:	16-19, 20-24, 25-29, 30-34, 35-39, 40-44, 45-49, 50-54, 55-59, 60-64, 65-69, 70-74, 75-79, 80-84, 85-89, 90+
Temperature:	42° - 80°
Aid/Splits:	6 / At summit

HIGHLIGHTS Once considered an impossibility by its namesake Zebulon Pike, ascending and descending Pikes Peak has become a mid-August tradition for the 800 adventurists in the Pikes Peak Marathon. Known as "America's Ultimate Challenge," our second rated most difficult marathon in North America climbs an imposing 7,815 feet in 13.4 miles from Manitou Springs to the summit (14,110 feet). Once there, the thin air and glorious view of Kansas, the Sangre de Cristo Mountains, and the Continental Divide leave you breathless. The very same view inspired Kathy Lee Bates to write "America the Beautiful" with "Purple Mountain's Majesty" referring to Pikes Peak. If you're thinking about running Pikes Peak, don't delay your entry. With its cult-like following, the race fills extremely early.

RACE HISTORY The first annual race up and down Pikes Peak occurred on August 10, 1956. Race originator Dr. Arne Suominen, of Del Ray Beach, Florida, had two distinct reasons for establishing the event. First, he wanted to commemorate the 150th anniversary of the discovery of America's most famous mountain by Zebulon Montgomery Pike. Second, as a former Finnish marathon champion and harsh critic of tobacco, he wanted to prove that smoking reduced one's physical endurance. By challenging smokers and nonsmokers to race Pikes Peak, he was confident of proving his point. Thirteen runners including Suominen accepted the challenge. As it turned out, not one of the three smokers who entered the race finished. Suominen, indeed, proved his point, and in so doing, started one of the most renowned marathons in the world.

COURSE DESCRIPTION One peek at the Pikes Peak Marathon's course profile gives you a good idea of what's in store. Although the average grade to the summit is 11%, it varies drastically including, believe it or not, some downhill portions. Don't get too excited on the downhills though, as the rule of the trail follows that for every downhill section there is an immediate steep climb. Most runners can expect to come within a few minutes of their best road marathon time during the 13.4 mile ascent. Adding 25% to your best road half marathon time gives you a good estimate of your time for the 12.9 mile descent.

Starting in front of the Manitou Springs City Hall (elevation 6,295 feet), the course travels along Manitou Avenue before turning left on Ruxton Avenue at approximately .5 miles. After passing Miramont Castle on the right, the route continues up a small hill. At the Cog Railway around 1.5 miles, a gravel road replaces the asphalt, marking the beginning of the steepest section of the course lasting almost a half mile before hitting the wild flowers and switchbacks of Barr Trail. Known as the Ws, the 13 switchbacks on Mount Manitou turn more than 90°, and the last rewards you with the first view of Pikes Peak since the start. The Ws end around 3 miles, but more switchbacks and a short downhill lead you to a natural rock arch at just under 4 miles up the trail (about 5.5 miles on the course). Just beyond the arch, another short but steep section awaits you, followed by two switchbacks to the Manitou Incline Trailhead. The Manitou Incline Trail quickly drops down to a brief flat section and then rises steeply to French Camp around 6 miles. Six steep switchbacks bring you to a welcomed flat to downhill stretch as you leave Mount Manitou for Barr Camp (mile 7). The downhill ends at the "1/2 Mile to Barr Camp" sign, and that half mile is extremely challenging. Barr Camp (10,200 feet) marks the beginning of what many runners describe as the toughest section of the course; from here it's all uphill. The terrain soon turns rocky as you make your way to the Bottomless Pit at the 8-mile mark. From here, 15 switchbacks, each one longer than the last, take you to the A-Frame (11,500 feet) at 10.5 miles. The "3 Miles to Summit" sign signals you will soon be above tree line. Several switchbacks take you to the east face of Pikes Peak. With two miles to go, the trail ascends straight to The Cirque (13,200 feet) at nearly 12 miles. Becoming quite rocky, the course winds to the Sixteen Golden Stairs — the 16 rocky switchbacks near the summit. After scrambling up the stairs, you head right to a short flat to downhill section before hitting the next series of switchbacks. These take you past a sign honoring the memory of Fred Barr, the builder of the Barr Trail. Two switchbacks and a few rocky zigzags after the sign and you've made it to the summit! Now it's time to catch your breath and retrace your steps to the finish on Manitou Avenue in front of Soda Springs Park just beyond the corner of Ruxton Avenue.

CROWD/RUNNER SUPPORT Since few spectators are crazy enough to climb the mountain to cheer you on, most of the crowd support is limited to the start and finish areas. Additional support comes in the form of aid stations along the route and race personnel at the summit. Six aid stations dot the course at the following locations: Manitou Incline — 2.4 miles; French Creek — 4.3 miles; Barr Camp — 7.6 miles, A-Frame — 10.2 miles; The Basin — 12.8; and the summit — 13.4. The rest of the time it's just you, nature, and 799 other runners challenging the mountain.

RACE LOGISTICS If you want a hassle-free race morning, try to stay in Manitou Springs. Most motels are within walking distance to the start line, affording you a satisfying shower soon after finishing. Pikes Peak maintains several time cutoffs at specific points on the route. Runners must reach these points by the indicated times or they will be pulled from the race: Barr Camp by 10:15 a.m., A-Frame by 11:30 a.m., and the summit by 1:30 p.m.

ACTIVITIES Race packets are available for pickup the week of the race at Runners Roost, 107 E. Bijou Street in Colorado Springs. On Friday and Saturday nights, the Manitou Springs Kiwanis Club holds a pre-race pasta party in Schryver Park for $10 per person. The awards ceremony begins at 2:00 p.m. in Soda Springs Park.

AWARDS All entrants receive T-shirts, and finishers receive medallions. The top three male and females receive belt buckles and bracelets, respectively. The top ten male and female finishers receive rock Kokopellis (Indian artifact depicting fertility). Age-division winners receive entry into the next year's race. Two special awards named after Walt Stack, legendary San Franciscan peak climber, and Rudy Fahl, longtime Pikes Peak race director, are awarded to two inspirational competitors.

ACCOMMODATIONS Although Pikes Peak has no official race hotel, accommodations abound in the Manitou Springs area. But, don't procrastinate; August is high-tourist season so rooms go fast. Some options near the race include: Santa Fe Motel, 3 Manitou Avenue (719-475-8185); Red Wing Motel, 56 El Paso Blvd. (719-685-9547); Park Row Lodge, 54 Manitou Avenue (719-685-5216); and El Colorado Lodge, 23 Manitou Avenue (719-685-5485).

RELATED EVENTS / RACES On Saturday, the day before the marathon, the Pikes Peak Ascent is held. The race is limited to 1,800 runners and, like the marathon, fills early.

AREA ATTRACTIONS If you're impatient and don't want to wait for race day to admire the summit view, reserve a seat on the Pikes Peak Cog Railway, the effortless way to the top. Another natural wonder, Garden of The Gods City Park, contains 300-million-year-old natural formations accessible by a 45-minute tram tour. The U.S. Olympic Training Center provides a different kind of wonder in the form of state-of-the-art athletic training techniques and equipment, with athletes to match. A 11/4 hour tour of the Center will fuel your training fire. If you're not toured out, head to the United States Air Force Academy and jaunt through its grounds.

LOCAL RUNNING STORE Runners Roost, 107 E. Bijou Street, Colorado Springs (719-632-2633).

SILVER STATE MARATHON

OVERALL: 83.7

COURSE BEAUTY: 8+

COURSE DIFFICULTY: 6-

APPROPRIATENESS FOR FIRST TIMERS: 7

RACE ORGANIZATION: 9-

CROWDS: 0+

RACE DATA

Contact:	Valentine Pisarski
	Silver State Striders
	2358 Camelot Way
	Reno, NV 89509
	(702) 849-0419
Date:	August 24, 1997
	August 31, 1998
Start Time:	6:00 a.m.
Time Course Closes:	11:00 a.m.
Number of Participants:	160 in 1996
Certification:	USATF
Course Records:	Male: (open) 2:37:58
	Female: (open) 3:07:27
Elite Athlete Programs:	No
Cost:	$15/20/30
Age groups/Divisions:	<19, 20-29, 30-39, 40-49, 50-59, 60-69, 70+
Temperature:	44° - 75°
Aid/Splits:	11 / mile 1

HIGHLIGHTS Tucked back in the beautiful Washoe Valley at the foot of the Sierra Nevada mountains, the Silver State Marathon quietly holds a wonderful event unbeknownst to the rest of the running world. Mere miles from Lake Tahoe, the course wraps around Washoe Lake and moves through an incredible arch of pine trees during the Franktown Loop. Finishers are treated to the best medallions in North America, which would fit nicely in the dollar slot machines in nearby Reno. Do not be tempted.

COURSE DESCRIPTION Silver State's loop course varies between 5,045 feet and 5,255 feet. Staged in Bowers Mansion County Park, the race proceeds north in the dawn on old highway 395 up an 85-foot climb at mile 1. Now awake, runners enjoy level going for the next 2 miles. Crossing closed U.S. Highway 395 just before mile 3, the route darts down a short steep hill onto a dirt road for a 1-mile diversion to U.S. 395 (mile 4). After trudging up 120 feet from mile 4.5 to 5.5, runners head to East Lake Blvd. for 2 miles beginning the trip around Washoe Lake. Slightly downhill from 5.5 to 9.5, the course goes right on Lakeshore Drive (mile 7.5) leading to a brief off-road section of .8 miles. A right turn at 11.2 miles brings runners back to East Lake Blvd., a gently rolling and winding two-lane country road (miles 12 to 18.5). Passing under U.S. 395 at 18.5, runners return north on old highway 395 preparing for the looming climb. At 20.1, you enter the gorgeous Franktown Loop, enveloped by a protective canopy of pine trees to mile 23.1. The loop welcomes you with a tough, 200-foot climb from mile 20.1 to 21.3. Bidding the curvy, rolling loop goodbye, runners detour down a private, dirt ranch road for .7 miles before heading for home on old highway 395 for the final 2.4 miles to the main gate of Bowers Mansion County Park.

CROWD / RUNNER SUPPORT The aid stations and the finish area provide the bulk of the crowd participation for the race. The 11 aid stations offer water, electrolyte replacement drink, and petroleum jelly in case you're rubbed the wrong way. Roving aid stations are available to the heavy footed.

RACE LOGISTICS All runners must find their own way to the start. Since parking is limited in Bowers Mansion County Park, it's best to head straight to the ranch field on the east side of old highway 395 where ample parking exists. Slower runners may start at 5:00 a.m., but they should bring their own fluids since aid stations may not be set up.

ACTIVITIES Late registration and packet pickup take place at the Atlantis Hotel and Casino, 3800 South Virginia Street in Reno, from noon until 6:00 p.m. on Saturday. Although discouraged, packets can be retrieved on race morning at the park entrance, but there is no race-day registration. An outstanding post-race picnic is held in the park, featuring free beer, food, music, massages, barbeque, and a raffle. Runners and their families can take advantage of the volleyball court, swimming pool, picnic tables among the pines, and large expanses of grass to relax and reflect on the day.

AWARDS Every participant receives a marathon T-shirt. Each finisher receives an encased solid copper medallion draped in a silver and blue ribbon. Minted on the silver dollar press at the Carson City Mint, the medal is the only non-government piece stamped with the official U.S. Government "CC" marking. Solid silver medals are presented to the top three age-group finishers. The top three overall runners receive gold-plated solid silver medals, solid silver medals, and solid nickel silver medals, respectively.

ACCOMMODATIONS Atlantis Hotel and Casino, 3800 South Virginia Street, Reno (800-723-6500) serves as the host hotel. Runners can stay in either Reno or Carson City since both are convenient to the start. In Carson City try: Best Western Trailside Inn, 1300 N. Carson Street (702-883-7300); Days Inn, 3103 N. Carson Street (702-883-3343); Motel 6, 2749 S. Carson Street (702-885-7710); or Super 8 Motel, 2829 S. Carson Street (702-883-7800). In Reno try: Best Western Continental Lodge, 1885 S. Virginia Street (702-329-1001); Comfort Lodge, 844 S. Virginia Street (702-786-6700); Holiday Inn Casino, 111 Mill Street (702-329-0411); Holiday Inn Convention Center, 5851 S. Virginia Street (702-825-2940); or Motel 6, 1901 S. Virginia Street (702-827-0255).

RELATED EVENTS / RACES The Silver State events menu also includes a half marathon, 10K Run, and 10K Walk. The two runs start at 7:00 a.m., and the 10K Walk starts at 7:10 a.m. Finishers in each of these events receive the famous commemorative medal from the Carson City Mint.

AREA ATTRACTIONS The area bursts with attractions and activities. Night owls will relish the casinos and shows in Reno, offering plenty of opportunities to blow some money. Nature enthusiasts will appreciate the region's proximity to Lake Tahoe and just about every outdoor activity imaginable.

LOCAL RUNNING STORES Fleet Feet Sports, 3771 S. Carson Street, Carson City, NV (702-883-3361); Eclipse Running, 937 West Moana, Reno, NV (702-827-2279).

MONSTER MARATHON

OVERALL: 77.8

COURSE BEAUTY: 9

COURSE DIFFICULTY: 10 (SEE APPENDIX)

APPROPRIATENESS FOR FIRST TIMERS: 2

RACE ORGANIZATION: 7+

CROWDS: 0

RACE DATA

Contact:	Monster Marathon
	c/o Finger Lakes Running Club
	Box 321
	Newfield, NY 14867
	(607) 257-3592
Date:	August 24, 1997
	August 30, 1998
Start Time:	7:00 a.m. - 8:30 a.m.
Time Course Closes:	None
Number of Participants:	40 in 1995
Certification:	None
Course Records:	Male: 3:27:00
	Female: 3:47:35
Elite Athlete Programs:	No
Cost:	$12/18/22, add $7 for optional "Trail Monster" T-shirt
Age groups/Divisions:	None
Temperature:	60°
Aid/Splits:	7 / none

HIGHLIGHTS If you're looking to qualify for Boston, look no further — at this entry that is. One glance at the course elevation profile, amusingly compared to Boston's, and you'll see that lack of USATF certification is not the only reason that qualifying is out of the question. Classified as the toughest marathon in the East, Monster features 5,560 feet of total climbing. Although you won't run a PR, you can still enjoy a beautiful run through hardwoods, hemlocks, and plantations of red pines, white pines, spruce, and tamarack along the double-out-and-back on the North Country National Scenic Trail and the Finger Lakes Trail. Since the Monster does not discriminate in its prey, the race handicaps runners to eliminate age and gender differences.

RACE HISTORY A 500-year-old Iroquois Indian legend tells how a "Forest Monster" chased the Indian brave Jost-du-it out and back twice along the present course. An incredibly accurate sundial recorded his time for the 26.2 miles at 3:26:59. Jost-du-it quickly vanished, presumably eaten by the "Forest Monster." Unlike his cousin whose similar disappearance led to signs reading Watch Out For Falling Rock, Jost-du-it was basically forgotten until 1989 when the Finger Lakes Running Club organized the Virgil Forest Monster Marathon in his honor.

COURSE DESCRIPTION The course profile does not lie; the Monster is not a friendly one. Starting and finishing at The Rafters restaurant on Route 392, the course consists of two out-and-backs on wooded trails with a total climb of 5,560 feet. The course follows Route 392 to Tone Road before joining the Finger Lakes Trail at .85 miles. Allowing your knees and chin to become well acquainted, the route climbs 800 feet in 1.5 miles to a course high of 2,134 feet. At 3 miles, you reach the Greek Peak summit and an aid station at 3.2 miles. Although remaining hilly, the course continues losing elevation to the turnaround and second aid station at 6.55 miles. After a quick refueling, it's back to The Rafter restaurant and one more out-and-back.

CROWD / RUNNER SUPPORT Believe it or not, race organizers have a hard enough time attracting runners to the race. Due to the nature of the course, crowd support is limited to the start and finish area. However, the volunteers at the aid stations along the way provide full "banquet" spreads and tremendous encouragement.

RACE LOGISTICS Since the race starts and finishes at the same location, your main concern is finding your way there. This is a sex/age group handicap race meaning start times are based on a formula to eliminate age and gender differences. Theoretically, this practice places every runner on equal footing, with 70-year-old females sprinting to the finish, neck and neck, with 25-year-old males.

ACTIVITIES As with most trail races, Monster places most emphasis on the race itself. Nevertheless, a pre-race pasta feed takes place Saturday night at The Rafters restaurant from 5:30 p.m. to 8:00 p.m., where you can also pick up your race packet. To top off your glycogen stores, coffee, juice and muffins are available race morning. After finishing, enjoy more food and drink.

AWARDS In keeping with the tongue-in-cheek nature of the race, only "joke" awards are presented to those who outrun the Monster.

ACCOMMODATIONS Monster does not have an official race hotel. Many hotels are available in the Courtland-Ithaca area, but call early as the race occurs on Labor Day weekend. Some hotels in Courtland include: Marathon Three Bear Inn, Exit 9 on I-81 (607-849-3258); Courtland Motor Court, 393 Tompkins Street (607-753-3351); and Courtland Super 8, Exit on I-81 (607-756-5622). In Ithaca try: Best Western University Inn, E. Hill (607-272-6100); Holiday Inn, 222 S. Cayuga Street (607-272-1000); Ramada Inn Ithaca Airport, 2310 N. Triphammer Road (607-257-3100); Sheraton Inn, 1 Sheraton Drive (607-257-2000); Econolodge, 2303 N. Cayuga Street (607-257-1400); or Springwater, Route 366 2 miles east of Cornell University (607-272-3721).

RELATED EVENTS / RACES If one trip up and back over Virgil Mountain summit is enough for you, try the accompanying half marathon. For marathoners reluctant to let the Forest Monster chase them for a second out-and-back, race officials allow them to stop midway with the half marathoners.

AREA ATTRACTIONS If you have some time, enjoy more of the area's natural beauty by staying at one of the state's parks in the Ithaca area. Buttermilk Falls and Robert H. Treman State Parks offer swimming, hiking and wonderful waterfalls. Wine-drinking runners must visit New York state's most acclaimed wine region on the nearby Cayuga Trail along Route 89 between Seneca Falls and Trumansburg. Do some wine tasting, and buy a bottle or two to complement your campside cooking.

LOCAL RUNNING STORE Pal's Sports Center, 8 West Pulteney, Corning.

MARATHON OF THE ROSES

OVERALL: 76.1

COURSE BEAUTY: 8

COURSE DIFFICULTY: 5+

APPROPRIATENESS FOR FIRST TIMERS: 7

RACE ORGANIZATION: 8-

CROWDS: 1-

R A C E   D A T A

Contact:	Marathon of the Roses
	Clay Shaw
	3035 Raintree Road
	York, PA 17404
	(717) 764-1181
Date:	September 14, 1997
	September 13, 1998
Start Time:	7:00 a.m.
Time Course Closes:	1:00 p.m.
Number of Participants:	400 in 1996
Certification:	USATF
Course Records:	Male (open) 2:36:44; (masters) 3:02:02
	Female (open) 3:15:21; (masters) 3:28:31
Elite Athlete Programs:	No
Cost:	$25/30
Age groups/Divisions:	18-29, 30-39, 40-49, 50-59, 60-69, 70+
Temperature:	50° - 70°
Aid/Splits:	14 / clocks at 13.1 & 20

HIGHLIGHTS Unlike the War of the Roses (1455-1485) in which the houses of Lancaster (whose badge was a red rose) and York (whose badge was a white rose) struggled for the English throne, the southern Pennsylvania counties of York and Lancaster display a friendly relationship when it comes to Marathon of the Roses. Neither county has the upper hand in this affair as the first 13.1 miles of the race take place in York and the second 13.1 miles in Lancaster. In fact, there's not even a draw bridge at the halfway point on top of the Susquehanna River. Besides featuring an attractive course through quaint small towns and pleasant countryside, this young race runs near many of Pennsylvania's famous tourist spots including Hershey, Philadelphia, Gettysburg, and Amish country.

COURSE DESCRIPTION Marathon of the Roses features a point-to-point course. From the start at Eastern High School near Wrightsville, the course travels over the challenging, rolling terrain of the historic Lincoln Highway through a mix of beautiful countryside and a series of small towns (Yorkana, Hellam, Wrightsville, Columbia, Mountville, and Centerville) in route to the finish in downtown Lancaster. You encounter a significant uphill at 4.5 miles, but are soon rewarded with a nice downhill between 5.5 and 7.5 miles. From here, the course continues rolling the rest of the way.

CROWD/RUNNER SUPPORT In 1983, a maverick marathon took place on the Marathon of the Roses course. Although devoid of permission and fees, the (non) event drew local media coverage. After thirteen years of anticipation, the first official Marathon of the Roses took place in 1996 drawing even greater coverage.

An estimated 2,000 spectators roamed the sidelines during the inaugural race. Most onlookers positioned themselves in Columbia (mile 14), Mountville (mile 18), and Lancaster (miles 24 to 26). Volunteers from the benefitting charity, Big Brothers and Big Sisters, provided tremendous support at the 14 aid stations along the course.

RACE LOGISTICS Buses to the start leave from the Hampton Inn Lancaster at 5:30 a.m. and from the finish in Lancaster at 5:45 a.m. If you don't have non-running friends to pick you up and are not staying at the Hampton Inn Lancaster, park at the finish and take the bus to the start. Bus transportation is provided back to the hotels from the finish.

ACTIVITIES Pick up your race packet at either The Inside Track in the Lancaster Shopping Center (take the Route 501/Lititz Pike exit south off US 30) from 10:00 a.m. to 6:00 p.m. on Saturday or at the Eastern High School start on race day from 6:00 a.m. to 7:00 a.m. Following the event, enjoy food, drink, and an awards ceremony.

AWARDS All marathoners receive T-shirts, while finishers receive medals. The top three overall males and females receive $1000, $500, and $250, respectively. The first place male and female masters runners receive $500. Age-group awards extend as deep as five places, depending on the number of entries in each division.

ACCOMMODATIONS The race maintains two official race hotels: Hampton Inn Lancaster, 545 Greenfield Road (717-299-1200) and Hampton Inn York, 1550 Mount Zion Road (717-840-1500). Other options in Lancaster include: Days Inn of Lancaster, 30 Keller Avenue (717-299-5700); Holiday Inn, 521 Greenfield Road (717-299-2551); and Quality Inn and Suites, 2363 Oregon Pike (717-569-0477). Possibilities in York include: Days Inn Conference Center, 222 Arsenal Road (717-843-9971); Holiday Inn, US 30 & Rte. 74 (717-846-9500); and Ramada Inn, 1650 Toronita Street (717-846-4940).

RELATED EVENTS/RACES If you're not interested in going the whole distance, consider joining a relay team. Teams consist of four runners, and exchange zones occur at 7.7, 14, and 20.3 miles. The relay starts with the marathon at 7:00 a.m. The first two teams earn $800 and $400, respectively.

AREA ATTRACTIONS Be sure to allow some extra time to see some of the area sites. Though they don't necessarily like the attention, the large Amish population in Lancaster County continues as a major attraction for modern-convenience loving tourists. Tour York's Harley Davidson Museum and Factory. Chocaholic or not, you won't want to miss visiting nearby Hershey, PA where even the street lamps resemble Hershey Kisses. Still more options include visiting historic Gettysburg and Philadelphia.

LOCAL RUNNING STORES The Inside Track, 1659 Lititz Pike, Lancaster (717-394-6439); Flying Feet Sport Shoes, 1511 Mount Rose Avenue, York (717-845-2833).

BURNEY CLASSIC MARATHON

OVERALL: 76.9

COURSE BEAUTY: 9

COURSE DIFFICULTY: 7-

APPROPRIATENESS FOR FIRST TIMERS: 6

RACE ORGANIZATION: 8

CROWDS: 0

RACE DATA

Contact:	Don Jacobs
	Burney Lions Club
	P.O. Box 217, Dept. M
	Burney, CA 96013-0217
	(916) 335-2825
Date:	September 21, 1997
	September 20, 1998
Start Time:	8:00 a.m.
Time Course Closes:	NA
Number of Participants:	25 in 1996
Certification:	USATF
Course Records:	Male: (open) 2:33:35; (masters) 3:00:04
	Female: (open) 3:19:40; (masters) 3:35:25
Elite Athlete Programs:	No
Cost:	$25/30
Age groups/Divisions:	<19, 20-29, 30-39, 40-49, 50-59, 60-69, 70+
Temperature:	38° - 70°
Aid/Splits:	12 / first five miles

HIGHLIGHTS A small mountain town provides the setting for the Burney Classic Marathon, a weekend of scenic running and family entertainment. Tucked away in the wilderness beyond Redding in Northern California, Burney offers a panoramic view of Mt. Shasta and Mt. Lassen. Though serene, the course challenges with an average elevation of 3,100 feet and plenty of hills over the first half. Looking for ways to attract more visitors to the beautiful Intermountain area, Race Director Don Jacobs and the Burney Lions founded the race in 1990. The beautiful Burney course leaves you wondering why the race hasn't grown over its brief history. Along with the marathon, the Burney Chamber of Commerce hosts a weekend of activities starting Saturday with a chili cookoff, crafts fair, live music, raffle and microbeer tasting. Race day includes a 5K, 10K, and half marathon. Though spectators are sparse and attendance is modest, the natural beauty and small town allure are enough to entice even the most competitive marathoner to Burney.

COURSE DESCRIPTION Surrounded by spectacular mountain peaks, this well-kept secret (until now) of a course journeys by expansive ranches and enchanting forests. Beginning behind the make-shift, start-line garden hose, the point-to-point route runs predominantly uphill for the first half with steep sections from mile 5.8 to 6.4 and mile 10 to 10.8. A steep downhill from mile 11.4 to mile 12 allows you to recuperate and enjoy a wonderful panorama before climbing to 12.6 miles. A precursor to the faster second half, a nice downhill occurs from mile 12.6 to 14. Rolling to mile 14.7, the route falls to mile 16.5 followed by a few rollers to the

17-mile mark. A left turn on Cassell Road at 17.3 miles takes runners through flat cattle ranches to the 20-mile mark. Here, runners turn right on Hwy. 89, climbing a short but steep hill before turning left at 20.9 miles. Veering onto the uneven dirt/gravel terrain of Mountain View Road, the route runs flat to slightly downhill with scattered pine trees to the right and open fields and distant mountains on the left. At 24.2 miles, the race rises sharply to 24.5, flattens briefly, and then continues up to mile 24.9. The final 1.3 miles travel downhill to the Burney High School track where the announcer has plenty of time to work on name pronunciation for each of the 25 periodic finishers.

CROWD/RUNNER SUPPORT With the exception of two or three bodies at each of the 10 aid stations, the course affords you virtual solitary appreciation of its beauty. Before becoming too lonely, however, you may join or pass some half marathoners who started at the marathon halfway point 75 minutes after the marathon start. You may also pass 10K and 5K runners over the final miles of the race. If you're a Gatorade drinker, note that not all aid stations want you to "Be like Mike."

RACE LOGISTICS If you're traveling by airplane, the nearest airports to Burney are located in Redding and Reno. Make your lodging arrangements early as accommodations are limited, and hunting season begins the next week. On race morning, one school bus is all that is needed to transport the field of runners to the start. The bus leaves at 7:00 a.m. from Burney High School. After the half-hour ride, you depart the bus knowing almost each one of your competitors.

ACTIVITIES Pick up your race packet Saturday at Mountain Footwear in Burney from 8:00 a.m. to 5:30 p.m. or at Veterans Hall during the Spaghetti Feed starting at 6:00 p.m. Be careful not to tire yourself the day before the race during all of the town festivities. Enjoy a postrace steak barbecue and plenty of beverages while awaiting the awards ceremony (almost everyone wins an award).

AWARDS Every runner receives a T-shirt, the top male and female in each division win medals, and second and third place division finishers receive rosette ribbons. The top three overall finishers receive $500, $200, and $100, respectively. Additionally, each runner is automatically entered for a chance to win a trip to Hawaii.

ACCOMMODATIONS Several small hotels lie on Main Street (Hwy. 89), only a few blocks away from the finish at Burney High School. Among them are: the newly refurbished Burney Motel, 37448 Main Street (916-335-4500); Clark Creek Lodge, Hwy. 89 (916-335-2574); Green Gable Motel, 37385 Main Street (916-335-2264); Shasta Pines Motel, 37386 Main Street (916-335-2201); and Sleepy Hollow Lodge, 36898 Main Street (916-335-2285).

RELATED EVENTS/RACES If 26.2 miles is further than you want to run, consider the accompanying half marathon, 10K or 5K. All races run on sections of the marathon course. The half marathon begins at 9:15 a.m. from the marathon halfway point. The 10K and 5K feature out-and-back courses leaving from Burney High School at 10:00 a.m. and 10:15 a.m., respectively.

AREA ATTRACTIONS Burney Falls State Park and Mt. Lassen National Park spoil the outdoor lover. You can't go wrong with hiking, mountain biking, fishing or plain sightseeing.

EQUINOX MARATHON

COURSE BEAUTY: 8+

COURSE DIFFICULTY: 10 (SEE APPENDIX)

APPROPRIATENESS FOR FIRST TIMERS: 2

RACE ORGANIZATION: 8+

CROWDS: 0

RACE DATA

Contact:	Steve Bainbridge
	Running Club North
	P.O. Box 84237
	Fairbanks, AK 99708
	(907) 452-8351
Date:	September 20, 1997
	September 19, 1998
Start Time:	8:00 a.m.
Time Course Closes:	6:00 p.m.
Number of Participants:	400 in 1995
Certification:	None
Course Records:	Male: (open) 2:41:30
	Female: (open) 3:25:19
Elite Athlete Programs:	No
Cost:	$15/25/35
Age groups/Divisions:	17-19, 20-29, 30-39, 40-49, 50-59, 60+
Temperature:	35°
Aid/Splits:	8 / none

HIGHLIGHTS The fourth most challenging marathon in North America, the Equinox Marathon appeals to those runners looking to test the limits of their strength and endurance, climbing about 4,500 feet from start to finish. Held just outside the middle of nowhere in Fairbanks, Alaska, Equinox runs mostly on trails, some of which could be covered with snow during the race. The race has been run every year for 33 years, except for 1992 when the race was "officially" canceled due to over 2 feet of snow on the course. Some local hard-core runners still "unofficially" ran the race. On clear days, Ester Dome's summit offers rousing views of the surrounding area if you can lift your head from your knees.

COURSE DESCRIPTION Equinox's loop course starts at the University of Alaska Fairbanks' athletic field. As a little taste test of the delights ahead, the race immediately heads up the 200-foot, college ski hill to warm up chilled runners. Hitting the densely forested ski trails north of the campus, the course reaches the second major hill at mile 2, a 300-foot incline over a mile. This hill is followed by a sharp downhill and another 300-foot climb near mile 4. Runners pass the Musk Ox Farm at mile 5, soon getting their first glimpse of Ester Dome. Continuing on the heavily wooded ski trail, runners begin the excruciating 1,800-foot climb over three miles to Ester Dome's summit by mile 9. In the higher elevations, runners should be prepared to encounter snow and wind. Once runners reach the summit, they begin a roller coaster, 5.5-mile out-and-back over hills and down valleys. Runners get no time to recover because at 17 miles, the course practically falls off a cliff, dropping 1,700 feet in four miles. Becoming slightly less unpleasant on the Aspen Trail between 18 and 20, good downhillers can make up some time. The dirt trails give way to pavement near mile 21 as runners enter the final section of the race. Around 23.5, runners can spot the satellite dish on top of UAF's Geophysical Institute signaling the end is near. Just to show who's the boss, race organizers throw in a final 100-foot climb over the UAF ski trail at mile 25, making the approaching finish line taste that much sweeter.

CROWD/RUNNER SUPPORT The two relay exchange points and the eight aid stations provide the biggest areas of support for the runners. Consider packing your own provisions to provide the energy necessary to complete the brutal course.

RACE LOGISTICS Runners must find their own way to the start, although there is plenty of parking at the university.

ACTIVITIES The day before the marathon, claim your race package and attend the pre-race Pasta Party ($7) at the Pump House Restaurant & Saloon, 1.3 Mile Chena Pump Road. Pick up your race packet or register late on race morning at UAF Patty Center Gym. After the marathon ordeal, replenish a little sugar at the dessert buffet held with the awards ceremony in the Wood Center.

AWARDS All entrants receive Equinox Marathon T-shirts, and runners finishing under 10 hours earn Equinox Marathon patches. The top three in each age division receive medals, and the top five overall winners earn trophies.

ACCOMMODATIONS Accommodations are available at the Fairbanks Princess Hotel, 4477 Pikes Landing Road (800-426-0500); Fairbanks Hotel, 517 Third Avenue (888-329-4685); Westmark Fairbanks, 813 Noble Street (907-456-7722); or Super 8 Motel, 1909 Airport Way (907-451-8888). Fairbanks has countless bed & breakfast inns. Among them are: Alaska 7 Gables B&B (907-479-0751); Fairbanks B&B (907-452-4967); Chena River B&B (907-479-2532); and Joan's (907-479-6918). For other B&B reservations call the Fairbanks Association of Bed & Breakfasts (907-452-7700).

RELATED EVENTS/RACES Runners not crazy enough to run the marathon can hike it or assemble a relay team of three members, either single sex or mixed. Relay runners complete legs of 8.5, 8.6, and 9.2 miles. Team members must provide their own transportation to the relay exchange areas.

AREA ATTRACTIONS While in Fairbanks, check out the Dog Mushing Museum above the Alaska Public Lands Information Center at Courthouse Square. Also, browse the surprisingly good University Museum at UAF. Then, hurry to Denali National Park, home of Mt. McKinley, before it closes for the season to view amazing wildlife and gorgeous scenery. Make sure to reserve your tour bus and lodging ahead of time.

LOCAL RUNNING STORE Beaver Sports, 3480 College Road, Fairbanks (907-479-2494).

DUTCHESS COUNTY MARATHON

OVERALL: 80.2

COURSE BEAUTY: 8

COURSE DIFFICULTY: 3+

APPROPRIATENESS FOR FIRST TIMERS: 7+

RACE ORGANIZATION: 9-

CROWDS: 1-

RACE DATA

Contact: Irvin Miller
Dutchess County Classic
11 Manor Drive
Poughkeepsie, NY 12603-3712
(914) 473-2568
Date: September 21, 1997
September 20, 1998
Start Time: 9:00 a.m.
Time Course Closes: 2:00 p.m.
Number of Participants: 200 in 1995
Certification: USATF
Course Records: Male: (open) 2:33:13; (masters) 2:38:54
Female: (open) 2:51:14; (masters) 3:08:59
Elite Athlete Programs: No
Cost: $20/23
Age groups/Divisions: 19-29, 30-39, 40-49, 50-59, 60+
Temperature: 70°
Aid/Splits: 7 / none

HIGHLIGHTS Many small marathons in North America get by on their requisite charm, offering few of the extras that runners expect in bigger affairs. Nothing wrong with that. However, if you like charm and appreciate special treatment (and who doesn't), consider the Dutchess County Classic held near Poughkeepsie, NY. A classic overachiever, Dutchess County does many little things that make a big difference. On top of a course featuring the picturesque scenery of the Hudson Valley, the race compiles a one-of-a-kind post-race yearbook with photographs of participants accompanied by an analysis of each runner's race (without the aid of the CHAMPI-ONCHIP). The professional singing of the National Anthem, permanent, artistic mile markers, and one of the most attractive race T-shirts anywhere, are a few of Dutchess County's attributes.

COURSE DESCRIPTION Dutchess County's double-loop country course travels through three towns, over several streams, and past schools, churches and historic homes. Starting at Wappinger Recreation Park in Wappinger, the course follows a mostly flat, rural route until two miles where it passes the Sons of Italy Joe DiMaggio Lodge and Van Wyck Junior High School. Here, runners enter a pleasant neighborhood for approximately 1 mile before returning to rural surroundings. At mile 4, the first of the course's two hills appears, lasting about .25 miles. After flattening briefly, the hill continues rising to the town of LaGrange. After the 5-mile mark coming off the upgrade, the course continues flat past the Karl Ehmer Farm and estate on the right and the Kinkead Farm located after the 6-mile mark. Between the two farms, runners pass the rock cut geological landmark while moving slightly uphill. From mile 7, the course continues flat and open until nearly the 9-mile mark when runners may encounter heavy traffic exiting the Presbyterian Church. A steep, .1-mile uphill greets runners after 9 miles (it can feel more like a mountain during the second loop) followed by a flat, narrow road through woodsy surroundings which most runners consider the loneliest part of the course. A slight, almost undetectable downhill lies after 11 miles, becoming flat by mile 12. Here, the scenic Secor Farm features a field of blazing sunflowers before the route returns to Wappinger Recreation Area and the start of the second loop.

CROWD/RUNNER SUPPORT DCC's rural nature means few spectators line the course. Most of the cheering comes at the halfway point as many of the 5K and half marathoners cheer on the marathon runners. Volunteers at the five aid stations offer additional support. To bolster community involvement, the Poughkeepsie Journal typically devotes several pages to DCC coverage before and after the race.

RACE LOGISTICS Several hotels lie in the vicinity but none within walking distance of the start; however, adequate parking areas exist around the start/finish area. Absolutely no vehicle parking is allowed on Robinson Lane in front of the park.

ACTIVITIES Race packet pickup takes place at the Wappinger Recreation Area on Robinson Lane on race day from 7:30 a.m. to 8:45 a.m. Following the race, enjoy individual food bags, beverages, rousing disc jockey music, and an awards ceremony.

AWARDS Runners preregistering up to a week before the event are guaranteed T-shirts. Additionally, each marathon finisher receives a medal, gloves, water bottle, certificate, food and a results booklet mailed after the race. The unique results booklet includes: a record of your position at different mile points along the course; the names of the runners that passed you or that you passed between the checkpoints; an analysis of the data and recommendations for future race strategy. In other words, if you go out too fast at DCC, you'll suffer in more ways than one. Overall and age-group winners receive trophies, and medals are awarded up to tenth place in some categories. The first local male and female runners receive clocks.

ACCOMMODATIONS Although the race maintains no official hotel, the area contains plenty of lodging choices. Some of your options include: Econolodge of Poughkeepsie, 418 South Road (914-452-6600); Best Western Inn and Conference Center, 679 South Road (914-462-4600); Holiday Inn Express, 341 South Road (914-473-1151); and Days Inn of Poughkeepsie, 418 South Road (914-454-1010).

RELATED EVENTS/RACES For runners not wanting to go the entire distance, the half marathon runs concurrently with the marathon, while the 5K begins at 9:15 a.m.

AREA ATTRACTIONS After the race, visit some of the area's historical sights including West Point Military Academy, FDR Historical site, Vanderbilt Mansion and other mansions along the scenic Hudson River. Treat yourself to a relaxing stay at one of the area's excellent bed and breakfasts after imbibing in some of the selections at the local wineries.

LOCAL RUNNING STORE Dick's Sporting Goods, Poughkeepsie Galleria (914-297-4767).

MARATHON DE L'ILE DE MONTREAL

OVERALL: 88.1

COURSE BEAUTY: 7+

COURSE DIFFICULTY: 4

APPROPRIATENESS FOR FIRST TIMERS: 9+

RACE ORGANIZATION: 9

CROWDS: 3-

RACE DATA

Contact:	Marathon de l'ile de Montreal
	Le club des coureurs sur route de Montreal
	C.P. 1383, Succ. Place d'Armes
	Montreal, Quebec
	Canada H2Y 3K5
	(514) 284-5272
Date:	September 21, 1997
	September 20, 1998
Start Time:	8:35 a.m.
Time Course Closes:	2:30 p.m.
Number of Participants:	3,000 in 1995
Certification:	Athletics Canada & AIMS
Course Records:	Male: (open) 2:15:19; (masters) 2:32:29
	Female: (open) 2:34:55; (masters) 2:52:49
Elite Athlete Programs:	Yes
Cost:	US $40/50
Age groups/Divisions:	18-39, 40-49, 50-59, 60+
Temperature:	50° - 65°
Aid/Splits:	15 / none

HIGHLIGHTS Experience unique Montreal, an island of French civilization in the New World, by running Marathon de l'ile de Montreal (The Island of Montreal Marathon). The city itself entices out-of-towners to make the trip. Urbane, lively, and slightly foreign to non-French speakers, Montreal offers a great deal to the visitor — sport, culture, beauty, and entertainment. The marathon courses through Montreal's suburbs, rolls past beautiful downtown (near mile 22), and finishes in the refurbished Old Port. Relatively fast, the well-organized race offers a good introduction to the city and boasts one of the few free pasta dinners in North America.

RACE HISTORY The Montreal Marathon began in 1972 with 150 runners to commemorate the coming 1976 Olympic Games. The race started on the future Olympic Stadium site but over the years has undergone a number of facelifts (there were even two races annually from 1979 to 1981) and name changes. The current name — which refers to the four cities the marathon bisects — was affixed in 1992. Designed to produce fast times, the present course debuted in 1995. The marathon grows by approximately 15% every year and attracted 3,000 runners in 1995.

COURSE DESCRIPTION The Montreal Marathon starts in the suburb of Saint-Laurent at the C.E.G.E.P. Saint-Laurent. The first mile travels down commercial Cote-Vertu before turning into a middle-class residential neighborhood until mile 3. Then, runners revisit Cote-Vertu for one mile. Miles 4 to 5.75 pass through another residential section, followed by a short, steep down and up. After a brief commercial district, the race enters a nice residential area on Graham. As runners enter Ville Mont-Royal (mile 6.5), the course becomes commercial and then quickly turns into a pleasant residential neighborhood. At 9.5 miles, the course enters the town of Outremont, traversing an overpass and rolling up for the next 1.5 miles. It skirts the University of Montreal and passes through downtown Outremont and the brick and stone town-houses of trendy St. Joseph, before entering Montreal's city limits. The now mostly flat race then enters its least scenic stretch, going through a warehouse district for over a mile and then a lower-income residential/industrial area. As runners make the turn onto Rachel, Olympic Stadium sits to the left. Runners soon welcome the beauty of Park LaFontaine (near 21 miles), knowing that the soul of the course, downtown Montreal, lies just ahead. The city's skyline appears on Sherbrooke. Past gorgeous McGill University, through downtown, the marathon finishes in the refurbished, festive Old Port, a wonderful spot for a night out.

CROWD/RUNNER SUPPORT Aid stations, located every 2.5 km (about 1.5 miles), carry water, electrolyte replacement, portable toilets, PowerBars, and minor first aid. Locals come out in force, with onlookers particularly dense at the start, near 5K, 5.5 miles, 13 miles, 19 miles, and the final half mile to the finish.

RACE LOGISTICS With limited parking and shuttle bus service to the start, race organizers strongly urge runners to take the subway to the Du College Station, which lies about 200 yards from the start line.

ACTIVITIES On Thursday, Friday, and Saturday before the race, attend the Health and Fitness Expo in the Old Port in order to retrieve your race packet. You may not register or pick up your packet on race day. On Saturday evening, carbo load at the free Pasta Party beginning at 5:00 p.m. The first-come, first-served dinner fills quickly, so arrive early. For $7.50, friends and family may join you for dinner. After the race, runners enjoy food and drink at the post-race party in the finish area.

AWARDS Every runner receives a T-shirt, marathon poster, and a pass to the pasta dinner. Runners who complete the race also earn finisher's medals and certificates. There are no age-group awards, although top runners vie for $20,000 in prize money.

ELITE RUNNERS INFORMATION Montreal offers special inducements to elite runners, which the race considers to be men under 2:16 and women under 2:39. The race could offer a combination of transportation expenses, lodging, entry, and other expenses.

ACCOMMODATIONS Le Centre Sheraton, 1201 Rene-Levesque West (514-878-2000), serves as the official marathon hotel. The hotel offers special rates for marathon runners.

RELATED EVENTS/RACES Companion events to the marathon include a marathon relay, a youth 3K, and an in-line skating 22K. The marathon relay consists of four-runner coed teams in open and corporate divisions. Only coed teams may win awards, and the final runner must be a woman. Boys and girls ages 6 to 17 run in the 3K Youth Challenge which begins at 8:15 a.m. and ends at the marathon finish. Finally, in-line skaters roll down the final 22K of the marathon course starting at 8:00 a.m.

LOCAL RUNNING STORES Boutique Courir, 4452 St. Denis (514-499-9600); Boutique Endurance, 6579 St. Denis (514-272-9267).

WALKER NORTH COUNTRY MARATHON

COURSE BEAUTY: 9

COURSE DIFFICULTY: 4+ (SEE APPENDIX)

APPROPRIATENESS FOR FIRST TIMERS: 7

RACE ORGANIZATION: 9-

CROWDS: 0+

R A C E   D A T A

Contact: Steve Bilbon
Walker North Country Marathon
P.O. Box 338
Walker, MN 56484
(218) 547-1851

Date: September 20, 1997
September 19, 1998

Start Time: 9:00 a.m.

Time Course Closes: 3:00 p.m.

Number of Participants: 193 in 1995

Certification: USATF

Course Records: Male: (open) 2:37:53
Female: (open) 3:01:20

Cost: $18

Age groups/Divisions: <14, 15-19, 20-24, 25-29, 30-34, 35-39, 40-44,
45-49, 50-54, 55-59, 60-64, 65-69, 70+

Temperature: 38° - 60°

Aid/Splits: 13 / none

HIGHLIGHTS Patterned after a German Black Forest festival celebrating life and land, the Walker North Country Marathon in northern Minnesota provides heartening views of remote forests, tranquil lakes and rolling farmlands for which Minnesota's famous. Run along a portion of the National Scenic Trail in the Chippewa National Forest, the course resonates with autumn's hues. Unique awards, handcrafted by local artists, further showcase the area's beauty.

COURSE DESCRIPTION Run on grass, gravel, dirt, and pavement, Walker North Country's loop course starts near the Walker-Hackensack-Akeley High School overlooking Walker Bay. After descending 75 feet to Main Street in the first half mile, runners turn south following State Hwy. 371 for the next 7.5 miles passing forest, lakes and an occasional home or business. Leaving the highway near 8 miles, the race veers onto the North Country Trail, a broad, grassy pathway. With several short steep hills, the difficult and scenic trail twists and turns the next 9 miles. At this stage, runners may take exception to the race's calling card, "The Celebration of Life and Land that is Northern Minnesota." At 16.6 miles, the route turns west onto the paved Heartland State Trail following an old railroad grade for approximately 1.5 miles. Minnesota's nickname, "Land of 10,000 Lakes," comes to mind as the race easily rolls through lake country to the finish. Around 18 miles, the course moves to a dirt road for 1.5 miles before briefly rejoining the North Country Trail and returning to the Heartland Trail at mile 21. The next 4.5 miles traipse mostly downhill to Walker where a challenging 75-foot rise in the last half mile leads to the finish line at Ostlund Field.

CROWD / RUNNER SUPPORT Except for the occasional couple in a canoe, runners are on their own as far as crowd support. The largest cheering section congregates near the start/finish with the crowd enhanced by the 10K runners. Thirteen aid stations provide medical personnel, first aid supplies, emergency communications, water and electrolyte replacement (fluids only at 3.5 and 8.8 miles).

RACE LOGISTICS Plenty of parking is available at the start/finish area at WHA High School. A shuttle service takes relay runners to and from the relay exchange points. Relay participants exchange a wristband in the transition area and turn it in at the finish. Showers are available in the school gym.

ACTIVITIES To encourage preregistration, all participants registered by September 1 are eligible to win a two-night stay at Tianna Farms Bed and Breakfast in Walker. All race activities take place at WHA High School. Race packet pickup takes place on Friday between 4:00 p.m. and 7:00 p.m. You can also pick up your packet on race day from 7:00 a.m. to 8:30 a.m. Carb up at the Spaghetti Feed Friday night from 5:00 p.m. to 8:00 p.m. After the race, stay for refreshments before the awards ceremony.

AWARDS All participants receive T-shirts, and finishers earn specially designed medallions, part of a continuing series. Overall male and female winners and division winners receive art pieces crafted by local artists.

ACCOMMODATIONS Although the race maintains no official race hotel, numerous motels and campgrounds exist in the popular resort community of Walker. Some of them include: AmericInn, Hwy. 371N, N Walker (218-547-2200); Tianna Farms Bed and Breakfast, Walker (218-547-1306); Chase on the Lake Lodge, Leech Lake (218-547-1531); Lakeview Inn, Hwy. 371E, E Walker (218-547-1212); Northwoods Beach Motel, Walker (218-547-1702); and Pioneer Inn Motel, Walker (218-547-1366). If you prefer to camp, consider the Acorn Hill Resort on Leech Lake (218-547-1015); or Shores Leech Lake Campground and Marina (218-547-1819).

RELATED EVENTS / RACES Walker North also conducts a 10K run/walk starting at 9:15 a.m. Traveling along portions of the Heartland Trail and past scenic Lake May, the race finishes with the famous half-mile uphill onto Ostlund Field. In 1996, race officials added Minnesota's only 2-Person Marathon Relay which starts with the marathon.

AREA ATTRACTIONS Camping, hiking, fishing and boating head the area's entertainment.

EAST LYME MARATHON

OVERALL: 79.6

COURSE BEAUTY: 9-

COURSE DIFFICULTY: 5

APPROPRIATENESS FOR FIRST TIMERS: 7-

RACE ORGANIZATION: 8

CROWDS: 0+

R A C E   D A T A

Contact:	Way Hedding
	East Lyme Marathon
	P.O. Box 186
	East Lyme, CT 06333
	(203) 739-2864
Date:	September 28, 1997
	September 27, 1998
Start Time:	8:30 a.m.
Time Course Closes:	NA
Number of Participants:	NA
Certification:	USATF
Course Records:	Male: (open) 2:23:56
	Female: (open) 2:48:51
Elite Athlete Programs:	No
Cost:	$22/25
Age groups/Divisions:	<29, 30-39, 40-49, 50-59, 60+
Temperature:	60°
Aid/Splits:	14 / miles 1, 6 & 13

HIGHLIGHTS Connecticut's oldest and most scenic marathon, East Lyme rolls past wooded farms, apple orchards, Rocky Neck State Park, coastline, and Black Point mansions. The cozy, relaxed ambiance makes for a serene experience. Kids can keep busy with the free timed track run.

COURSE DESCRIPTION East Lyme's completely paved, loop course promenades several of the area's most scenic back roads. Starting at East Lyme High School, the route heads northwest over winding and rolling Pataguanset Road. A small lake (at mile 1), several attractive country homes, and an occasional grazing cow characterize the rural, early miles. Two notable uphills (with corresponding downhills) occur between 1.2 and 1.8 miles on Pataguanset Road and 3 miles and 3.6 miles on Scott Road. Near 4.8 miles, the route turns left on Post Road beginning a 3-mile loop through the tree-canopied residential area of Lovers Lane and Dean Road. Around the 8-mile mark, the course turns left embarking on a nice rolling to mostly downhill stretch on Bride Brook Road. Flattening around the 11-mile mark, the course loops around Rocky Neck State Park for 3 miles before heading east another 3 miles to the exclusive Black Point residential area near 17.5 miles. Flat narrow roads, luxury homes and ocean glimpses mark the next few miles — the fastest and most scenic on the course. After a couple of quick ups and downs, the route exits Black Point near 21.5 miles, rises for a brief stint, and then heads east for .5 miles through downtown Niantic after 22 miles. At 22.5 miles, the course turns left heading north on

Penn Avenue. Flat to gradually rolling for the next 3.5 miles, the race cuts through a commercial area around 24.6 miles and finishes at the high school.

CROWD/RUNNER SUPPORT Spectators spread along sections of the rural route. The 14 aid stations supply water, electrolyte replacement, diluted soda, oranges, and additional encouragement.

RACE LOGISTICS A hassle-free race, East Lyme starts and finishes within 100 yards of East Lyme High School where plenty of parking is available. Runners may take advantage of the high school's hot showers and locker rooms.

ACTIVITIES A spaghetti dinner is held on marathon eve from 6:00 p.m. to 8:00 p.m. at East Lyme High School (about $5). You can pick up your race packet or register while at the dinner or on race day from 7:00 a.m. to 8:00 a.m. Plenty of food and refreshments await the runners following the race.

AWARDS Every registered runner receives a marathon T-shirt, and marathon finishers receive high-quality medals. Merchandise prizes go to the top finishers, and the top three in each age group and overall winners receive other awards.

ACCOMMODATIONS While there is no official race hotel, several offer special rates for East Lyme Marathon entrants: Connecticut Yankee Inn (203-739-5487); Days Inn — East Lyme (203-739-3951); Howard Johnson Lodge (203-739-6921); and Motel 6 (203-739-6991).

RELATED EVENTS/RACES Non-marathoners can enter the 5K Run and Health Walk which starts immediately after the marathon. The free Children's Track Run starts at 9:30 a.m. with ribbons and refreshments for all runners.

AREA ATTRACTIONS Coastal Connecticut offers some interesting diversions, such as the USS Nautilus Submarine Museum and the Mystic Seaport. Gamblers can test their luck at the huge Fox Woods Resort Casino.

LOCAL RUNNING STORE Kelley's Pace, Olde Mystick Village, Bldg. 15-C, Mystic (203-536-8175).

PORTLAND MARATHON

OVERALL: 92.1

COURSE BEAUTY: 8

COURSE DIFFICULTY: 4- (SEE APPENDIX)

APPROPRIATENESS FOR FIRST TIMERS: 10

RACE ORGANIZATION: 10+

CROWDS: 3

RACE DATA

Contact: Les Smith
Portland Marathon
P.O. Box 4040
Beaverton, OR 97076
(503) 226-1111
e-mail: pdxmar@teleport.com
http://www.teleport.com/~pdxmar

Date: September 28, 1997
September 27, 1998

Start Time: 7:00 a.m.

Time Course Closes: 12:00 p.m.

Number of Participants: 5,665 in 1995

Certification: USATF

Course Records: Male: (open) 2:17:23; (masters) 2:26:03
Female: (open) 2:36:39; (masters) 2:54:57

Elite Athlete Programs: No

Cost: $40/75

Age groups/Divisions: <19, 20-24, 25-29, 30-34, 35-39, 40-44, 45-49, 50-54, 55-59, 60-64, 65-69, 70-74, 75-79, 80-84, 85-89, 90+, Clydesdale (185+ lbs.) and Bonnydale (145+ lbs.)

Temperature: 50° - 56°

Aid/Splits: 16 / every mile including pace

HIGHLIGHTS With Portland known as the City of Roses, it's appropriate that the Portland Marathon never fails to come off smelling as sweet as a rose. Boasting twenty-five years of experience, the race is one of the premier marathon events in the United States. No stranger to adulation, Portland annually hosts the National Race Director's Conference during race weekend. What better way to learn how to produce a successful event than to watch first hand Portland's masterful organization. And, with Portland offering more running and non-running events over race weekend than any other marathon in North America, effective organization is a must. The second largest non-prize money marathon in the country (Marine Corps is larger), Portland definitely believes in its motto "Everybody is a winner." This fact is, undoubtedly, the reason why 70% of participants come from points 100 miles or further; 46 states and 15 countries in all. The race also offers friendliness all-year round. What other marathon sends Christmas cards to past participants?

RACE HISTORY One of the many races under the auspices of the Oregon Road Runners' Club, the Portland Marathon premiered in 1972 with 173 runners. However, due to rapid growth, the marathon was forced to change courses numerous times in its formative years. Add to this the frequent shifting of the race date and race director, and Portland topped out in the late seventies with 1,219 runners, then declined to a five-year low of 481 in 1981. Ironically, that same year marked the first time the course entered the downtown area, a dream of the race's founding fathers but continually squelched by city officials. That year also signaled the beginning of a new era for the Portland Marathon. As strange as it may sound, it started when one of the 481 runners quit mid-race. Runner Les Smith, president of the ORRC, did not quit from exhaustion. He quit because he felt that race management could be doing much more for the runners. He spent the next few hours assisting at an undermanned aid station and cheering on his fellow runners all the while visualizing the transformation of Portland into a world-class marathon. After assuming the position of race director in 1984, Les completely overhauled the race. Fifteen years later, Les continues at the helm of the race that treats every runner like a champion.

COURSE DESCRIPTION The Marathon and Marathon Walk begin and end at charming Chapman/Lownsdale/Schrunk Parks, which are actually one big park in downtown Portland. Starting at the corner of SW Madison and Fourth, the course traces a route that embraces the many faces of a beautiful and friendly city, including the scenic riverfront, historic Old Town, and various residential neighborhoods. Broad panoramas of the city and dramatic views of the Cascade Mountain Range (Mt. Hood and Mt. St. Helens) and the St. Johns Bridge, one of the most beautiful suspension bridges in the world, inspire runners. Well-marked, the race provides large signs covered by balloons to signal each mile. The first 5 miles of the course are downtown. A gentle 1-mile downhill starts the race, with the next 2.5 miles gradually gaining 140 feet. An immediate, 2-mile downhill takes runners along the waterfront. The next section, from mile 5.5 to 12, travels through the industrial northwest section of town. You hardly notice this least scenic area of the course since the music and the adrenaline rush from eyeing other runners approaching from the opposite direction easily divert your attention. Making another gradual downhill, the course heads along the flat border road of the Forest Park area through mile 15. The principal elevation gain on the course occurs over the next mile as runners climb 150 feet over the beautiful St. Johns Bridge. Thereafter, you run along Portland's spectacular east bluff that faces the Willamette River from mile 18 through 24. There is an elevation loss of approximately 140 feet from mile 22 to 24.5, with a slight rise as runners go over Portland's Steel Bridge. You then turn back down to Marathon Avenue which leads to Front along the waterfront to the finish. Entirely run on well-maintained asphalt, the majority of the course is closed to vehicular traffic. Because the course records are relatively slow, you might surmise that the course is slow. But, remember, fast times are partly a function of prize money, one of the few things Portland doesn't offer. Make no mistake about it, Portland is a potential PR course.

CROWD/RUNNER SUPPORT Enthusiastic spectators, numbering upwards of 50,000, line the streets throughout the course with the greatest percentage in the downtown area for the first 5 miles and for the last 1.5 miles. Large neighborhood crowds gather between 18 and 21 miles. Various musical groups and street performers entertain along the course and appear to enjoy the event as much as the runners. Les Smith no longer has to work an aid station for the race as Portland fashions 19 of them manned by volunteers from businesses and organizations around the city. The stations compete for awards, including best organized, best decorated, and most enthusiastic. The aid stations are tremendous (some have cups with lids and straws), and depending on the weather, sponge and spray stations are also available.

RACE LOGISTICS Because the race starts and ends near all the hotels in downtown Portland, transportation is not a concern. Clothing storage is provided starting at 6:00 a.m. and closing at 3:00 p.m. in the basement area of the Portland Building.

ACTIVITIES Featuring more pre-race activities than any marathon in North America, the Portland Marathon offers something for the whole family, including: a golf tournament, Big Band Jazz Night, Pasta Party and International T-shirt Exchange, National Race Director's Conference (2 days), and Sports and Fitness Expo. A post-race party for finishers takes place in the finish area. Portland offers a novel approach to the post-race food frenzy. Instead of shepherding the finishers along in extended lines through various food tables, large, sealed plastic bags containing a plethora of goodies are handed to each runner. Massage practitioners provide foot/leg massages in the finish area for a nominal donation. A party open to all entrants, volunteers and their guests begins at 1:00 p.m. at the Portland Hilton, with the awards ceremony at 3:00 p.m.

AWARDS Each finisher receives a long-sleeve T-shirt, finisher medallion, race pin, Pacific Redwood sapling, and red rose. Race certificates and post-race results publications are mailed to finishers at a later time. Awards go as deep as 15 depending on the number and percentage of entrants in each age division.

FIRST-TIMERS INFORMATION The large field, broad crowd support, outstanding aid stations, plentiful entertainment, usually good weather, and scenic course with only one significant hill, translate into a superb race for a maiden voyage. While the course closes at noon, runners can proceed on well-marked sidewalks. Aid stations continue to provide aid to those within an 8-hour pace.

ACCOMMODATIONS The Portland Hilton, 921 SW 6th Avenue downtown (503-226-1611), serves as race headquarters. Specially priced rooms are reserved for marathoners and their guests at $130 per night. Other hotels in the area include: Days Inn, 11455 SW Pacific Highway (503-246-8451); Marriott, 1401 SW Front Street (503-226-7600); Heathman Hotel, 1009 SW Broadway (503-241-4100); and the Benson Hotel, 309 SW Broadway (503-228-9611).

RELATED EVENTS/RACES Portland features six separate events in addition to the marathon. The fun includes a Marathon Walk, Niketown 5-miler, 10K Mayor's Walk, and Marafun Kids' run (2 miles), all of which take place on race Sunday. The Run & Shoot Summer Biathlon and 24 Hour Track Ultra & Corporate Relay take place on Saturday.

AREA ATTRACTIONS Portland is a great destination city. If you have a few extra days, we recommend embarking on a trip to Mt. Hood, Mt. St. Helens or the beautiful Oregon coast. Additionally, you can view the spectacular waterfalls of the Columbia Gorge only thirty minutes east of Portland on I-84. Oktoberfest at Oak Park is another entertainment option.

LOCAL RUNNING STORES Finish Line Sports, 333 S. State, Lake Oswego (503-635-3577); Pacesetter Athletics, 4431 SE Woodstock (503-777-3214); Niketown, 6th and SW Salmon (503-234-4567).

PORTLAND MARATHON

ENTRY FORM

Be a part of our festival of events in the City of Roses!

Future Dates: Sept. 28, 1997 • Oct. 4, 1998 • Oct. 3, 1999 • Oct. 1, 2000

Please read carefully before completing form. Please print clearly. Please note deadlines for sending applications and late fees. Marathon and Marathon Walk entries by mail ($50) must be postmarked on or before midnight, September 8 for 1997's event; Sept. 14 for 1998; Sept. 13 for 1999; and Sept. 11 for 2000. Note: runners and walkers may enter in person for all events at a late fee rate (double the usual rate) at the Marathon Expo held at the Portland Hilton on the two days before the event.
(No refunds, exchanges or transfers)

(Please begin your name in the large box)   Check one box: ☐ Marathon Run   ☐ Marathon Walk

1. Last Name   First Name   M.I.

2. Address

   City   State   Zip   Country

3. Date of Birth   4. Age   Sex M   F

6. Total years of school   7. Shirt Size S M L XL XXL   (100% cotton)

8. Phone (work)   (home)

9. Best Previous Marathon Time: hr.   min.   sec. | Office use only

10. Predicted Time: hr.   min.   sec.   11. Completed Marathons:

12. Completed Portland Marathons:

Training For Portland Marathon Shirts (check size)

Entry Fee ($50)	$ _____
"Training For" Shirt ($15/$20)	$ _____
Souvenir Shirt ($15/$20/$30)	$ _____
Postage & Handling (see chart)	$ _____
Total Enclosed:	$ _____

(US Dollar amounts only: No foreign checks or money orders)

A. S☐ M☐ L☐ XL☐ Short Sleeve $15.00
B. S☐ M☐ L☐ XL☐ Long Sleeve Crew Neck T-Shirt $20.00

Portland Marathon Souvenir Shirts (check size)

A. S☐ M☐ L☐ XL☐ Short Sleeve $15.00
B. S☐ M☐ L☐ XL☐ Long Sleeve Crew Neck T-Shirt $20.00
C. S☐ M☐ L☐ XL☐ Sweatshirt $30.00

Make checks payable to: Portland Marathon; Mail to: P.O. Box 4040, Beaverton, OR 97076

	US/Canada	Foreign
Shirt Postage & Handling Fees	$15-25 ... $5	$7
Allow 5-6 weeks for delivery	$26-$40 ... $6	$9
Over $40	$7	$11

Signature _____   Date _____

Parent (if under 18)

 **PowerBar** ® ATHLETIC ENERGY FOOD **The Portland Hilton**

This form may be reproduced, duplicated or enlarged.
MARATHON HOTLINE: (503) 226-1111
e-mail address: pdxmar @ telport.com
www: http://www.telport.com/~pdxmar

 Crown Pacific

 VoiceStream AHEAD OF THE CURRENT

DON RASMUSSEN

 Albertson

*IF YOU WOULD LIKE A COPY OF OUR 16 PAGE MARATHON ENTRY BOOKLET OR AN ENTRY BOOKLET THAT ALSO DESCRIBES THE FIVE-MILER, MAYOR'S WALK, MARAFUN, KIDS' RUN, OR THE 26.2-MILE MARATHON WALK, PLEASE SEND A LEGAL SIZE SASE (55¢) TO THE ABOVE ADDRESS.

DUKE CITY MARATHON

OVERALL: 73.4

COURSE BEAUTY: 7-

COURSE DIFFICULTY: 6-

APPROPRIATENESS FOR FIRST TIMERS: 7

RACE ORGANIZATION: 8-

CROWDS: 1

RACE DATA

Contact:	Duke City Marathon
	P.O. Box 4543
	Albuquerque, NM 87196
	(505) 890-1018
Date:	September 28, 1997
	September 27, 1998
Start Time:	6:45 a.m.
Time Course Closes:	1:45 p.m.
Number of Participants:	497 in 1995
Certification:	USATF
Course Records:	Male: (open) 2:24:40
	Female: (open) 3:11:15
Elite Athlete Programs:	Yes
Cost:	$26/36
Age groups/Divisions:	18-24, 25-29, 30-34, 35-39, 40-44, 45-49, 50-54, 55-59, 60-64, 65-69, 70-74, 75-79, 80+, Cardiac special category.
Temperature:	73°
Aid/Splits:	16 / none

HIGHLIGHTS Recently becoming a training mecca for many of the world's top long distance runners, high altitude Albuquerque hosts one of the Southwest's most popular running events, the Duke City Marathon. With seven races to choose from, Duke City allows everyone to participate. Although the marathon course rises and falls only 300 feet throughout, the 5,000-foot average elevation provides little hope for PR chasers. Instead, relax and enjoy a route that takes you past a nature center and waterpark, along the Rio Grande bike path, past the University of New Mexico and trendy Nob Hill, and through downtown Albuquerque on legendary Route 66.

RACE HISTORY Named for the Duke of Albuquerque, the first Spanish Viceroy in the 17th Century, the Duke City Marathon was started in 1984 by a group of local runners who wanted to put Albuquerque on the national marathon map. That first race attracted 250 runners, one of whom was a young Kenyan named Ibrahim Hussein. Although known more for his subsequent wins at Boston and New York, few people know that he got his start at Duke City. His distinguished name remains in the record book as the winner of the inaugural Duke City Marathon.

COURSE DESCRIPTION Featuring two separate out-and-backs, Duke City provides a nice tour of downtown Albuquerque and the surrounding area. Generally flat for the first 15 miles before gradually rising 300 feet to 20 miles, the course returns downhill and then flat for the finish. The course's elevation, which hovers around 5,000 feet, provides perhaps the race's greatest challenge. After starting in the heart of downtown near Civic Plaza, the route heads west through Old Town before hitting the Paseo del Bosque bike path along the Rio Grande at 1.5 miles. The 11.5-mile out-and-back along the bike path traipses through a cottonwood forest and nature center, with glimpses of the Rio Grande River. After returning to the downtown area, the route turns right on Central Avenue, formerly historic Route 66, and continues east toward the University of New Mexico and Nob Hill. After finishing the southeastern loop, it's a return to downtown and the finish at 4th and Marquette at Civic Plaza, in front of City Hall.

CROWD / RUNNER SUPPORT Due to the large number of events on race morning, Duke City provides continuous action for spectators. Most spectators clamor about the start and finish areas near Civic Plaza. Another area of the course with high crowd concentration is Central Avenue. Additional cheering and refueling assistance comes from the 14 motivation stations along the route.

RACE LOGISTICS Duke City starts and finishes in the heart of downtown Albuquerque within walking distance from major hotels. Plenty of parking is available for those arriving by car on race morning. A booth is available for safekeeping of warm-up clothing.

ACTIVITIES The Family Fitness Expo happens Saturday from 9:00 a.m. to 6:00 p.m. at the Albuquerque Convention Center. Race packets must be picked up at the Expo unless previously received by mail for an additional fee. There is no race-day registration or packet pickup. An awards ceremony takes place at noon at Civic Plaza.

AWARDS Each entrant receives a T-shirt. Finishers receive pins. The top three overall and first masters runners receive special awards. Age-group awards extend three deep. All participants' places and times are published in a special section of the Albuquerque Tribune the day after the event.

ELITE RUNNERS INFORMATION The race offers free lodging and entry to elite runners. Elite status is determined by race organizers on an individual basis.

ACCOMMODATIONS The Merv Griffin DoubleTree Hotel, 201 Marquette Street NW (800-222-TREE), serves as the host hotel for the event and offers special marathon rates. Other nearby hotels include: Hyatt Regency Albuquerque, 330 Tijeras Avenue NW (505-842-1234); and La Posada de Albuquerque, 125 2nd Street NW (800-777-5732).

RELATED EVENTS / RACES There's no shortage of race options at Duke City. To kick things off, a 1K race for kids under 12 takes place the day before the marathon. In addition to the marathon, a half marathon is a popular event for many world-class runners training for the major fall marathons. The race, an out-and-back course on the second half of the marathon route, starts at 7:45 a.m. A 20K competitive walk, held on the half marathon course, begins at 8:10 a.m. For those favoring the shorter distances, a 5K run and separate 5K walk start at 7:00 a.m. and 7:50 a.m., respectively. In 1996, a 5-person marathon relay was added to the mix. The relay consists of four 5-mile and one 6.2-mile segments and starts jointly with the marathon. All routes are closed to vehicular traffic.

AREA ATTRACTIONS Adobe-laden Old Town, one of the more popular Albuquerque attractions, contains an assortment of shops, restaurants, Native American art galleries, and three museums. The Albuquerque Museum of Art and History displays New Mexican art and Albuquerque history, while the New Mexico Museum of Natural History presents a geologic and evolutionary history of New Mexico. The Rattlesnake Museum is home to the world's largest collection of these venomous reptiles. If you prefer to spend more of your time outdoors, head to the Petroglyph National Monument on Albuquerque's west side where you'll get a Native American history lesson, assuming you can read the over 17,000 petroglyphs carved into lava rock. If you're not worn out yet, hike to the 10,378-foot summit of Sandia Mountain. We suggest riding the Sandia Peak Aerial Tramway which affords spectacular views of Albuquerque and the Rio Grande.

LOCAL RUNNING STORES Fleet Feet Sports, 8238 Menaul Blvd. NE, Albuquerque (505-299-8922); Gil's Runners World, 3515 Lomas Blvd. NE, Albuquerque (505-268-6330).

Fox Cities Marathon

Overall: 88.8

Course Beauty: 8-

Course Difficulty: 4- (see appendix)

Appropriateness for First Timers: 10

Race Organization: 10

Crowds: 3+

RACE DATA

Contact:	Community First Fox Cities Marathon
	835 Valley Road
	Menasha, WI 54952
	(414) 954-6790
Date:	September 28, 1997 (tentative)
	September 27, 1998 (tentative)
Start Time:	10:00 a.m. (8:00 a.m. walkers)
Time Course Closes:	4:00 p.m.
Number of Participants:	1,500 in 1995
Certification:	USATF
Course Records:	Male: (open) 2:15:52
	Female: (open) 2:39:03
Elite Athlete Programs:	Yes
Cost:	$30/40
Age groups/Divisions:	<19, 20-24, 25-29, 30-34, 35-39, 40-44, 45-49, 50-54, 55-59, 60-65, 66+, Cruiserweight (men 200+, women 150+), Walkers
Temperature:	46° - 65°
Aid/Splits:	23 / every mile including pace, clocks every 5 miles

HIGHLIGHTS The upper Midwest hosts some heavyweight marathons in early fall, including the Chicago, Detroit, Twin Cities, and Lakefront Marathons. With these well-established races, you might think that a relative newcomer like Fox Cities, held in the paper communities in eastern Wisconsin, would get overlooked in the shuffle. But it doesn't, and it shouldn't. Not only a nice marathon for runners, Fox Cities serves as a community event for local residents of seven towns that dot the Fox River. Exceptionally well-organized, the race contains 23 aid stations and digital clocks every 5 miles as it crosses seven decorated bridges. Though Fox Cities is an urban marathon, the fall foliage radiates along the course. Among the number of excellent fall marathons in the Midwest, Fox Cities proves itself as one of the best.

RACE HISTORY Race founder Gloria West believed that a marathon provided the perfect vehicle to bring together the communities that share the Fox River near Lake Winnebago in the heart of Wisconsin's paper country. So, in 1990 she approached First Community Credit Union and convinced it to sponsor the event. One year later, the first Fox Cities Marathon welcomed 1,382 runners to eastern Wisconsin. The theme of the race was, and still is, "Seven Cities, Seven Bridges."

COURSE DESCRIPTION Starting in Neenah, WI, the Fox Cities Marathon meanders along the Fox River passing through seven communities along the way, and finishes in Appleton, WI. Brilliant fall colors punctuate the entire area. The point-to-point course is entirely paved and closed to traffic. The starting line is located in Neenah's beautiful, tree-filled Riverside

Park on the shores of Lake Winnebago. Mansions line the road opposite the park. Miles 1 through 4 wind through commercial and residential areas of Neenah and Menasha, with runners crossing two of the seven bridges in this stretch. As you pass through Jefferson Park (between miles 3 and 4), admire the view of Lake Winnebago to your right and the slight downhill. The next 5 miles (5 through 9) offer homes in a rural setting in Appleton and include the first hill along the course. Runners climb approximately 30 feet over a 2-mile span (4 to 6); many runners will not even notice the change. Miles 9 through 17 cut through more subdivisions and residential areas on a gradual decline of 80 feet. Here, runners traverse Combined Locks and Kaukauna and experience plenty of entertainment. Between miles 15 and 16, you cross bridge number 3, slightly climbing across the river. Mile 18 marks the beginning of the most difficult section of the course as you go past Little Chute and Kimberly, home of the "wall." Runners climb 50 feet in this section, with the Washington Street bridge at 19 a particularly tough spot for some. You have a chance to recover as you head back toward Appleton before another 50-foot incline between miles 22 and 23, highlighted by the fifth bridge of the course. After mile 23, it's mostly flat through commercial areas in Appleton. You cross the last two bridges, and finish after the Oneida Skyline Bridge. You can now rejoice at having conquered the river you have been tracing for 26.2 miles!

CROWD/RUNNER SUPPORT As a bona fide community event, Fox Cities attracts thousands of spectators, more or less depending on who the Packers play that day, to cheer the runners and walkers. No part of the course is left uncovered. Costumed characters provide a humorous lift for the runners. The race also organizes hoopla along the course, with themes for aid stations and bridges, each of which is dressed-up by local civic groups and businesses for the occasion. The 23 (!) water stations are well-stocked with water and electrolyte replacement. Medical vehicles travel the course prior to mile 13, and there are six medical aid stations after that point.

RACE LOGISTICS The race offers free shuttle buses to the start from official hotels in the area, and then back to the hotels from the finish area. Buses are also available to transport runners from the finish back to the start. The race also stores any belongings you may have at the start and transports them for retrieval at the finish area.

ACTIVITIES Fox Cities holds a two-day (Saturday and Sunday) Sports and Fitness Expo, where you can attend informational clinics on fitness, nutrition, and race details. You can also pick up your race packet at the expo on Saturday. Note that there are no race-day entries. On Saturday evening, the traditional pasta dinner at the Paper Valley Hotel in Appleton typically features a guest speaker of some repute. After the race, runners may opt for a well-deserved massage. The awards ceremony occurs on Sunday evening also at the Paper Valley Hotel. Race organizers provide refreshments and entertainment for recuperating runners.

AWARDS Every entrant receives a Fox Cities Marathon T-shirt, with finishers also earning medals. Age-group awards are given to the top three finishers in each division. The race offers approximately $50,000 in prize money.

ELITE RUNNERS INFORMATION Trying hard to recruit elite athletes, Fox Cities offers special packages for men under 2:20 and women under 2:39. Depending on your credentials, race officials could provide a combination of appearance money, travel expenses, accommodations, and free entry. And, of course, there is the quite generous $50,000 in prize money that is up for grabs. Prize money is allocated to the top ten open runners (male and female), with winners receiving $5,000, second $4,000, third $3,000, fourth $2,500, fifth $2,000, sixth $1,500, seventh $1,250, eighth $1,000, ninth $750, and tenth $500. Masters runners also earn prize money to third place, Wisconsin Division to third place, and Seniors, Cruiserweight and Wheelchair Division winners also receive some prize money.

ACCOMMODATIONS The race headquarters hotel is the Paper Valley Hotel in Appleton (414-733-8000). Rates range from about $79 to $89. If you prefer to stay near the start line, try the Valley Inn in Neenah (414-725-8441), about $62 to $72. The race provides a list of ten other hotels that also offer shuttle service to/from the start/finish, and discounts to runners.

RELATED EVENTS/RACES Fox Cities is more than just a marathon. On Saturday, there is a popular 1% Kids Marathon for children ages 14 and under. The actual distance varies depending on the age of the child. Kids receive their own race number, T-shirt, and goody bag. The 1% Marathon is held in Jones Park, Appleton, behind the Paper Valley Hotel. Then, on Sunday at 11:00 a.m., the 10% Marathon kicks off from the Paper Valley Hotel. The race covers the final 2.62 miles of the marathon course, finishes at the Oneida Skyline Bridge, and is a great way for friends and family members to share your day. Runners receive finisher's T-shirts and medals. Finally, the race offers a unique Marathon Relay for two to five-member teams. There are five exchange points at approximately the 5, 10, 15, and 20-mile points. Teams can decide which exchange points to utilize, depending on their number of runners. Race officials provide free transportation to/from relay exchange points. Relay team divisions are: open, corporate, credit union, and pulp and paper.

AREA ATTRACTIONS While you're in the Fox Cities area, visit a cheese factory, stroll Huidini's haunts, or take a city tour offered to the runners.

LOCAL RUNNING STORE Athletics North, Fox River Mall, 4301 W. Wisconsin Avenue, Appleton (414-738-0750).

NEW HAMPSHIRE MARATHON

OVERALL: 85.4

COURSE BEAUTY: 9+

COURSE DIFFICULTY: 6 (SEE APPENDIX)

APPROPRIATENESS FOR FIRST TIMERS: 6

RACE ORGANIZATION: 8

CROWDS: 0

RACE DATA

Contact:	Executive Director
	Newfound Region Chamber of Commerce
	P.O. Box 454
	Bristol, NH 03222
	(603) 744-2150
Date:	October 4, 1997
	October 3, 1998
Start Time:	10:00 a.m.
Time Course Closes:	3:00 p.m.
Number of Participants:	175 in 1995
Certification:	USATF
Course Records:	New Course
Elite Athlete Programs:	No
Cost:	$20
Age groups/Divisions:	<39, 40+
Temperature:	50° - 65°
Aid/Splits:	14 / none

HIGHLIGHTS The deep golden ponds and lakes sparkling throughout central New Hampshire lured Hollywood to the region to shoot the famous movie with Kathryn Hepburn and Henry Fonda. One of the purest and deepest of them all, Newfound Lake, serves as the centerpiece of the New Hampshire Marathon, with about 16 rolling miles set around the lake. The fiery leaves at water's edge make for inspiring beauty, and you will welcome every morsel of motivation to get through the difficult course.

COURSE DESCRIPTION The New Hampshire Marathon's course wraps around Newfound Lake in a modified out-and-back configuration that traces the lake's eastern shore out and its western shore back. The race, run in the shoulder of country roads, starts near central Bristol, NH on Lake Street (Route 3A) immediately in front of Newfound Memorial Middle School. Runners go north on Route 3A through a brief commercial area, climbing from .3 miles to mile 2. After running along the river, you reach Newfound Lake at 2.5 miles, where you climb to mile 2.8 and then have a gentle descent to 3.4. From the start to mile 4, the course gains about 250 feet. The course undulates to the 8-mile mark, with a tough 100-foot rise from 8 to 8.6. Turning left on North Shore Road at 8.5 miles, the route continues on this road until the turnaround at Sculptured Rocks (14 miles). A sharp downhill lies from 8.9 to 9.3; enjoy it because another stiff ascent awaits from 9.6 to mile 10, followed by a corresponding downhill. The course flattens or gently rolls through the town of Hebron before turning uphill from 12.8 to 13.8. A brief downgrade leads to the turnaround, with runners coming back the same way until West Shore Road at 16.8.

Back along the lake, West Shore Road contains a good hill from 17.5 to 17.8, then mostly rolls with a few nice downhills thrown in. The area offers some great views of Newfound Lake. By the time the race returns to Route 3A just after mile 24, it is mostly a gentle downgrade to the finish through Bristol in Kelley Park.

CROWD/RUNNER SUPPORT The 14 aid stations inject some enthusiasm into runners in the sparsely populated Bristol area. Some spectators do scatter along the course, particularly in Hebron village, with its quaint village green and gazebo, and at the Inn on Newfound Lake (mile 6), where people gather on the porch to watch the race and enjoy the view. Every mile is marked, so those of you with watches can catch your split times.

RACE LOGISTICS Most runners will need to drive to the start, but plenty of parking exists at Newfound Memorial Middle School, opposite the race start. Additional parking is located at the elementary school a block to the east on School Street.

ACTIVITIES On Friday evening, the Masonic Hall hosts a pasta dinner ($5) from 5:00 p.m. to 7:30 p.m. Pick up your race package on marathon morning at Newfound Memorial Middle School. You may register on race morning, but if you want a T-shirt it will cost you extra (about $5) to cover shipping costs. After you run, enjoy a free massage, shower, refreshments, and bluegrass concert.

AWARDS Every early-registered entrant receives a New Hampshire Marathon T-shirt, and finishers sport medals. Approximately $2,500 in prize money is awarded to the top five open and masters finishers, with overall winners receiving $500.

ACCOMMODATIONS The race does not have an official host hotel. Most of the lodging in the area consists of small motels or private cottages. Among those in the vicinity are: Bungalo Village Cottages and Motel, West Shore Drive, Bristol (603-744-2220); Cliff Lodge, HC 60, Bristol (603-744-8660); Lakeside Cottages, 68 Lake Street, Bristol (603-744-3075); Pleasant View B&B, Hemphill Road, Bristol (603-744-5547); The Inn on Newfound Lake, 1030 Mayhew Turnpike, Bridgewater (603-744-9111); Whip-O-Will Motel, 1755 Mayhew Turnpike, Bridgewater (603-744-2433); and Whittemore Inn, 367 Mayhew Turnpike, Bridgewater (603-744-3518). For rentals try Century 21 Country Lakes Realty, 130 Lake Street, Bristol (800-342-9767); or Greenan Realty (603-744-8144).

RELATED EVENTS/RACES The New Hampshire 10K Road Race starts with the marathon and runs on an out-and-back route over the first 5K of the marathon course. Winners receive $150 in prize money. The race also holds an informal, noncompetitive 10K Fun and Health Walk at 10:15 a.m. to benefit the Camp Mayhew Program for at-risk boys and the D.A.R.E. program.

AREA ATTRACTIONS You come to New Hampshire this time of year to relax (after the marathon) and enjoy the change of seasons. Those with some energy reserves can find plenty of hiking and canoeing.

LOCAL RUNNING STORE Joe King Shoe Shop, 18 Pleasant Street, Concord (603-225-6012).

ST. GEORGE MARATHON

OVERALL: 92.1

COURSE BEAUTY: 9-

COURSE DIFFICULTY: 5- (SEE APPENDIX)

APPROPRIATENESS FOR FIRST TIMERS: 7

RACE ORGANIZATION: 10-

CROWDS: 2

RACE DATA

Contact:	Kent E. Perkins
	St. George Marathon, Leisure Services
	86 South Main Street
	St. George, UT 84770
	(801) 634-5850
Date:	October 4, 1997
	October 3, 1998
Start:	6:45 a.m.
Close Time:	12:45 p.m.
Number of Participants:	3,908 in 1995
Certification:	USATF
Course Records:	Male: (open) 2:15:16; (masters) 2:22:52
	Female: (open & masters) 2:37:13
Elite Athlete Programs:	Yes
Cost:	$24
Age groups/Divisions:	Male: <12, 13-14, 15-18, 19-24, 25-29, 30-34, 35-39, 40-44, 45-49, 50-54, 55-59, 60-64, 65-69, 70-74, 75+, Heavyweight (200+); Female: <18, 19-24, 25-29, 30-34, 35-39, 40-44, 45-49, 50-54, 55-59, 60-64, 65-69, 70+, Heavyweight (140+)
Temperature:	37° - 80°
Aid/Splits:	13 / every 2 miles

HIGHLIGHTS St. George has garnered quite a reputation recently as the fastest marathon in the United States (to its credit, St. George never billed itself as such). Whoever said that probably has not run the course. For the vast majority of runners, St. George is not the fastest marathon in the country, probably not even in the top 20. A couple of long, taxing uphills and sharp, quad-killing downhills see to that. But that shouldn't detract from what it is — a distinctively beautiful, well-organized, fun community event within an easy drive of some of the country's top destinations (see AREA ATTRACTIONS). The race provides unique touches that runners love, such as bonfires at the start for warmth. Race organizers go all out to accommodate everyone's needs, as many runners can attest. Sunrise over the barren mountains, the brilliant red rock formations of Snow Canyon, and several ancient volcanos make the scene spectacular in places. All of these combine to place the St. George Marathon at the top of many runners' lists.

Andre Tocco of San Pedro, California says, *"I have been going to this race for the past 14 years, and I have seen it grow .... But every year the quality of the race was never affected."*

COURSE DESCRIPTION The St. George Marathon runs point-to-point on Highway 18 from Pine Valley Road near Central, UT, to Worthen Park in St. George. Entirely closed to traffic with excellent asphalt, the course begins at an elevation of 5,240 feet and ends at 2,680 feet, an elevation loss of 2,560 feet. This impressive figure excites everyone about the speed of the race. However, the course contains two significant hills at miles 7 and 21.5, slowing down most runners.

The first small rise on the course occurs at .7 miles, then it levels out for a half mile. Runners hit a noticeable .33-mile hill, then it's mostly flat or gently downhill (except 3.2 to 3.7) to mile 5.6. You descend quickly into the town of Veyo at the 7-mile mark. Upon leaving Veyo, a challenging 1-mile climb (about 500 feet) awaits you, making you doubt talk of fast, downhill courses. The hill crests near 8 miles. You then have some time to recover on flat to slightly downhill roads to mile 9, where the road inclines gradually with some intermittent bumps to 12.3. The next essentially flat 2 miles become a sharp downhill from 13.7 to 15.4. Hope you did your downhill training! At 14.4, you negotiate a right curve and come face to face with interesting rock formations. The course flattens out from mile 15.4 to 16.7 and then declines just perceptively to 18.2. Another hill looms between 18.2 and 18.6, and then it's mostly downhill with a few bumps from 18.6 to 21.5. Just before the 20-mile mark, notice the beautiful rock formations to your right. Yet another strenuous, steep climb must be conquered between 21.5 and 22.1. Your legs are then hit immediately with a sharp downhill for .25 miles that eases slightly for the rest of the way to St. George at 23.4. Here, Highway 18 becomes Bluff Street, the main drag in St. George. Enjoy the sound of the crowds as you check out the impressive red rock bluffs overlooking the town. Bluff Street provides a nice, easy slope for a downhill finish. Before mile 25 you can see the white tip of the Mormon Temple against the red rock backdrop. At mile 25, you make a sharp left onto 300 South Street straight into Worthen Park for the finish.

CROWD/RUNNER SUPPORT The marathon is the community event in St. George. Over 1,400 volunteers cater to the runners, while the locals turn out in droves in downtown St. George. Due to limited access, relatively few spectators perch along Highway 18. The two exceptions are at Veyo, where a large and supportive crowd turns out, and at Snow Canyon (mile 15). Aid stations stock water, electrolyte replacement, petroleum jelly, sponges, and first aid supplies, and nurses are available for medical aid. Approximately 80 portable toilets dot the course.

RACE LOGISTICS All runners must take the buses from Worthen Park to the start, unless camping in the Pine Valley area. Buses begin departing at 4:30 a.m. with the last bus leaving around 5:40 a.m. The race must bus 4,000 runners to the start, so arrive early. And remember, if you are staying in Nevada, St. George's clocks are one hour ahead. The bus ride provides an excellent opportunity to get an idea of what you're in for since it drives the course in reverse, although you can only see so much in the dark. Of course, the race transports your personal belongings from the start to the finish.

ACTIVITIES St. George sponsors a race expo on Friday, from 9:00 a.m. to 9:00 p.m. at the Smith's Auditorium, Dixie Convention Center. A pasta feed with entertainment and all-you-can-eat food and drink is also at the Convention Center ($6). The race hosts a number of running clinics, including "Marathon 101" offering advice on how to run the St. George course. Runners keep warm by bonfires near the start in the morning chill and darkness. St. George hosts an excellent post-race party in Worthen Park. Good food, fresh fruit, drinks and entertainment preface the awards ceremony. Runners can relax with a complimentary 15-minute massage after the race before viewing the results at the Recreation Center.

AWARDS All entrants receive T-shirts and race posters. Finishers earn special medallions to commemorate their achievement. Age-group awards go up to ten deep. Overall winners typically receive an all-expenses paid trip to run in the Ibigawa Marathon in Japan. A Special Achievement Award recognizes a particularly exceptional effort. After completing 10 St. George marathons, you are eligible for the Ten-Year Club. Club members are entitled to special T-shirts, photos, discounts on entry fees, and a post-marathon party.

FIRST-TIMERS INFORMATION St. George offers a couple of challenges for the first-timer — a demanding course (see Course Description) at moderate altitude and few spectators over the first 25 miles (except for miles 7 and 15). These factors are tempered by a supportive race organization with excellent aid stations, a scenic course, a sizeable field of runners, and usually good weather conditions. Prepare yourself for the course by doing plenty of hill training (both up and down). In one of St. George's many distinctive touches, first-timers are given special T-shirts, products and prizes.

ELITE RUNNERS INFORMATION St. George provides limited assistance to elite runners, possibly including entry, transportation, lodging, and/or expenses. Funds are limited, so contact Kent Perkins for more information on obtaining elite status.

ACCOMMODATIONS For accommodations in St. George, call (800-259-3343). Entry forms also have a complete listing of lodging in Washington County. For dorm lodging, try the Dixie College Elderhostel (801-673-3704). Hotels in St. George fill extremely early, so many runners stay in Nevada, a 45-minute drive from St. George (remember the time difference). You shouldn't have much trouble obtaining a reservation there.

RELATED EVENTS/RACES A 2-mile Mayor's Walk from Bluff Street Park to the marathon finish line begins at 7:00 a.m. Walkers receive T-shirts, walker numbers, and post-walk refreshments, and are eligible for random drawings. The walk draws over 1,200 participants.

AREA ATTRACTIONS St. George sits within a modest drive of two completely dichotomous attractions — Zion National Park and Las Vegas. Definitely worth the short trip from St. George, Zion offers some spectacular hiking, camping, and just plain sightseeing. If you have an extra couple of days, you can also visit Bryce Canyon National Park, which lies just beyond Zion. If you feel like a little more city action, Las Vegas lies just 2 hours away. Make the drive during the daylight, if you can, to admire the stunning gorge just outside of St. George on Interstate 15. The incredible bluffs envelope you in their majesty. Unforgettable!

LOCAL RUNNING STORES The Locker Room, 514 N. Bluff, St. George (801-628-4221); Elite Feet, 435 N. 1680 E. #6, St. George (801-652-9449).

MAINE MARATHON

OVERALL: 82.9

COURSE BEAUTY: 9-

COURSE DIFFICULTY: 6-

APPROPRIATENESS FOR FIRST TIMERS: 7-

RACE ORGANIZATION: 9-

CROWDS: 1

RACE DATA

Contact:	Jim McCorkle
	NYLCare Maine Marathon
	P.O. Box 8654
	Portland, ME 04104
	(207) 781-5887
Date:	October 5, 1997
	October 4, 1998
Start Time:	8:00 a.m.
Time Course Closes:	1:00 p.m.
Number of Participants:	600 in 1995
Certification:	USATF
Course Records:	Male: (open) 2:35:00; (masters) 2:41:01
	Female: (open) 2:51:44; (masters) 3:14:02
Elite Athlete Programs:	No
Cost:	$30/35
Age groups/Divisions:	<19, 20-29, 30-34, 35-39, 40-44, 45-49, 50-54, 55-59, 60-64, 65+
Temperature:	53°
Aid/Splits:	12 / display clocks at miles 5, 10, 13.1 & 20

HIGHLIGHTS The home of marathon great Joan Benoit Samuelson and boasting a beautiful craggy coast, Maine hosts one of the most easterly marathons in the United States — the Maine Marathon. The Atlantic Ocean, rural communities, and urban Portland, punctuated with fall's changing colors, dominate the scenery along the loop course. Although the route never exceeds an elevation of 180 feet, its rolling hills make it challenging for most runners. Race weekend starts with the Martin's Point Kick-Off Festival featuring live music, family-oriented entertainment, food, and a sports expo, all overlooking pretty Casco Bay.

COURSE DESCRIPTION The Maine Marathon begins adjacent to the University of Southern Maine (USM), running along flat, scenic Back Cove for 2 miles with downtown's skyline rising to your right. After traversing an on-ramp to Route 1, the course continues flat with Casco Bay to the right. Exiting Route 1 after mile 4, runners head down less busy Route 88 (miles 4 through 13). Here, the course begins to roll gently, passing through rural woodsy residential areas most of the way, with particularly beautiful homes near mile 9. A good hill awaits from mile 8.5 to mile 9.1, followed by a steep descent from 9.3 to 9.6. Two more uphills lie on this stretch from 10.5 to 11.1 and from 12.5 to 12.7. Runners enter the town of Yarmouth traversing mostly flat North Road and Leighton Road, where the street and the scenery deteriorate slightly. The course turns rolling again on West Elm Street as it goes through a middle-class neighborhood. At mile 17, the course briefly bisects an industrial area, and then returns to rolling through rural communities. Mile 18 to 18.7 is largely uphill, while miles 18.7 to 19.8 mostly undulate. Flat to mile 21.5, the course crosses a beautiful waterscape with a wonderful bridge back to the right and then contains a few short rollers. Runners face a challenging climb from mile 22.8 to 23.2, past modern homes, and then have mostly level running through Payson Park, along Back Cove, and to the finish.

CROWD/RUNNER SUPPORT The small crowds mostly gather at the start/finish line, and residents come out of their homes at scattered parts of the course to support the runners. Otherwise, the best encouragement comes from the aid station volunteers placed approximately every 2 miles.

RACE LOGISTICS You will need to drive to the start; parking is available at the USM on Bedford Street. The race provides a bag check service so you can leave your sweats at the start without having to return to your car.

ACTIVITIES Race weekend gets underway on Saturday with the Martin's Point Kick-Off Festival (see HIGHLIGHTS above) from 10:00 a.m. to 4:30 p.m. If you need to register on Saturday, go to Martin's Point Health Care, 331 Veranda Street, between noon and 7:00 p.m. You get a T-shirt until they run out. You may register or pick up your packet on race morning in the USM Gym on Falmouth Street. Race-day registrants will probably not get a T-shirt, however. Organizers are working to develop a street fair to coincide with the race finish starting in 1997. At the very least, enjoy refreshments and a massage after the race.

AWARDS All preregistered runners receive Maine Marathon T-shirts. The top three finishers in each age group and the top five overall runners receive awards. Note that the race may offer prize money and/or a course record bonus beginning in 1997. Contact the race director for more information.

ACCOMMODATIONS While there is no official race hotel, several in the area may offer a special rate to Maine Marathon runners: The Ramada Inn (207-774-5611); The Inn at Portland (207-775-3711); and Comfort Inn (207-775-0409).

RELATED EVENTS/RACES On Saturday prior to the marathon, the Lifeline 5K and Kids 1K and 1 Mile Fun Run are held near USM. The Casco Bay Half Marathon (about 750 entrants) starts with the marathon on Sunday. The women's course record holder is, of course, Joan Benoit Samuelson. A four-person marathon relay (with legs of 6.5, 6.5, 6, and 7.2 miles) runs with the full marathon.

AREA ATTRACTIONS Literature lovers may consider the Wadsworth-Longfellow House, 487 Congress Street. At the other end of the spectrum, the Portland Pirates hockey team plays at the Civic Center. For a gorgeous getaway, cruise to one of the many offshore islands, or drive south to Kennebunkport. The shopping outlets in Freeport lie an hours drive north.

LOCAL RUNNING STORE 5K Sports, 190 U.S. Route 1, Falmouth (207-781-3134).

SACRAMENTO MARATHON

OVERALL: 76.1

COURSE BEAUTY: 8

COURSE DIFFICULTY: 3

APPROPRIATENESS FOR FIRST TIMERS: 6+

RACE ORGANIZATION: 8-

CROWDS: 1-

RACE DATA

Contact:	Sacramento Marathon
	P.O. Box 995
	Dixon, CA 95620
	(916) 678-5005
Date:	October 5, 1997
	October 4, 1998
Start Time:	7:30 a.m.
Time Course Closes:	NA
Number of Participants:	350 in 1995
Certification:	USATF
Course Records:	Male: (open) 2:28:30; (masters) 2:36:57
	Female: (open) 3:00:28; (masters) 3:00:41
Elite Athlete Programs:	No
Cost:	$25/35
Age groups/Divisions:	13-15, 16-18, 19-24, 25-29, 30-34, 35-39, 40-44,
	45-49, 50-54, 55-59, 60-64, 65-69, 70+
Temperature:	60° - 80°
Aid/Splits:	10 / every mile

HIGHLIGHTS The Sacramento Marathon has an admittedly sentimental appeal for us. It was at this race in 1977 where a short, scrawny thirteen-year-old boy named Rich Hanna ran his first marathon in 3:01:14 on a bacon and eggs breakfast. Perhaps this wisp of nostalgia compelled us to place the Sacramento Marathon among the Top 100 races. After all, most locals now run the Sacramento Half Marathon as a tune up for the larger, more prestigious California International Marathon in December. However, the Sacramento Marathon still has plenty to commend — a pleasant course, flat terrain (no elevation change greater than 25 feet), and a decidedly relaxed atmosphere.

COURSE DESCRIPTION Essentially a double out-and-back route, the Sacramento Marathon starts in shady William Land Park — home to the Sacramento Zoo and Fairytale Town for children — running through its grassy landscapes for the first 1.75 miles. The course then winds through nice area neighborhoods to mile 4.5, turning slightly industrial for a short period. Hitting the edge of riverside Miller Park after mile 5, runners head along the Sacramento River toward Old Sacramento, a restored, riverfront Old West district of shops, saloons, museums, cobblestones, and restaurants. After mile 6, runners veer right for a quick down and up preceding the loop turnaround on the cusp of Old Sacramento. Runners now retrace their way back to William Land Park, where full marathoners double back for the second time.

CROWD / RUNNER SUPPORT The double out-and-back course makes it a good race for spectators. You find most onlookers in the neighborhoods outside William Land Park. On warm days, area residents turn on sprinklers for runners to dash through. Participants find portable toilets and 10 aid stations with water and electrolyte replacement drink along the route.

RACE LOGISTICS Runners staying at the host hotel may take advantage of the shuttle service from the hotel to the race start. Others will need to drive to the race. Plenty of parking is available at Sacramento City College across the street from the starting line.

ACTIVITIES A packet pickup and mini expo is held at the race headquarters hotel all day on Saturday. Out-of-towners only may pick up their numbers on race morning near the start. After the marathon, take advantage of the free massage; showers are available at Sacramento City College across the street. Then enjoy lots of refreshments, live music, and a picnic in the park. The awards ceremony and a drawing take place at 11:30 a.m.

AWARDS Every runner receives a long-sleeve T-shirt or a cap, and marathon finishers earn medals. The top three division winners and the first runner overall are awarded special prizes.

ACCOMMODATIONS The Best Western Harbor Inn & Suites, 1250 Halyard Drive in West Sacramento (800-371-2101), serves as the official race hotel. Other possibilities nearby in Sacramento include: Best Western Sandman Motel, 236 Jibboom Street (916-443-6515); Days Inn Discovery Park, 350 Bercut Drive (916-442-6971); La Quinta Inn, 200 Jibboom Street (916-448-8100); Motel 6, 227 Jibboom Street (916-441-0733); and Holiday Inn, 300 J Street in downtown (916-446-0100).

RELATED EVENTS / RACES The Sacramento Half Marathon attracts the largest contingent of runners — approximately 1,000. The half consists of a single out-and-back on the marathon course. Others may opt for the 5K Fun Run.

AREA ATTRACTIONS See California International Marathon entry for things to do in Sacramento. A popular fall ritual for area residents is a visit to Apple Hill, about an hour drive on Highway 50 east of Sacramento. With the apple harvest in full swing, wander from orchard to orchard sampling just about every conceivable apple concoction.

LOCAL RUNNING STORES Fleet Feet Sports, 2311 J Street (916-442-3338), 513 2nd Street, Davis (916-758-6453), 8128 Madison Avenue, Fair Oaks (916-965-8326), 1730 Santa Clara Drive, Roseville (916-783-4558), or 2222 Francisco Drive, El Dorado Hills (916-939-1967).

TWIN CITIES MARATHON

OVERALL: 99.5

COURSE BEAUTY: 10

COURSE DIFFICULTY: 3- (SEE APPENDIX)

APPROPRIATENESS FOR FIRST TIMERS: 10

RACE ORGANIZATION: 10

CROWDS: 4+

RACE DATA

Contact:	Twin Cities Marathon
	708 North First Street, Ste. CR-33
	Minneapolis, MN 55401
	(612) 673-0778
	e-mail: scott26pt2@aol.com
	http://www.doitsports.com/marathons/twincities
Date:	October 5, 1997
	October 4, 1998
Start Time:	8:00 a.m.
Time Course Closes:	2:00 p.m.
Number of Participants:	6,962 in 1995
Certification:	USATF
Course Records:	Male: (open) 2:10:05; (masters) 2:15:15 (U.S. Masters Record)
	Female: (open) 2:27:59; (masters) 2:35:08 (U.S. Masters Record)
Elite Athlete Programs:	Yes
Cost:	$30/35/45
Age groups/Divisions:	<19, 20-24, 25-29, 30-34, 35-39, 40-44, 45-49, 50-54, 55-59, 60-64, 65-69, 70+
Temperature:	43° - 64°
Aid/Splits:	12 / digital clocks at miles 1, 2, 3, 4, 10, 13.1, 15, 20 & 25

HIGHLIGHTS "Beautiful" and "urban" are two words that cannot often be used together to describe marathons. When applied to the Twin Cities Marathon (TCM), however, beautiful and urban are as harmonious as Minneapolis and St. Paul — they have blended into a single, inseparable phrase. More than just another pretty race, TCM is one of the three finest marathons in the country. Gorgeous, fast, flawless, and loud, over 200,000 spectators surround the route. Toss in all of the amenities of the Twin Cities area and you have an irresistible destination marathon. Few races should be on every marathoners' must-run list; TCM is one.

RACE HISTORY The Minnesota Distance Running Association created the Land of Lakes Marathon, Twin Cities' antecedent, in 1963. The first race had a rather modest three finishers. Over the next several years Land of Lakes was held at various locations in the Twin Cities. In 1976, the race was recast as the City of Lakes Marathon and moved to a four-lap course around Lakes Calhoun and Harriet. It had 178 finishers. Then came the running boom. In 1981, City of Lakes reached its 1,700 runner limit in only one month. That same year, St. Paul held its own marathon, the St. Paul Marathon, which attracted nearly 2,000 runners. Organizers soon realized that a race which spanned the two cities straddling the Mississippi River would be a much greater attraction than two separate events. In 1982, the modern Twin Cities Marathon was born, drawing more than 4,500 entrants — a then-record for a first-time marathon. Since then, Twin Cities has blossomed into one of America's premiere races. It has been the site of numerous national marathon championships, and is the site of the U.S. Masters Marathon Championship from 1996 to 2000. More U.S. records have been set on its course than any other marathon.

COURSE DESCRIPTION The bulk of TCM traces parkways in bursting autumn brilliance, passing four lakes, a creek, and the Mississippi River on its trek from Minneapolis to St. Paul. The course is nothing short of spectacular. The race is run entirely on asphalt and is completely closed to vehicle traffic. TCM starts at the Hubert H. Humphrey Metrodome, home of the Minnesota Twins (MLB) and Vikings (NFL). The first 1.5 miles course through downtown Minneapolis, where you encounter the world renown Guthrie Theater and the Walker Art Center and Sculpture Garden. You complete one of the route's biggest inclines, an 80-foot climb in a half mile, as you reach the first aid station at 2.5 miles. Then it's slightly downhill until just past mile 3, where you come to the first lake on the course: Lake of the Isles, site of some of the finest homes in the Twin Cities. It's also the first step on the cities' parkway system, where you will run the next 19 miles of the race. After leaving Lake of the Isles behind, you soon reach Lake Calhoun (miles 4 to 6). The sun's reflection off the lake creates an inspirational setting. Shortly after the 6-mile point, a quick 20-foot climb brings you to Lake Harriet, where you pass the Rose Garden, a popular area for spectators and the media. As you depart Lake Harriet at 7.5 miles, you may feel a bit envious knowing that the three lakes are the most popular training sites for area runners. But try to remember that they have to endure the local winters. See, it all works out in the end!

With a smile on your face, the course turns east, starting a 4.5-mile stretch on Minnehaha Parkway, a tree-lined boulevard along beautiful Minnehaha Creek. This gently rolling piece (including a good 40-foot drop) leads to lake number four on the course: Lake Nokomis. After circling Nokomis, you pass the 13.1-mile mark — you're half way home! Then it's back to Minnehaha Parkway for the next two miles before turning north to run along the Mississippi River (miles 15 to 19).

Crossing the Mississippi at mile 19, runners may be tempted to stop to view the bank of trees in full fall colors along the Mississippi. You then head south for two miles on the river road to begin the toughest part of the course — an incline of 130 feet over a two-mile stretch up Summit Avenue and its stately mansions (miles 21 to 23). You may see the governor as you puff past his mansion; he's usually out there watching the race. It's mostly downhill from this point to the finish, with a small rise at mile 25.

Seeing St. Paul Cathedral means you've done it. As you turn the corner at mile 26, the finish line, with the state capitol as a backdrop, is an awesome and welcomed sight. Bask in the glory the last two tenths of a mile as some of the 200,000 spectators cheer your arrival.

CROWD/RUNNER SUPPORT Over 200,000 Twin City residents come out to cheer on the runners, quite a large turnout for communities of this size. TCM is not big on hoopla, the loud and crazy entertainment that lines so many courses these days. But it is big on volunteers, with more than 4,000 people helping out along the way. Twelve aid stations speckle the course at miles 2.5, 5, and every two miles thereafter, carrying water, electrolyte replacement, portable toilets, and medical aid. In addition, first aid is available at every mile marker. Medical personnel will be wearing red shirts, and communications personnel (should you need a ride to the finish) will be decked in yellow shirts. Digital clocks which show the elapsed time are located at miles 1, 2, 3, 4, 10, 13.1, 15, 20, and 25.

RACE LOGISTICS Race organizers provide shuttle bus service to the starting line from official race hotels, and then from the finish area back to the hotels. Transportation is also available from the finish to the start following the race. The race transports your belongings from the start to the finish area.

ACTIVITIES TCM sponsors the large, two-day (Friday and Saturday) Marketplace and Fitness Fair at the headquarters hotel that attracts 20,000 people. The fair has more than 75 exhibitor booths with great deals on running gear, hands-on exhibits, free health screenings, and hourly drawings for free merchandise and services. You must pick up your race packet at the fair as there is no race number pickup on race day. On Saturday, attend seminars on a variety of running topics presented by Running Times magazine. On Saturday evening, devour all the pasta you can at the carbo-load party (about $10). The post-race party and awards ceremony begin at 11:30 a.m. near the finish line in the National Guard Armory on Cedar Street. Preliminary results are posted in the Armory.

AWARDS Every entrant receives a TCM Results Book. Finishers also receive T-shirts, medallions, and official results cards. TCM offers approximately $155,000 in prize money to at least 22 division winners. Division winners also receive merchandise awards. Masters runners make out particularly well at TCM. The first three finishers in each five-year age group, starting at age 40, receive prize money — $250 for first, $100 for second, and $50 for third — a nice, and rare, little bonus for many masters runners.

FIRST-TIMERS INFORMATION Twin Cities is one of the best marathons in the country for first-timers (our only nit-pick is there could be more than 12 aid stations), with about 2,000 in the race each year. All of the conditions are optimal for a positive experience: usually cool weather, abundant company, gentle course, supportive crowds, exceptional scenery, and top-flight organization.

ELITE RUNNERS INFORMATION TCM extends several benefits to elite runners (men under 2:20, women under 2:40), including hotel, transportation, expenses, free entry, and generous prize money. Priority is given to previous TCM participants. Open division prize money is offered to tenth place, with overall winners earning $20,000, then $12,000 for second, $7,000 for third, $5,000 for fourth, $4,000 for fifth, $3,000 for sixth, $2,000 for seventh, $1,500 for eighth, $1,000 for ninth, and $500 for tenth. The top five masters runners receive prize money from TCM ($5,000; $3,000; $2,000; $1,000; $500), and the top three masters also win prize money as part of the USATF American Masters Championship ($2,000; $1,000; $750). Contact David Coyne, Vice President — Runner Recruiting (612-698-5467), for more information.

ACCOMMODATIONS The headquarters hotel for the 1997 race is the Radisson St. Paul, 11 E. Kellogg Blvd. (800-333-3333). For the 1998 race, the Minneapolis Hyatt Regency, 1300 Nicollet Mall (800-233-1234), serves as the headquarters hotel. Both offer special rates to marathon runners, but you must book extremely early. Several other hotels in St. Paul give runners special rates, including the Days Inn Civic Center, 177 W. Seventh Street (800-325-2525); The Saint Paul Hotel, 350 Market Street (800-292-9292); Crown Sterling Suites, 175 E. Tenth Street (800-433-4600); and the Radisson Inn, 411 Minnesota Street (800-333-3333). If you prefer to stay near the start in Minneapolis, the following offer special rates: Regal Minneapolis Hotel, 1313 Nicollet Mall (800-522-8856); Luxeford Suites Hotel, 1101 LaSalle Avenue (800-662-3232); The Marquette, 710 Marquette Avenue (800-328-4782); Holiday Inn Metrodome, 1500 Washington Avenue S. (800-448-3663); and Sheraton Minneapolis, 1300 Industrial Blvd. (800-777-3277).

RELATED EVENTS/RACES On Saturday, the day before the marathon, organizers hold a 5K Race/Walk, Kids' Half-Mile Fun Run, and Toddlers' Trot. The 1997 events will be held at Harriet Island in St. Paul, while the 1998 version will be at Lake Nokomis in Minneapolis. Every participant receives a T-shirt and post-race refreshments. In addition, every child who enters receives a "Number 1" bib and ribbon. You may register at the Fitness Fair, or on race day.

AREA ATTRACTIONS If you need more sports while in the Twin Cities, attend a Minnesota Vikings game. It is possible that the Twins will still be playing, if they make the playoffs. On the cultural side, see the Guthrie Theater, Walker Art Center, Minnesota Orchestra, St. Paul Chamber Orchestra, or the St. Paul Science Museum. Or, if you need to shop, check out the country's largest shopping center, The Mall of America, about 20 minutes from either city.

LOCAL RUNNING STORES Forget your shoes? Check out the following: Marathon Sports, 2304 W. 50th Street, Minneapolis (612-920-2606); Gear, 4510 Excelsior Blvd., St. Louis Park (612-926-2645); Run 'n Fun, 868 Randolph, St. Paul (612-290-2747); Runner's Edge, 794 Grand, St. Paul (612-224-1971).

It's the annual running of the most scenic 26.2 urban miles in the country

It's more than 6,000 runners coursing along 26.2 miles of winding parkways, stunning foliage, blue lakes, and the majestic Mississippi River. It's a weekend packed with events, including a health and fitness expo, a 5K race, and a Kids' Half-Mile Fun Run. It's the lightning-fast course for the USA Track & Field Masters' Championship. It's over 200,000 colorful fans and 4,000 volunteers.

It's the Annual Twin Cities Marathon.

Minneapolis–St. Paul, Sunday, October 5, 1997, 8:00 A.M.

Minneapolis–St. Paul, Sunday, October 4, 1998, 8:00 A.M.

The Most Beautiful Urban Marathon in America®

For more information, contact TCM, 708 N. 1st Street, Minneapolis, MN 55401 (612) 673-0778.

http://www.doitsports.com/marathons/twincities

WINEGLASS MARATHON

OVERALL: 87

COURSE BEAUTY: 9+

COURSE DIFFICULTY: 3+ (SEE APPENDIX)

APPROPRIATENESS FOR FIRST TIMERS: 8+

RACE ORGANIZATION: 9

CROWDS: 1

RACE DATA

Contact:	Mark E. Landin
	Wineglass Marathon
	P.O. Box 117
	Corning, NY 14830-0900
	(607) 974-4668
Date:	October 5, 1997
	October 4, 1998
Start Time:	9:00 a.m.
Time Course Closes:	3:00 p.m.
Number of Participants:	800 in 1995
Certification:	USATF
Course Records:	Male: (open) 2:27:33; (masters) 2:47:03
	Female: (open) 2:59:16; (masters) 3:31:13
Elite Athlete Programs:	Yes
Cost:	$25/35/50
Age groups/Divisions:	14-24, 25-29, 30-34, 35-39, 40-44, 45-49, 50-59, 60+
Temperature:	40° - 60°
Aid/Splits:	14 / miles 1 & 13.1

HIGHLIGHTS New York's Finger Lakes clasp the Wineglass Marathon like a goblet of fine Cabernet as fall's burnt red and orange hues sprinkle the surrounding hills. The region, famous for its incredible gorges, tasty wine, and glass making, plays generous host to this rural marathon with big-time amenities. Generous corporate sponsorship makes terrific awards possible, such as $4,500 in prize money, crystal trophies, commemorative glass medallions, and local wine. Designed to maximize the chances for a tailwind, the rolling course boasts a net elevation loss of 200 feet.

COURSE DESCRIPTION The point-to-point Wineglass Marathon course starts at Philips Lighting, just north of Bath. Adrenaline and a 40-foot drop over the first mile should get you going as you travel through Bath, while flat miles 2 through 4 should allow you to get into a good rhythm. With a 40-foot uphill lying from mile 4.75 to mile 5, the next 4 miles proceed through the countryside to Savona (mile 9). During this stretch, the course falls 90 feet, but includes two small hills. Upon leaving Savona, runners continue through the countryside while the course gradually descends 40 feet over the next 4 miles. Runners reach the halfway point in Campbell, home of Polly-O String Cheese, and then it's back to nature. Runners ascend about 30 feet just beyond mile 14, before gradually losing 80 feet in elevation as they reach Coopers Plains (mile 18.2). Painted Post lies only a short distance from Coopers Plains; after a brief, 25-foot hill, runners enter a local park and tour a residential neighborhood. A bike path (mile 22.5) leads runners through the village of Riverside and into Corning, providing a flat journey to the finish line. Once in Corning, runners proceed through several neighborhoods before hitting the downtown area. At mile 25.4, they turn onto historic Market Street and then proceed several blocks before turning left to Centerway Square. After passing through Riverfront Park and across the Chemung River, the finish line lies just ahead at the Corning Glass Center.

CROWD/RUNNER SUPPORT Runners encounter particularly energetic crowds in the numerous small towns dotting the route, while cheerleaders and bands entertain you in downtown Bath. The countryside between the towns leaves runners to their own thoughts. The course is a convenient one for family and friends to follow your progress in a car, allowing them to inspire you at several points. The 14 aid stations offer water and electrolyte replacement.

RACE LOGISTICS The race provides bus transportation from the finish line near Corning Glass Works Center to the start on race morning. Buses leave from 6:30 a.m. to 8:00 a.m. and cost $6. If your friends can't drop you off at the start, you need to drive to the finish and take the bus. The race transports your gear from the start for you to pick up in the finish area.

ACTIVITIES Race weekend starts on Saturday from 2:00 p.m. to 5:00 p.m. with the Runners Expo, packet pickup, registration, and a visit by a noted running personality, held at the Union Hall — Local #1013 at Pulteney Square in Bath. Immediately following the expo, the Pasta Party goes from 5:00 p.m. to 8:00 p.m. at the Knights of Columbus Hall, a short walk from Pulteney Square on W. Washington Street. The dinner costs $6 and includes live music, door prizes, and carbos. After you finish the race, cool down with refreshments and food. If you want to clean up, showers are available at the Corning YMCA next to the Glass Center. Free massages are also available. The awards ceremony starts around 1:30 p.m.

AWARDS All marathon runners receive T-shirts, and finishers also take home long-sleeve finisher's T-shirts, commemorative glass medallions, finisher's certificates, and Souvenir Wineglass Editions of Runner's Gazette. Age-group awards go to the top 10% of age-group finishers and include local wine and champagne. Approximately $4,500 in prize money goes to the top overall and masters runners.

ELITE RUNNERS INFORMATION The race offers free lodging and race entry to elite runners, generally those with times under the current course record. Overall winners earn $1,000, Steuben Crystal, and champagne, with $500 for second, $250 for third, and $125 for fourth. Masters winners take home $250 and Steuben Crystal, with $125 for second.

ACCOMMODATIONS There is no official race headquarters hotel. In Corning try: Comfort Inn (607-962-1515); or Radisson Hotel Corning (607-962-5000). In Bath try Old National Hotel (607-776-4104). In Painted Post try: Hampton Inn (607-936-3344); Econo Lodge (607-962-4444); or Holiday Inn (607-962-5021).

RELATED EVENTS/RACES Wineglass also holds a Marathon Team Relay in conjunction with the marathon, with teams of three runners completing legs from 8 to 9 miles. Starting at 9:15 a.m., the relay offers male, female, and mixed divisions in open and masters age groups. The race transports runners from the start line to the relay exchange points.

AREA ATTRACTIONS Apart from the scenic beauty of the area, visit the fascinating Corning Glass Center, the third largest tourist attraction in New York state. You can also tour area wineries (over 20), possibly catching them during the harvest season, and browse the Rockwell Museum of Western Art.

LOCAL RUNNING STORE Pal's Sports Center, 8 West Pulteney, Corning.

YONKERS MARATHON

OVERALL: 70.1

COURSE BEAUTY: 6+

COURSE DIFFICULTY: 6

APPROPRIATENESS FOR FIRST TIMERS: 5+

RACE ORGANIZATION: 8-

CROWDS: 0+

RACE DATA

Contact:	A.J. Cambria
	Yonkers Marathon
	Yonkers Parks & Recreation
	285 Nepperhan Avenue
	Yonkers, NY 10701
	(914) 377-6430
Date:	October 5, 1997
	October 4, 1998
Start Time:	9:00 a.m.
Time Course Closes:	2:00 p.m.
Number of Participants:	200 in 1995
Certification:	USATF
Course Records:	Male: (open) 2:29:52
	Female: (open) 2:53:13
Special Programs for Elite Athletes:	No
Cost:	$15/20
Age Groups/Divisions:	18-29, 30-39, 40-49, 50-59, 60-69, 70+
Temperature:	60° to 70°
Aid/Splits:	25 / every 5 miles

HIGHLIGHTS For a good part of its history, the Yonkers Marathon rivaled Boston as the country's most prestigious marathon. Many of running's most celebrated heroes challenged Yonkers' pitiless hills in the hot, muggy climate each May. Today, Yonkers' runners confront a new course at a new time — October. While remaining hilly, the race draws only a fraction of its former numbers, but still offers the chance to run in one of the most storied marathons in the world.

RACE HISTORY Essentially, only two marathons mattered in the United States during much of the post-WWII period — Yonkers and Boston. Held merely one month apart, both races started at noon over challenging courses. To earn a space in the Olympics, American hopefuls had to compete in both races with the team decided by competitors' average place. Given the heroic task of being a top finisher in two marathons in two months, no American ever placed among the top ten Olympic finishers during that era. Yonkers last served as the U.S. Olympic Trials in 1964 and as the U.S. National Championship in 1966.

The Yonkers Marathon debuted almost 90 years ago on Thanksgiving Day in 1907, sponsored by the Mercury Athletic Club. The race, then 25 miles, started and finished in Getty Square in downtown Yonkers. Some of the hills were so tough that automobiles of the era couldn't conquer them. In 1908, the Mercury Athletic Club moved the marathon to the Empire City Race Track in order to charge spectators admission to the event. Included in the prize offerings that year was a live pig to the Mercury Club member who crossed the finish line first — it was even stipulated in the awards agreement that he must invite fellow members to the pig-roasting party. So extraordinarily popular were marathons in the early 1900s, Yonkers held two of them in 1909, one scheduled on New Year's Day, the other on Thanksgiving. Nineteen seventeen marked the last Yonkers Marathon until the Chippewa Democratic Club resurrected it in 1935 using the old race track course and the Thanksgiving date. The Yonkers Marathon celebrated its 60th anniversary in 1996 even though Yonkers missed a race in 1948 when the National Championship and Olympic Trials were relocated to a course that ran from Idlewild Airport to Flushing Meadows in New York City. The running craze has waned somewhat in Yonkers; only 200 runners showed up in 1996. Nonetheless, the Yonkers Marathon is still notorious as the "marathoner's marathon," unique for its brutal battleground.

COURSE DESCRIPTION Yonkers' new loop course debuted in 1995. Still relentlessly hilly, the course travels on city streets through most sections of Yonkers, primarily industrial and business districts. Runners find the most significant hills at miles 6, 9.5, 11.5, 13.5, and 25 (the largest hill on the course). Miles 15 and 16 forge Yonkers' downtown district, while miles 17 through 19 roll near a golf course.

CROWD/COMMUNITY SUPPORT Most crowds typically gather around aid stations, downtown, and at the finish line, but are sparse at other points along the course.

RACE LOGISTICS The race offers shuttle bus service from 90th Street and Fifth Avenue in New York City to the start for those preregistered runners who request shuttle service. Boarding starts at 6:30 a.m. and the shuttle leaves at 7:00 a.m. The bus leaves the finish at 2:30 p.m. for the return.

ACTIVITIES Pick up your race packet or register on race morning 6:30 a.m. to 8:30 a.m. at Court Sports II by the starting line. After the race, enjoy the post-race lunch and the awards luncheon.

AWARDS Every entrant receives a Yonkers Marathon T-shirt, and each finisher earns a commemorative finishers award, certificate and results. Cash prizes and other awards are presented to winners at the post-race luncheon. Total prize money of $2,000 is divided among the top three open and masters finishers according to the percentage of division registration compared to overall registration. Once prize money for each division is determined, cash awards will be subdivided into the following categories: 50% for first place, 35% for second place and 15% for third place. Overall male and female winners receive a bonus of $250. Also, the top three winners in each age group receive engraved plaques.

ACCOMMODATIONS Lodging is available at the Holiday Inn on Tuckahoe Road (914-476-3800) at a special rate.

RELATED EVENTS/RACES A marathon team relay of five runners — four legs of 5 miles each and one of 6.2 miles — also runs on race day. Teams compete for $1,000 in prize money.

AREA ATTRACTIONS After the marathon, watch the Columbus Day Parade make its way down Yonkers' main thoroughfares.

GREATER HARTFORD MARATHON

OVERALL: 78.2

COURSE BEAUTY: 8-

COURSE DIFFICULTY: 4- (SEE APPENDIX)

APPROPRIATENESS FOR FIRST TIMERS: 9-

RACE ORGANIZATION: 10-

CROWDS: 2

RACE DATA

Contact:	Beth Shluger
	Hartford Marathon Foundation
	221 Main Street
	Hartford, CT 06106
	(860) 525-8200
Date:	October 18, 1997
	October 10, 1998
Start Time:	7:50 a.m.
Time Course Closes:	12:50 p.m.
Number of Participants:	1,400 in 1995
Certification:	USATF
Course Records:	Male: (open) 2:22:08; (masters) 2:41:48
	Female: (open) 2:47:41; (masters) 3:23:34
Elite Athlete Programs:	Yes
Cost:	$20/25/30/35
Age groups/Divisions:	<19, 20-29, 30-39, 40-49, 50-59, 60-69, 70+
Temperature:	41° - 65°
Aid/Splits:	12 / every two miles with six digital clocks

HIGHLIGHTS The Greater Hartford Marathon features five different races sandwiched between some of the best tasting pre- and post-race parties in North America. The pre-race pasta party showcases over two dozen of the city's finest restaurants serving up their favorite pasta dishes. As one of the fastest courses in New England, Hartford features a dramatic start and finish near the golden-domed State Capitol building while treating runners to a memorable stretch along a beautiful country road dotted with 17th century homes, pumpkin farms, and stunning autumn foliage.

COURSE DESCRIPTION A loop course (completely closed to traffic), Hartford starts downtown in Bushnell Park amongst the golden-domed State Capitol building and landmark Memorial Arch. After a short tour of downtown, including a stint on the brick-covered pedestrian walkway of Pratt Street, the route crosses Founders Bridge spanning the Connecticut River — the most difficult upgrade on the course — at the 2-mile mark. After a brief stretch on a bike path beside the Connecticut River, the course loops around an office park before heading north through a business/commercial area on Rt. 5/Main Street. Gently rolling past a middle-class neighborhood on King Street, the course veers left onto Old Main Street at mile 7. For the next 11 miles, Old Main Street, with its impressive 17th century homes, rural pumpkin farms and colorful autumn foliage, hosts the most scenic area of the course, heading slightly downhill to the turnaround at 12.5 and slightly uphill back. After a pleasant stint along the bike path, runners return over Founders Bridge at mile 22. The course meanders through an industrial/warehouse area which ushers in the finish under the grand Memorial Arch.

CROWD / RUNNER SUPPORT Nearly 15,000 spectators cheer the marathoners, with most, including participants from the related races, stationing themselves near the start/finish area where they can see the runners several times. In addition, over 700 volunteers ensure that each marathoner is supported along the course. Live music in route is another encouraging feature.

RACE LOGISTICS The start/finish in Bushnell Park lies within walking distance of downtown hotels. If you're arriving by car on race morning, sufficient parking is available.

ACTIVITIES In conjunction with the packet pickup and late registration, a Sports & Fitness Expo featuring health screening, sport vendors, and running clinics takes place at the Hastings Hotel & Conference Center beginning Friday from 11:00 a.m. to 8:00 p.m. Race-day packet pickup and late registration extend from 6:00 a.m. to 7:30 a.m. under the tent in Bushnell Park. The Passion for Pasta Carbo-Load Supper, one of the finest in North America, with over 24 of Hartford's finest restaurants offering their favorite dishes, begins at 5:30 p.m. with a second seating at 7:00 p.m. The party-like atmosphere continues after the race with the Post-Race Picnic, including food, drink, music, awards, and Sports Expo in Bushnell Park from 10:30 a.m. to 2:00 p.m. Before you start dancing to the music, take advantage of the free massages offered to runners on a first-come, first-served basis.

AWARDS All marathon entrants receive T-shirts. Finishers are awarded commemorative medals and certificates. Top runners vie for $12,000 in prize money, and top age groupers earn marathon lithographs and merchandise prizes (watches for first and marathon baseball caps for second). Individual result postcards are mailed to all finishers within ten days of the race. Results of all races are mailed to registered runners within 45 days.

ELITE RUNNERS INFORMATION Males under 2:30 and females under 2:45 receive complimentary entries and consideration for transportation and accommodations. Open prize money extends to seventh place with the following breakdown: $1,500, $1,000, $700, $500, $300, $200, and $100, respectively. The winner collects an additional $500 bonus for times under 2:22 for men and under 2:45 for women. Masters prize money stretches four deep: $400, $250, $100, and $50, respectively.

ACCOMMODATIONS The Hastings Hotel & Conference Center, 85 Sigourney Street (806-727-4200), serves as headquarters of the marathon and related festivities. Within walking distance of the race start/finish, Hastings Hotel offers a rate of $75 which includes parking and continental breakfast. Other hotels with special rates include: Ramada Inn Capitol Hill, 440 Asylum Street (203-246-6591); Sheraton Hartford Hotel, 315 Trumbull Street (203-728-5151); Super 8 Motel, 57 West Service Road (203-246-8888); Susse Chalet, 185 Brainard Road (203-525-9306); Holiday Inn — East Hartford, 363 Roberts Street (203-528-9611); Ramada Inn East Hartford, 100 East River Drive (203-528-9703); or Wellesley Inn, 333 Roberts Street (203-289-4950). Also, local runners house out-of-town participants on a space-available basis. Details may be obtained from the Marathon Hotline (860-525-3435).

RELATED EVENTS / RACES Race day provides several options for would-be runners. If you're a team player, enter the marathon relay consisting of 2 to 5 runners tackling any combination of 5 legs varying in length from 4 to 6.5 miles. The Kids K, a .7-mile, noncompetitive run for children aged 3 to 7, begins at 8:45 a.m. Youngsters aged 8 to 11 run 1.4 miles around Bushnell Park. A 5K run takes place at 8:15 a.m. and starts in Bushnell Park. With so many options, no one is left out!

AREA ATTRACTIONS If the events surrounding the marathon are not enough, take in one or more of the fall festivals in the area. Those desiring a little culture should visit the Wadsworth Atheneum, 600 Main Street, the oldest public art museum in the country, featuring collections of Monet, Renoir and Degas. Literary buffs may want to tour the homes of Mark Twain and Harriet Beecher Stowe, both of whom wrote their most famous works in the area.

LOCAL RUNNING STORE The Run In, 2172 Silas Deane Highway. (203-536-6136).

LAKEFRONT MARATHON

OVERALL: 85.9

COURSE BEAUTY: 8+

COURSE DIFFICULTY: 3- (SEE APPENDIX)

APPROPRIATENESS FOR FIRST TIMERS: 8

RACE ORGANIZATION: 9

CROWDS: 2-

RACE DATA

Contact: The Lakefront Marathon
c/o Badgerland Striders
9200 W. North Avenue
Milwaukee, WI 53226
(414) 783-5009

Date: October 12, 1997
October 11, 1998

Start Time: 8:00 a.m.

Time Course Closes: 1:00 p.m.

Number of Participants: 1,523 in 1995

Certification: USATF

Course Records: Male: (open) 2:14:09
Female: (open) 2:39:15

Elite Athlete Programs: No

Cost: $30/32/37/40

Age groups/Divisions: 18-24, 25-29, 30-34, 35-39, 40-44, 45-49, 50-54, 55-59, 60-64, 65+; Clydesdale

Temperature: 43° - 64°

Aid/Splits: 10 / every mile, digital clocks at 1, 5, 10, 13.1, 15 & 20

HIGHLIGHTS You will find much more than beer in Milwaukee. The U.S. Beer Capital houses a large ethnic population with their accompanying cuisines, a terrific summer of festivals, and an excellent fall marathon — the Lakefront Marathon. Despite the packed autumn marathon season in the Midwest, Lakefront manages to draw more than 1,500 runners. Mostly paralleling the shore of Lake Michigan, the point-to-point course finishes downtown at the Milwaukee Art Museum and offers a reasonable shot at a PR.

COURSE DESCRIPTION Traveling through rural countryside and quiet northshore neighborhoods, Lakefront starts at Grafton High School (26 miles north of downtown Milwaukee). Heading east, the course presents a slight downhill before climbing the steepest hill (Hwy. 43 overpass) at 1.2 miles. Hwy. 60 then becomes Uleo Road which leads to two short hills at 1.7 miles. Turning right, the course goes south on rolling to downhill Hwy. C. Cornfields and llama farms on the right and views of Lake Michigan on the left provide scenic variety. By mile 4.5, the route parallels Hwy. 43, running very close to Lake Michigan while continuing flat until a .1-mile hill at 7.1. Runners continue on long, straight stretches, filing by lovely lakefront homes. A gradual rise occurs from 9.5 to 9.8 miles, and near mile 10.7, runners tour a new subdivision. Be alert for a few sharp turns before the course changes from open-road running to a one-lane, coned course. From mile 15 to 24, the course features some of Milwaukee's finest homes, many of which are palatial lakeshore estates. During this stretch, the race goes downhill near 18.2 miles, before rising at

20.6. Runners have a great view of Lake Michigan from mile 23 to 23.4 accompanied by a steep downhill. The mostly flat final 2.5 miles bring runners through McKinley Marina and the finish line in front of the Milwaukee Art Museum in Veterans Park.

CROWD/RUNNER SUPPORT The Lakefront Marathon doesn't pass through any highly populated areas, so most of the crowds are centered around the four relay exchange points and the finish (with the exceptions being miles 15 and 21.5). The ten aid stations feature cups with lids and straws, water, electrolyte replacement, and petroleum jelly. Digital clocks show the elapsed time at six points on the course, and split timers call out at every other mile.

RACE LOGISTICS Runners may park south of the Milwaukee Art Museum and take the free race shuttle to the start. Buses leave between 6:00 a.m. and 7:15 a.m. Runners with friends or family along can drive directly to the start at Grafton High School, but note that there is no bus transportation back to the start after the race. Organizers transport your sweats to the finish for you to reclaim.

ACTIVITIES Pick up your race packet on Saturday from 10:00 a.m. to 6:00 p.m. at the Milwaukee Hilton, 509 W. Wisconsin Avenue (north of I-794 at 5th and Wisconsin), and breeze through the small expo. You may also retrieve your packet or register at Grafton High School on race morning. After the race, munch on fruit, cookies, veggies, and cheese, while washing it down with good ol' Milwaukee beer (soda or water if you prefer).

AWARDS All marathon entrants collect colorful, long-sleeve sweatshirts and official results programs mailed at a later date. Each finisher also gets a medal hung around his neck in the finish chute. Age-group awards go three deep in most divisions and two deep in a few of the less-populous ones.

ACCOMMODATIONS The Milwaukee Hilton, 509 W. Wisconsin Avenue (414-271-7250), serves as the official race hotel. Other possibilities include: Exel Inn (414-961-7272); Hilton Inn (414-962-6040); Holiday Inn (414-273-2950); Manchester East (414-351-6960); Hyatt Regency (414-276-1234); Park East Hotel (414-276-8800); Residence Inn (414-352-0070); Sheraton Inn (414-355-8585); and Super 8 Motel (414-481-8488).

RELATED EVENTS/RACES Get in on the action by running the marathon relay for five-member teams. Relayers run legs of 5, 5.7, 4.3, 5, and 6.2 miles. Divisions include Male, Female, Mixed (at least two females), and Corporate. The race provides bus transportation from the start to each of the relay exchange points and from the exchange points to the finish.

AREA ATTRACTIONS You must tour one of the many beer factories — Miller Brewery is located at 4251 W. State Street, and Pabst Brewing Company is at 915 W. Juneau Avenue. Friday nights in Milwaukee mean fish fry. Go to just about any restaurant to join in the tradition. Top it off with some frozen custard. Sneak a peek in the Pettit National Ice Center, 500 S. 84th Street, where some local runners do their winter training.

LOCAL RUNNING STORE Rodiez's Running Store, 10903 W. Lincoln Avenue, West Allis (414-321-1154).

ROYAL VICTORIA MARATHON

OVERALL: 91.8

COURSE BEAUTY: 9

COURSE DIFFICULTY: 4 (SEE APPENDIX)

APPROPRIATENESS FOR FIRST TIMERS: 8+

RACE ORGANIZATION: 9

CROWDS: 2

RACE DATA

Contact:	Victoria Marathon Society
	c/o #182-911 Yates Street
	Victoria, B.C.
	Canada V8V 4X3
	(604) 382-8181
Date:	October 12, 1997
	October 11, 1998
Start Time:	8:00 a.m.
Time Course Closes:	12:00 p.m.
Number of Participants:	2,000+ in 1995
Certification:	B.C. Athletics
Course Records:	Male: (open) 2:19:31
	Female: (open) 2:42:32
Elite Athlete Programs:	No
Cost:	$55
Age groups/Divisions:	<29, 30-34, 35-39, 40-44, 45-49, 50-54, 55-59, 60-64, 65-69, 70+; Walkers; Teams: Open, Masters, Husband & Wife
Temperature:	50° - 65°
Aid/Splits:	17 / miles 1, 5, 10K, 13.1, 15, 30K, 20 & 25.2

HIGHLIGHTS A truly unique marathon experience in North America awaits you on Vancouver Island, northwest of Seattle by car and ferry. The elegant and beautiful Royal Victoria Marathon, held in quaint, seaside Victoria, British Columbia, will delight and transport you to the Old World's heart. Victoria, a British enclave of pubs and afternoon tea, enchants visitors with its immaculate gardens, monumental air, and English manner. That marvelous setting, a healthy dose of ocean views, and typical Canadian hospitality unite to produce one of marathoning's rising stars.

COURSE DESCRIPTION Containing no serious hills, RVM's modified out-and-back course rolls for much of its 26.2 miles posing a challenge for many runners. The race starts alongside the B.C. Parliament Building, a monumental, gray stone structure that lends a decidedly British air to the city. After a downhill start passing famous, stately Empress Hotel, the course heads along Wharf Street, bordering Victoria's beautiful harbor. The first 2.3 miles proceed through downtown Victoria, passing shops, restaurants, and hotels with some long, gentle ups and downs. Runners then come up behind Beacon Hill Park, enter it by mile 2.8, and enjoy the gardens while passing through it. As you leave the park (mile 3.5), the ocean greets you until 4.3 when you traverse residential Oswego Street to the scenic Inner Harbor at mile 5. Following the line of hotels around the point, runners hit the shoreline at mile 6 and hug the coast for 2.3 miles. About mile 6.2, runners begin a gentle 60-foot incline to the 7-mile mark and then descend to mile 8. Ross

Bay at 7.8 offers a great vantage to Hollywood Cove's hillside homes overlooking the ocean. Winding through residential Oak Bay from 8.3 to 11.4, the course rolls, rising about 50 feet. You're back along the water by 11.5 miles, passing expensive houses and entering the exclusive and scenic Royal Victoria Golf Course at 12.2. Runners roll through the golf course and reach RVM's halfway point at the marina on Oak Bay. The next five miles are mostly flat through an upscale neighborhood until you return to the marina (mile 18) and face the 50-foot climb to the golf course. Runners retrace their steps the rest of the way and finish in front of the Parliament Building at the Inner Harbor.

CROWD/RUNNER SUPPORT As the race grows, Victorians turn out in larger numbers to cheer the runners. While onlookers still speckle most of the route, the start/finish area and Oak Bay attract good crowds. Runners pass aid stations 17 times. Besides carrying the usual water and electrolyte replacement drink, aid stations, after mile 16, also provide PowerBars to energy-flagged runners.

RACE LOGISTICS The small downtown area and the proximity of several hotels to the Inner Harbor make race-morning transportation unnecessary for many runners. If you stay further out, you must provide your own means to the start, but abundant, free parking exists in the area.

ACTIVITIES On Friday or Saturday, runners may pick up their race packets at the headquarters hotel. Otherwise, retrieve your packet on the legislative grounds near the start on race morning. Bus tours of the marathon course depart Saturday afternoon and cost $5. On Saturday evening, attend the pasta dinner for about $20. After the marathon, stop by the free post-race social at the Harbour Towers, featuring a video of the race, finishers' certificates, and race results.

AWARDS Early registrants receive original design sweatshirts, with finishers earning RVM medals engraved with the shirt design and certificates. Age-group awards go up to 10 deep depending on the number of entrants in each category. All runners are eligible for several raffle prizes, including a trip to the London Marathon. A one-ounce gold coin goes to the runner who sets a new course record.

ACCOMMODATIONS Located about four blocks from the RVM start, the Harbour Towers, 345 Quebec Street (800-663-5896), serves as the sponsoring hotel, offering marathoners special rates of about $95 per night. Other lodging possibilities include: Ocean Point Resort, 45 Songhees Road (800-667-4677), about $100 a night; The Coast Victoria Harbourside Hotel, 146 Kingston Street (800-663-1144), about $110; Clarion Hotel Grand Pacific, 450 Quebec Street (800-663-7550), about $110; Quality Inn Harbourview, 455 Belleville Street (800-663-7550), about $90; Dashwood Seaside Manor, #1 Cook Street (800-667-5517); Dominion Hotel, 759 Yates Street (800-663-6101); Hotel Douglas, 1450 Douglas Street (800-332-9981); and Strathcona Hotel, 919 Douglas Street (604-383-7137). For cheaper accommodations, try one of Victoria's many bed & breakfast inns, most of which lie outside downtown.

RELATED EVENTS/RACES RVM welcomes walkers to stride the full marathon. Royal Victoria sponsors an 8K run beginning at 8:30 a.m. on Sunday. Early registered 8K runners receive original shirts, and all 8K entrants participate in the random drawing for a trip for two on Air BC. Kids may do the Children's 1K Run for Charity, beginning at 9:30 a.m.

AREA ATTRACTIONS A great tourist city, charming Victoria contains numerous attractions for marathoners. Flower lovers will delight in the hanging flower baskets throughout the city and world-renowned Butchart Gardens. The British-like Old Town area contains scores of pubs, shops, and restaurants. Join in an English tradition and take afternoon tea at the Empress Hotel, or stroll the Inner Harbor and Beacon Hill Park.

LOCAL RUNNING STORES Frontrunners, 911 Yates Street #182 (604-382-8181); Island Runner, 1576 Fairfield Road (604-595-2378); Running Room, 1008 Douglas Street (604-383-4224).

TOE TO TOW MARATHON

OVERALL: 83.7

COURSE BEAUTY: 9

COURSE DIFFICULTY: 2+

APPROPRIATENESS FOR FIRST TIMERS: 8

RACE ORGANIZATION: 8+

CROWDS: 0+

RACE DATA

Contact: Toe to Tow Marathon
Ohio Canal Corridor
P.O. Box 609420
Cleveland, OH 44109
(216) 348-1825

Date: October 12, 1997
October 11, 1998

Start Time: 9:00 a.m.

Time Course Closes: 2:30 p.m.

Number of Participants: 760 in 1995

Certification: USATF

Course Records: Male: (open) 2:27:59
Female: (open) 2:50:42

Elite Athlete Programs: No

Cost: $30/35

Age groups/Divisions: <19, 20-24, 25-29, 30-34, 35-39, 40-44, 45-49, 50-54, 55-59, 60-64, 65-69, 70+; Clydesdale (M: 195+; F: 145+)

Temperature: 55°

Aid/Splits: 10 / none

HIGHLIGHTS Nestled between Cleveland and Akron, the Cuyahoga Valley National Recreation Area hosts a wonderful marathon largely undiscovered by the outside world — the Toe to Tow Marathon. Run on the Towpath Trail along the historic Ohio & Erie Canal and the Cuyahoga River, Toe to Tow cushions runners with the ultimate running surface, a soft path of decomposed gravel. The trail envelops runners with exploding orange and gold leafed trees. Leonard Fisher of Dublin, OH, a 15-marathon veteran, calls Toe to Tow, *"The most beautiful course I've run."* Toe to Tow puts runners in the right mood straight off by transporting them through the valley to the start via the Cuyahoga Valley Scenic Railroad, allowing glimpses of some of the coming splendor. The event benefits the Ohio Canal Corridor, a nonprofit organization whose mission is to create a legacy park system along the historic Ohio and Erie Canal from Cleveland to Zorr.

COURSE DESCRIPTION Starting at the Special Events Site, Toe to Tow rolls two miles down winding Riverside Road. The course then makes a U-turn onto the towpath at Bath Road, heading north. Runners follow the twisty towpath, where mules pulled boats packed with the area's commerce in the mid 1800s, for the next 24 miles. Notice the old locks along the canal, many of which are hidden by overgrowth. Turning around at Wilson Mill near the 18-mile mark, runners head back south to the finish at Boston Mill Ski Resort. In the future, Toe to Tow may become a point-to-point race as additional sections of the towpath trail are completed.

CROWD/RUNNER SUPPORT As you would expect, this rural race does not draw large crowds, but the enthusiastic race volunteers provide much needed support. Friends and family can also access the route at several points along the canal to support you.

RACE LOGISTICS Runners must take the Cuyahoga Valley Scenic Railroad to the start. Park at the Boston Mills Ski Resort finish line and catch the train there. Be warned! The train leaves promptly at 8:00 a.m.!

ACTIVITIES There are no pre-race activities associated with the race. You may pick up your race packet from the Athlete's Shoe Specialist or at Boston Mills Ski Resort on race morning. You may also register on race day in the finish area. The race offers post-marathon refreshments and free massages for spent legs.

AWARDS The first 500 entrants receive long-sleeve T-shirts, and every finisher earns a special medallion. The top three in each age group receive commemorative awards, as do the overall and masters winners.

ACCOMMODATIONS You may stay within the Cuyahoga Valley National Recreation Area at two places: the Historic Wallace farmhouse, now the Inn at Brandywine Falls, 8230 Brandywine Road (216-467-1812); or the Stanford House Hostel, an American Youth Hostel Association member which accepts adults as well. Located at 6093 Stanford Road (216-467-8711), the hostel offers simple lodging and food preparation facilities. Outside the park, try the Holiday Inn, just south of Ohio Turnpike exit 11 at 4742 Brecksville Road, Richfield, OH (216-659-6151).

RELATED EVENTS/RACES Friends can join forces and enter the marathon relay, consisting of two- and four-person teams. Teams may be unisex or coed.

AREA ATTRACTIONS The area offers numerous opportunities for hiking, bike riding, and bird watching. Football fans can dissect the Pro Football Hall of Fame in nearby Canton, and music lovers may want to check out the new Rock and Roll Hall of Fame in Cleveland. Cleveland also offers a variety of professional sports.

LOCAL RUNNING STORE The Athlete's Shoe Specialist, 5525 Warrensville Center Road, Maple Heights (216-663-2282).

CANADIAN INTERNATIONAL MARATHON

OVERALL: 85.4

COURSE BEAUTY: 7

COURSE DIFFICULTY: 3 (SEE APPENDIX)

APPROPRIATENESS FOR FIRST TIMERS: 9-

RACE ORGANIZATION: 9+

CROWDS: 2

RACE DATA

Contact: Jay W. Glassman
The Canadian International Marathon
240 Heath Street West, Suite 802
Toronto, Ontario
Canada M5P 3L5
(416) 972-1062

Date: October 19, 1997
October 18, 1998

Start Time: 9:00 a.m.

Time Course Closes: 2:00 p.m.

Number of Participants: 1,418 in 1995

Certification: AIMS, Athletics Canada, and Ontario Roadrunners Association

Course Records: Male: (open) 2:23:15; (masters) 2:28:16
Female: (open) 2:49:19; (masters) 2:52:06

Special Programs for Elite Athletes: No

Cost: $40 Cdn./$30 US; $50 Cdn./$40 US; $70 Cdn./$50 US

Age Groups/Divisions: 18-29, 30-39, 40-49, 50-59, 60+

Temperature: 50° - 70°

Aid/Splits: 14 / mile 1, then every 5K

HIGHLIGHTS The youthful Canadian International Marathon offers a relatively quick course through perhaps Canada's most exciting city, Toronto. Approximately 10 miles of the race travel down Yonge Street, Toronto's main thoroughfare. Along the way, the course takes in York University, Toronto's financial district, St. Lawrence Market, and the Ontario Legislature. The recent demise of the Toronto Marathon, although a spring race, should bolster CIM in the future.

COURSE DESCRIPTION The race, on mostly coned streets, begins on Yonge Street (reputed to be the longest street in the world) just north of Mel Lastman Square. Runners head south .6 miles to Sheppard Avenue and turn right, rolling through residential streets to 2.5 miles. The course then flattens, passing through Downsview Air Force Base to emerge at Keele Street. Going north on Keele Street, runners follow a gradual uphill for 1.9 miles past the York University campus. At Steeles Avenue, the course turns back toward Yonge Street, a distance of about 3.75 miles, passing parks interspersed with shopping malls and apartment complexes. Back on Yonge Street, the route gradually descends past the half marathon point just north of Mel Lastman Square continuing under the Highway 401 overpass. At Hogg's Hollow, at the 25K point, runners face the largest hill on the course, a tough 100-footer. Once over the hump, the course turns downhill once again. Runners then scurry through the upscale neighborhoods of Lawrence Park, Forest Hill, and Rosedale. The only left turn of the course lies at the 32K mark (19.84 miles) at Aylmer Avenue. Here, the course follows the scenic and forested Rosedale Valley Road to Bayview Avenue. The course meanders along the Don River Valley, before turning onto Front Street, marked by abandoned factories and warehouses. As the city approaches, runners pass the historic St. Lawrence Market, Gooderham, Worts Flatiron Building, and the trendy stores and restaurants of the area. Front Street gives way to Wellington Street through the heart of Toronto's financial district. Turning on University Avenue, you encounter cheering crowds while passing stately Osgoode Hall Provincial Courts, hospitals, and finish after a brief loop around the top of Queen's Park, home to the Ontario Legislature.

CROWD / RUNNER SUPPORT Approximately 20,000 supporters come out to bolster the marathoners. You also receive a warm reception by the 20 to 30 entertainment stations stretched along Yonge Street. The new 9:00 a.m. start should boost audience attendance. You won't go unattended at aid stations as typically over 800 volunteers offer their help along the course, handing out water, sports drink, fruit, medical assistance, and transportation every 5K, then more frequently in the last 15K of the race. The course is marked every kilometer and every 5th mile.

RACE LOGISTICS Public transportation starts at 9:00 a.m. on Sundays so you need to find some other way to the start. Parking is provided near the start if you plan to drive. Otherwise, shuttle buses depart the race headquarters hotel starting at 7:00 a.m. Take the bus from the finish area back to the hotel or to Mel Lastman Square. The marathon also provides a bag check at the start; your bag will be waiting for you at the finish.

ACTIVITIES Pick up your race packet, register, and attend the Runners' Expo on Thursday, Friday or Saturday preceding the marathon at the race headquarters hotel from 10:00 a.m. to 7:00 p.m. Out-of-town runners may retrieve their packets on race morning at Mel Lastman Square. A free feast is provided for runners the evening before the marathon (non-runners may attend for $10). A workshop is also held to orient newcomers to the course and to talk about running generally. Food and refreshments are plentiful at the finish line in Queen's Park, and showers and a changing room are available at nearby Hart House.

AWARDS Every entrant takes home a Canadian International Marathon T-shirt. All full marathoners receive medals as they cross the finish line, and certificates of completion are mailed later. Though only two years in the running, the CIM offers generous sums of cash to winners.

ELITE RUNNERS INFORMATION Elite athletes may receive complimentary entry to CIM. Top runners compete for about $50,000 to $60,000 in prize money. The top three overall finishers are awarded $6,000, $4,000, and $2,000 respectively. The top three masters earn $2,000, $1,500, and $1,000.

ACCOMMODATIONS The official race hotel is the Holiday Inn, 370 King Street West (800-263-6364). If you can't reserve a room (they go fast!), try: Sheraton Centre Toronto Hotel & Towers, 123 Queen Street West (416-361-1000); Toronto Hilton, 145 Richmond Street West (416-869-3456); or Royal York, 100 Front Street West (416-386-2511).

RELATED EVENTS / RACES Also featured on the same day as the marathon are a half marathon, the Canadian Wheelchair Marathon Championships, as well as a corporate/school marathon challenge (for teams of up to eight runners).

AREA ATTRACTIONS Renowned as one of the most culturally diverse cities on the planet, Toronto offers a dizzying array of activities to keep you busy. An extremely active theater scene can be enjoyed at a number of places, including O'Keefe Centre, St. Lawrence Centre, and Canadian Stage. Toronto also has outstanding ballet, symphony, and opera. Catch the tremendous view from the 553-meter CN Tower, the tallest freestanding building in the world. Strewn with museums, Toronto boasts the Royal Ontario Museum, Art Gallery of Ontario, Ontario Science Center, and the Bata Shoe Museum. Hockey fans will want to visit the Hockey Hall of Fame and then catch a Toronto Maple Leafs game. Even if the Blue Jays are not playing, check out the amazing Sky Dome with its retractable roof.

LOCAL RUNNING STORES Running Room, 2629 Yonge Street (416-322-7100); Runner's Shop, 180 Bloor Street W (416-923-9702); Runners' Choice, College Park Mall, 777 Bay Street (416-597-0023).

CHICAGO MARATHON

OVERALL: 94.5

COURSE BEAUTY: 8

COURSE DIFFICULTY: 2

APPROPRIATENESS FOR FIRST TIMERS: 10

RACE ORGANIZATION: 10

CROWDS: 4+

RACE DATA

Contact:	The LaSalle Banks Chicago Marathon
	P.O. Box 10597
	Chicago, IL 60610-0597
	(312) 243-0003
Date:	October 19, 1997
	October 18, 1998
Start Time:	7:45 a.m.
Time Course Closes:	1:15 p.m.
Number of Participants:	11,108 in 1995
Certification:	USATF
Race Records:	Male: (open) 2:07:13
	Female: (open) 2:21:21
Elite Athlete Programs:	Yes
Cost:	$35/40
Age groups/Divisions:	<19, 20-24, 25-29, 30-34, 35-39, 40-44, 45-49, 50-54, 55-59, 60-64, 65-69, 70+
Temperature:	53°
Aid/Splits:	12 / digital clocks every mile and at 10K, 20K & 13.1

HIGHLIGHTS Chicago's dead population notoriously arises at opportune times; John F. Kennedy could have attested to that! Not limited to Chicago politics, however, resurrection extends to Chicago sports — Michael Jordan, the Bulls, and the Chicago Marathon. Sponsorship problems forced the cancellation of the 1987 race, but Chicago has regained its place as one of the country's top, big-city marathons; and if you like big cities, Chicago is a must. The city of big shoulders' impressive architecture, skyline, lakefront, sports, entertainment, history, and culture make it a destination town par excellence. Our fastest-rated race, Chicago's lightning fast course (North American records for male and females have been established here) tours numerous ethnic neighborhoods that most visitors never see. With the exception of the disqualified women's winner from 1992, rarely will you hear a negative comment about the Chicago Marathon. Alive and well, Chicago is yours to enjoy.

COURSE DESCRIPTION Taking runners through many of the city's most historic and diverse neighborhoods, the Chicago Marathon's flat, loop course passes through Lincoln Park, Old Town, Greektown, Little Italy, Pilsen, Chinatown, Bridgeport and the Gap District. Starting in Grant Park, site of famous Buckingham Fountain, near the shore of beautiful Lake Michigan, runners head north traveling past the Hard Rock Café, Planet Hollywood and other chic restaurants and night spots during the three miles in the River North area. Continuing north, the route heads through Lincoln Park past the Lincoln Park Zoo and Diversey Harbor. Coffee shops, bookstores, and restaurants characterize the Lakeview area between miles 4.5 and 6. Heading south from Lakeview, runners return to Lincoln Park passing the world-renowned dance and blues clubs and international restaurants on Clark Street. Still early in the race, your sense of humor should be intact as you pass the great comedy clubs in Old Town Chicago around 8 miles. After cruising past The Loop (shoppers' paradise), Merchandise Mart, City Hall, and Sears Tower near mile 10, the course heads west, crossing the Chicago River into Greektown. After hitting the halfway point in Little Italy, expect great spectator support, including music and dancing as the route enters Pilsen, Chicago's largest Hispanic area, around mile 15. The rainbow tour proceeds, cutting through Chinatown's Lion and Dragon dancers at mile 17. Bridgeport, the mayor's neighborhood, Comiskey Park, home of the White Sox, and the Southside, home of Bad Bad Leroy Brown, lie between miles 18.5 and 20. Heading east toward Lake Michigan, runners enter the supportive Gap District, a large black community, near the 23-mile mark. The last three miles head north on Lakeshore Drive with a beautiful view of the Chicago skyline, passing McCormick Place and Soldier Field before finishing in Grant Park.

C R O W D / R U N N E R   S U P P O R T Chicago's legendary sports-town image extends to the marathon; over 200,000 onlookers line the streets or hang out of apartment windows encouraging the marathoners. The twelve aid stations stretch an entire block in places, while numerous musical groups entertain. The course layout makes it very easy for spectators to view the race from several spots along the way. In fact, onlookers can watch the start, saunter six blocks, and cheer at the ten-mile mark.

R A C E   L O G I S T I C S Convenient Grant Park makes arriving at the start relatively hassle free with the major hotels nearby. If you're arriving by car, you'll find ample parking in the area.

ACTIVITIES Chicago features a two-day Health and Fitness Expo and race registration at the Chicago Hilton & Towers. The expo includes over 100 exhibitors displaying the latest products and services from the sports, health and fitness industries. Runners may register or pick up their packets at the expo on Friday between 11:00 a.m. and 8:00 p.m. and Saturday from 9:00 a.m. to 6:00 p.m. A spectacular pasta carbo-load dinner is held on Saturday night from 6:00 p.m. to 8:00 p.m. at the Chicago Hilton. The dinner includes a three-course, sit-down meal, special guest appearances by celebrity runners, and a drawing for prizes. Runners, family, and friends are welcome, but the limited $15 tickets sell quickly. After the race, a great post-race finishers party takes place at a local hot spot (Hard Rock Cafe in 1996) with free food, wine, and beer. The overall winners' checks are presented along with a raffle for exciting prizes.

AWARDS Every marathoner receives a race T-shirt, goody bag, official race results booklet and entry into the post-race party. Participants finishing under 5:30 receive medallions, results cards and finisher's certificates. Age-group winners receive special prizes which are mailed soon after the event. Elite runners compete for $275,000 in prize money.

ELITE RUNNERS INFORMATION Chicagoan's have come to expect big-time sports with big-time players. Chicago Marathon organizers realize this and actively recruit some of the top names in marathoning. The race executive director holds complete discretion in conferring elite status. To be considered for expense money, you must contact Carey Pinkowski between January 1st and September 15th. A fast course and $275,000 in prize money, including generous time incentive bonuses, do not hurt Chicago's recruitment efforts. Prize money goes 10 deep in Open Divisions and five deep in Masters Divisions. Open winners earn $40,000, $25,000 for second, $15,000 for third, $12,000 for fourth, $10,000 for fifth, $6,000 for sixth, $5,000 for seventh, $3,000 for eighth, $2,000 for ninth, and $1,000 for tenth. The top American receives an additional $4,000. Masters winners take home $1,500, down to $250 for fifth. Time bonuses are awarded to any male runners under the qualifying times, ranging from $1,000 for a sub 2:13 to $75,000 for a world record. For women, the times range from sub 2:33 ($1,000) to a world record ($75,000).

ACCOMMODATIONS The Chicago Hilton and Towers, 720 S. Michigan Avenue (800-445-8667), only two blocks from the start/finish line, acts as the official race hotel. It offers special rates to marathon runners, but don't procrastinate. Other convenient hotels with special marathon rates include: Best Western Grant Park, 1100 S. Michigan Avenue (312-922-2900); Holiday Inn Chicago City Center, 300 E. Ohio Street (312-787-6100); River North Hotel, 125 W. Ohio Street (312-467-0800); Ramada Congress, 520 S. Michigan Avenue (312-427-3800); and the Sheraton Chicago, 301 E. North Water Street (312-464-1000).

RELATED EVENTS/RACES Race weekend begins Saturday with the Youth Mile Run open to children 5 to 14 years of age. Starting at 11:00 a.m. in Grant Park, the course loops Buckingham Fountain on Chicago's spectacular lakefront.

For those not bitten by the marathon bug, Chicago offers a popular 5K starting at 8:15 a.m. on race day. If you're running the marathon, consider recruiting a few friends or co-workers and enter the Team Challenge. For an extra fee, corporate or open teams of three to five members compete in this uniquely scored event. Team members are scored according to their place within their age group, relative to the number of finishers in that division. The top three performances are then added together, and the team with the lowest total points wins.

AREA ATTRACTIONS Spicy Chicago offers something for everyone: architecture, art galleries, museums, fine restaurants, Chicago Pizza, theaters, night clubs, blues music, sports, ethnic neighborhoods, shopping, and the lakefront beach. Save a little race energy, and allow time to take in some of the attractions.

LOCAL RUNNING STORES Vertel's, 2001 N. Clybourn Avenue (312-248-7400); Fleet Feet, 241-243 W. North Avenue (312-587-3338).

Run Chicago

20th ANNIVERSARY
Sunday, October 19, 1997

Sunday, October 11, 1998

1-888-243-3344

The LaSalle Banks

The LaSalle Banks
Chicago Marathon & 5K Run

P.O. Box 10597
Chicago, IL 60610-0597
Local Phone (312) 243-0003
Toll-Free Phone 1-888-243-3344
http://www.chicagomarathon.com

Chicago Marathon & 5K Run

COLORADO MARATHON

OVERALL: 75

COURSE BEAUTY: 6-

COURSE DIFFICULTY: 8-

APPROPRIATENESS FOR FIRST TIMERS: 3+

RACE ORGANIZATION: 8+

CROWDS: 0

RACE DATA

Contact:	Lesley Fuller
	Colorado Marathon
	P.O. Box 4184
	Englewood, CO 80155
	(303) 694-2030
Date:	October 19, 1997
	October 18, 1998
Start Time:	8:00 a.m.
Time Course Closes:	1:00 p.m.
Number of Participants:	1,650 in 1995
Certification:	USATF
Course Records:	Male: (open) 2:28:54
	Female: (open) 3:09:12
Elite Athlete Programs:	No
Cost:	$24/40
Age groups/Divisions:	18-19, 20-24, 25-29, 30-34, 35-39, 40-44, 45-49,
	50-54, 55-59, 60-64, 65-69, 70+
Temperature:	35° - 40°
Aid/Splits:	12 / every mile

HIGHLIGHTS Few races can claim as unique a genesis as the Colorado Marathon, the sole purpose of which is to heal the wounds caused by the defunct Denver International Marathon. In 1993, the race director of DIM disappeared with the race proceeds without paying the winners' prize money or the necessary police fees. Colorado race director Lesley Fuller stepped into this raw situation, creating the Colorado Marathon to raise money to pay the athletes. To date, nearly half the debt to the runners has been settled. The challenging race itself, winds, rolls, and loops through office parks and an outlying subdivision. You can make your own conclusions about the desirability of the setting from a runner's perspective.

COURSE DESCRIPTION Starting in front of the Inverness Hotel in suburban Englewood, the marathon strongly undulates through the surrounding office park for over 13 miles before crossing Interstate 470. After passing through a second office park and open space, runners enter a subdivision after mile 18. This section contains some significant grades, exacerbated by the sparse air. Exiting the residential community, the course follows a bike path paralleling I-470 (mile 21.7 to mile 24). Back now in the original office park, runners finish at the Inverness Athletic Club.

CROWD/RUNNER SUPPORT Have you ever been to an office park on a weekend? It's kind of like being in the mall on the first bright day of spring after a long, hard winter — deserted. While not quite that drastic, don't expect much in the way of crowd support here. All twelve aid stations offer water, while electrolyte replacement is available at seven of the stations.

RACE LOGISTICS You will likely need to drive to the race start; plenty of parking exists around the finish area. It's then a half mile trot to the start, but before heading over, take advantage of the portable toilets since there may not be any near the start.

ACTIVITIES You may attend the Carbo Load Buffet on Saturday evening at an undetermined location. Pick up your race packet or register on race morning from 6:30 a.m. to 7:30 a.m. Post-race refreshments are provided, and runners may take advantage of the Athletic Club facilities to change or shower.

AWARDS Everyone who pays the fee and shows up on race day receives a long-sleeve T-shirt. Marathon finishers also receive medals. The top three in each age division, top three overall, and top masters finisher earn special awards.

ACCOMMODATIONS The official race hotel remains undetermined at press time. Convenient to the start/finish in Englewood are: the Inverness Hotel and Golf Club, 200 Inverness Drive West (303-799-5800); Westin Resort, 384 Inverness Drive South (303-799-8041); Hyatt Regency Tech Center, 7800 E. Tufts Avenue (303-799-1234); Radisson Hotel Denver South, I-25 and Arapahoe Road (303-799-6200); Woodfield Suites Denver Tech, 9009 E. Arapahoe Road (303-799-4555); Hampton Inn Hotel, 9231 E. Arapahoe Road (303-792-9999); and Motel 6, 9201 E. Arapahoe Road (303-790-8220).

RELATED EVENTS/RACES If the idea of running a full marathon in Englewood's office parks doesn't sound appealing, you may consider the Colorado Half Marathon and the accompanying 5K. The half starts with the full marathon, with the 5K commencing just after.

AREA ATTRACTIONS Mile-high Denver offers tremendous entertainment and recreation options. Catch a Denver Broncos football game, Colorado Avalanche hockey game, or maybe a Nuggets basketball game. Outdoor lovers may want to hike one of the many nearby trails or head to Rocky Mountain National Park. Plan for chilly conditions.

LOCAL RUNNING STORES Runner's Roost, 1685 S. Colorado Blvd., Denver (303-759-8455); Fleet Feet, 1201 16th Street #202, Denver (303-623-5380).

DETROIT MARATHON

OVERALL: 81.2

COURSE BEAUTY: 8

COURSE DIFFICULTY: 2+

APPROPRIATENESS FOR FIRST TIMERS: 9-

RACE ORGANIZATION: 10-

CROWDS: 1+

RACE DATA

Contact: Detroit Free Press/Mazda International Marathon
300 Stroh River Place
Suite 4000
Detroit, MI 48207
(313) 393-7749
Date: October 19, 1997
October 18, 1998
Start Time: 8:00 a.m.
Time Course Closes: 1:30 p.m.
Number of Participants: 2,773 in 1995
Certification: USATF
Course Records: Male: (open) 2:13:07; (masters) 2:19:25
Female: (open) 2:34:55; (masters) 2:45:21
Elite Athlete Programs: Yes
Cost: $25/30/35
Age groups/Divisions: <19, 20-24, 25-29, 30-34, 35-39, 40-44, 45-49,
50-54, 55-59, 60-64, 65-69, 70+
Temperature: 42° - 57°
Aid/Splits: 25 / every mile

HIGHLIGHTS The Detroit Free Press/Mazda International Marathon may surprise you. Boasting one of the fastest courses and most unique starts in North America, Detroit begins in Windsor, Ontario and makes a dramatic entrance into the United States via a well-ventilated traffic-free, one-mile tunnel beneath the Detroit River. The pounding echo of runners' feet inspires you for the long journey ahead. The recent addition of International Management Group and Mazda North America have provided organizational expertise and financial muscle, resulting in an extremely well-organized event. As the race and the city revitalize, hopefully the Detroit community will give the marathon the support it deserves.

RACE HISTORY While the first Detroit Free Press Marathon took place in 1978, its roots stretch back to 1963 and the Motor City Marathon ("MCM"). Held on Thanksgiving Day, the first MCM attracted 23 starters with only half finishing the four-and-three-quarter loop course around Belle Isle Park. In 1969, the race was moved to October to take advantage of better weather. Also that year, Jerome Drayton, formerly Peter Buniak, of Canada, set a North American record of 2:12:00. Early in 1978, during the height of the running boom, the Detroit Free Press contacted the race sponsor, Motor City Striders Running Club, about putting on a major race in Detroit. The two groups joined forces, and on October 21, MCM became the Detroit Free Press International Marathon and was held on a new course starting in Windsor, Ontario and ending in Belle Isle Park. The new race attracted a field of 1,942, up dramatically from the previous year's total of 428 entrants. It reached its peak in 1981 with 4,953 runners. Today the race has a new course, including a downtown finish in Hart Plaza.

COURSE DESCRIPTION The Detroit Marathon starts at Jackson Park in Windsor, Ontario, and loops around retail and residential areas before descending into the Detroit/Windsor Tunnel at the 5-mile mark. Closed to vehicles and well-ventilated, the tunnel offers a surreal running experience. After a moderate quarter-mile climb, runners leave the tunnel and enter downtown Detroit to the roar of the large crowd. From here, the course proceeds eastward past business districts and ethnic neighborhoods to Belle Isle Park near the halfway point. Designed by Frederick Olmstead, designer of New York's Central Park, and built near the turn of the century, Belle Isle hosts 5.4 miles of the marathon. Leaving the park shortly past 18 miles, the race heads back toward downtown, eventually hitting Woodward Avenue (formerly an Indian trade trail and the oldest road in Michigan) around 22 miles. After a short out and back on Woodward Avenue and a small loop near the Civic Center, the race finishes near the gleaming Renaissance Center in Hart Plaza. Flat and fast, Detroit's course contains only three small uphills which occur at the tunnel exit and the entrance and exit to Belle Isle Park.

CROWD/RUNNER SUPPORT If your performance depends on heavy doses of spectator support, we suggest finding a different race. For a big-city marathon, Detroit's crowd participation is disappointing. Only 6,000 spectators lend support, with the majority situated at the Detroit/Windsor tunnel exit and the finish in Hart Plaza. To the race organizers' credit, aid stations are located every mile, and one dozen "morale stations" with entertainment and cheering spectators support your effort.

RACE LOGISTICS The race provides bus transportation to the start from the Westin Hotel at the Renaissance Center. The Westin is conveniently located near the finish line, where ample parking is available.

ACTIVITIES Detroit holds a Health & Fitness Expo at the Westin beginning Friday from 4:00 p.m. to 7:00 p.m. and continuing Saturday from 10:00 a.m. to 6:00 p.m. The site for race packet pickup, the expo also hosts running clinics and the usual sports-related vendors. There is no late registration since all entries must be inspected by customs and immigrations before anyone can cross the Canada - U.S. border. In fact, the entry deadline is always set two weeks prior to race day to help expedite the process. A pre-race pasta dinner begins at 6:00 p.m. Saturday evening. A brief awards ceremony for top finishers follows the event at Hart Plaza.

AWARDS Every marathon entrant receives a T-shirt which may be picked up at the expo or at the finish line after the race. All finishers receive medals and finisher certificates. The latter are mailed to marathoners 3-4 weeks after the race. Finish times of marathoners are published in the Monday Detroit Free Press, which can be mailed to runners for a $5 fee. A new Mazda car lease and $18,000 in prize money await the top finishers. Age-group awards extend as deep as 12 depending on the number of entrants in the division. Top division finishers are awarded plaques, mailed after the race.

ELITE RUNNERS INFORMATION Male runners under 2:22 and female runners under 2:50 qualify for elite status and may receive some expense money and lodging assistance. Overall male and female winners receive a 12-month Mazda 626LX auto lease and $3,000. Second through ninth place finishers earn $2,000, $1,500, $1,000, $750, $500, $250, $100, and $50, respectively. Masters prize money stretches four deep: $1,000, $500, $250, and $100, respectively.

ACCOMMODATIONS The Westin Hotel in Detroit's Renaissance Center (313-568-8200), serves as the host hotel. Conveniently located near the finish line, the hotel offers a package that includes a complimentary breakfast on race morning. Depending on the number of persons, rates range from $81 to $91. Other nearby hotels offering special marathon rates include: DoubleTree Hotel, 333 E. Jefferson Avenue (312-222-7700); The Atheneum Suite

Hotel, 1000 Brush Avenue (313-962-2323); and Crown Plaza Pontchartrain, 2 Washington Blvd. (313-965-0200).

RELATED EVENTS/RACES Race day includes a 5K and 1 Mile Fun Run, both of which take place at Hart Plaza, finish location for the marathon. The 5K begins at 8:00 a.m. and the 1 Mile Fun Run at 7:45 a.m. The races finish in time to allow participants to cheer for the marathoners emerging from the nearby tunnel.

AREA ATTRACTIONS Have you known anyone to vacation in Detroit? Neither have we. However, the city is not completely devoid of entertainment. The Henry Ford Museum lies in nearby Dearborn. Also of historical significance is the Motown Museum on W. Grand Blvd. The nation's largest movie theater hall, the Fox, stands on Woodward Avenue. Belle Isle Park, located three miles from downtown on the marathon course, holds many attractions, including a small zoo, aquarium and nature center. Sports fans may see the Wolverines of the University of Michigan or the Detroit Lions of the NFL, both of which play in neighboring towns. Another option involves heading across the Detroit River to the clean, charming Canadian city of Windsor, Ontario. Windsor, which recently legalized gambling, maintains a casino in an old art gallery and a riverboat casino on the Detroit River.

LOCAL RUNNING STORES Total Runner, 29207 Northwestern Hwy., Southfield (810-354-1177); Hanson's Running Shop, 3407 Rochester Road (810-616-9665).

HUMBOLDT REDWOODS MARATHON

OVERALL: 92.2

COURSE BEAUTY: 10

COURSE DIFFICULTY: 3- (SEE APPENDIX)

APPROPRIATENESS FOR FIRST TIMERS: 9

RACE ORGANIZATION: 9

CROWDS: 0+

RACE DATA

Contact:	Humboldt Redwoods Marathon
	P.O. Box 4989
	Arcata, CA 95518-4989
	(707) 443-1220
Date:	October 19, 1997
	October 18, 1998
Start Time:	9:00 a.m.
Time Course Closes:	2:00 p.m.
Number of Participants:	444 in 1995
Certification:	USATF
Course Records:	Male: (open) 2:27:28
	Female: (open) 2:46:16
Elite Athlete Programs:	No
Cost:	$30/40
Age groups/Divisions:	<18, 19-24, 25-29, 30-34, 35-39, 40-44, 45-49,
	50-54, 55-59, 60-64, 65-69, 70-74, 75-79, 80-84,
	85-89, 90-94, 95-99, 100+
Temperature:	45° - 60°
Aid/Splits:	10 / miles 1, 5, 10, 15, 20 & 25

HIGHLIGHTS Noble, old growth redwood groves provide a protective canopy almost every step of the way in one of North America's top 20 destination marathons, the Humboldt Redwoods Marathon. The ultimate nature lover's race, Humboldt's fast course offers the perfect setting for inspired running and tranquil introspection as you weave among the creaking giants. The filtered light cascades down runners like worshipers in an outdoor cathedral. After the race, explore the rugged beauty of California's northern coast and surrounding parks.

COURSE DESCRIPTION The Humboldt Redwoods Marathon starts and finishes at the Dyerville Bridge on the Avenue of the Giants (a Hwy. 101 alternative scenic route). After crossing the south fork of the Eel River, the race immediately enters a canopy of centuries-old redwoods that recedes only for a quarter mile at 2.2 and 10.6. The mostly flat, extremely fast, completely closed first half contains some gentle ups and downs that impart an interesting illusion. *"The first half seems downhill both out and back! Really fast,"* says Jeff Hildebrandt of Roseville, California. Returning to the Dyerville Bridge at mile 13, runners proceed left down Bull Creek Road for the second out and back passing through Rockefeller Forest. Monitored by CHP pilot cars, this section of the course is narrower, quieter, and more winding and rolling, gaining about 150 feet from mile 14 to 20 and losing the same amount from mile 20 to the finish.

CROWD/RUNNER SUPPORT Other than the thousands of ancient redwoods witnessing your quest, spectators are pretty much limited to the start, halfway, and finish. In addition to the usual water and electrolyte replacement, the aid stations near miles 17 and 22 carry energy bars and fruit to help get you through the final miles. Portable toilets are located at every aid station.

RACE LOGISTICS The undeveloped race site in Redwoods State Park means facilities in the area are fairly limited. You will need to drive to the start since lodging is scattered throughout the area. If you are traveling north on Highway 101, take the Founder's Tree exit, while southbound travelers should take the second Redcrest exit. You immediately hit upon the staging area and parking monitors will direct you to the parking location. Try to arrive before 8:00 a.m. to avoid traffic hassles.

ACTIVITIES Runners can register late on Saturday afternoon at the Burlington Campground Visitor's Center or on race day near the start area. On late Saturday afternoon, attend a slide show and discussion of the course at the Visitor's Center. Saturday evening you can choose between the Weott American Legion's Spaghetti Feed ($5) or the Scotia Inn's pasta dinner (about $11), both all-you-can-eat affairs. After the race, there are refreshments, a raffle, and awards ceremony.

AWARDS Marathon entrants receive T-shirts, finishers earn medallions, and the top three in each age group receive special medals. The overall winners are awarded merchandise prizes, and the top three overall, top two masters, and top seniors take home commemorative awards.

ACCOMMODATIONS The two race sponsor hotels are the Scotia Inn, 100 Main Street, Scotia (about 15 miles from the start) (707-764-5683); and Hotel Carter, 301 L Street, Eureka (about 40 miles from the start) (707-445-1390). Possibilities in Fortuna (about 24 miles from the start) include: the Best Western Country Inn, 1528 Kenmar Road (800-528-1234); Holiday Inn Express, 1859 Alamar Way (800-465-4329); and Super 8 Motel, 1805 Alamar Way (800-800-8000). In Eureka (about 40 miles from the start) try the: Eureka Inn, 7th and F Streets (707-442-6441); Comfort Inn, 2014 4th Street (800-424-6423); Red Lion Inn, 1929 4th Street (800-547-8010); Carson House Inn, 4th and M Streets (800-772-1622); and Motel 6, 1934 Broadway (707-445-9631). Possibilities in Myers Flat (8 miles away) include: Log Chapel Inn, Avenue of the Giants (707-943-3315); and Myers Flat Country Inn, Avenue of the Giants (707-943-3259). Redcrest (4 miles away) houses the Redcrest Motor Inn on the Avenue of the Giants (707-943-4208); and Garberville (25 miles away) offers the Benbow Inn, 445 Lake Benbow Drive (707-923-2124); and Motel Garberville, 948 Redwood Drive (707-923-2422). Campgrounds dot the area; campsite assignments are made at Burlington Campground near Humboldt Redwoods State Park Headquarters, 1.5 miles south of Weott on the Avenue of the Giants. See Avenue of the Giants entry for more accommodations.

RELATED EVENTS/RACES You may want to run in the super-fast Humboldt Redwoods Half Marathon which covers the first half of the full marathon course. The popular half, the USATF Pacific Association Half Marathon Championship, regularly attracts over 1,000 entrants and runs concurrently with the marathon. In addition, $4,000 in prize money is offered to the top half marathon finishers (must be USATF Pacific Association members to receive prize money).

AREA ATTRACTIONS Spend some time wandering amongst the redwoods, such as the Founder's Grove Nature Trail for starters. If you have the energy and time, we highly recommend driving north to Prairie Creek Redwoods State Park (south of Klamath) and hiking the incomparable Fern Canyon Trail with 50-foot precipices covered by immense ferns.

LOCAL RUNNING STORE The Jogg'n Shoppe, 1090 G Street, Arcata (707-822-3136).

CAPE COD MARATHON

OVERALL: 88.9

COURSE BEAUTY: 9+

COURSE DIFFICULTY: 6-

APPROPRIATENESS FOR FIRST TIMERS: 8

RACE ORGANIZATION: 8+

CROWDS: 1

RACE DATA

Contact:	Courtney & Carolyn Bird
	Cape Cod Marathon
	P.O. Box 699
	West Falmouth, MA 02574
	(508) 540-6959
Date:	October 26, 1997
	October 25, 1998
Start Time:	11:00 a.m.
Time Course Closes:	4:00 p.m.
Number of Participants:	905 in 1995
Certification:	USATF
Course Records:	Male: (open) 2:17:35; (masters) 2:30:49
	Female: (open) 2:37:06; (masters) 3:02:29
Elite Athlete Programs:	No
Cost:	$25/30
Age groups/Divisions:	14-39, 40-49, 50-59, 60+
Temperature:	45° - 60°
Aid/Splits:	10 / miles 1, 5, 10, 15, 20 & 25

HIGHLIGHTS Windswept coast, cranberry bogs, pulsing lighthouses, and clapboard homes provide the backdrop for New England's most charming marathon, the Cape Cod Marathon. Offering spectacular scenes, fall in the Cape often treats runners to fair weather for race day. After completing the challenging course and reloading at the post-race meal, head to the race directors' home for an evening of beer, snacks, and camaraderie. Such personal touches make for an experience that few marathons can match.

COURSE DESCRIPTION Cape Cod's loop course, open to residential traffic, starts at Village Green in downtown Falmouth, a wonderfully quaint town of wood and brick shops and restaurants. By .3 miles, the course enters a beautiful residential community before tracing Falmouth harbor (with a short, steep hill at 2.7) and fronting the coast until near mile 4. Here, the course turns inland through a scenic residential area, crossing one of the area's numerous finger inlets. Runners go down a short hill at 7.6, leading to cranberry bogs, woods, and farm land in rolling terrain. On Thomas Landers Road, from about mile 11 to 13, the course gains 70 feet over rolling hills. The course goes gently down from 13 to 13.5 and then rolls again as it becomes more residential. From mile 15.2 to 15.5, runners go up newly-paved Old Palmer Road and then drop from 15.8 to 16.1. As the course heads south toward Woods Hole, the rolling hills become more pronounced. At mile 20, a tough, .33-mile hill greets runners as they pass a nicely manicured golf course. Following part of the Falmouth Road Race course, runners enter Woods Hole at mile 21, go past the harbor, along the shore, and around Nobska Point and its lighthouse at mile 22. The short uphill provides spectacular views for runners. The course has a few steep rollers left before leveling off after mile 24 as it hugs the coast until mile 25.3. The course then turns up, away from the water, briefly cutting through a residential section before arriving downtown for the finish at Village Green.

CROWD/RUNNER SUPPORT Since the course goes through several residential areas, the race attracts good crowds for a small community, about 4,000 to 5,000 people. Portable toilets are available at the second, third, and fourth relay exchange points. A medical team roams the course as does a sag wagon for race victims.

RACE LOGISTICS Held in a small town, the race neither requires nor offers transportation to the start. Many accommodations are within walking distance of the start/finish. There is plenty of parking at the Lawrence School.

ACTIVITIES The Gus Canty Recreation Center, 790 East Main Street in Falmouth, serves as pre-race headquarters for most race activities. On Friday evening and Saturday afternoon, pick up your race packet, register late, or get info on things to do in the area. The race does not have an organized pasta party, but does cooperate with several local restaurants for pasta specials and free beer. The Lawrence School on Lakeview Avenue serves as race-day headquarters. You may register or pick up your packet on race day. Let one of the race massage therapists work out the kinks from the challenging course. Afterwards, enjoy a great meal of pasta, clam chowder, salad, juice, and soda in the school cafeteria. The awards ceremony starts at 3:30 p.m. in the school gym. After the mess at the school is cleaned up, head to the home of race directors Courtney and Carolyn Bird for a post-race party of free beer and leftover race tidbits.

AWARDS Every marathoner receives a Cape Cod Marathon long-sleeve T-shirt, and finishers receive medallions and certificates. A random drawing is held for various merchandise. Trophies and merchandise prizes go to the top age-group finishers, with the overall open and masters winners competing for about $6,000 in prize money. Overall winners earn $1,300, with $600 for second, and $300 for third. Fourth-place man receives $200 and fifth receives $100. Masters winners earn $400, runner-ups $200, and third-place man receives $100. All winners also receive individually inscribed coffee mugs.

ACCOMMODATIONS The Quality Inn — Falmouth, 291 Jones Road (800-854-1507), is the official race hotel. Located about a half mile from Village Green, the inn offers specials rates to Cape Cod runners. Also convenient are: Ramada on the Square, 40 North Main Street (508-457-0606); Elm Arch Inn, Elm Arch Way (508-548-0133); Inn at One Main Street, 1 Main Street (508-540-7469); Capt. Tom Lawrence House, 75 Locust Street (508-540-1445); Village Green Inn, 40 West Main Street (508-548-5621); and Palmer House Inn, 81 Palmer Avenue (508-548-1230). B&Bs dot the entire area, and the race can provide additional suggestions.

RELATED EVENTS/RACES The five-leg marathon relay runs concurrently with the marathon. Teams of two to five members run legs of 3, 6.5, 5.5, 5.8, and 5.4 miles. Each member can run from one to four legs in any order.

AREA ATTRACTIONS You can avoid the tourist mob on the Cape by visiting in the fall at marathon time. For unspoiled beaches, head to the Cape Cod National Seashore. Visit one of the many historic towns, such as Provincetown, Sandwich, and Truro. You can also explore the offshore islands, Martha's Vineyard and Nantucket. If you prefer your action a little faster, head north to Boston, about 90 minutes away.

LOCAL RUNNING STORE Burt's Sports Specialty, 850 Main Street, Falmouth (508-540-0644).

MARINE CORPS MARATHON

OVERALL: 99.2

COURSE BEAUTY: 10-

COURSE DIFFICULTY: 3+

APPROPRIATENESS FOR FIRST TIMERS: 10

RACE ORGANIZATION: 10

CROWDS: 3-

RACE DATA

Contact:	Marine Corps Marathon
	P.O. Box 188
	Quantico, VA 22134-0188
	(800) RUN-USMC
Date:	October 26, 1997
	October 25, 1998
Start Time:	8:30 a.m.
Time Course Closes:	3:00 p.m.
Number of Participants:	16,700 in 1995
Certification:	USATF
Course Records:	Male: (open) 2:14:01
	Female: (open) 2:37:00
Elite Athlete Programs:	No
Cost:	$30/40
Age groups/Divisions:	<19, 20-24, 25-29, 30-34, 35-39, 40-44, 45-49,
	50-54, 55-59, 60-64, 65-69, 70+
Temperature:	49° - 68°
Aid/Splits:	20 / miles 1, 3, 5, 10, 15, 20, 22 & 24

HIGHLIGHTS Nicknamed "The People's Marathon®" and "Marathon of the Monuments," the Marine Corps Marathon has established itself as one of the country's finest marathons. As the name implies, the U.S. Marine Corps hosts this Washington, D.C. classic, drawing about 15,000 runners, about half of whom are first-timers. The Marines execute the race splendidly, from race organization to providing encouragement along the course. Topping perhaps all other marathons in North America for first-timers (Oprah ran her first marathon here), Marine Corps also provides a great race for veterans. The course tours the nation's capital, passing Arlington Cemetery, Georgetown, the Kennedy Center, Lincoln Memorial, Jefferson Memorial, U.S. Capitol, Washington Monument, Union Station, and Smithsonian Museums. The Washington, D.C. location and the Marines' dedication combine for an unbeatable destination marathon.

RACE HISTORY Twenty one years ago, a group of Marines got together to find a way to celebrate the 200th anniversary of the U.S. Marine Corps. They decided that a marathon would be a good choice as it illustrates the Marine Corps' credo. The determination, endurance, and strength required to train for and complete a marathon lead to the same healthy lifestyle and pride in accomplishment that the Marines have long known and respected. Like the Marine Corps, anyone can join, but only the few, the proud, those who are willing to ask the most of themselves, succeed in meeting the challenge. The Marines thought a race touring the monuments would not only be beautiful, but it would give the runners a chance to reflect on the history of the country and those who have defended it. MCM's strong reputation has made it the fourth-largest marathon in North America, with over 15,000 runners.

C O U R S E   D E S C R I P T I O N MCM's closed course starts and finishes near the Marine Corps War Memorial marked by the Iwo Jima Monument in Arlington, VA. The marathon first passes through sobering Arlington National Cemetery where many of the nation's great soldiers and John F. Kennedy are buried. Then it's past the Pentagon, the world's largest office building (after mile 1), Pentagon City, a large shopping mall (mile 2), and the mostly commercial surrounding areas between miles 2 and 3. During miles 4 to 6, runners wind around the Pentagon before returning to Arlington Cemetery (near mile 7). The course passes the starting area and the high-rise office buildings of Rosslyn, VA, at mile 8. At this point, the heart of the MCM course begins. Runners enter Key Bridge after mile 8 on a slight incline. Crossing the bridge, the stone spire of prestigious Georgetown University, the nation's oldest Catholic university, looms above you. Runners exit Key Bridge onto M Street, one of fashionable Georgetown's main thoroughfares. The course then cuts down to scenic Rock Creek Parkway, skirting the Potomac River, and passing the Kennedy Center's bright white classicism just after mile 10. Around 10.66 miles, the course turns left past the Lincoln Memorial to the famous Mall (miles 10.66 to 13 and 14.66 to 17.66). At about 11.5 miles, runners can glimpse the White House beyond the Ellipse on the left and the towering Washington Monument on the right. During mile 12, the course heads by many of the Smithsonian Museums, and mile 13, runners have an excellent view of the U.S. Capitol. Then, with a slight incline, it's on to Union Station (about 13.5 miles) before circling the Capitol and returning down to the Mall on the opposite (south) side. At mile 17.5, look across the Tidal Basin for a nice view of the Jefferson Memorial. Completely flat, miles 18 to 22.5 are run in scenic East Potomac Park, around Hains Point, the site of many of the area's top road races. The course crosses the 14th Street Bridge (mile 23) with a gentle incline, and then it's past the now very familiar Pentagon as runners retrace their steps to finish, on an incline, at the Iwo Jima Monument.

CROWD / RUNNER SUPPORT Most of MCM runs in the historic sections of Washington, so the course doesn't pass through many residential neighborhoods. Despite this, local spectators turn out in surprisingly good numbers at several points. Nearly 10,000 spectators pack the start/finish area, and large numbers also turn out along the Key Bridge. Particularly strategic, the Mall attracts many onlookers as they can cheer for their favorite runner three times. Right before the 14th Street Bridge is another prime spectator spot, since it is scenic and near accessible parking. Friends and family can take the Metro to several of these and other points on the course to support their runner. Helpful, polite, and enthusiastic, the Marines along the course provide the best inspiration (besides your fellow runners). Tall, 12-foot yellow poles with large mile indicators mark the course.

RACE LOGISTICS Several hotels have shuttle buses to the start. Check with race officials for the most recent list. You can park in the Pentagon's North and South parking lots and then take a shuttle from there to the start (6:30 a.m. to 8:30 a.m.). The Metro does not run early on marathon day, so it is not a solution to make it to the start. However, runners could take a taxi to the start and take the Metro from Rosslyn Station or Arlington Cemetery Station after the race. The race has a bag drop for your belongings. After the race, meet your family in the post-race linkup area, marked by red banners indicating first letters of your last name.

ACTIVITIES Runners can pick up their race packets at the Sheraton National Hotel, the week prior to the marathon, on Thursday from 4:00 p.m. to 8:00 p.m., Friday from 10:00 a.m. to 10:00 p.m., or Saturday from 8:00 a.m. to 10:00 p.m. There is no race-day packet pickup or registration. On Friday and Saturday, attend the runner's expo and symposium while picking up your race packet. On Saturday night, the Sheraton hosts a pasta dinner (about $10). After the race, hang out at the post-race party with refreshments, drink, and fruit. The awards ceremony is held on the west steps of the War Memorial at 1:00 p.m.

AWARDS Every entrant receives a T-shirt, and finishers receive medals, certificates and results books. Over 400 trophies are awarded in individual and 11 team categories. MCM presents Middendorf Trophy replicas to the overall winners. Among the categories of awards are: age groups (men up to 10 places and women up to 5 places), first Virginia, Maryland, and D.C. residents, U.S. military, U.S. Marine Corps, Canadian military, Clydesdale, and retired military.

ACCOMMODATIONS The Sheraton National Hotel, Columbia Pike & Washington Blvd. in Arlington (703-521-1900), serves as the race headquarters hotel ($100). Also convenient are the: Holiday Inn Key Bridge, 1850 N. Fort Myer Drive, Rosslyn (703-522-0400), $100; Sheraton Crystal City, 1800 Jefferson Davis Hwy., Arlington (800-862-7666), $110; and the Courtyard Marriott, 2899 Jefferson Davis Hwy., Arlington (800-847-4775), $90.

RELATED EVENTS / RACES MCM sponsors the Special Olympics Mini Marathon, where Special Olympics athletes from around the country compete in 5K, 10K, and unified road races after the marathon start.

AREA ATTRACTIONS Washington, D.C. is a tourist's heaven, and many of the city's premiere attractions are free! Be sure to visit your favorite Smithsonian Museum (Air & Space, Natural History, American History, and Holocaust are the most popular), the National Gallery, U.S. Capitol, White House, Mount Vernon, and Arlington National Cemetery. You could easily spend weeks here without getting the least bit bored. For a short getaway, try Skyline Drive in Shenandoah National Park for spectacular autumn foliage and excellent hiking. Take I-66 West and follow the signs (about 1.5 hours). In the evening, head to Adams-Morgan for some ethnic flavor, Georgetown for urban chic, and Old Town Alexandria for slightly more staid fun.

LOCAL RUNNING STORES Fleet Feet Sports, 1840 Columbia Road, NW, Washington, D.C. (202-387-3888); Racquet & Jog, 3225 M Street, NW, Washington, D.C. (202-333-8113); Pacers, 1301 King Street, Alexandria, VA (703-836-1463); Fleet Feet Sports, 7516 Leesburg Pike, Falls Church (703-790-3338).

SH WAR 1898 × PHILIPPINE·INSURRECTION·1898-1902 × BOXER·REBELLION·1900 × NICARAGUA·1912·1933

N REPUBLIC 1965 × LEBANON·1981-1984 × GRENADA·1983

"THE PEOPLES MARATHON"®
1-800-RUN-USMC

Marine Corps Marathon

4th Sunday in October • Tour Your Nation's Capital

OCEAN STATE MARATHON

OVERALL: 88.8

COURSE BEAUTY: 9-

COURSE DIFFICULTY: 5- (SEE APPENDIX)

APPROPRIATENESS FOR FIRST TIMERS: 8

RACE ORGANIZATION: 9

CROWDS: 1+

RACE DATA

Contact: Gerry Beagan
Ocean State Marathon
5 Division Street
East Greenwich, RI 02818
(401) 885-4499
Date: October 26, 1997
October 25, 1998
Start Time: 9:00 a.m.
Time Course Closes: 2:30 p.m.
Number of Participants: 880 in 1995
Certification: USATF
Course Records: Male: (open) 2:16:31; (masters) 2:25:20
Female: (open) 2:41:23; (masters) 3:04:55
Elite Athlete Programs: Yes
Cost: $30/40
Age groups/Divisions: <39, 40-49, 50-59, 60+
Temperature: 47° - 63°
Aid/Splits: 12 / digital clocks at miles 5, 10, 13.1, 15, 20 & 25.2

HIGHLIGHTS Believe in reincarnation? Ocean State Marathon ("OSM") organizers do. OSM, which traces Rhode Island's coast from Narragansett to Warwick, springs from the original Ocean State race held in Newport from 1976 to 1986. The current Ocean State offers a scenic, point-to-point, moderately difficult course. Weather can play a real factor in Rhode Island — you may face a Nor-Easter head on, or you may be blessed with a tailwind all the way to Warwick. Quickly on the road toward recapturing its former glory, OSM already ranks as one of the top races in New England.

RACE HISTORY The Ocean State Marathon started in 1976 in Newport, Rhode Island. Very successful, the race peaked with more than 2,500 runners in 1979. After losing its primary sponsor, the race was canceled in 1987 when no alternative sponsor emerged. Revived in 1988 as the Rhode Island Marathon ("RIM"), the race was run on a variety of courses on Aquidneck Island until 1992 when it looped from Warwick to Providence. Around that time, several race committee members became disillusioned with the direction the RIM had taken. They began exploring the possibility of resuscitating the Ocean State Marathon. In 1993, the new Ocean State threw down the gauntlet, holding its race one week prior to RIM and within miles of each other. RIM folded the following year, and Ocean State doubled to over 1,100 entrants.

COURSE DESCRIPTION Ocean State's scenic, moderately challenging, point-to-point course starts on Kingstown Road at Sprague Park in Narragansett (adjacent to the high school). Gaining 28 feet in the first mile, runners then go downhill about 60 feet to the sea-wall at mile 2. As you turn onto the shoulder of Ocean Road (Scenic Route 1A), you will either be nailed by a stern headwind or graced with a pleasant tailwind. The next mile and a half along the coast remain flat and beautiful. At 3.5 miles, the course rises 40 feet and then falls 30 feet at 4 miles. Now begins the first real climb on the course, a 105-footer over 2 miles. Mostly flat, the next 3 miles (6 to 9) provide a nice respite before the second big climb from mile 9 to 10. Just after the 9-mile mark, look to your right for a great view of Narragansett Bay and the Newport Bridge. From the Casey Farm at 9 to Heffie's at 10, you climb another 85 feet. Then you face a steep downhill (120 feet) to mile 11 on a newly paved road. Try not to get too carried away here. Enjoy the flat stretch from mile 11 to 12.7 since you climb another 44 feet to 13, before dropping 30 feet into the charming village of Wickford. Savor these next two miles because the course's complexion soon changes. At 14.2, runners turn right on Route 1 climbing 40 feet in the process. The next five miles on Route 1 roll with about four noticeable ups and downs. This relatively tedious section may be the most difficult psychologically for many runners since it runs by fast-food joints, stores, bowling alleys, and lots of concrete. Just before mile 20, runners face the toughest hill on the course, a short, steep 80-footer. The next mile proceeds down affluent East Greenwich's Main Street. Mostly flat until mile 22.5, the route features two more down and ups from 22.5 to 23.2 and from 23.8 to 24 while becoming flat again the final 2.2 miles through residential Warwick.

CROWD/RUNNER SUPPORT Approximately 5,000 to 10,000 people come out to support the runners, with the largest clumps at 10K, miles 10, 13.1, 14, 20, 21 and the finish. Twelve aid stations offering water and electrolyte replacement dot the course at approximately miles 2.5, 4.5, 7, 9, 11.5, 14, 16, 18.5, 19.5, 21, 23, and 25. Digital clocks are located at miles 1, 5, 10, 15, 20, and 25.2, and every mile is marked. Music and other entertainment provide inspiration at several points, while four medical units provide mending.

RACE LOGISTICS You can either drive to the start or take the race bus from the finish area. Buses leave from Warwick Veterans Memorial High School from 6:30 a.m. to 7:30 a.m. If you drive to the start, park at Narragansett High School parking lot, and make sure someone will pick you up at the finish since there is no bus from the finish back to the start after the race. To get to the starting line, walk a short distance down Prospect Avenue at the back of the school to Kingstown Road. The race transports your sweats and other gear to the finish for you to retrieve.

ACTIVITIES The Health and Fitness Fair goes from 11:00 a.m. to 5:00 p.m. on Saturday. Browse informational booths, buy race apparel, pick up your race packet, or register late for the race. You can register on race morning at Narragansett High School from 7:00 a.m. to 8:30 a.m. Saturday evening, dine at the pasta dinner (about $10) at a local restaurant. After the marathon, enjoy a well-deserved massage, shower, and food, such as clam chowder, donuts, and pizza. At 2:00 p.m., the awards ceremony kicks off in the auditorium, followed by a raffle.

AWARDS Every entrant receives a long-sleeve T-shirt and a race program book. Finishers garner unique medallions, certificates, and complete results, including individual performance data. OSM offers approximately $30,000 in prize money for individuals and teams.

ELITE RUNNERS INFORMATION OSM may award elite status to men under 2:20 and women under 2:50. Elites may be offered some travel money, lodging, and free entry and compete for about $30,000 in prize money. The top five overall runners earn $5,000, $2,500, $1,250, $750, and $500; the top two masters runners (40-49) garner $500 and $400; the top two seniors (50-59) earn $300 and $200; and the top veteran (60+) earns $200. Special awards also go to the top Rhode Island finishers.

ACCOMMODATIONS The Sheraton Tara Airport Hotel, 1850 Post Road, Warwick (800-THE TARA), serves as the host hotel. The Tara offers discount packages to Ocean State runners, about $80 a night. Other possibilities include: Comfort Inn, 1940 Post Road (401-732-0470); Radisson Hotel, 2081 Post Road (401-739-3000); Master Hosts Inn, 2138 Post Road

(401-737-7400); Holiday Inn at the Crossings, 800 Greenwich Avenue (401-732-6000); Marriott Residence Inn, 500 Kilvert Street (401-737-7100); Susse Chalet Inn, 36 Jefferson Blvd. (401-941-6600); and Crossroads Inn, 20 Jefferson Blvd. (401-467-9800).

AREA ATTRACTIONS The 400 miles of coastline attract most people to Rhode Island. Perhaps most famous is Newport, site of some of the most monied homes on the East Coast and one of the world's best music spectacles, the Newport Jazz Festival held every Spring. Block Island, an excellent daytrip, lies southeast of Newport. Perhaps best toured by bicycle, Block Island offers wild natural splendor packed into 21 square miles.

LOCAL RUNNING STORES Camire's Athletic Soles, 533 Pontiac Avenue, Cranston, north of Warwick (401-467-5582); Camire's Athletic Soles, 20-B Main Street, Belmont Plaza, Wakefield (401-782-8353); Feet First, 153 Old Tower Hill Road, Wakefield (401-783-8074); Feet First, 5600 Post Road, E. Greenwich (401-885-0606).

NEW YORK CITY MARATHON

OVERALL: 97.9

COURSE BEAUTY: 8-

COURSE DIFFICULTY: 4+ (SEE APPENDIX)

APPROPRIATENESS FOR FIRST TIMERS: 10-

RACE ORGANIZATION: 10+

CROWDS: 5+

RACE DATA

Contact:	New York City Marathon
	New York Road Runners Club
	9 E. 89th Street
	New York, NY 10128
	(212) 860-4455
Date:	November 2, 1997
	November 1, 1998
Start Time:	10:50 a.m.
Time Course Closes:	NA
Number of Participants:	27,900 in 1995
Certification:	USATF
Course Records:	Male: (open) 2:08:01
	Female: (open) 2:24:40
Elite Athlete Programs:	Yes
Cost:	$35/45 plus USATF membership
Age groups/Divisions:	18-19, 20-29, 30-39, 40-49, 50-59,
	60-69, 70-79, 80+
Temperature:	42° - 55°
Aid/Splits:	24 / digital clocks every mile

HIGHLIGHTS Perhaps the most exciting marathon in the world, the New York City Marathon overwhelms the senses with its sights, smells, sounds, and excitement. Over 60,000 runners vie for the 29,000 slots each year. The first Sunday each November, the lucky winners fill the upper and lower spans of the Verrazano-Narrows Bridge anxiously awaiting their trek through the five boroughs that comprise New York City and over the five bridges that connect each borough to the next. Over 2 million cheering spectators surround the course, buoying your every step.

RACE HISTORY The New York City Marathon's humble beginnings may surprise runners new to the sport. Legendary runner Fred Lebow, who died of brain cancer in 1994, founded the marathon in 1970. Held entirely within Central Park, the race vanquished 72 of its 127 starters. One hundred hard-core spectators witnessed Gary Muhrcke's victory in 2:31:38, with the top finishers earning cheap wrist watches and recycled bowling trophies. With grueling 80° temperatures, the survivors rushed to the waiting cans of soda only to find there were no can openers! In 1976, the race finally left Central Park for the five boroughs of the city. To keep things interesting, however, organizers threw in a flight of stairs on the course. Bill Rodgers won his first of four in a row that year, only to discover afterward that his car had been towed. In 1979, Grete Waitz of Norway entered her first marathon here, the start of her nine victories in eleven years. In 1981, both the men's and women's winners broke the then-world marathon record, with Alberto Salazar finishing in 2:08:13 and Allison Roe recording a 2:25:29. In 1994, eventual winner German Silva

of Mexico nearly blew it at the end when he took his eye off the blue line and took a wrong turn in Central Park. He quickly recovered and snatched the victory in the closest finish in NYC's history. Things are never dull in New York.

C O U R S E   D E S C R I P T I O N Located on Staten Island, the marathon's three starting lines lie at the Verrazano-Narrows Toll Plaza. Runners use both the upper and lower spans of the bridge, the longest single suspension bridge in the world. Elite men and men under 3:30 start at the blue line on the Brooklyn-bound, right-side upper level. Local elite men and men over 3:30 start at the green line on the Staten Island-bound lower level. All women start at the red line on the Staten Island-bound upper level. After going up the bridge, about a 180-foot climb, runners hit the first mile mark at its midpoint and the second mile mark at the exit ramps. Miles 3 through 13 course through Brooklyn, passing Bay Ridge at mile 3, Fort Greene at mile 8, Bedford-Stuyvesant at mile 9, and Williamsburg at mile 11. The half marathon point lies on the Pulaski Bridge (about a 40-foot incline) connecting Brooklyn and Queens (13.1 to 15.5). The course heads through Long Island City, a manufacturing area since the industrial revolution and now home to the Silvercup Studios, often referred to as Hollywood East. At mile 15, runners climb 130 feet up the Queensboro Bridge, spanning the East River and Roosevelt Island, bringing them to Manhattan (16 to 20). North on First Avenue, you pass through the Upper East Side, known as the silk stocking district; Yorkville in the East 80s, formerly a thriving German community; and then Spanish Harlem. Just before mile 20, the Willis Avenue Bridge spans the Harlem River, posing a challenge to many runners. You then make a quick trip through the ethnically diverse Bronx, mile 20, before hitting the final bridge, the Madison Avenue Bridge, just prior to mile 21 leading back into Manhattan. The next two miles traverse Harlem, the center of black culture famous for its dance and music. The final miles tour rolling, challenging Central Park, one of the world's great urban retreats, finishing at Tavern on the Green.

H O W   T O   E N T E R Request an entry form with a self-addressed envelop beginning on January 1st. The first 14,000 runners are accepted on a first-come, first-served basis, with 8,000 drawn from New York, New Jersey, and Connecticut, and 6,000 drawn from the rest of the country. Get your application in the day you receive it in the mail. The next 5,000 runners are determined by a lottery held in July or August. The last 10,000 entries are reserved for international runners based on a quota system by country. Accepted runners are notified beginning in early July. The race maintains a wait list to fill spaces vacated by runners who are forced to cancel. Note that runners must belong to USATF to enter the race.

C R O W D / R U N N E R   S U P P O R T Banners hang prominently along the race course and in midtown Manhattan, gearing up community support for the marathon. On race day, spectators turn out in tremendous numbers, with approximately 2 million viewing the race. More than 40 bands of all flavors speckle the course, providing a lift to tired runners. Twenty-four water stations line the course every mile starting at mile 3, with electrolyte replacement available every two miles beginning at mile 4 and every mile beginning at mile 22. A sponge station lies just after mile 18; sponges can be replenished in the kiddie pools from miles 19 to 25. Digital clocks indicate the elapsed time every mile, and several video checkpoints ensure race integrity.

R A C E   L O G I S T I C S Since the Verrazano-Narrows Bridge closes at 9:00 a.m., we recommend taking the race buses to the start area. Although unfortunately an expensive ride at $7 a head, it will eliminate much worry and aggravation on race morning. Buses pick up runners at the New York City Public Library at Fifth Avenue and 42nd Street between 5:30 a.m. and 7:30 a.m. You must purchase a ticket ahead of time at the Runner's Expo. The race will transport your warmups to the finish area.

A C T I V I T I E S On Wednesday through Saturday before the marathon, you can attend the marathon expo at the New York Coliseum. Bring your registration card and a photo ID to retrieve your race packet, and check out the approximately 80 exhibitor booths. You can also buy NYC Marathon souvenirs at the marathon Gift Shop in the Coliseum. The race holds a number of clinics and seminars which may interest you. See your information package for this year's topics. On Saturday evening from 4:30 p.m. to 9:30 p.m., join 17,000 other runners and guests at the pasta party at Tavern on the Green under the big tent. On race morning, munch on bagels at the start area to fuel your journey. After your race, meet your family and friends at the Family Reunion Festival on Central Park West from Columbus Circle to 72nd Street. The festival features food, beverage, music, and a giant screen projecting the race. An awards ceremony is held inside the Sheraton Hotel at 7:30 p.m., followed by the Celebration Party at 8:30 p.m. in the Roseland Ballroom and Disco, 239 West 52nd Street.

AWARDS Every NYC Marathon entrant receives an official race T-shirt and poster. Those who complete the race also receive finisher medals. Age-group winners receive Tiffany trophies as do the top runners from each New York borough. Awards also go to the top three international teams, USATF-sanctioned teams, top five NYRRC local runners, and the oldest male and female to finish the race.

ELITE RUNNERS INFORMATION As expected, the NYC Marathon actively recruits the top runners from around the world. Elites are offered transportation, lodging, expenses, and the chance to take home a sizeable paycheck. The top five overall finishers respectively earn: $20,000 plus a new automobile, $15,000, $10,000, $5,000, and $2,500. American citizens who finish in the top five earn double the above amounts. Furthermore, any American who wins the race receives a $60,000 bonus, bringing their total earnings to $100,000 plus an auto. The race has established time bonuses for runners breaking 2:15 for men and 2:33 for women (from $2,500 up to $65,000 for sub 2:07 and 2:22 times respectively). The top three masters are awarded $3,000, $2,000, and $1,000. Prize money also goes to the top local teams and individuals, including time incentives.

ACCOMMODATIONS Two hotels serve as the NYC Marathon co-headquarters, the New York Hilton and Towers, 1335 Avenue of the Americas, between 53rd and 54th Streets (212-586-7000); and the Sheraton New York Hotel & Towers, 811 Seventh Avenue, between 52nd and 53rd Streets (212-581-1000). Runners who would like to stay at either hotel must complete an application provided with their acceptance notification. The race also provides a Hotel Guide listing scores of other possible lodgings.

RELATED EVENTS / RACES The race sponsors the International Friendship Run, a four-mile fun run held the day before the marathon at 8:00 a.m. Exclusively for international runners and their families, runners follow their country's flag from the United Nations to Tavern on the Green in Central Park. After the jaunt, runners swap T-shirts and pins with fellow marathoners from around the world.

LOCAL RUNNING STORES Super Runners Shop, 360 Amsterdam Avenue, New York City (212-787-7665); Super Runners Shop, 1337 Lexington Avenue, New York City (212-369-6010); Super Runners Shop, 416 Third Avenue, New York City (212-213-4560).

WARWICK MARATHON

OVERALL: 76.1

COURSE BEAUTY: 8-

COURSE DIFFICULTY: 4- (SEE APPENDIX)

APPROPRIATENESS FOR FIRST TIMERS: 7+

RACE ORGANIZATION: 9

CROWDS: 1-

R A C E   D A T A

Contact: Warwick Marathon
P.O. Box 561
Warwick, NY 10990
(914) 986-8572
Date: November 2, 1997
November 1, 1998
Start Time: 10:40 a.m.
Time Course Closes: 4:40 p.m.
Number of Participants: 720 in 1995
Certification: USATF
Course Records: Male: (open) 2:32:13
Female: (open) 2:58:00
Elite Athlete Programs: Yes
Cost: $35/40
Age groups/Divisions: 16-19, 20-29, 30-39, 40-49, 50-59, 60-69, 70+
Temperature: 45° - 50°
Aid/Splits: 24 / miles 5, 10, 13.1 & 20

HIGHLIGHTS You're all trained, ready to go, but got shut out of the NYC Marathon sweepstakes. What do you do now? The folks in Warwick think you should head to their 18th century village 50 miles north of New York City for the Warwick Marathon. Held on the same day and at the same time as New York, Warwick was started to attract all the disgruntled NYC hopefuls and those who prefer open space and fresh air. The rural course rolls past countless farms, meadows, and forest, well supported by 24 aid stations, 400 volunteers, and numerous forms of entertainment.

COURSE DESCRIPTION Starting down Warwick's Main Street, runners quickly reach the country, slightly descending during mile 1 and gradually rising in mile 2. Flat from mile 2 to mile 5, the course climbs slightly before turning onto Jones Road preceding a small downward pitch to mile 7.5 (interrupted by a good, 100-yard bump near 6). A sharp hill precedes the right turn onto Blooms Corner through beautiful meadows and forest. Watch the cows graze while readying for the steep quarter-mile hill at mile 9. Rolling to mile 11.5, the course runs mostly flat through fertile, black dirt onion fields to 24 (except some gentle undulations at miles 13, 15, and 17 and a 100-yard incline at 21). A short, steep hill wakes runners at 24, with a final bump at 25.5. Back in town, runners finish at Town Park.

CROWD/RUNNER SUPPORT Small town Warwick shows off its community support by supplying 400 volunteers, several bands, two bagpipers, clowns, and comedians to entertain and support the runners. The residents also throw block parties to amuse themselves.

The race buses spectators to various points along the course so they can catch their runners, and returns them to the finish ($6). Portable toilets sit ready at miles 6 and 16, and there is food for sale for hungry race watchers. The generous 24 aid stations offer water, electrolyte replacement, and minor first aid.

ACTIVITIES Pick up your race packet or register late at the Warwick Center, Friday evening and all day Saturday. (You may also register on race day at the start from 8:00 a.m. to 10:00 a.m.) While there, breeze through the race expo with merchandise and informational booths. The pasta party dishes out Saturday evening from 5:30 p.m. to 8:00 p.m. at the Warwick Center, 60 Hoyt Road. Unwind with a free post-race massage, refreshments, and music. The awards ceremony follows the festivities.

AWARDS Each runner receives a long-sleeve T-shirt, and finishers also receive medals. The top three age-group finishers are awarded trophies. The top three runners compete for $1,750 in prize money: $500 for first, $250 for second, and $125 for third.

ELITE RUNNERS INFORMATION Men under 2:30 and women under 2:45 are offered lodging and complimentary entry. Contact the race director for more information.

ACCOMMODATIONS The marathon headquarters, Warwick Center, 60 Hoyt Road (914-986-1164), offers inexpensive, hostel-like lodging for Warwick Marathon entrants. Other accommodations in the area include: Howard Johnson, 551 Route 211 East, Middletown (914-342-5822 or 800-654-2000); Seasons Resort at Great Gorge, Route 517, McAfee, NJ (201-827-6000); Peach Grove Inn, 205 Route 17A, Warwick (914-986-7411); Chateau Hathorn, 33 Hathorn Road, Warwick (914-986-6099); Yesterday's, 29 Main Street, Warwick (914-986-1904); Warwick Valley B&B, 24B Maple Avenue, Warwick (914-987-7255); Inn at 40 Oakland, 40 Oakland Avenue, Warwick (914-987-8269); and Day's Inn, Route 17M and Route 6, New Hampton (914-374-2411).

AREA ATTRACTIONS Pick your own apples at one of the many orchards that speckle the area while enjoying the fall foliage. Antique lovers may give Sugar Loaf Arts and Crafts Village a try, or the many antique dealers around Warwick. You will also find plenty of opportunities for golf and hiking.

LOCAL RUNNING STORES Dick's Sporting Goods, Middletown Galleria, 1 Galleria Drive, Middletown; Sneakers to Boots, 30 Forester Avenue, Warwick.

CITY OF SANTA CLARITA MARATHON

OVERALL: 78

COURSE BEAUTY: 7

COURSE DIFFICULTY: 3+ (SEE APPENDIX)

APPROPRIATENESS FOR FIRST TIMERS: 7

RACE ORGANIZATION: 9+

CROWDS: 1+

RACE DATA

Contact: City of Santa Clarita Marathon
P.O. Box 800298
Santa Clarita, CA 91380
(805) 259-5441

Date: November 9, 1997
November 8, 1998

Start Time: 7:00 a.m.

Time Course Closes: 1:00 p.m.

Number of Participants: 600 in 1995

Certification: USATF

Course Records: Male: (open) 2:30:54; (masters) 2:47:38
Female: (open) 3:06:28; (masters) 3:15:22

Elite Athlete Programs: No

Cost: $35/45

Age groups/Divisions: 18-24, 25-29, 30-34, 35-39, 40-44, 45-49, 50-54,
55-59, 60-64, 65-69, 70+

Temperature: 44° - 60°

Aid/Splits: 26 / every mile, 10K & 13.1

HIGHLIGHTS You had hoped to go to Orlando this winter for the Walt Disney World Marathon. Maybe you live in California and just don't have the funds for the trip. The next best thing may be Six Flags California and its Colossus roller coaster, which lies on the path of the City of Santa Clarita Marathon. This fresh, exuberant race burst on the Southern California running scene in 1995 with an impressive debut and envious budget for a first-time affair. With grand growth plans, the race may eventually become a national draw, but for now it is a nice alternative for Californians worried about spending too much money around Christmas.

COURSE DESCRIPTION The City of Santa Clarita Marathon's point-to-point course journeys through all four Santa Clarita communities — Saugus, Newhall, Valencia, and Canyon Country — utilizing streets, trails, and paseos. Nestled among mountain ranges in view throughout the course, the rural-flavored course is completely closed to traffic. Beginning at the historic Lang Station area in Canyon Country, the route follows a gentle, downhill slope on tree-lined streets past residential communities and the flowered hillsides of Canyon Country Park. At the first intersection on the course, runners glimpse a continuous parade of restaurants, shopping centers, and homes. The course drops off the street onto the Santa Clara River trail and remains on this asphalt bike path to Golden Oak, where it jumps back onto Soledad Canyon Road. As they continue past the infamous Saugus Speedway, runners catch a peek at the bargain hunter's paradise, the Saugus Swap Meet. At mile 10, the course begins a gentle ascent until its peak at mile 16.

Runners soon jump onto the South Fork Trail and eventually pass through Old Town Newhall. Again passing through tree-lined, residential streets, runners practically tiptoe through backyards as they run on the Valencia paseo system. The paseo system includes several overpass bridges and under-passes, after which runners pass the renowned California Institute of the Arts while encountering their toughest hill at 18.5. But, it's a downhill relief for the next mile into the main entrance of College of the Canyons, through its campus and past the baseball field to Valencia Blvd. and the Old Road. While crossing the Golden State Freeway, runners hear the roar of 30,000 Harley Davidsons as their riders motor through on their annual Love Ride. Another downhill slope leads into Six Flags California, where runners come within yards of the rollercoaster Colossus, Hurricane Harbor, and the new Superman ride. At last, the course passes through the Valencia Business Park, a flat, secluded complex of large buildings and home of several movie and sound studios. From the business park, runners emerge into a mix of empty fields and retail centers and finish at the Valencia Town Center shopping mall in the heart of Santa Clarita.

CROWD/RUNNER SUPPORT The Santa Clarita communities genuinely support the marathon, with spectators dotting most of the course. CSCM offers outstanding runner support with 26 water stations along the course including electrolyte replacement drink from mile 5 through 25. There are five medical aid stations, toilets at every mile, and a sponge station at mile 22. Mile splits are called every mile, at 10K and the halfway point.

RACE LOGISTICS The race designates a parking area near the finish line and offers shuttle bus service from the assembly area to the start from 5:30 a.m. to 6:15 a.m. Don't worry about your warm-ups; the race transports them from the start to the finish for you to retrieve.

ACTIVITIES The Business, Sports, and Fitness Expo goes on Saturday, noon to 6:00 p.m., and Sunday from 6:30 a.m. to 3:00 p.m., at the Valencia Town Center. A pasta dinner is held Saturday evening. There is no race-day registration. Family music and entertainment keep you occupied after the marathon. Expo booths also sit around the finish area for you to browse while you await the awards ceremony at noon. You can also stroll through Valencia Town Center for food, shopping, and movies.

AWARDS All race entrants receive T-shirts, while finishers earn commemorative medals. Overall winners receive trophies, while the top five age-group finishers are awarded plaques.

ACCOMMODATIONS The official race hotel is the Best Western Ranch House Inn, 27413 Tourney Road, Valencia (805-255-0555). Others convenient to the course are: Hampton Inn, 25259 The Old Road, Newhall (805-253-2400); Marriott Fairfield, 25340 The Old Road, Stevenson Ranch (805-290-2828); Residence Inn, 25320 The Old Road, Stevenson Ranch (805-290-2800); Valencia Hilton at Six Flags, 27710 The Old Road, Valencia (800-445-8667); and Country Inn, 17901 Sierra Highway, Santa Clarita (800-537-8930).

RELATED EVENTS/RACES Santa Clarita holds two related events at the marathon finish line — a 10-Mile Run on an out-and-back route covering the final five miles of the marathon course (designated an official training run for the LA Marathon), and a Kiddie K Fun Run for children 12 and under.

AREA ATTRACTIONS Kids and grownups alike will enjoy the Six Flags California amusement park in Valencia and Mountasia Fun Center in Canyon Country. Bargain hunters may want to check out the Saugus Swap Meet on Sundays. Several film studios mark the area, including Melody Ranch. Los Angeles lies only a short drive away.

LOCAL RUNNING STORE In-Motion, 25834 McBean Parkway, Santa Clarita (805-255-3353).

COLUMBUS MARATHON

OVERALL: 91.3

COURSE BEAUTY: 9-

COURSE DIFFICULTY: 3- (SEE APPENDIX)

APPROPRIATENESS FOR FIRST TIMERS: 10-

RACE ORGANIZATION: 10

CROWDS: 4-

R A C E   D A T A

Contact: Joan Riegel
Columbus Marathon
P.O. Box 26806
Columbus, OH 43226
(614) 433-0395
http://www.columbuspages.com/marathon

Date: November 9, 1997
November 8, 1998

Start Time: 9:00 a.m.

Time Course Closes: 2:30 p.m.

Number of Participants: 6,500 in 1995

Certification: USATF

Course Records: Male: (open) 2:11:02; (masters) 2:20:23
Female: (open) 2:30:54; (masters) 2:38:07

Elite Athlete Programs: Yes

Cost: $35/45, plus USATF membership

Age groups/Divisions: 18-19, 20-24, 25-29, 30-34, 35-39, 40-44, 45-49,
50-54, 55-59, 60-64, 65-69, 70+; Clydesdales
(males 200+, females 140+): 18-39, 40+

Temperature: 42° - 53°

Aid/Splits: 19 / digital clocks every mile & 5K, including pace
& projected finish

HIGHLIGHTS Fast, detailed, and runner-friendly, the Columbus Marathon regularly attracts 5,000 runners, many looking to improve their marathon mark. Columbus' excellent reputation led to its designation as the U.S. Men's Olympic Marathon Trials in 1992. The unique course design, called a cloverleaf by organizers, resembles the profile of a roadrunner, with the three loops depicting its tail, body/head, and leg. The layout allows runners to cover many of Columbus' most interesting neighborhoods, such as Short North, Ohio State University, Bexley, and German Village. Those not familiar with the city may be pleasantly surprised at what it offers, including museums, theater, shopping, and diverse dining. Weather, the biggest variable, can range from cold and blustery to unseasonably warm.

COURSE DESCRIPTION Columbus' layout makes it spectator friendly, easy for tired runners to drop out, and more scenic than many loop courses. Completely closed to traffic, the race begins on High Street, the city's main drag, in front of the Nationwide Insurance Building. After a gentle down and up start through the Short North, with its galleries, trendy shops, and restaurants, the race turns flat until about 2.5 miles. A short rise, followed by a quick downhill, leads to 3.7 miles. The runners pass the Ohio State agricultural areas here as they prepare for the 100-foot ascent into Upper Arlington, a quiet suburban community with tree-lined streets and some interesting homes. Beginning at mile 4, the climb concludes at mile 6.2. After a few minor ups and downs, the course descends gradually to the Ohio State University, passing Ohio Stadium, home of perennial Big Ten power Ohio State Buckeyes football team, at 10 miles. Leaving the campus, runners pass down Neil Avenue and Victorian Village, with its renovated, turn-of-the-century homes. Passing by shady Goodale Park, the course returns to High Street, retracing its path through the Short North. Runners return downtown at mile 13.5 and turn east for a peek into the original Wendy's restaurant, followed by the Columbus Museum of Art. At mile 16, runners make a circuit around Franklin Park, home of the beautifully restored 1895 conservatory. Affluent Bexley, site of the Ohio Governor's Mansion and other distinguished homes, awaits at mile 17. The course from downtown to Bexley is generally flat with a few minor grades. Runners exit Bexley at mile 20. From here, the race features long, gentle rolls. At mile 22, the course passes Olde Towne East, one of Columbus' oldest neighborhoods and Topiary Garden on East Town Street, reaching German Village at mile 23. The largest privately-funded restoration project in the country, German Villages' cobbled streets (none on the runners' route), beer halls, and proud brick homes will beckon your return after the race.

CROWD/RUNNER SUPPORT Columbus' course gives downtown onlookers a chance to catch their favorite runner four times during the race — the start, mile 13.5, mile 23, and the finish — by walking only a few blocks. Crowd support at other sections of the course is also surprisingly strong, with approximately 100,000 people cheering the runners. Runners also find entertainment, including professional and high school bands, at a number of areas, especially at Schiller Park. Many of Columbus' 2,400 volunteers man the 19 aid stations, which stock water and electrolyte replacement drink, and the 13 portable toilet stations at even miles. Columbus' enthusiastic helpers consistently receive high marks from runners year after year. Among the race's other notable details are the digital clocks located every mile and 5K, including overall time, pace, and projected finish.

RACE LOGISTICS Columbus' compact downtown means most hotels lie near the race staging area, making transportation to the start unnecessary. However, a shuttle bus from the finish area will return you to the Hyatt Regency (pickup at Broad and High Streets). For those driving into town, there is plenty of inexpensive, convenient, garage parking.

ACTIVITIES Packet pickup and late registration are located at the Marathon Expo in the Hyatt Regency Ballroom. Runners may retrieve their packets on Friday, 4:00 p.m. to 9:00 p.m., Saturday, 10:00 a.m. to 8:00 p.m., and Sunday, 6:00 a.m. to 8:00 a.m. There is no race-day registration, and remember, you must belong to USATF to run the marathon. On Saturday, attend clinics on a variety of subjects, including the popular Columbus Marathon 101 which gives advice to Columbus first timers on how to run the race. Saturday night, the race holds a pasta party (about $10) in the Nationwide Insurance Cafeteria, connected by walkway to the Hyatt Regency. An awards ceremony follows the marathon.

AWARDS Every marathon entrant receives a high-quality, embroidered T-shirt, results magazine, and official race program, and finishers earn medals. Age-group awards go mostly five deep. Finally, about $70,000 in prize money is up for grabs.

ELITE RUNNERS INFORMATION Male runners under 2:20 and female runners under 2:45 may qualify for elite status at Columbus. Elites may be offered travel, accommodations, and free entry. Promising young runners may also receive a complimentary entry. In addition, Columbus offers prize money totaling approximately $70,000, doled out to the top 10 overall finishers, top five Ohioans, and top five masters, with bonuses for U.S. finishers in the top three overall and for males under 2:14 and females under 2:35. Specifically, the top ten finishers earn $10,000, $6,000, $3,000, $1,500, $750, $500, $350, $250, $150, and $100, respectively. Masters winners and top Ohioans receive $500, $300, $200, $150, and $100. Runners under the time bonus receive $2,000, and U.S. runners finishing first, second, or third overall earn an additional $2,000, $1,000, or $500.

ACCOMMODATIONS Conveniently located at the start and a few blocks from the finish, the Hyatt Regency, 350 North High Street (614-463-1234), serves as the host hotel. Also convenient are the Hyatt on Capitol Square, 75 East State Street (614-228-1234); Holiday Inn City Center, 175 E. Town Street (614-221-3281); Holiday Inn Crowne Plaza, 33 E. Nationwide Blvd. (614-461-4100); Hojo Inn Downtown, 1070 Dublin Road (614-486-4554); Courtyard by Marriott, 145 N. High Street (614-228-2244); Sheraton Suites Columbus, 201 Hutchinson Avenue (614-436-0004); Holiday Inn, 175 Hutchinson Avenue (614-885-3334); and Hampton Inn, 1100 Mediterranean Avenue (614-848-9696). Alternatively, call Peoples Travel (800-336-7662) for assistance finding other accommodations.

RELATED EVENTS / RACES Two or three runners can band together to form a marathon relay team in either corporate or non-corporate divisions. Teams may be male, female, or mixed. Relay legs run 13.9, 9.3, and 3 miles. Team members do not need to belong to USATF to participate. Others may choose to run in the 5K, which starts immediately after the marathon/marathon relay. Kids may want to join in the Kilometer Fun Run following the marathon start. Register at the marathon expo.

AREA ATTRACTIONS Those not familiar with Columbus may be pleasantly surprised. A clean, wholesome city, Columbus contains lots of museums, theaters, shopping, and other places of interest. Among them are the Columbus Museum of Art, 480 E. Broad Street; Wexner Center for the Arts on the Ohio State University campus at North High Street and 15th Avenue; the hands-on Center of Science and Industry, 280 E. Broad Street; a replica of Christopher Columbus' Santa Maria at the Riverfront; German Village south of Capitol Square; Short North; and the State Capitol building.

LOCAL RUNNING STORES Galyan's, 611 Sawmill Road, Dublin (614-798-1111); Frontrunner, 1328 W. Lane Avenue, Columbus (614-486-0301); Second Sole, 4367 Westland Mall (614-279-7225).

SAN ANTONIO MARATHON

OVERALL: 84.5

COURSE BEAUTY: 8-

COURSE DIFFICULTY: 3+ (SEE APPENDIX)

APPROPRIATENESS FOR FIRST TIMERS: 8-

RACE ORGANIZATION: 9-

CROWDS: 2

R A C E   D A T A

Contact:	San Antonio Marathon
	1123 Navarro
	San Antonio, TX 78205-2196
	(210) 246-9652
	http://www.texas.net/~sarun
Date:	November 9, 1997
	November 8, 1998
Start Time:	7:00 a.m.
Time Course Closes:	12:30 p.m.
Number of Participants:	1,300 in 1995
Certification:	USATF
Course Records:	Male: (open) 2:25:13; (masters) 2:32:35
	Female: (open) 2:48:46; (masters) 3:10:20
Elite Athlete Programs:	No
Cost:	$25/30/35
Age groups/Divisions:	<19, 20-24, 25-29, 30-34, 35-39, 40-44, 45-49,
	50-54, 55-59, 60-64, 65-69, 70+
Temperature:	62°
Aid/Splits:	12 / every mile including pace

HIGHLIGHTS The cradle of Texan independence, San Antonio retains many monuments to its frontier past, and the San Antonio Marathon passes most of them. The Alamo, Mission Concepcion, Fort Sam Houston, King William District, and historic downtown all lie on the course, as well as some more modern monuments like the Alamodome and the Tower of the Americas. After the race, plenty of San Antonio remains to be explored, and we believe you will quickly understand why San Antonio is becoming one of the United States' top tourist destinations.

COURSE DESCRIPTION The San Antonio Marathon starts north of the Alamodome, workplace of the NBA San Antonio Spurs, and heads to HemisFair Plaza, site of the 1968 World's Fair and current home to the Tower of the Americas and the renowned Institute of Texan Cultures (mile 1). After completing a semicircle of the plaza, the course returns to the Alamodome (mile 3). After crossing the freeway again, the race proceeds through historic downtown and passes the San Antonio Museum of Art (miles 4 to 5). Winding through an older commercial district (mile 5) and older residential neighborhood (mile 6), runners reach the first hill of the course, a 100-foot climb over 300 yards just before Fort Sam Houston (miles 7 to 11). Runners enter Fort Sam at the historic quadrangle and proceed slightly downhill for 100 yards. The course takes in the most scenic sections of the fort, passing stately houses of base bigwigs, the parade grounds, and the Brooke Army Medical Center (BAMC). The marathon exits Fort Sam and heads to beautiful Brackenridge Park (miles 12 to 14), passing the Witte Museum, San Antonio Zoo, and Japanese Tea

Gardens. Runners then go straight down North St. Mary's Street, a fairly nice commercial road, from miles 14 to 17, with the Tower of the Americas looming ahead. By mile 16 you're back downtown and go right past HemisFair Plaza into the historic south section of town (miles 18 to 23). The turn-around point is located at Mission Concepcion, which dates from 1731. The runners then head back to the finish in the North Plaza of the Alamodome.

CROWD/RUNNER SUPPORT Several thousand race fans cheer on the runners, with the greatest concentrations near the start/finish, downtown, and the half marathon point. The aid stations, well stocked for San Antonio's weather, carry water, electrolyte replacement, fruit, and medical aid. Portable toilets are also located near each aid station.

RACE LOGISTICS The start and finish are located near many downtown hotels so transportation is not an issue unless you are staying further out. If you drive to the start, try parking on Durango Street across from the Federal Office Building or around the Alamodome.

ACTIVITIES On Friday evening and all day Saturday, you can register, pick up your race packet, and attend the Sports Expo and Health Fair at the Gunter Hotel. There is no race-day registration or packet pick up. On Saturday evening from 6:30 p.m. to 8:00 p.m., the Gunter hosts the pre-race Pasta Party ($12). On race afternoon, enjoy music, beverages, baked potatoes, cookies, fruit, and other tidbits.

AWARDS The San Antonio Marathon is a pretty good deal at $25. Every marathon entrant receives a short-sleeve T-shirt, while each finisher also receives a long-sleeve T-shirt and a medal. Age-group awards range from three to five deep, with winners receiving trophies. Top runners compete for approximately $5,000 in prize money. The top four overall runners earn: $1,000, $500, $250, and $125. The top three masters runners take home $250, $125, and $75. Awards are not duplicated.

ACCOMMODATIONS The Gunter Hotel, 205 East Houston (800-222-4276), is the host hotel, offering special rates to San Antonio Marathon runners. Other convenient hotels include: Best Western Historic Crockett Hotel, 320 Bonham Street (800-292-1050); Days Inn at the Alamo Riverwalk, 902 E. Houston Street (210-227-6233); the historic Fairmont Hotel, 401 S. Alamo (210-224-8800); Holiday Inn Riverwalk, 217 North St. Mary's Street (210-224-2500); Howard Johnson Riverwalk Plaza-Hotel, 100 Villita Street (800-554-HOST); Hyatt Regency, 123 Losoya Street (210-222-1234); and Radisson Downtown Market Square, 502 West Durango (800-333-3333) or (210-224-7155).

RELATED EVENTS/RACES Two runners can join together to compete in the marathon relay, with each runner completing a half marathon. Teams may be same sex or co-ed. Road runners may consider the San Antonio Mayor's 5-mile Challenge Run, starting at 7:30 a.m., through downtown San Antonio. Walkers may be interested in the Celebration for Fitness Walk, a three-mile fun walk beginning at 7:50 a.m. Finally, keep the kids happy with the Roger Soler's Sports Kids Klassic, a quarter-mile run adjacent to the Alamodome for children 10 and under (8:30 a.m.).

AREA ATTRACTIONS San Antonio boasts lots of tourist points of interest, most of which center around its rich history. Every visitor must visit the Alamo, site of that famous stand against General Santa Anna. You will also want to explore the local missions founded by Spanish missionaries in the 18th century, among them Mission San Jose, Mission Concepcion, Mission San Juan Capistrano, and Mission San Francisco de la Espada. Stroll or cruise down San Antonio's teeming urban canal, the famous Riverwalk, a great place to get a bite to eat, shop, or simply people watch. Worthwhile museums include Witte Museum, Pioneer Hall, Institute of Texan Cultures, and San Antonio Museum of Art. Spelunkers may want to check out the Natural Bridge Caverns about 17 miles outside of San Antonio. Basketball fans may be able to catch a San Antonio Spurs game at the Alamodome.

LOCAL RUNNING STORES Roger Soler's Sports, 2589 Jackson-Keller (210-366-3701); Run-A-Way Runners Store, 3428 N. St. Mary's (210-732-1332).

PHILADELPHIA MARATHON

OVERALL: 88.1

COURSE BEAUTY: 8+

COURSE DIFFICULTY: 3- (SEE APPENDIX)

APPROPRIATENESS FOR FIRST TIMERS: 9-

RACE ORGANIZATION: 9-

CROWDS: 2+

RACE DATA

Contact:	Philadelphia Marathon
	P.O. Box 21601
	Philadelphia, PA 19131-0901
	(215) 685-0054
Date:	November 23, 1997
	November 22, 1998
Start Time:	8:30 a.m.
Time Course Closes:	2:00 p.m.
Number of Participants:	2,900 in 1995
Certification:	USATF
Course Records:	Male: (open) 2:20:15; (masters) 2:37:10
	Female: (open) 2:39:44; (masters) 2:55:36
Elite Athlete Programs:	No
Cost:	$35/40
Age groups/Divisions:	<19, 20-29, 30-39, 40-49, 50-59, 60+
Temperature:	54°
Aid/Splits:	12 / digital clocks every mile

H I G H L I G H T S Run through history in the Philadelphia Marathon, a tour of the original U.S. capital city. The U.S. Mint, Betsy Ross House, Benjamin Franklin's Grave, Independence Hall, University of Pennsylvania, and Fairmount Park all lie on the marathon trail. Fairly flat, the loop course includes a 12-mile out-and-back along the Schuylkill River. City-run, the fledgling Philadelphia Marathon cannot match the organizational mastery of other major races, but it is a growing regional race that could become a national draw, particularly given its setting in America's fifth largest city.

C O U R S E   D E S C R I P T I O N Starting at the Philadelphia Museum of Art, the race courses down stately, flag-lined Benjamin Franklin Parkway toward downtown, loops Logan Circle and heads back to the start line. Circling the museum oval, runners return down the parkway to Arch Street (mile 2.5), glimpsing City Hall before passing through Independence National Historical Park after mile 3. Proceeding by the U.S. Mint, Benjamin Franklin's Grave, and Betsy Ross House, the course turns right on Front Street for about two-thirds mile going by the brick federal-style townhouses of Society Hill. Briefly on South Street, runners travel down 6th catching glimpses of Norman Rockwell Museum and Independence Hall. Near 5.5 miles, the course heads left on Chestnut crossing the Schuylkill River at 7 into University City. Rising 34 feet between 7 and 8, runners hit the edge of the University of Pennsylvania as they turn right on 34th. Traveling by the Philadelphia Zoo, the course drops about 48 feet between 8 and 9, then climbs 78 feet between 9 and 10. Winding for 2 miles through the Horticultural Center area, runners descend about 80 feet between miles 11 and 12, when the course finds West River Drive on the edge of Fairmount Park. Crossing the Schuylkill River just before 14, the race passes in front of the start before heading north on Kelly Drive tracing the river through the eastern section of Fairmount Park for a 12-mile out-and-back. Passing Boathouse Row, Sailboat House, and Falls Bridge, runners turn around near mile 20 in Manayuk, retrace their steps and finish at the Philadelphia Museum of Art.

CROWD/RUNNER SUPPORT The thickest crowds gather around the Philadelphia Museum of Art, which includes the first 2 miles, mile 14, and the finish line. Music entertains runners at Memorial Hall, West River Drive, and Kelly Drive. The aid stations, located every 2 miles, generally offer water, electrolyte replacement, and minor first-aid.

RACE LOGISTICS Runners can walk from the Embassy Suites Hotel, the Wyndham Franklin Plaza, and the Holiday Inn Express Midtown to the start, about six to eight blocks away. Runners staying elsewhere have to find their own way to the start. Parking exists around the museum, but arrive early.

ACTIVITIES Go to Memorial Hall in Fairmount Park on Friday, 11:00 a.m. to 8:00 p.m., or Saturday, 10:00 a.m. to 6:00 p.m., to pick up your race packet. Memorial Hall also features a Health and Fitness Expo those same times, including massages and the usual products. On Saturday evening, see how much you can eat at the pasta party ($10) in the Wyndham Franklin Plaza on 17th and Race Streets. Unknot yourself with a free post-race massage, and then enjoy music, refreshments, and an awards ceremony.

AWARDS Every runner who pays the entry fee receives a marathon T-shirt; those who actually finish also take home a medal and receive a certificate and individual result postcard. Up to the top five finishers in each age group receive trophies, and the frontrunners compete for $5,000 in prize money.

ACCOMMODATIONS The Embassy Suites Center City, 18th Street and Benjamin Franklin Parkway (215-561-1776), serves as the headquarters hotel (about $110). Other hotels offering marathon discounts are: Wyndham Franklin Plaza (about $100), 17th and Race Streets (215-448-2000); Holiday Inn Express Midtown (about $80), 1305 Walnut Street (215-735-9300); and Sheraton University City (about $80), 36th and Chestnut Streets (215-387-8000).

RELATED EVENTS/RACES Those not wanting to compete in the marathon should consider joining the approximately 750 other runners in the Rothman Institute 8K, which starts a half hour after the marathon. There is also a Celebration of Mobility 2-Mile Walk in which participants raise money through pledges for the Orthopaedic Research and Education Foundation.

AREA ATTRACTIONS Much more than a capsule to America's revolutionary past, Philadelphia offers exceptional activities for almost all tastes. Sports fans can catch one of Philadelphia's many professional teams, the 76ers basketball team, Eagles football team, and Flyers hockey team. Cultural buffs should consider the Museum of Art, the Academy of Music which houses the excellent Philadelphia Orchestra, Rodin Museum, Science Center in the Franklin Institute, the Horticultural Center, and the Norman Rockwell Museum. Philadelphia also boasts outstanding restaurants, clubs, and theaters.

LOCAL RUNNING STORES Sneak Preview, 6511 Ridge Avenue, Roxborough (215-482-8887); Rittenhouse Sports Specialties, 132 S. 18th Street, Philadelphia (215-569-9957).

ATLANTA MARATHON

OVERALL: 83.5

COURSE BEAUTY: 7+

COURSE DIFFICULTY: 6+

APPROPRIATENESS FOR FIRST TIMERS: 6+

RACE ORGANIZATION: 9+

CROWDS: 1

R A C E   D A T A

Contact:	Atlanta Marathon
	c/o Atlanta Track Club
	3097 East Shadowlawn Avenue, NE
	Atlanta, GA 30305
	(404) 231-9064
Date:	November 27, 1997
	November 26, 1998
Start Time:	7:30 a.m.
Time Course Closes:	12:30 p.m.
Number of Participants:	1,000+ in 1995
Certification:	USATF
Course Records:	Male: (open) 2:30:54; (masters) 2:40:29
	Female: (open) 2:56:28; (masters) 3:17:51
Elite Athlete Programs:	No
Cost:	$25/40
Age groups/Divisions:	<19, 20-24, 25-29, 30-34, 35-39, 40-44, 45-49,
	50-54, 55-59, 60-64, 65-69, 70+
Temperature:	42°
Aid/Splits:	10 / miles 1, 5, 10, 13.1, 15, 20 & 25

HIGHLIGHTS Held on Thanksgiving morning, the Atlanta Marathon may be the best appetite enhancer for your holiday feast. Littered with hills sporting names like Cardiac Arrest and Capitol Punishment, the race challenges the most seasoned marathoner. Designed for the 1996 Olympic Marathon, the Atlanta course uses over 90 percent of the route used for the Games. Once post-Games restructuring of Centennial Stadium is completed in 1997, the Atlanta Marathon will put the finishing touches on its course.

RACE HISTORY The eighth oldest marathon in the United States, the Atlanta Marathon humbly began with a handful of runners completing a ten-ring merry-go-round around North Fulton Golf Course. No entry blank was needed for the March 1963 race, and no T-shirts or trophies were awarded. The race took on more formal dimensions the following year, and from 1964 to 1980, the marathon ran on a difficult two loops in North Atlanta. In the mid-1970s, the race became the Peach Bowl Marathon and moved to the week between Christmas and New Years. In a bid to attract more than 200 runners, the race moved downtown in 1981 and the race date moved to Thanksgiving. By 1982, 902 hardy souls finished the race. The race faced another course change in the early 1980s, and then in 1992, the present course debuted. The marathon now attracts about 1,000 entrants, and its accompanying half marathon draws nearly 7,000.

COURSE DESCRIPTION The Atlanta Marathon's loop course begins and ends at Centennial Olympic Stadium. The route goes north on Capitol, gently rising until .6 miles, then falling gently until mile 2, passing the State Capitol along the way. The ups and downs become more pronounced between miles 2 and 8, including the 100-foot Early Riser from 4.3 to 4.6, 40-foot Colina Latina before the 6-mile mark, and 125-foot Hill Too Pharr from 6.5 to 7.7. Piedmont Park, home of the Atlanta Botanical Garden, lies prior to Early Riser, and Atlanta's oldest Hispanic community surrounds Colina Latina. From miles 8 to 19, the course gently rolls giving runners a nice break for the hills ahead. Just before mile 19, the course's major downhill appears, a fairly steep drop of about 220 feet to mile 20.4. Then, runners mount short, steep Cardiac Hill, a 125-footer over half a mile. From 22 miles to 25, the course contains a series of hills, climbing approximately 175 feet. Near mile 23, the race passes Atlanta's arts district, including the High Museum, the Memorial Arts Center, and the Alliance Theatre. The final mile or so is mostly flat or downhill to the finish. Note that the course is not closed to traffic. Runners typically stick to the right-hand lane of a broad road.

CROWD/RUNNER SUPPORT Arising extra early on Thanksgiving morning does not appeal to many people, especially with the planning and preparations many must go through that day. So don't expect large crowds along the course. Aid stations are located every 2.5 miles or so and carry water, electrolyte replacement, Vaseline, and minor first aid. Portable toilets also sit at every aid station.

RACE LOGISTICS Plenty of parking exists at the Centennial Olympic Stadium for those who have cars. Alternatively, you can take MARTA to the Georgia State University station and walk ten minutes to the start. MARTA tokens are on sale at the race expo. You can check your bags at the Stadium.

ACTIVITIES The Atlanta Marathon Expo goes on Tuesday and Wednesday before the race from 11:00 a.m. to 9:00 p.m. at the Sheraton Colony Square Hotel. Pick up your race packet at the expo. If your training hasn't gone so well, or has gone better than expected, you may switch between the marathon and the half marathon prior to 2:00 p.m. on Wednesday. There is no packet pickup or registration on race day. After the race, go home and enjoy Thanksgiving dinner because there is no awards ceremony or other post-race party.

AWARDS All participants receive long-sleeve T-shirts, and finishers receive medals in the finish chute. The top masters runner and the top three finishers in each age group are mailed awards. Overall winners receive trophies and merchandise.

ACCOMMODATIONS Race headquarters is the Sheraton Colony Square Hotel, 14th and Peachtree (800-422-7895 or 404-892-6000). The Sheraton offers Atlanta Marathon runners a special rate of $60 per night. Other possibilities include: Ramada Hotel Downtown, 175 Piedmont Avenue NE (404-659-2727); Travelodge Downtown, 311 Courtland Street NE (404-659-4545); Westin Peachtree Plaza, 210 Peachtree Street NW (404-659-1400); Best Western American Hotel, 160 Spring Street NW (404-688-8600); Comfort Inn, 101 International Blvd. NE (404-524-5555); and Days Inn, 683 Peachtree Street NE (404-874-9200).

RELATED EVENTS/RACES The Atlanta Half Marathon covers the second half of the marathon course and begins at 7:00 a.m. on Peachtree near Chamblee-Tucker Road. The half attracts almost 7,000 runners, making it the largest in the South and the third largest in the United States.

AREA ATTRACTIONS While in Atlanta, you may want to witness the lighting of the Big Tree, signifying the start of the Christmas season. Or, you could visit the usual Atlanta sights: Martin Luther King, Jr. National Historical Site, Stone Mountain Park, Georgia State Capitol, Carter Presidential Center, Piedmont Park and its Atlanta Botanical Garden, the Science and Technology Museum of Atlanta (SciTrek), the High Museum of Art, the Center for Puppetry Arts, the Governor's Mansion, Atlanta History Center in Buckhead, and the New Museum of Atlanta History.

LOCAL RUNNING STORES Fleet Feet Sports, 6221-A Roswell Road (404-255-3338); Phidippides, 1544 Piedmont Road NE (404-875-4268).

NORTHERN CENTRAL TRAIL MARATHON

OVERALL: 78.2

COURSE BEAUTY: 8

COURSE DIFFICULTY: 2-

APPROPRIATENESS FOR FIRST TIMERS: 8+

RACE ORGANIZATION: 8-

CROWDS: 0

RACE DATA

Contact:	David Cooley
	Northern Central Trail Marathon
	P.O. Box 5464
	Towson, MD 21285
	(410) 377-8882
Date:	November 29, 1997
	November 28, 1998
Start Time:	9:30 a.m.
Time Course Closes:	NA
Number of Participants:	361 in 1995
Certification:	USATF
Course Records:	Male: (open) 2:25:18; (masters) 2:36:00
	Female: (open) 3:00:28; (masters) 3:27:06
Elite Athlete Programs:	No
Cost:	$25/30
Age groups/Divisions:	16-19, 20-29, 30-39, 40-49, 50-59, 60+
Temperature:	54°
Aid/Splits:	8 / miles 1, 5, 10, 13.1, 15, 20 & 25.2

HIGHLIGHTS Amid the spirit of Thanksgiving, the Northern Central Trail Marathon takes place in Gunpowder Falls State Park, a mere 15 miles north of Baltimore, Maryland. This fast, out-and-back marathon travels along a hard-packed former railroad bed, beautifully surrounded by the telltale signs of the season. Destroyed in 1972 by Hurricane Agnes, the tracks have been converted to a multi-use recreational trail. Local lore claims that this same route was traced by the train that carried President Lincoln's body back to his Illinois home after his assassination.

COURSE DESCRIPTION To thin out the crowds, the first 1.5 miles of the marathon lead to the trail via country roads. The balance of the course is a wide, hard-packed dirt path decorated with trees sparsely covered with the last vestiges of fall. The soft, forgiving surface is gentle on your legs. Along a stream that runs beside the course at several points, depots of a once glorious railroad past mark the trail. To make this rustic scene complete, if you look closely, you might even spot deer along your path. Though the trail ascends gently for the first 14 miles, the second half of the course is downhill, making for a fast finish.

CROWD/RUNNER SUPPORT Small gatherings of fans cheer at various road crossing points and at the finish line. However, because the trail is somewhat prohibitive to spectators, you have to go it alone for most of the race. Aid stations dot the course approximately every 3 to 3.5 miles. Generally, water and electrolyte replacement fluids are available at each station, which competes for the best runner support. Splits are provided at miles 1, 5, 10, 13.1, 15, 20 and 1-mile-to-go mark along the course so you can conveniently monitor your progress.

RACE LOGISTICS Park your car at Advanced Manufacturing, 14600 York Road. From there, a shuttle van transports you to and from the start/finish.

ACTIVITIES You may pick up your packet or register on race morning at Advanced Manufacturing. On Friday evening, there is a pasta dinner. Replenish yourself at the finish line with complimentary refreshments and massages. Afterwards, find a comfortable space to sit and enjoy the awards ceremony.

AWARDS Every runner receives a T-shirt, and finishers receive medals. Awards for the top five overall and top three in each age group are announced on race day at the finish line tent, but the actual awards (usually plaques) will be engraved and mailed to award winners after the race.

ACCOMMODATIONS Lodging facilities include the Marriott Hunt Valley Inn, exit 20 off I-83 (410-785-7000); Red Roof Inn, exit 16 off I-83 (410-666-0380); Holiday Inn, exit 16 of I-83 (410-252-7373); Days Inn, exit 17 off I-83 (410-560-1000); and the Hampton Inn, exit 20 off I-83 to 11200 York Road (410-527-1500). In each case, request rooms for the Northern Central Trail Marathon. All hotels are conveniently located near the marathon start/finish.

AREA ATTRACTIONS Nearby Baltimore offers plenty to do. Browse the Inner Harbor, with its National Aquarium, the U.S.S. Constellation (the first commissioned U.S. Navy ship), and numerous shops and restaurants. Make sure to sample Maryland's famous crab cakes. A great area for fun, Fells Point offers quaint streets and historic buildings. In addition, Washington, D.C. lies about an hour and a half away.

LOCAL RUNNING STORE Hess Running Center, Towson Town Center (401-821-6473).

SEATTLE MARATHON

OVERALL: 84.8

COURSE BEAUTY: 9-

COURSE DIFFICULTY: 2+ (SEE APPENDIX)

APPROPRIATENESS FOR FIRST TIMERS: 8

RACE ORGANIZATION: 8+

CROWDS: 1

RACE DATA

Contact:	Seattle Marathon Association
	P.O. Box 31849
	Seattle, WA 98103-1849
	(206) 524-RUNS
	http://www.wolfenet.com/~sea_mara/
Date:	November 29, 1997 (tentative)
	November 28, 1998 (tentative)
Start Time:	9:00 a.m./9:10 a.m.
Time Course Closes:	3:00 p.m.
Number of Participants:	2,885 in 1995
Certification:	USATF
Course Records:	Male: (open) 2:20:45
	Female: (open) 2:41:04
Elite Athlete Programs:	NA
Cost:	$38/45/55
Age groups/Divisions:	<19, 20-24, 25-29, 30-34, 35-39, 40-44, 45-49, 50-54, 55-59, 60-64, 65-69, 70+
Temperature:	44°
Aid/Splits:	12 / NA

HIGHLIGHTS Like a talented runner with a questionable work ethic, the Seattle Marathon could be one of the top destination marathons in North America. The fact that it currently isn't largely results from a sub-par course and some organization snafus. The course follows bike trails in suburban Seattle. While pretty, it pales in comparison to what a Seattle Marathon course could be given the tremendous beauty of the area and the city. In our dealings with the marathon organization, we have found them to be among the most unresponsive of any major race in North America — quite an accomplishment. Supplier problems created some ruffled feathers with runners in 1995 as the race director let be known for months after the fact. This is not to say that Seattle is a bad race — it isn't. It merely underachieves.

COURSE DESCRIPTION Entirely paved and mostly flat, the Seattle Marathon's point-to-point course follows the Sammamish River Trail and the Burke-Gilman Trail, dropping down the west side of Lake Washington before finishing at the University of Washington. Starting in Marymoor Park near Redmond, the course completes an out-an-back within the park for just over 2 miles before picking up the Sammamish River Trail. Runners go through Woodinville and Bothell, joining the Burke-Gilman Trail in Kenmore. This attractive trail, lined with trees, tops Lake Washington and comes down parallel with its western shore. The course gently rises 85 feet from about mile 17 to mile 23 before dropping about 60 feet to mile 24. A short rise to 25 precedes the finish at the University of Washington at Rainier Vista.

CROWD / RUNNER SUPPORT With any bike trail course, spectator involvement is limited to a few access areas, and Seattle is no exception. The well-stocked aid stations carry water, electrolyte replacement, Band-Aids, Vaseline, and blister protection. Portable toilets are also available.

RACE LOGISTICS The Seattle Marathon utilizes a wave start: one at 9:00 a.m. and another at 9:10 a.m. The race will assign you to one of the waves based on your expected finish time. Parking at the start is extremely limited so don't even try it unless you are being dropped off. Instead, take advantage of the free bus service leaving between 7:30 a.m. and 8:15 a.m. from two locations — the Westin Hotel and the University of Washington Parking Lot E-1. If you are not staying at the Westin, drive to Lot E-1, E-5 or Padelford Parking Garage, park for free, and take the free bus. Shuttle buses run all day between Lot E-1 and the finish area, and from Lot E-1 to the Westin Hotel. Check your gear at the start if you would like the race to transport it to the finish area.

ACTIVITIES Pick up your race packet, register, and browse the expo at the Westin Hotel on Friday from 11:00 a.m. to 9:00 p.m. There is no race-day entry. Friday evening the Westin serves an all-you-can-eat pasta buffet ($12), with seatings at 5:00 p.m., 6:00 p.m., and 7:00 p.m. The lower level of the UW Medical Center Parking Garage serves as the post-race recovery area, where finishers can receive massages ($15), get medical help, pick up their sweatshirts, and get some hot soup and refreshments. At 3:00 p.m., the "Brag and Whine" lounge opens at the Westin with refreshments and snacks. Here, you can check the official results, and division winners can pick up their awards later that evening.

AWARDS Every finisher receives a Seattle Marathon sweatshirt, medallion, and certificate. The top 10 in each age division receive an award or "acknowledgment." You must run in the first wave to be eligible to receive an age-division award. A special award is given to the oldest finisher.

ACCOMMODATIONS The Westin Hotel, 1900 Fifth Avenue (206-728-1000), serves as the host hotel, offering special rates to Seattle Marathon runners (about $85). If the Westin is full, try: Best Western Executive Inn, 200 Taylor Avenue N (206-448-9444); Travelodge By The Space Needle, 200 6th Avenue N (206-441-7878); Hilton Seattle Downtown (206-624-0500); Sheraton Seattle Hotel & Tower, 1400 6th Avenue (206-621-9000); Stouffer Renaissance Madison, 515 Madison Street (206-583-0300); Travelodge University, 4725 25th Avenue NE (206-525-4612); Inn at the Market, 86 Pine Street (206-443-3600); and Inn at Queen Anne, 505 1st Avenue N (206-282-7357).

RELATED EVENTS / RACES Attracting nearly 4,000 entrants, the Seattle Half Marathon starts at 8:00 a.m. (with three wave starts) in St. Edward State Park. Bus transportation to the start is provided to half marathon runners. An 8K Walk starts at the finish area at 9:00 a.m.

AREA ATTRACTIONS Famous for its coffee houses, brewpubs, and music, Seattle offers much more to the visitor. Check out the Museum of Flight near Boeing Field, and take a tour of the huge Boeing complex. Stop by the Pike Place Market for fresh fruits, vegetables, seafood, or just plain browsing. The Pacific Science Center is great for the kids, or maybe take them to a Seattle Supersonics basketball game at KeyArena or a Seahawks game at the Kingdome. Green Lake Park offers great jogging, rollerblading, bike riding, or people watching opportunities, and be sure to wander downtown along the waterfront.

LOCAL RUNNING STORES Super Jock 'n Jill, 7210 E. Greenlake Drive N, Seattle (206-522-7711); Fast Lady Sports, 2710 NE University Village, Seattle (206-522-2113); Niketown, Sixth and Pike, Seattle (800-352-NIKE).

WHITE SANDS / ALAMOGORDO MARATHON

OVERALL: 72.3

COURSE BEAUTY: 8-

COURSE DIFFICULTY: 4+

APPROPRIATENESS FOR FIRST TIMERS: 6+

RACE ORGANIZATION: 8

CROWDS: 0+

R A C E   D A T A

Contact:	Clint Burleson
	White Sands/Alamogordo Marathon
	P.O. Box 1589
	Alamogordo, NM 88311-1589
	(505) 382-8869
Date:	December 6, 1997
	December 5, 1998
Start Time:	9:00 a.m.
Time Course Closes:	NA
Number of Participants:	210 in 1995
Certification:	USATF
Course Records:	Male: (open) 2:30:57; (masters) 2:46:10
	Female: (open) 3:07:27; (masters) 3:26:19
Elite Athlete Programs:	No
Cost:	$14/17/20
Age groups/Divisions:	12-18, 19-29, 30-39, 40-44, 45-49, 50-59, 60+
Temperature:	32° - 60°
Aid/Splits:	14 / miles 1, 5 & 13.1

HIGHLIGHTS Run amok amongst the wavy white sand dunes in southern New Mexico in the White Sands/Alamogordo Marathon. However, beach lovers won't find the lapping ocean. In fact, the only water you'll find sits on the aid station tables. Much of the race takes place in White Sands National Monument near the site of the first atomic bomb explosion. The marathon awards utilize the local skills of native culture, and the T-shirts feature petroglyph designs.

COURSE DESCRIPTION WSA Marathon's point-to-point course starts in the White Sands National Monument (at elevation 4,000 feet about the lowest point in the basin) and finishes at the Alameda Zoo in Alamogordo, gradually gaining 300 feet along the way. The first 10 miles, run in the Monument, pass through rolling, brilliant white sand dunes that would seem more appropriate in Antarctica; you'd swear you were surrounded by snow drifts! You run most of the early miles on hard grated sand, a very comfortable running surface. The course exits the Monument near mile 10, heading northeast on Route 70 (miles 10 to 22). At that junction lies the park visitors center where you can learn more about the geological formation of the park. On Route 70, runners, passing through high desert scrub brush, see the snow-capped Sierra Blanca rising from the barren desert floor. Near mile 16, runners pass the entrance to Holloman Air Force Base, home of the Stealth Fighter. You reach the Alamogordo city limits near mile 22, going through mostly outlying commercial areas. At mile 23, you pass the Coulston Foundation, pioneers in using monkeys for space and medical research. Just before mile 25, runners make a detour under tracks and then continue for the next mile on a gravel railroad alley. When you cross the Albertsons' parking lot, you have .2 miles to the finish at the Alameda Zoo.

CROWD/RUNNER SUPPORT You find the best crowds congregated at the finish in the Alameda Zoo. The 14 exuberant aid stations and marathon relay points at miles 5, 10, 15, and 20 provide most of the cheerleading along the route. All stations carry water and electrolyte replacement, while selected others offer orange slices, ice, and petroleum jelly.

RACE LOGISTICS Park at the First National Bank or Norwest Bank parking lots near the finish, and take the free bus to the start. The last bus leaves at 8:00 a.m. You must arrange your own transportation from the Alameda Zoo to the start if you drive to the Monument. Place your sweats in the Runners' Clothing vehicle and then retrieve them at the finish.

ACTIVITIES Pick up your packet at the race headquarters on Thursday evening or Friday, or at the start on race day. Go to school for the pasta dinner on Friday evening, 6:00 p.m. to 8:00 p.m., at Alamogordo High School ($5). After the race, wander the zoo for free or follow the crowd to the informal get-together at a local microbrewery.

AWARDS All marathoners receive unique T-shirts using a petroglyph design, and finishers corral two-sided custom medals. Local pottery is awarded to the second and third place age-group finishers, and Indian Kachinas go to overall, masters, and age-group winners. The top three overall runners also earn prize money of $300, $200, and $100.

ACCOMMODATIONS The Holiday Inn, 1401 S. White Sands Blvd. in Alamogordo (505-437-7100), serves as the host hotel. If that is full, try the Best Western Desert Aire (505-437-2110); Motel 6, 251 Panorama Blvd. (505-434-5970); or All American Inn, 508 S. White Sands Blvd. (505-437-1850).

RELATED EVENTS/RACES On top of the marathon, White Sands/Alamogordo features a five-person marathon relay, half marathon, marathon and half marathon walk, 5K Run and Walk, and kids' 1-Mile run.

AREA ATTRACTIONS The major attractions in the area are Carlsbad Caverns, the White Sands National Monument, the Three Rivers Petroglyph Site, and Trinity Site (about 70 miles away), location of the first atomic bomb test.

DALLAS WHITE ROCK MARATHON

OVERALL: 90.2

COURSE BEAUTY: 9+

COURSE DIFFICULTY: 5- (SEE APPENDIX)

APPROPRIATENESS FOR FIRST TIMERS: 8+

RACE ORGANIZATION: 9

CROWDS: 3

RACE DATA

Contact:	Dallas White Rock Marathon
	3607 Oak Lawn, Ste. 204
	Dallas, TX 75219
	(214) 528-2962
Date:	December 7, 1997
	December 6, 1998
Start Time:	8:00 a.m.
Time Course Closes:	1:30 p.m.
Number of Participants:	3,500 in 1995
Certification:	USATF
Course Records:	Male: (open) 2:12:18
	Female: (open) 2:33:39
Elite Athlete Programs:	Yes
Cost:	$35/45/55
Age groups/Divisions:	<19, 20-24, 25-29, 30-34, 35-39, 40-44, 45-49, 50-54, 55-59, 60+ (F), 60-64 (M), 65-69, 70+
Temperature:	45° - 70°
Aid/Splits:	15 / none

HIGHLIGHTS The Dallas White Rock Marathon ranks as one of the top six most beautiful urban marathons in the country and is our highest-rated destination race in Texas. No small feat given the competition — Houston-Methodist, Motorola Austin, Cowtown, and San Antonio, among others. In fact, Texas trails only California in the high number of quality marathons. Houston-Methodist may be bigger and faster, but The Rock (as it is affectionately known) has class, starting with its eclectic course. The Rock proves that an urban marathon does not need to pass through slums or mile upon mile of strip malls. It can encompass parkways, pleasant communities, refurbished districts, and even a lake.

RACE HISTORY As runners, we have found that some of our best thinking is done during a run. Clearly, Talmage Morrison, founder of the Cross Country Club of Dallas, agrees. Running around White Rock Lake one bright morning in 1970, Morrison had a moment of clarity. He walked to a now famous flagpole at Winfrey Point, gazed out at the picturesque lake and the flat roads that ring it, and saw the perfect setting for a marathon. He paid $25 for a quarter-page ad in Runner's World (boy, that was a long time ago!) and had the course certified by the Amateur Athletics Union. Eighty-two runners showed up at the inaugural Dallas White Rock Marathon in 1971 to loop around White Rock Lake three times. Twenty-seven years later, The Rock has matured to more than 3,500 runners, has added two relay events, and has changed its course. But the inspiration that launched it hasn't changed.

COURSE DESCRIPTION Completely closed to traffic, The Rock offers a loop course that starts and finishes at City Hall. Race organizers have put a lot of thought into the course and it shows. Showcasing the best of Dallas, the race passes through Highland Park Township, White Rock Lake, Swiss Avenue, and downtown. In short, the deceptively difficult course is the most scenic and entertaining in Texas. The start is slightly downhill on Young, a wide street that can handle the large number of entrants. Between miles 1 and 2, runners pass through West End, downtown's entertainment district, and face a 60-foot climb over a half mile. After a right turn on Olive, runners barrel down a 60-foot drop over 200 yards, and then go right back up. At Cedar Springs (miles 2 to 3), a quarter-mile downhill leads to beautiful, woodsy, Turtle Creek. Around the 3-mile mark, the course begins a 3.5-mile, general upward trend, gaining about 200 feet over rolling terrain through the exclusive Township of Highland Park. At mile 6, runners swing onto commercial Mockingbird Lane and begin a long (about 2 miles) downhill toward White Rock Lake. After mile 8, the course returns to a neighborhood before a short, good uphill entering White Rock Park. The next 10 miles loop the running trails around beautiful White Rock Lake. Completely flat (except for a rolling downhill between 19 and 20), this part of the course can be windy since it is relatively unprotected. At mile 20, you regret leaving the inspiration of White Rock Lake, especially as you begin two steep hills and the gradual climb through Lakewood to mile 22. Your spirits will soar again at mile 22, the head of historic Swiss Avenue with its refurbished houses, tree-laden median strip, and best of all, a long, two-mile gradual downhill. About 23.5, the course gradually becomes more commercial, and downtown and the City Hall finish are not far. Dallas' skyline comes into view about mile 25, near the renovated Farmer's Market. Although the street consists of cobblestones, they are easy to run on (though slippery when wet). After the cobblestones, weary runners have pretty much a straight shot to the finish line at City Hall.

CROWD/RUNNER SUPPORT Fifteen very enthusiastic aid stations sponsored by businesses and other groups highlight The Rock. Many of the aid stations have different themes every year. Some past themes include the Dancing Cowgirl, The Beverly Hillbillies, Christmas in Toyland, and Comedy Club. The aid stations compete against each other in three categories, with the winners chosen by the runners. Aid stations offer water, electrolyte replacement, fruit, medical personnel, and portable toilets. A variety of entertainment along the course ranges from live bands to residents blasting boom boxes. Scattered along the course, crowds are particularly thick along Turtle Creek near the entrance to Highland Park, the entrance to White Rock Lake, and from Lakewood to the finish.

RACE LOGISTICS The Rock is a loop course so little transportation is required. The headquarters hotel and other race affiliated hotels all have shuttles to the start/finish areas. Furthermore, sag wagons search the course for those unable to finish. Relay teams must provide their own transportation to the relay exchange points and from the exchange points to the finish.

ACTIVITIES Race weekend begins on the Saturday before the race with a Sports Expo from 9:00 a.m. to 5:00 p.m. at the Plaza of the Americas adjacent to the Harvey and Le Meridien Hotels. The expo features seminars, running clinics, exhibits, running apparel and footwear vendors. Saturday night features the Pasta Dinner and the popular Sports Style Show. Doled out during the Pasta Dinner, the annual Award for Excellence honors an individual who has made significant contributions to distance running. Past award winners include Frank Shorter, Dave Scott, Joan Benoit Samuelson, Fred Lebow, Dr. Kenneth Cooper, and Dr. George Sheehan. An awards banquet featuring food and refreshments follows the marathon.

AWARDS Every runner receives a terrific Rock T-shirt. Those able to finish also earn a finisher's medallion, certificate, and a well-conceived results booklet. Special age-group awards go up to 15 deep, depending on the number of entrants in each age group. The Rock's poster won second place in Runner's World's annual contest in 1995.

ELITE RUNNERS INFORMATION The Rock recruits elite runners — men who have recently run under 2:20 and women under 2:35. Depending on your credentials, the race could offer transportation, hotel, expenses, and/or complimentary entry.

ACCOMMODATIONS The Harvey Hotel, 400 N. Olive Street (800-922-9222), serves as the official race headquarters hotel. Or, try the Le Meridien, 650 N. Pearl Street (800-543-4300); or The Fairmont Hotel, 1717 N. Akard (800-527-4727). All offer special rates for Rock runners and are within 4 to 6 blocks of City Hall. Other possibilities include: Holiday Inn-Aristocrat Hotel, 1933 Main Street (214-741-7700); Ramada Hotel-Convention Center, 1011 S. Akard (214-421-1083); Best Western Market Center, 2023 Market Center Blvd. (214-741-9000); and Quality Hotel Market Center, 2015 Market Center Blvd. (214-741-7481).

RELATED EVENTS / RACES On Sunday, there are two marathon relays starting simultaneously with the marathon. Five and two-person teams in various categories compete on the marathon course.

AREA ATTRACTIONS Dallas is a great sports town. Check out the NFL Cowboys (if they are in town), the NBA Mavericks, or NHL Stars. Dallas is also something of a shopping mecca if you need to take your mind off the big race with some mindless money-blowing.

LOCAL RUNNING STORES Luke's, 3607 Oak Lawn, Dallas (214-528-1290); Run On, Old Town Shopping Center, 5500 Greenville Avenue #600, Dallas (214-361-6493).

WESTERN HEMISPHERE MARATHON

OVERALL: 69.9

COURSE BEAUTY: 6+

COURSE DIFFICULTY: 4+

APPROPRIATENESS FOR FIRST TIMERS: 7-

RACE ORGANIZATION: 7+

CROWDS: 1

RACE DATA

Contact:	Western Hemisphere Marathon
	4117 Overland Avenue
	Culver City, CA 90230
	(310) 253-6650
Date:	December 7, 1997
	December 6, 1998
Start Time:	8:00 a.m.
Time Course Closes:	1:00 p.m.
Number of Participants:	573 in 1995
Certification:	USATF
Course Records:	Male: (open) 2:28:27
	Female: (open) 2:59:09
Elite Athlete Programs:	No
Cost:	$20/25/30
Age groups/Divisions:	<10, 11-13, 14-18, 19-24, 25-29, 30-34, 35-39, 40-44, 45-49, 50-54, 55-59, 60-64, 65-69, 70-74, 75-79, 80+
Temperature:	70°
Aid/Splits:	25 / None

HIGHLIGHTS Quietly aging, the Western Hemisphere Marathon reveals few signs of its significant place in marathon annals. Reigning as the second oldest consecutively run marathon in the United States, the race celebrates its golden anniversary in 1997. Its golden years, however, date far back when the race finished in the glamorous confines of the Los Angeles Coliseum before 70,000 fans attending the Coliseum Relays track and field meet. The modern, convoluted course consists of a series of out-and-backs and a loop. Beginning in front of the Culver City Veteran Memorial Auditorium, the race runs unceremoniously through the main venues of Culver City, passing historic movie studios before heading to the coastline of the Pacific Ocean and then back.

RACE HISTORY With 49 races under its elastic waistband, it's not surprising that WHM's scrapbook is chock full of entertaining stories. One of the best emanates from the inaugural run. For added drama, the race was timed so the winner would arrive at the Los Angeles Coliseum just before the one-mile run of the 1948 Coliseum Relays. Slowed by heavy traffic, the lead runner arrived only to find the Coliseum gates locked. After finally gaining entry, Gerald Cote of Canada found himself in the midst of the 100-yard high hurdles race. Before 70,000 cheering fans, Cote proceeded to clear a series of 39-inch hurdles finishing two races in one. The mood of the boisterous crowd soon changed to quiet dismay, however, when Cote celebrated his accomplishment by puffing on a cigar during his victory lap. Another memorable race occurred three years later when China's Lan Wen Ngau, while leading the race, suddenly veered off course. Unable to understand instructions to turn around, Ngau continued running until race officials physically altered his direction — forcing his disqualification. Sponsored by the People's Party of China, Ngau feared harsh consequences upon his return so, instead, he stayed. He's rumored to be living in the California mountains to this day.

COURSE DESCRIPTION After reading WHM's race literature, you may think you're in for an amazingly beautiful course. "A setting that is unparalleled," or "One of the most picturesque and enjoyable routes in American history." We can only surmise that these descriptions have been carried over from the days when WHM stood as one of the few marathons in the country. In reality, with the exception of a 6-mile stretch along the coastline, the course is not particularly attractive. Appropriately starting in front of Culver City's Veterans Memorial Auditorium, the veteran race loops the city passing its historic movie studios before heading west toward the ocean. Much of the course runs on Culver Blvd., a mostly flat, secondary road with two lanes in each direction, lined on both sides with retail areas, apartments, duplexes, schools, and car lots. The scenery improves as you meet a wetlands preserve before heading south up a gradual hill on Vista Del Mar. Near the halfway point, runners overlook the beach at Playa Del Rey as they make their way along the Pacific coast. Descending slightly near the Imperial Hwy., runners negotiate an out-and-back on both a service access road and Pershing Drive. Hopefully, the 6 miles along the scenic coastal bluffs inspire you for your return to the Veterans Memorial Auditorium as you encounter much of the same urban sprawl which characterized earlier miles.

CROWD/RUNNER SUPPORT Don't expect much crowd support on race day. Most of the encouragement comes from the volunteers at the aid stations which dot the course each mile. Although impressive in number, be aware that the aid stations don't provide electrolyte replacement drinks.

RACE LOGISTICS Race participants have to get themselves to the start. This should not pose too much of a problem since plenty of parking is available near the Veterans Memorial Auditorium.

ACTIVITIES You may pick up your race packet or register late during the small race expo held on Saturday from 9:00 a.m. to 3:00 p.m. at the Culver City Veterans Memorial Auditorium. Race-day registration and packet pickup starts at 6:30 a.m. Food and display booths and a pancake breakfast (for a fee) begin at 7:00 a.m. After the race, enjoy a well-deserved massage before refueling on the traditional stew lunch beginning at noon at the Senior Center. The awards ceremony, also held at the Senior Center, begins at 12:30 p.m.

AWARDS Every participant receives a T-shirt and goodie bag, and finishers receive medals. The first overall male and female finishers receive the coveted Culver City Heart of Screenland Trophy. The first three males and females in all age divisions receive trophies.

ACCOMMODATIONS You shouldn't have a problem finding accommodations in the area. Lodging options near the start/finish include: Culver City Travelodge, 11180 Washington Place (310-839-1111); Holiday Inn, 3930 Sepulveda Blvd. (310-390-2189); and Ramada Inn, 6333 Bristol Parkway (310-839-1111).

RELATED EVENTS/RACES Starting with an in-line skating marathon at 7:00 a.m., race day features an event for almost everybody. In one of the only in-line skating marathons in California, skaters navigate a separate course from the marathon runners. Shortly after 8:00 a.m., the Bruce Robinson Memorial 5K runs through the heart of Culver City. A separate, elite 5K begins at 9:00 a.m. Sandwiched between the two 5Ks is a 1 Mile Fun Run for Kids.

AREA ATTRACTIONS People watching at Venice Beach, star gazing on Sunset Blvd., or shopping on Rodeo Drive are but a few activities to consider before or after the race.

LOCAL RUNNING STORES The Starting Line, 114-A Washington Street, Marina Del Rey (310-827-3035); Frontrunners, 11640 San Vicente Blvd., Los Angeles (310-820-7585).

MEMPHIS MARATHON

OVERALL: 86.2

COURSE BEAUTY: 7-

COURSE DIFFICULTY: 5-

APPROPRIATENESS FOR FIRST TIMERS: 8

RACE ORGANIZATION: 10-

CROWDS: 2+

R A C E   D A T A

Contact:	First Tennessee Memphis Marathon
	P.O. Box 84
	Memphis, TN 38101
	(800) 893-7223
Date:	December 7, 1997
	December 6, 1998
Start Time:	8:00 a.m.
Time Course Closes:	1:00 p.m.
Number of Participants:	1,407 in 1995
Certification:	USATF
Course Records:	Male: (open) 2:26:24; (masters) 2:31:19
	Female: (open) 2:49:39; (masters) 2:56:43
Elite Athlete Programs:	No
Cost:	$20/25/35
Age groups/Divisions:	16-19, 20-24, 25-29, 30-34, 35-39, 40-44, 45-49,
	50-54, 55-59, 60-64, 65+
Temperature:	38° - 56°
Aid/Splits:	12 / every mile

HIGHLIGHTS Billed as a running tour of the city, the Memphis Marathon fulfills its promise. The only problem being that the tour includes some areas you may not want to visit! The consensus on Memphis? Great city, great race, not-so-great course. David Williams of Little Rock sums up the general feeling, *"Great little marathon with only one drawback — the course! If you like hills, exhaust fumes from 10 to 20, cobblestones at 21 and 22 … and some bad parts of town …, then by all means — go for it!"* Runners do rave about the finish inside The Pyramid arena and the excellent race organization. Runners also appreciate the excitement and history of Memphis as the birthplace of blues and rock 'n' roll. Now, if we could just do something about that course.

COURSE DESCRIPTION Despite what you may have read elsewhere, Memphis' loop course is not particularly fast. Heading east from the start outside the majestic Pyramid arena, runners traipse the flat, tree-lined residential neighborhoods along North Parkway. Near 3.5 miles, runners may hear a baboon's howl or a lion's roar as they pass the Memphis Zoo in Overton Park. Scenic residential neighborhoods continue on East Parkway before the route heads west on South Parkway around 7.25 miles. After passing still more beautiful homes along South Parkway for two miles, the route turns left on the 4 to 6 lane-wide Elvis Presley Blvd. — full of heavy, Sunday traffic. The challenging hills and suffocating vehicle exhaust on EPB leaves one wondering whether changing the course to incorporate Graceland was a wise decision. Nonetheless, runners can have their picture taken in front of the Graceland Wall as they head for the turnaround. Police and course officials have their hands full with angry motorists at the highly congested and cruelly positioned U-turn atop a difficult hill on EPB (about 14.5 miles). Still rolling along Winchester Road between 15 miles and 16.5 miles, the race turns right starting the most unappealing section of the course along the highly commercial and lower-income areas of Third Street (another byproduct of the Graceland addition). Six miles later, the scenery improves when entering flat, cobblestone-laden Beale Street at 22.5 miles. Be careful, as the uneven edges of the cobblestones can have you singing the blues at this point in the race. Around 23 miles, the route heads southwest passing the fashionable storefronts on newly revitalized Front Street before hitting the posh South Bluffs neighborhood. Runners encounter more treacherous cobblestones (made more tricky by temporary astroturf, which, despite the good intentions of the race organizers, only hides the bumps) while passing Cybill Shepherd's home before 24 miles. After a right turn onto Riverside Drive at 24 miles, the course heads north for the final 2 miles along the breathtaking Mississippi River to the spectacular finish inside the Pyramid Arena.

CROWD / RUNNER SUPPORT Crowds along the course tend to congregate around the aid stations, with sparse support in between. The best throng can be found inside The Pyramid as runners finish at half court. Aid stations, about every two miles, offer water, electrolyte replacement, Vaseline, and band-aids. Portable toilets are located at the start/finish, miles 3.5, 13.5, and 19.5. The water stations at 13.5 and 19.5 also carry cookies and fruit.

RACE LOGISTICS Most hotels are located within walking distance of The Pyramid. If you do need to arrive by car, plenty of parking exists at The Pyramid. After the race, you can shower at The Pyramid, provided you bring your own soap, towel, and lock.

ACTIVITIES Every pre-race event on Saturday is held at the Memphis Cook Convention Center, 255 N. Main, near The Pyramid. You may pick up your race packet between 2:00 p.m. and 7:30 p.m. While you can retrieve your packet on race day (at The Pyramid), you may not register for the race. Saturday night, attend the pasta dinner which features a noted guest speaker (about $8). The awards ceremony starts at 1:30 p.m. at The Pyramid, immediately followed by the rock 'n' roll victory party held one block away at High Point Finch.

AWARDS Every entrant receives a long-sleeve T-shirt. Each finisher also receives a medallion, certificate, and results. Approximately $25,000 in prize money is awarded to open, masters and age-group winners, with first place overall earning $2,000, down to $225 for fifth place. Masters winners earn $1,500, down to $225 for fifth. Age-group winners receive $125, $100 for second, and $75 for third. Masters runners are eligible for both open and masters prize money. There is also a random drawing for $4,000 in cash prizes for all finishers under 5 hours.

ACCOMMODATIONS Several convenient hotels offer discounts to Memphis Marathon runners, including: Brownstone Hotel, 300 N. Second Street (800-HOTEL-15), about $60; Comfort Inn, 100 N. Front Street (901-526-0583), about $75; Crowne Plaza, 250 N. Main Street (901-527-7300), about $75; The Peabody, 149 Union Avenue (800-PEABODY), about $110; Radisson Hotel, 185 Union Avenue (901-528-1800), about $75; and Ramada Convention Center Hotel, 160 Union Avenue (901-525-5491), about $70. You can obtain a list of other hotels in the area from the Visitor's Information Center, 340 Beale Street (800-873-6282).

AREA ATTRACTIONS Loaded with things to do, Memphis could keep you moving for some time. Make sure you check out the Beale Street Historic District, fountainhead of the blues. Visit Graceland, that beacon for Elvis lovers around the world. Tour the National Civil Rights Museum, located in the Lorraine Motel, site of Dr. Martin Luther King, Jr.'s assassination. Watch the charming duck parade in the Peabody Hotel every day at 11:00 a.m. and 5:00 p.m. For gamblers, roll the dice at nearby Tunica, Mississippi, offering several casinos with individual themes.

LOCAL RUNNING STORES Run For Your Life, 597 Erin Drive (901-761-0078); Breakaway Athletics, 1708 Union Avenue (901-722-8797).

CALIFORNIA INTERNATIONAL MARATHON

OVERALL: 82.4

COURSE BEAUTY: 7+

COURSE DIFFICULTY: 3- (SEE APPENDIX)

APPROPRIATENESS FOR FIRST TIMERS: 8

RACE ORGANIZATION: 9+

CROWDS: 2+

RACE DATA

Contact: California International Marathon
P.O. Box 161149
Sacramento, CA 95816
(916) 983-4622

Date: December 7, 1997
December 6, 1998

Start Time: 7:00 a.m.

Time Course Closes: 12:00 p.m.

Number of Participants: 3,800 in 1995

Certification: USATF

Course Records: Male: (open) 2:10:26; (masters) 2:15:35
Female: (open) 2:29:29; (masters) 2:41:09

Elite Athlete Programs: Yes

Cost: $30/40/50 plus USATF membership

Age groups/Divisions: <19, 20-24, 25-29, 30-34, 35-39, 40-44, 45-49,
50-54, 55-59, 60-64, 65-69, 70+

Temperature: 38° - 56°

Aid/Splits: 12 / every mile

HIGHLIGHTS The California International Marathon, one of the 15 fastest marathons in North America, attracts a multinational field to the Golden State's capital every December. The mostly rolling course, which starts near Folsom Dam and ends in front of the State Capitol, loses approximately 300 feet. Containing few turns, CIM runs even faster than it appears, and runners have the entire road to work with. With solid crowd support, CIM is an excellent choice to go for a PR in a winter marathon.

COURSE DESCRIPTION CIM's point-to-point course begins on a gradual downhill near Folsom Dam. Turning at a right angle up a steep incline on Oak Avenue, the course gently rolls through rural residential neighborhoods. At the 6-mile mark, the course turns left on Fair Oaks Blvd., following it for the next 15.5 miles. The next noticeable hills on the route occur from mile 6.8 to 7 and from 7.5 to 7.7. Again rolling, the race enters Fair Oaks Village on an upgrade, passing antique shops, book sellers, and other small stores. At 10.4 miles, take advantage of the terrific downhill to 11.1. Back to rolling, the course reaches the halfway point during a commercial stretch on Fair Oaks Blvd., and the hills tend to roll more gently thereafter. Continuing to go through a mixture of residential and commercial areas, the route passes a particularly nice neighborhood between 15 and 21. At this point, CIM enters the City of Sacramento. Just before mile 22, runners face a slight hill that could prove tough at this point as they cross the American River via the H Street Bridge. Past the entrance to Sacramento State University, runners soon reach one of the city's most exclusive neighborhoods, the Fabulous Forties, former home to Governor Ronald Reagan. As you turn left on Alhambra Blvd. and enter midtown, you have 2 miles to go. At 24.6, the course passes historic Sutter's Fort, nucleus of the man who started the California Gold Rush. Runners soon reach scenic Capitol Park, which supposedly contains at least one example of every tree species found in California, and can see the Capitol dome. After passing Capitol Park, the course makes two turns to a beautiful finish in the Capitol's shadow.

CROWD/RUNNER SUPPORT The Sacramento community warmly supports the marathon; spectators are found most of the way along the route while over 1,500 volunteers take care of runners' needs. Since the Sacramento Bee newspaper usually prints the names and numbers of entrants the day before the race, some onlookers can be seen with paper in hand, cheering for the runners by name. Various music along the course provides added inspiration, particularly the high school band playing in Old Fair Oaks just after the 10-mile mark. Marathon parties along the route are also common. Look for the John McCarthy Memorial Party at the 17-mile mark. Held in honor of the longtime Sacramento runner, cyclist, and marathon supporter, the party brings together over 50 friends and family members to cheer the runners.

RACE LOGISTICS Runners may not park at the marathon start, which leaves two ways to get there. You can either have someone drop you off about a half mile away, or you can take the race-provided bus ($4) which leaves from the headquarters hotel. Tickets for the race bus must be purchased in advance. The race provides free transportation for all runners from the finish back to the headquarters hotel. CIM transports your sweats to the finish area.

ACTIVITIES On Friday afternoon and all day Saturday, register, pick up your race packet, and browse the Sports and Fitness Expo at the Red Lion Hotel. All marathon entrants must join USATF to run ($15), and there is no race-day registration. After the race, plenty of food including tomato soup (a favorite in colder years), can be found in the Capitol Rotunda. Massages are also available. The awards ceremony takes place at the headquarters hotel.

AWARDS Every runner receives a T-shirt, while finishers earn medallions. The top three age-group finishers are awarded plaques.

ELITE RUNNERS INFORMATION Men under 2:20 and women under 2:50 could receive lodging, transportation, and free entry. The top five overall finishers take home about $50,000 in prize money. The precise breakdown varies year to year.

ACCOMMODATIONS The headquarters hotel is the Red Lion Hotel, 2001 Point West Way (Arden Way at the Capital City Freeway) (800-733-5466) or (916-929-8855). Other hotels near the Red Lion are: Red Lion's Sacramento Inn, 1401 Arden Way (916-922-8041); The Beverly Garland Hotel, 1780 Tribute Road (800-972-3976); Expo Inn, 1413 Howe Avenue (800-643-4422); and the Radisson Hotel, 500 Leisure Lane (800-333-3333). Near the finish line are the Hyatt Regency, 1209 L Street (800-233-1234); and the Clarion Hotel, 700 16th Street (800-252-7466).

RELATED EVENTS/RACES Four-person teams can enter the Corporate Relay Challenge, with three 10K legs and one 12K leg. Family and friends may want to enter the 2.62-mile Marafun Run/Walk while they wait for their marathoner. The Marafun Run starts at 8:00 a.m. and is held at the marathon finish line. Kids under 13 may enter free.

AREA ATTRACTIONS While in Sacramento, get a taste of the Old West in Old Sacramento, just off the Sacramento River in downtown. Wood walkways, cobblestone streets, shops, restaurants, and horse-drawn carriages highlight the area. Don't miss the Railroad Museum while there. Other possibilities include State Capitol tours, and kids may enjoy exploring Sutter's Fort to learn about life in the frontier days. Centrally located, Sacramento provides easy access to Lake Tahoe for skiing or gambling, the Napa Valley and Sonoma wine country, and San Francisco.

LOCAL RUNNING STORES Fleet Feet Sports, 2311 J Street (916-442-3338); Fleet Feet Sports, 8128 Madison Avenue, Fair Oaks (916-965-8326).

HONOLULU MARATHON

OVERALL: 97.5

COURSE BEAUTY: 9+

COURSE DIFFICULTY: 5-

APPROPRIATENESS FOR FIRST TIMERS: 8

RACE ORGANIZATION: 10

CROWDS: 3

RACE DATA

Contact:	Honolulu Marathon Association
	3435 Waialae Avenue, Room 208
	Honolulu, HI 96816
	(808) 734-7200
Date:	December 14, 1997
	December 13, 1998
Start Time:	5:00 a.m
Time Course Closes:	2:30 p.m.
Number of Participants:	34,434 in 1995
Certification:	USATF
Course Records:	Male: (open) 2:11:43; (masters) 2:17:24
	Female: (open) 2:31:01; (masters) 2:48:00
Elite Athlete Programs:	Yes
Cost:	$30/40/50
Age groups/Divisions:	<14, 15-19, 20-24, 25-29, 30-34, 35-39, 40-44, 45-49, 50-54, 55-59, 60-64, 65-69, 70-74, 75-79, 80-84, 85-89, 90-94, 95-99, 100+
Temperature:	65° - 85°
Aid/Splits:	17 / every mile, clocks every 5 miles

HIGHLIGHTS Like the swallows' yearly pilgrimage to San Juan Capistrano, runners from East and West flock to Hawaii for the burgeoning Honolulu Marathon. In 1995, nearly 35,000 runners made the flight to the tropics, perhaps to escape the pre-winter cold or to place the ultimate bookend on their marathon year. The painfully early 5:00 a.m. start, necessary because of the impending heat and humidity, is tempered by the most entertaining staging area of any marathon. Each year, upwards of 20,000 Japanese runners add a colorful flair to the race, providing more vitality than a hummingbird on honey as they proudly sport their brightly colored running club duds, wave club banners and bellow club chants. If this spectacle doesn't get you going, the gust of fireworks will surely put some bounce in your stride as you embark on a course that includes the world-famous sights of Waikiki Beach, Diamond Head and Koko Head Crater.

COURSE DESCRIPTION Most runners congregate in the darkness of Ala Moana Beach Park or the Ala Moana Shopping Center, listening to the lively military band. Amidst a torrent of fireworks and a Howitzer cannon blast, the 30,000 runners stampede west toward downtown and Aloha Tower. Runners enter the Capitol District (miles 2 and 3) on South King Street, passing the Kamehameha Statue, Alliolani Hale (the Judiciary Building), Iolani Palace, the Hawaii State Library, Kawaihao Church, and Honolulu Hale (City Hall). With Christmas only weeks away, local businesses and merchants get into the marathon spirit by leaving on their Christmas lights to illuminate this predawn section of the course. Returning near the start after 5K, runners cross the Ala Wai Canal into the world-famous Waikiki strip just after 4 miles. The Hilton Hawaiian Village and Fort DeRussy lie on the way to your first glimpse of the balmy Pacific waters at Kuhio Beach (mile 5). Leaving the ocean behind, the course makes its first trip through Kapiolani Park, the eventual finish, six miles into the race. Virtually flat up to this point, the course begins ascending Diamond Head Road at 7.25 miles and peaks just past the lighthouse near mile 8 (93 feet). At 8.6 miles, the course veers left of Ft. Ruger Triangle Park, climbing to its highest point (108 feet) at 15K. A quick turn onto 18th Avenue leads runners past the Diamond Head Film Studio, home of Hawaii Five-O and Magnum P.I. The lonely next 3 miles on Kalanianaole Hwy., although barely 10 feet above sea level and absolutely flat, afford only a few places to see the ocean. Your spirits soon rise as you reach the half marathon point just before the Aina Haina Shopping Center. After passing the Niu and Kuliouou Valleys around 14 miles, the course turns off the highway into residential Hawaii Kai, christened by a 200-yard climb over a short bridge. After retracing your steps on the lonely highway, a slight incline occurs past the Waialae Country Club (21.5 miles) before the course descends toward the ocean. At the bottom of the short decline sits the Aloha Gasoline station, site of a Hawaiian band and hula dancers in grass skirts. At mile 23, the course turns right onto Kahala Avenue, better known as the Million Dollar Mile because of the high value of its real estate. By mile 23.75, you begin the 1-mile climb up Diamond Head, gaining a modest 50 feet. From the cliffs to your left, watch the surfers and windsurfers in the water below. A 3-mile downhill from Diamond Head and you're in the homestretch — only flat Diamond Head Road (mile 25) and Kalakaua Avenue remain before the finish in Kapiolani Park.

CROWD/RUNNER SUPPORT Over 30,000 fellow runners and 50,000 spectators do their best to give you company on the course. The thousands of spouses, friends and other spectators left behind at the start get their next chance to cheer their runner at the 5K mark when the course returns near the start. Here, cheering sections from the Japanese running clubs shout, chant, blow whistles, sound horns, and jingle bells. Others cheer from their high-rise condos and hotel lanais along Ala Moana and Kalakaua Avenue in Waikiki. Not only do they cheer you on, but their camera flashbulbs light up your predawn path. More applause and encouragement come from residents of Hawaii Kai (15-18 miles) and the Million Dollar Mile (23-24 miles). As the day grows older and the temperature rises, each of the 17 aid stations becomes more of a welcomed sight. You'll especially enjoy the enthusiastic stations in Hawaii Kai around miles 15 and 17.

RACE LOGISTICS Free bus service from Kapiolani Park to the start begins at 2:00 a.m. The last bus leaves at 4:00 a.m. Kapiolani Park is located within walking (hobbling for the return) distance of major hotels along Waikiki Beach.

ACTIVITIES Early arrivers to Honolulu have first pick at arguably the best collection of souvenirs (most display Honolulu's signature Polynesian runner) of any North American marathon. An all-in-one Sports Expo, Souvenir Sale and Packet Pickup extends from Wednesday to Saturday 10:00 a.m. to 6:00 p.m. There is no race-day registration for the marathon. Souvenir sales also take place at Kapiolani Park, Thursday through Saturday from 11:00 a.m. to 6:00 p.m. and race day from 6:00 a.m. to 4:00 p.m. On Friday evening, join runners from around the world at the Carbo-Loading and International T-shirt Exchange Party at the Waikiki Shell from 5:30 p.m. to 9:00 p.m. Bring a few of your race T-shirts to exchange for foreign ones that will truly impress your running buddies. After the race, speed your recovery with post-race refreshments and a well-deserved massage as you await the awards ceremony, starting at 1:00 p.m., at the Kapiolani Park Bandstand.

AWARDS Every finisher receives a T-shirt, shell lei, and medallion. Finisher certificates are also awarded and available the day after the race at race headquarters. Elite runners compete for several thousand dollars in overall prize money, while the top three in each age group receive trophies. Additionally, the top 5% of each age division receive medals.

ELITE RUNNERS INFORMATION The race maintains no official criteria establishing elite status. Instead, race organizers determine elite status and appropriate expenses on an individual basis. The usually substantial prize money purse fluctuates annually depending on sponsorship commitments.

ACCOMMODATIONS As of our press date, the official race headquarters hotel had not been determined. In the past, the Outrigger Hotel chain has played a major role in the marathon and related events. Located at 2169 Kali Road (808-668-7444), the Outrigger Reef Hotel normally offers special marathon rates. Additional nearby hotels include: Sheraton Waikiki, 2255 Kalakaua Avenue (800-325-3535); Hyatt Regency Waikiki, 2255 Kalakaua Avenue (800-233-1234); Royal Hawaiian Hotel, 2259 Kalakaua (800-325-3535); Hawaiian Waikiki Beach Hotel, 2570 Kalakaua Avenue (800-877-7666); and Continental Surf Hotel, 2426 Kuhio Avenue (808-922-2755).

RELATED EVENTS/RACES To insure that you're not overly peaked for the marathon, run the Diamond Head Duet couples run. This is a free, 4.2-mile run on Thursday at 8:00 a.m. in Kapiolani Park. On race day, family and friends braving the early marathon start may consider participating in the 10K Mayor's Walk, benefitting Hawaii's Special Olympics, held immediately following the start of the marathon. The walk course covers the first 10K of the marathon and finishes in Kapiolani Park in plenty of time to watch the marathon finish.

AREA ATTRACTIONS While catching some rays will surely be near the top of your ' to do' list, wait until after the race for sun worshiping on famous Waikiki Beach or snorkeling at nearby Hanauma Bay. In the meantime, take in the Kodak Hula Show at the Waikiki Shell Amphitheater in Kapiolani Park on Tuesday, Wednesday or Thursday at 10:00 a.m., or head to the U.S.S. Arizona National Memorial in Pearl Harbor. Although you'll pass Diamond Head Crater during the marathon, take time to hike the one mile into the crater for a gorgeous sunrise or sunset and spectacular view of Waikiki. The souvenir shops, restaurants and nightclubs scattered along Waikiki will also keep you occupied. However, don't forget the main reason you're in Honolulu, to run the marathon!

LOCAL RUNNING STORE The Running Room, 819 Kapahulu Avenue, Honolulu (808-737-2422).

KIAWAH ISLAND MARATHON

OVERALL: 90.2

COURSE BEAUTY: 9+

COURSE DIFFICULTY: 3-

APPROPRIATENESS FOR FIRST TIMERS: 9-

RACE ORGANIZATION: 9

CROWDS: 1

R A C E   D A T A

Contact:	Dylan Jones
	Kiawah Island Resort
	12 Kiawah Beach Drive
	Kiawah Island, SC 29455
	(803) 768-6001
Date:	December 13, 1997
	December 12, 1998
Start Time:	8:00 a.m.
Time Course Closes:	3:00 p.m.
Number of Participants:	1,160 in 1995
Certification:	USATF
Course Records:	Male: (open) 2:21:24
	Female: (open) 2:52:08
Elite Athlete Programs:	Yes
Cost:	$22
Age groups/Divisions:	13-17, 18-23, 24-29, 30-34, 35-39, 40-44, 45-49,
	50-54, 55-59, 60-69, 70+
Temperature:	45° - 60°
Aid/Splits:	12 / every 2 miles

HIGHLIGHTS Chances are you have never heard of the Kiawah Island Marathon. Until now. Offering one of the most unique marathon experiences in North America, the race runs entirely on this 10,000 acre resort barrier island off the coast of South Carolina. Using just about every inch of road on the isle, the winding course passes salt marshes, semitropical wilderness, breathtaking golf courses, and maybe even an alligator! The elegant, post-race banquet knows no equals. And after the marathon, Kiawah Island is a terrific place to relax and savor your accomplishment. So if you want to escape the December frost, the Kiawah Island Marathon may be the perfect destination.

COURSE DESCRIPTION Covered by salt marshes, wilderness, beaches, and golf courses, environmentally sensitive Kiawah Island consists entirely of a world-class resort and exclusive residential communities. The controlled marathon course, open to limited residential traffic, consists of a series of inventive loops and out-and-backs up and down the island. Since the barrier isle has relatively few roads, the race covers many twice, providing ample opportunity to view the other runners. The course has many curves and turns which could annoy faster runners. However, runners should love the excellent footing and the flat route (the highest elevation on the island is 14 feet), with the largest grades consisting of golf cart paths. If you want it any flatter you'd have to send out for it!

The marathon starts and finishes in front of the East Beach Conference Center. The first six miles of the course cover the western end of the island passing 21-acre Night Heron Park, the Cougar Point Golf Course, and the tree-lined roads of Kiawah's first residential area. The following 10 miles weave through the middle and eastern sections of the island, now comprised of second and third growth maritime forest and quintessential Southern Living homes. Indigo and cotton fields covered this area over 150 years ago. The next four miles (16-20) take runners down and back on spectacular Ocean Course Drive, providing vistas of marshland, salt water creeks, gracious oaks, and the famous Ocean Course where America claimed the 1991 Ryder Cup. The final stretch guides marathoners down beautiful Flyway Drive with ponds and gators motivating runners to the East Beach Conference Center finish line.

CROWD/RUNNER SUPPORT Kiawah Island has a small local population so most of the crowds consist of runners' families and friends. An excellent spectator course, the runners pass most points at least twice. Located every 2 miles, aid stations offer runners the choice of water, electrolyte replacement and fruit. Splits are called roughly every two miles.

RACE LOGISTICS There is a free shuttle service to the start area for those runners staying on the island. If you are staying in Charleston, there is plenty of parking near the conference center, but as always, you should arrive early.

ACTIVITIES On Friday evening, attend the Pasta Bash at the East Beach Conference Center. The resort catering staff does a superb job with the dinner (about $13). Kiawah Island hosts an excellent awards ceremony and party following the marathon. A generous buffet of hot and cold food and beverage highlights the festivities.

AWARDS Each preregistered marathon entrant receives a long-sleeve T-shirt, with finishers earning medals. Kiawah "Proud Pelican" awards go to the top five open males, top three open females, and the male and female masters winners. Age-group awards are also given to the top three finishers in each age division. Ten percent of all preregistered runners receive awards..

ELITE RUNNERS INFORMATION Kiawah Island Marathon does not actively recruit elite runners, nor does it offer prize money. The race will, however, assist with on-site expenses such as lodging and entry fees on a case-by-case basis. Contact the race director for more information.

ACCOMMODATIONS The Kiawah Island Inn offers special accommodation packages for marathon runners and their families. The resort also offers numerous villa and home options, starting at about $40 per person, per night. For resort reservations call (800-654-2924). Other companies also offer home and villa accommodations, including Ravenel Associates (800-845-3911); Pam Harrington Exclusives (800-845-6966); Benchmark Rentals (800-992-9666); Beachwalker Rentals (800-334-6308); and Charleston Resort Properties (800-845-7368). Budget lodging can be found in Charleston a short drive away.

RELATED EVENTS/RACES Kiawah Island also sponsors a half marathon and 5K, both held on the same day as the marathon.

AREA ATTRACTIONS A true resort, Kiawah Island offers four world-class golf courses ranked among the top in the country, numerous tennis courts, ten miles of beach, and an outstanding children's program, Kamp Kiawah.

LOCAL RUNNING STORE The Extra Mile, 336 King Street, Charleston, South Carolina (803-853-9987).

ROCKET CITY MARATHON

OVERALL: 81.5

COURSE BEAUTY: 7+

COURSE DIFFICULTY: 3 (SEE APPENDIX)

APPROPRIATENESS FOR FIRST TIMERS: 8+

RACE ORGANIZATION: 9+

CROWDS: 2+

RACE DATA

Contact:	Harold & Louise Tinsley
	Huntsville Track Club
	8811 Edgehill Drive
	Huntsville, AL 35802
	(205) 881-9077
Date:	December 13, 1997
	December 12, 1998
Start Time:	8:00 a.m.
Time Course Closes:	1:30 p.m.
Number of Participants:	1,474 in 1995
Certification:	USATF
Course Records:	Male: (open) 2:12:21; (masters) 2:17:01
	Female: (open) 2:32:22; (masters) 2:45:35
Elite Athlete Programs:	Yes
Cost:	$20/25/30
Age groups/Divisions:	<19, 20-24, 25-29, 30-34, 35-39, 40-44, 45-49,
	50-54, 55-59, 60+, Father-Son, Husband-Wife
Temperature:	45°
Aid/Splits:	10 / every mile, 10K, 13.1 & 25.2

HIGHLIGHTS Huntsville, Alabama, a.k.a. Rocket City, USA. Home to the launch vehicles that carried man to the moon and the Space Shuttle. With such a high-flying history, you would expect the Rocket City to host a real barnburner of a marathon. And they do. It's just that most people outside the Southeast don't know it. The Rocket City Marathon is a true sleeper. Its race organization is among the most friendly and thorough in the country. Only the warm and supportive community surpasses the fast course that boasts no significant hills. No other marathon provides runners with as much information about the race, course, history, and surrounding area in the form of an 84-page information book. Trained handlers greet and attend to every finisher, providing personalized care that usually can only be found at races one-tenth Rocket City's size. Rocket City sports one of the fastest courses in the country, as attested to by the numerous age-group records that have been set here. If you are looking for an early winter marathon to bust a PR, we suggest you give Rocket City a try.

RACE HISTORY Following World War II, 100 ex-German scientists were brought to Huntsville to develop the U.S. rocket and space program. Among the results: Saturn rockets that powered man to the moon and the Space Shuttle. These achievements earned Huntsville the nickname, Rocket City. The Rocket City Marathon began in 1977 with a healthy 482 runners, becoming the first marathon held in Alabama. Participation peaked in 1981 with nearly 2,000 entrants. Lured by the fast course, many runners hoping to qualify for the 100th Boston Marathon increased participation numbers by 50% in 1995.

COURSE DESCRIPTION Run on a mixture of downtown streets (13.4%), broad avenues (21%), and residential roads (65.6%), the course consists almost entirely of asphalt. Relatively flat, with a few modest inclines and descents, the route contains no steep hills. The difference between the lowest and highest point on the course is 93 feet, with a total elevation change of 563 feet (includes ups and downs) over the 26.2 miles. The race has a large number of curves and turns, especially for a fast course, but it is well marked and patrolled.

The start/finish lies outside the Huntsville Hilton. After the start, look for the rocket launches in the park that let you know you are indeed running the Rocket City Marathon. The first 2.5 miles loop through downtown Huntsville. As you run north on Monroe Street, you pass Big Spring International Park and the Von Braun Civic Center. The course veers left, and you hit the first incline of the race, an 18-foot rise. Immediately following the 1-mile marker and a short downgrade, you turn left on Holmes Avenue and cross through the Old Town Historic District, the only predominantly Victorian neighborhood remaining in Huntsville, with most of the residences dating from 1870 to 1930. Within a few blocks, runners enter the Twickenham Historic District, one of the largest concentrations of antebellum homes in the South, through tree-canopied Randolph Avenue, accompanied by a nice downward slope. That is, until you reach Green Street and climb 20 feet. At the Madison County Courthouse, you traverse Cotton Row to the 2-mile mark in front of the 1835 Greek Revival First Alabama Bank. Runners then have a nice half-mile descent leading to a section of the course called the Downtown Connection. As you pass the Huntsville Hospital, a 24-foot climb over .3 miles precedes Governors Drive, the busiest intersection on the course. Largely flat and residential, the next 3 miles include some of Huntsville's older neighborhoods. Just before 6 miles, you encounter a short, 33-foot climb, and then you drop 41 feet over the next mile. At 6.85 miles, you begin the 58-foot climb to the highest point (668 feet) on the course at about 7.6 miles. As you cross the pedestrian tunnel under Whitesburg Drive, you are entering the 14.5-mile southern loop. The next 2 miles are through tree-lined residential streets. From the highest point to just before mile 9, the course follows a nice downward pitch. After a slight rise between 9 and 10, the course again dips to the lowest part on the route, 575 feet between miles 14 and 15. At mile 15, runners reach the biggest climb on the course, an 88-foot rise over 2 miles as you make the turn back toward downtown Huntsville. From the crest just before 17 to 19 miles, you drop 72 feet on the Chickamauga Trail. The next 3 miles roll slightly, and at 21.5, you return to the pedestrian tunnel and do the Downtown Connection in reverse. This last section of the course leading to downtown is mostly flat until the home stretch and a downhill, red carpet finish at the Hilton. Announcers call out your name as you cross the line.

CROWD/RUNNER SUPPORT Rocket City provides excellent support to the runners. Race organizers distribute 18,000 spectator flyers to homes along the course, and they promote a contest for the best spectator signs (many of which are extremely well done) boosting the runners. Crowd turnout is decent for a city of this size. The Friday paper lists all entrants so that spectators can cheer on runners by name. In addition, more than 1,000 volunteers, nearly one volunteer per runner, allows Rocket City to provide personalized service, such as the trained handlers for each and every marathon finisher.

RACE LOGISTICS Since the course is a loop, with the start and finish at the Huntsville Hilton, transportation is not required for the vast majority of runners. If you are staying elsewhere, you need to get to the start on your own. Portable toilets are located at four locations along the course. Belongings may be left in the Runner's Check-In area and picked up after the race. Aid stations every 2.4 miles offer water, electrolyte replacement, and minor medical supplies.

ACTIVITIES Rocket City offers a number of pre-race activities. On Friday evening, members of the Huntsville Track Club lead noncompetitive group runs around historic Huntsville. The emphasis is on sightseeing and socializing. The runs begin at 4:00 p.m. and leave from the covered bridge at the Hilton. A "gabfest" greets runners at the race headquarters where they pick up their race packets, get information about the course, and browse the expo. The Carbo Loading Supper and clinic (about $9) at the Hilton features a noted guest speaker. After finishing the race, runners receive a snack while the official results are posted after every 50 finishers. Following the race, a panel of experts provides informal advice on any questions you may have. The awards presentation begins at 2:30 p.m. inside the Hilton. Finally, marathon weekend concludes with the Award Winners' Banquet and Party.

A W A R D S One of the best marathon values around, Rocket City presents runners with an 84-page Marathon Information book that contains everything you need to know about the race, a 40-page Results Book, long-sleeve T-shirt, race packet, and original art poster all for the low $20 entry fee. Every finisher also receives a medallion, finisher's cap, and finish certificate. Rocket City offers $16,000 in prize money, plus $4,000 course record bonuses. There are special age-division awards (3 to 5 deep), including special medallions, winners' sweatshirts and merchandise. Winners must be present to receive their awards.

E L I T E   R U N N E R S   I N F O R M A T I O N Rocket City maintains fairly explicit policies for elite runner recruitment. Recently, the race has moved toward offering more prize money and less in travel expenses in the hopes of encouraging faster performances. Essentially, the race offers lodging (at a hotel or possibly with a host) and entry to open males under 2:25, master males under 2:35, open females under 2:55 and master females under 3:05. Past winners also receive travel expenses. Complimentary entry and race functions are available to open males under 2:30, master males under 2:40, open females under 3:00, and master females under 3:10. The race offers prize money of approximately $16,000, with money going to the top ten open males and females, the top five master's males, and the top three master's females. Overall winners earn $2,000 for their efforts. There is also a $1,000 bounty for any open or masters runner who sets a new course record. Contact Harold Tinsley for more information.

A C C O M M O D A T I O N S Try to stay at the Huntsville Hilton if you can. All race activities begin and end there, including the marathon. A good value at $52 or so, the Hilton is located at 401 Williams Avenue (205-533-1400), and fills very early so make your reservations far in advance. Two other hotels offer special rates to marathoners: the Huntsville Marriott Hotel, 5 Tranquillity Base (205-830-2222); and the Courtyard by Marriott, 4804 University Drive (205-837-1400). The Huntsville Marriott is located next to the U.S. Space and Rocket Center Museum and offers shuttles to and from the marathon. The Marathon Information Book contains a list of other hotels in the area.

A R E A   A T T R A C T I O N S While in Huntsville, you should visit the Space Museum which is the largest in the world. The Museum contains more than 60 hands-on exhibits, space flight simulations, and a 354-foot Saturn V rocket. The Von Braun Civic Center also hosts a large craft show on race weekend.

L O C A L   R U N N I N G   S T O R E Foot Locker, Parkway City Mall (205-539-2610).

THE MID PACK

80 LOCAL MARATHONS

TALLAHASSEE MARATHON

Contact: Dana Stetson
Gulf Winds Track Club
3218 Albert Drive
Tallahassee, FL 32308
(904) 668-3839
Date: February 1, 1997
February 7, 1998

Catering to the mid-pack marathoner since 1974, the Tallahassee Marathon attracts more than 300 participants for both the full and half marathons. Featuring a flat, out-and-back course starting and finishing at Wacissa Springs, the race travels over paved country roads. Aid stations occur every 2 miles, and splits are called at 1, 2, 3, 4, 5, 10, 15, 20, and 25 miles. Every entrant receives a T-shirt and race results, and finishers earn achievement certificates. Packet pickup occurs Friday from 3:00 p.m. to 7:00 p.m. at Sports Beat, 2020 W. Pensacola Street #20. Following the race, enjoy food, beverages and a massage while awaiting the awards ceremony.

TYBEE MARATHON

Contact: Anna Boyette
Savannah Striders Track Club
P.O. Box 15785
Savannah, GA 31416
(912) 232-0070
Date: February 8, 1997
February 14, 1998

Originally called the Savannah Marathon, the race moved five years ago to the friendly and less congested surroundings of Tybee Island, Savannah's beach. From 50 to 75 runners line up in front of City Hall for the flat, double-loop course along mostly paved roads through island marshlands and residential areas. Aid stations dot the route every 2 to 3 miles. For those not interested in going a full 26, race day includes a larger half marathon(250 runners) starting with the marathon at 8:00 a.m. All entrants receive T-shirts, and marathon finishers receive either commemorative medals or mugs. The top three overall and age-group winners receive plaques.

After the race, enjoy the many tourist sites of Tybee Island, including the: Coney Island-type amusement park, water park or Marine Science Center. For more entertainment, head to River Street or the City Market in Savannah where street-side food stands and local band performances regularly attract large crowds.

VALLEY OF THE SUN MARATHON

Contact: Rob Wallack
Raceplace Events
6505 N. 16th Street
Phoenix, AZ 85016
(602) 277-4333
Date: February 16, 1997
February 15, 1998

Debuting in 1996, the Valley of the Sun Marathon features a USATF-certified, flat, figure-8 loop in Scottsdale, Arizona's temperate wintertime climate. Starting at the Scottsdale Civic Center Plaza, the course traipses the main streets of central and northeast Scottsdale. After offering an easy rise of 80 feet over the first 13 miles, the route gradually drops back down to the finish. Aid stations occur every 2.5 miles through mile 22, then every mile thereafter. Runners not wanting to tackle the entire distance may consider taking part in the accompanying marathon relay, half marathon or 5K run and walk.

All entrants receive T-shirts and results booklets. Runners finishing under 5.5 hours receive commemorative mugs. The top three male/female finishers in each age group are recognized at an awards ceremony in the Scottsdale Civic Center amphitheater adjacent to the finish line. Post-race activities include music, food and the camaraderie of fellow competitors.

HUDSON MOHAWK MARATHON

Contact: Lori Christina
Hudson Mohawk Road Runners
2A Ramsgate — London Sq. Apts.
Clifton Park, NY 12065
(518) 383-4514
Date: February 23, 1997
February 22, 1998

There's a 30° F below zero wind chill and the weather report urges you to stay inside. Do you suddenly feel compelled to run 26 miles? If you answer yes, then join the 75 or so brazen competitors (and 20 to 30 3-person relay teams) at the Hudson Mohawk Marathon in Albany, New York. Despite the harsh climate, the race has been canceled only once in 23 years. Perseverance is essential when tackling not only the adverse weather conditions but also the mentally-challenging, flat, four-loop course around the state university and New York state office campuses. Post-race refreshments and awards are presented at the athletic center. Bundle up and come equipped with sardonic wit to the Hudson Mohawk Marathon for a coffee mug is your compensation for completing the race!

OLYMPIAD MEMORIAL MARATHON

Contact: Gateway Athletics — St. Louis
c/o Marathon Sports
13453 Chesterfield Plaza
Chesterfield, MO 63017
(314) 434-9577
Date: February 23, 1997
February 22, 1998

The Olympiad Memorial Marathon, a tribute to those who participated in the 1904 St. Louis Olympic Marathon, runs on a USATF-certified, loop course that was new in 1995. Commencing in Chesterfield Plaza, the race runs on rolling residential roads for the first 5 miles before proceeding onto a flat river bottom over lightly-traveled roads for the next 20 miles. At mile 25, you encounter a major hill preceding the Chesterfield Plaza finish. Starting at mile 5, aid stations are positioned along the course every 2 to 2.5 miles, and splits are called out at miles 1, 5, 10, 13.1, 15, and 20. Upon completion of the course, you receive a finisher's award and certificate. The open, masters, and age-group winners are presented awards at a post-race ceremony. The St. Louis Marriott West, about 2 miles from the race start (800-352-1175), serves as the host hotel. The hotel offers free shuttle service to and from the airport if you're flying in from out of town.

NANTUCKET MARATHON

Contact: Paul K. Daley
Nantucket Marathon
P.O. Box 401
Norton, MA 02766-401
(508) 285-4544
Date: March 1, 1997
March 7, 1998

Historic Nantucket Island, located 30 miles off the coast of Cape Cod, plays host to about 350 marathoners each spring. The beautiful course on this former whaling bastion lazily rolls along paved roads in the crisp salt air. Arrive early, and pick up your race packet and T-shirt at the Jared Coffin House, the host hotel. After check-in, mosey over to the official island greeting and Friday night Five Star CarboLoad feast, where you can ask any last minute questions about the race. Each finisher is awarded a medal, and personalized certificates are mailed to participants after the race. Other prizes go to the top five overall runners and to age-group winners. Nantucket is accessible from Hyannis, MA by express ferry (1 hr.), air (15 min.) and steamship (2.7 hrs.).

TRAIL'S END MARATHON

Contact: Gordon Lovie
Oregon Road Runners Club
P.O. Box 549
Beaverton, OR 97075-0549
(503) 646-7867
Date: March 1, 1997
March 7, 1998

Named for the wintering spot of the Lewis & Clark expedition, the Trail's End Marathon was created by a group of runners from the Portland area who eventually formed the Oregon Road Runners Club. The marathon attracts approximately 500 participants with the same number in the accompanying 8K race. Made up of gently rolling country roads, the double-loop course travels through several beachside communities and finishes near the beach. You have some great vantage points of lakes, golf courses, and the Pacific Ocean as you make your way along the route. You also encounter 13 aid stations supplying your fluid needs. All finishers are adorned with commemorative medals, and the usual post-race refreshments and awards presentation follow.

This area is Oregon's most popular seaside resort, so be sure to make your lodging reservations early. After the race, head over to the jazz festival or indulge in other activities including: kite flying, surfing, beach combing, hiking or shopping.

B & A TRAIL MARATHON

Contact: Thomas Bradford
Annapolis Striders
746 Mimosa Court
Millersville, MD 21108-1883
(410) 987-0674
Date: March 9, 1997
March 1, 1998

Originally created to accommodate Boston Marathon hopefuls who hadn't yet made the cut, the B & A Trail Marathon now runs on its own since Boston has moved up its qualifying date. The paved course has an unusual configuration. Technically a loop, the route contains two out-and-backs for the marathon on the B & A Trail. Starting on the residential streets of Severna Park, you embark on the B & A Trail, an asphalt bike and running path along the Rails-to-Trails Park, at mile 3. Runners complete an out-and-back from miles 3 to 13.1; half marathoners finish on the trail, while full marathoners continue on for another out-and-back. Marathoners finish near the race start. Though mostly level, the race contains a couple of slight grades at miles 2 and 7. Take care on the course as you share it with cyclists, rollerbladers and walkers. Volunteers greet you at miles 3, 7, 11, 13.1, 15, 20 and 24 with refreshments, first aid and other necessities. Though crowd participation is small, the race allows doting friends and relatives to cheer you on at numerous spectator access points.

All registered runners receive T-shirts, and each finisher earns a medal. Additional awards are presented to the first three finishers in each age group, and bonus prizes go to the overall and masters winners. All winners are recognized at the post-race awards ceremony held at noon.

MUSIC CITY MARATHON

Contact: Greater Nashville Athletic Club
P.O. Box 150867
Nashville, TN 37215-0867
(615) 298-3435
Date: March 15, 1997
March 21, 1998

If you like your running accompanied by a twang, then mosey to Nashville, Tennessee for the Music City Marathon. Staged in Riverfront Park on the banks of the Cumberland River, the two-loop course circles the State Capital and then saunters out-and-back over city streets. Although moderately hilly with an occasional long gradual grade, the route hides no "heartbreak" hills along the way. Medallions and certificates await all finishers, while only preregistered runners are guaranteed T-shirts. The post-race reception recognizes the open and masters winners.

For country music fans, the real race begins after the marathon. Start off at Music Row, or marvel at the classic memorabilia housed at the Country Music Hall of Fame. Amuse yourself at Opryland USA, gather at the Grand Ole Opry, or brave the crowds at the Blue Bird Cafe where Garth Brooks and many other famous country singers got their start. The Courtyard by Marriott, 1901 West End Avenue (615-327-9900), serves as the host hotel. Other downtown hotels include: DoubleTree Hotel, 315 4th Avenue North (615-244-8200); Holiday Inn Crowne Plaza, 623 Union Street (800-447-9825); The Hermitage Hotel, Union Street and 6th Avenue (800-251-1908); and Stouffer Renaissance Hotel, 611 Commerce Street (615-255-8400). Make your reservations early or you'll only be singing the blues!

ATHENS MARATHON

Contact: Tom Wolf
c/o Athens Marathon Committee
44 Grosvenor Street
Athens, OH 45701
(614) 594-3042
Date: March 30, 1997
March 29, 1998

Greece is beyond your budget? Will Athens, Ohio do? Each year this community hosts a marathon and half marathon starting at high noon in front of the Athens County Courthouse. The USATF-certified marathon heads straight for the country and finishes in Ohio University's Peden Stadium. Aid stations and medical assistance are provided every three miles. To save you from splashing yourself uncontrollably, the water cups come equipped with lids and straws.

Cash prizes are presented to the top three overall finishers, top two masters runners, and age-division winners. Wreaths (from Greece, of course) are also presented to the marathon winners. All preregistered marathoners receive long-sleeve T-shirts. Located 75 miles southeast of Columbus, Athens contains several hotels near the course. Most convenient is the Ohio University Inn (614-593-6661).

MULE MOUNTAIN MARATHON

Contact: Leslie H. Woods
Dept. of Army
P.O. Box 12100
Ft. Huachuca, AZ 85613
(520) 533-2442
Date: April 5, 1997
April 4, 1998

Since its inaugural event in 1975, the Mule Mountain Marathon has seen participation grow from a meager 30 to more than 1,200 runners in its marathon, dual Mule (52.4 miles), half marathon, and fun run. Many elite runners come to "the mule," if not for the desert scenery, then for its $10,000 prize money. Starting in the southeastern Arizona town of Bisbee (5,300 feet), the challenging, point-to-point course follows the same route (now paved) once used by Apache Indians, the U.S. Calvary and mining prospectors. After climbing 2.5 miles to the Mule Mountain Tunnel at 6,000 feet, the race descends over the next 17 miles to the San Pedro River Basin at 4,000 feet. From here, the race heads predominately uphill for the final 7 miles ending at Veteran's Memorial Park in Sierra Vista. Aid stations are provided every 2.5 miles along the traffic-free course. All entrants receive T-shirts, and finishers earn commemorative medallions. Division winners are presented trophies during the Festival of the Southwest, an event created around the marathon and related races.

Located only 12 miles from Tombstone and Mexico, this region offers a plethora of activities to the tourist, including the mile-high bird sanctuary, San Pedro River Riparian Area, as well as Ft. Huachuca (home of the buffalo soldier).

LONGEST DAY MARATHON

Contact: Scotty Roberts, M.D.
1345 1st Street
Brookings, SD 57006
(605) 692-2334
Date: April 19, 1997
April 18, 1998

With a net elevation change of only 70 feet, the Longest Day Marathon offers the chance to run a personal best in a small-town, prairie setting. The two-loop course travels mostly over paved roads with two miles on gravel. It starts near the campus of South Dakota State University (SDSU) and for the first 10 miles alternates between the university, surrounding residential neighborhoods, and highway bypasses. The race then proceeds for about a mile over gravel through cornfields, and then the first loop ends on highways and bypasses past agricultural areas. Upon completing the second loop, you have a spectator-friendly finish as you make your victory lap around the track at SDSU's Sexauer Field. Aid stations are provided every 3.5 miles along the course.

Prepare for your "longest day" by hitting the pre-race, pool-side pasta feed, followed by a guest lecturer, at the host hotel, the Staurolite Inn (605-692-9421). Every marathon participant receives a long-sleeve T-shirt, and finishers earn medallions. The race offers a $500 bonus for new open or masters course records (OM 2:22:29; OF 2:48:26; MM 2:37:23; MF 3:07:36). Longest Day also hosts four other events including: a marathon relay, half marathon, 10K, and 5K. The events benefit the Easter Seals.

GLASS CITY MARATHON

Contact: Pat Wagner
130 Yale
Toledo, OH 43614
(419) 385-1072
Date: April 20, 1997
April 19, 1998

The Glass City Marathon runs along the Maumee River through the communities of Rossford, Perrysburg, and Maumee. Traveling over a mix of city and country roads, the loop course starts in downtown Toledo at Summit and Jefferson Streets and finishes on Water Street.

Arrive on Saturday at the host hotel, The Holiday Inn Crowne Plaza Hotel (800-HOLIDAY), where you can pick up your race packet, enjoy the daylong expo, and receive a massage for $5. Then ramble to the Regatta Restaurant where you can appease your pre-race appetite with the pasta dinner. Included in your entry fee is a T-shirt, a finisher's award, and post-race refreshments. Don't forget to attend the awards ceremony, where cash is awarded to the top three overall finishers ($100 for first, $75 for second and $50 for third). Division awards are also presented.

PINE LINE MARATHON

Contact: Bob Linaberry-Charis
Pine Line Sports
351 N. 8th
Medford, WI 54451
(715) 748-3400
Date: April 26, 1997
April 25, 1998

The Pine Line Marathon, formerly known as the Dairyland Marathon, originally reflected both Wisconsin's famous dairy industry and the German ancestry of the local community. Upon the development of the Pine Line Rail Trail, the name was changed to reflect the huge quantities of white pine shipped over its ground by the Wisconsin Central Railroad between 1876 and 1988.

The point-to-point marathon runs through the glacial hills between Prentice and Medford, Wisconsin and presents very little elevation change. The majority of the trail is covered with crushed gravel except the southernmost 3 miles which are surfaced with limestone screenings. The northern part of the route travels through the terminal moraine left by the Wisconsin glacier more than 12,000 years ago. Hardwood forests, and the unusual wetland vegetation of numerous cedar swamps and bogs, characterize the first half of the course. If you're lucky, you might spot a beaver building its proverbial dam adjacent to the trail. Picturesque Wisconsin dairy farms dot the second half of the route. Only six aid stations adorn the path, so if you require more frequent replenishment, consider carrying supplies or recruiting a helpful friend. A marathon relay of up to six persons runs concurrently with marathon.

Every participant receives a T-shirt, a chance to win one of several door prizes, and a free lunch at the post-race picnic.

ARMY MEDCOM MARATHON

Contact: Roger Soler
Roger Soler Sports
2589 Jackson Keller Rd.
San Antonio, TX 78230
(210) 366-3701
Date: April 27, 1997
April 26, 1998

In the historic quadrangle of Ft. Sam Houston in San Antonio, Texas, your 26.2-mile journey in the Army Medcom Marathon begins. Held entirely within the fort, the out-and-back course challenges those accustomed to flat races in cool, dry weather. Completely paved, the route winds through the affluent, tree-lined neighborhoods of the local military community and the base parade grounds for the first few miles, before turning toward the Brook Army Medical Center. The first several miles contain several long, gentle grades, while miles 14 to 18 feature a series of easy to moderate hills. If hills haunt you, lay your apprehensions to rest at the base cemetery located just past the halfway point. Finish before the stately beauty of the 1879 quad tower as your friends and family applaud your performance. Aid stations and split times are offered every mile. Several aid stations carry fruit to help you through the race.

At a post-race ceremony, awards are presented to the top overall male, female, military, wheelchair, masters and age-group winners. Top relay teams are also presented with prizes.

CBK COUNTRY WALNUT CREEK TRAIL MARATHON

Contact: Bill & Cheri Kissell
301 N. Jenifer Avenue
Covina, CA 91724
(818) 339-5251
Date: April 27, 1997
April 26, 1998

Originally a 21-mile course, the CBK Country Walnut Creek Trail event, a fundraiser for local charities, was lengthened to marathon distance in 1996. Though only in its third year, the race is well on its way to reaching its 200 runner limit by virtue of its growing reputation as a trail marathon conveniently located in the midst of a city. Race day begins with a flag ceremony by local boy scouts and the singing of our National Anthem. The safe yet challenging, out-and-back passage starts with a 3-mile trek through downtown Covina, then travels through country terrain, across bubbling streams, and over the rolling hills of pristine Bonelli Regional Park. As you make your way through the second half of the course, the sight of the cool waters of Puddingstone Lake and Raging Waters Park rejuvenate and push you toward the live entertainment at the Covina Park finish line. All runners are treated to race T-shirts, a post-race pancake breakfast and live entertainment, and all finishers receive medallions.

IDAHO GREAT POTATO MARATHON

Contact: Tim Severa
YMCA
1050 State St.
Boise, ID 83702
(208) 344-5501
Date: May 3, 1997
May 2, 1998

Beginning in 1978 as a Boise YMCA fitness challenge, the Idaho Great Potato Marathon features a relatively fast, point-to-point course (shuttle buses are provided to the start) with a net drop of 500 feet. Starting outside of Boise, the City of Trees, the race provides beautiful views of the city and the Boise foothills. Runners enjoy more of the area's springtime beauty while running along the Boise River Greenbelt System, which comprises 40% of the race course. Approximately 150 runners typically compete in the marathon with hundreds more participating in the accompanying half marathon, 10K run and walk, and 2.2-mile run and walk. Every entrant receives a T-shirt, unless choosing the reduced entry fee, while division winners receive plaques and bags of potatoes. If you're not fast enough to win your division, you're still eligible to go home a winner. Sport your best Mr. Potato Head garb and enter the costume contest to win dinner at one of Boise's finest restaurants. Speaking of food, post-race activities include a carbo reload party with, you guessed it, a large potato feed. So, if you're a potato lover and a marathoner, consider placing the Idaho Great Potato Marathon on your race menu.

SHIPROCK MARATHON

Contact: Nancy Krivo
2800 N. Dustin #205
Farmington, NM 87401
(505) 327-5595
Date: May 3, 1997
May 2, 1998

Named for the sacred mountain of the Navajo people, the Shiprock Marathon starts at 6,000 feet on Red Rock Highway, two miles east of Red Rock Trading Post in Arizona, and makes its way through the rolling terrain of the Navajo Indian Reservation, losing about 1,000 feet over the entire course. The 1,800-foot Shiprock, in Navajo legends the "rock with wings" or the great bird that brought them from the north, is visible nearly the entire way. Aid stations are provided every 2.5 miles, then every mile from mile 20. Supported by Navajo tribal authorities, the pounding of Navajo drummers sends the runners off. All participants receive unique southwestern design T-shirts, and each finisher receives a medal. Overall and age-group winners receive Native American Pottery. Race day also includes a marathon relay and half marathon walk. Buses take runners from the finish to the start. A pasta dinner is held at the headquarters hotel, the Anasazi Inn, 903 West Main (505-325-4564), on Friday night. After the race, enjoy the Native American arts and crafts fair at the finish area.

WHISKEY ROW MARATHON

Contact Jenny Huq
Prescott YMCA
750 Whipple Street
Prescott, AZ 86301
(520) 445-7221
Date: May 3, 1997
May 2, 1998

Named "Whiskey Row" in the late 1800s, downtown Prescott's Montezuma Street marks the site of the Whiskey Row Marathon. The challenging out-and-back course travels over primarily dirt roads and winds amongst the fragrant pines of the Prescott National Forest. Only the first and last 3.5 miles cover paved roads. For those not acclimated to high elevation, be forewarned — this course starts at 5,280 feet, climbs to 7,000 feet by mile 7, and then descends to 5,600 feet by the turnaround point. Aid stations appear every 2 miles along the route. After arriving back in downtown Prescott, enjoy the post-race refreshments and awards ceremony. All participants receive T-shirts, and finishers earn ribbons. The top male and female in each age division win special awards. Other race services provided for a small fee include a pre-race pasta bar dinner and child-care. Race day also includes a half marathon, 10K and 2-mile fun run/walk.

LONG ISLAND MARATHON

Contact: Patti Kemler
NC Recreation & Parks, Sports Unit
Eisenhower Park
East Meadow, NY 11554
(516) 572-6251
Date: May 4, 1997
May 3, 1998

The Long Island Marathon (originally called the Earth Day Marathon) attracts more than 7,500 participants to one of New York's most popular sandy summer refuges. The loop course starts in Eisenhower Park, winding through suburban streets on its way to Wantagh Parkway. Here, with water on both sides, you make an out-and-back to Jones Beach with the Jones Beach tower in the background. Aid stations await you at least every 2 miles. Runners can also choose to do the half marathon in mid race. Starting together, the full and half races split near mile 7.7; you may go in either direction depending on how you feel that day. After the race, runners receive refreshments prior to the awards ceremony.

With the race behind you, set out to see the sights of Long Island. Start at Nassau's Jones Beach State Park with its 1.5 miles of boardwalk offering activities such as miniature golf, deck games and rollerblading. If you haven't quite recovered from your run, head to Fire Island to enjoy the national seashore and protected wilderness of this 32-mile barrier island. If you want to toast your accomplishment, then work your way to wine country where the vineyards of the North Fork produce wines from Riesling to Chardonnay.

WILD WILD WEST MARATHON

Contact: Lone Pine Chamber of Commerce
P.O. Box 749
Lone Pine, CA 93545
(619) 876-4444
Date: May 4, 1997
May 3, 1998

As the United States' third oldest trail marathon behind Pikes Peak and Catalina Island, the Wild Wild West Marathon features a challenging loop starting in Lone Pine, California (220 miles east of Los Angeles) and traversing the eastern Sierra foothills. A favorite among ultra runners, the route includes several steady climbs and moderate declines with one long downhill from mile 7 to 12. Despite the demanding conditions — lofty elevation (4,000 to 6,200 feet), hills, and typical heat (85° by high noon) — the spectacular scenery may be worth the discomfort. Striking vistas, the snow-capped eastern Sierras, and the expansive Owens Valley are just a few of the sites along the way. The clearly marked trail contains aid stations every 3 miles serving water and oranges.

Race registration and a pre-race meal take place Saturday at Lo-Inyo Elementary School in Lone Pine from 5:00 p.m. to 7:00 p.m. You may also register on race day from 5:30 a.m. to 6:30 a.m. at the race start in Tuttle Creek Campground. If you prefer running a shorter distance, an accompanying 10-mile run leaves with the marathon at 7:00 a.m. All entrants receive T-shirts and free entry to the post-race picnic and awards ceremony held at 12:00 p.m. in Lone Pine Park.

JOHNNY MILES MARATHON

Contact: Johnny Miles Marathon
P.O. Box 7
New Glasgow, Nova Scotia
Canada B2H 5E1
(902) 755-8363
Date: May 10, 1997
May 9, 1998

As a tribute to the sensational victory of the young Nova Scotian who, as a 19-year-old under-dog, won the 1926 Boston Marathon, the Johnny Miles Marathon is held each spring to remind us of what may be accomplished through strength, courage and dedication. Offering a loop course entirely within the New Glasgow town limits, the marathon starts at Union Race Track at the Scott Weeks Parkdale Sports Center. Fully certified, the route contains a few steep hills along the way. Several local musicians provide entertainment for spectators and runners alike. Every finisher receives a T-shirt, commemorative medal, certificate and finishing photo. Trophies, medals and special gifts are presented to the top three overall finishers, and the first masters runners. Random prizes are also presented. A half marathon takes place an hour after the marathon start. The night before the events, join other runners and their families for a carbo-loading feast ($5) starting around 5:00 p.m. at the Curling Club on Park Street.

If you have time before or after the race events, Pictou County has plenty to offer including the white sandy beaches of Big Island or Melmerby and several historic mills and homesteads.

GAGE ROADRUNNER MARATHON

Contact: Janet Pierce
Gage Chamber of Commerce
P.O. Box 328
Gage, OK 73843
(405) 923-7727
Date: May 24, 1997
May 23, 1998

Leading a fight in the late 1960s to save rural schools in Oklahoma, the Gage community and the local Chamber of Commerce wanted to start a project to unite the towns' citizens. An article in the Wall Street Journal about the growth of the Boston Marathon launched an effort to put together a marathon in Gage. Locals believed such an event would spark community participation, promote "Save Rural Oklahoma", and improve the industrial growth of small communities. A telegram was sent to Chicago's Mayor Daley challenging him to race against Gage Mayor Loris Shafer as a unique way to publicize the event. Though Mayor Daley's staff suspected the challenge was a hoax, they notified the media and called Mayor Shafer. Shafer verified the telegram's authenticity; however, Daley declined the invitation to compete. Out of this unique experience, the first Gage Roadrunner Marathon was born. More than 1,500 spectators came out to celebrate the marathon's debut on May 21, 1969. Though the course was originally only 21 miles (it has since been extended and certified by USATF), only four of eighteen runners could muster enough energy to finish it. The traditional race date of Memorial Day weekend has remained in place since 1979. To the delight of Gage residents, the oldest Oklahoma marathon continues to satisfy its original purpose of focusing attention on its rural areas, schools and industry.

Starting in downtown Gage (located near the panhandle in northeast Oklahoma) at 6:00 a.m., around 50 runners tackle the completely paved, double out-and-back course on State Hwy. 46. Although hilly in parts, the scenery along the course is pleasantly distracting. Average temperatures range from 55° to 65°, and aid stations are positioned every 2 miles.

Few people come out for the early start of the marathon, but typically good crowds gather by 9:00 a.m. in preparation for the related festivities — a parade, baseball games, arts & crafts show and the crowning of the Gage Roadrunner Queen. Every entrant receives a T-shirt, and finishers earn certificates. The top three age-group finishers and overall winners receive gold, silver or bronze medals. Gage City Hall has traditionally served as the race headquarters.

LONE STAR PAPER CHASE MARATHON

Contact: Heather Sells
Amarillo Globe-News
P.O. Box 2091
Amarillo, TX 79166
(806) 345-3451
Date: May 24, 1997
May 23, 1998

Founded by a veteran long-distance runner who worked for the Amarillo Globe-News, the Lone Star Paper Chase Marathon benefits the Newspapers in Education (NIE) program which supplies subscriptions to area schools. Featuring a point-to-point course starting in the local medical complex, the race runs through Amarillo's newly-constructed neighborhoods before heading toward historic Route 66 residential and shopping areas. Aid stations are positioned at least every 2 miles. Though this USATF-certified marathon normally attracts a small field of around 40 runners, more competitors take part in the accompanying half marathon, 10K and 2-mile runs.

The Ramada Inn traditionally serves as the race headquarters. Transportation is available from the airport to the hotel and back. Transportation is also available to and from the start/finish for all runners staying at the Ramada Inn. A finish line celebration and awards ceremony follows the race. If you plan on extending your stay, consider visiting the Wonderland Amusement Park and Palo Duro Canyon State Park.

BAYSHORE MARATHON

Contact: Deb Seyler
1019 Pine Street
Traverse City, MI 49684
Date: May 24, 1997
May 23, 1998

Celebrating its 15th anniversary in 1997, Traverse City Track Club's Bayshore Marathon features a scenic, flat USATF-certified course. Taking place entirely within Traverse City (producers of half of our nation's cherries), the race starts at Northwestern Michigan College and finishes on the high school track. Aid stations dot the course every 2 miles, and splits are provided at miles 1 and 3. Be aware if you're running in the back of the pack; the course stays open only five hours. For those not wanting to run the full 26 miles, the race includes an accompanying 10K event. After the race, snacks are provided, and an awards ceremony is held to recognize the top five male and female finishers. In addition, special medals are awarded to a minimum of three places up to 20% of each age group. All participants receive T-shirts, and finishers receive medals. Race results are mailed approximately 2 to 4 weeks after the event. Host hotels include the Days Inn (616-941-0208) and Hampton Inn (616-946-8900). If you would rather enjoy the nearby sandy beaches of Grand Traverse Bay, then stay at the campgrounds at Traverse City State Park or drive 20 miles west to the Sleeping Bear Dunes National Lakeshore.

WYOMING MARATHON

Contact: Brent Weigner
Wyoming Distance Runners
3204 Reed Avenue
Cheyenne, WY 82001
(307) 635-3316
Date: May 25, 1997
May 24, 1998

The primarily paved point-to-point course negotiates 10 miles of Interstate 80 before meandering through the Medicine Bow National Forest, with its beautiful mountain scenery, and finishing on aptly-named Happy Jack Road. A sparse annual field of about 25 runners tackles the challenging course which starts at 7,100 feet, gains 1,855 feet by the 11-mile mark, and finishes at 7,500 feet. If the hills don't bother you, then the absence of aid stations might. So remember to bring your own crew or carry your supplies during the race. Each finisher is presented with a medal in the finish chute, and the top three age-group winners earn special awards. Sip post-race refreshments before catching a car pool back to the start. Bring warm clothes; the weather is typically chilly (40° to 55°), especially with the 6:00 a.m. race start.

ANDY PAYNE MEMORIAL MARATHON

Contact: J.R. Cook
United National Indian Tribal Youth, Inc. (UNITY)
P.O. Box 25042
Oklahoma City, OK 73125
(405) 424-3010
Date: May 31, 1997
May 30, 1998

When Andy Payne, a Cherokee from Claremore, Oklahoma, stepped across the finish line first at the 1928 Los Angeles to New York City "Great Cross-Country Marathon Race," he could not have anticipated that nearly 70 years later runners would come out to Lake Overholser in Oklahoma City to pay tribute to his life. In an effort to uphold Andy Payne as a role model, the United National Indian Tribal Youth, Inc. has sponsored the Andy Payne Memorial Marathon and related 10K and 5K runs since 1978.

Starting along the shore of Lake Overholser, this paved, USATF-certified course, dubbed the "Bunion Run," loops around the lake three times before taking a short, out-and-back to finish at the start. Four aid stations are positioned throughout each loop.

An awards ceremony is held after the race where prizes are presented to the overall male and female winners and the top three in each age division. Every participant who preregisters receives a commemorative T-shirt.

GOLD COUNTRY MARATHON

Contact: Nick Vogt
Christian Team Ministries
1025 Grange Road
Meadow Vista, CA 95722
(916) 878-0697
Date: June 1, 1997
June 7, 1998

One of our top ten most difficult marathons, Northern California's Gold Country Marathon climbs over 2,600 feet during its figure-8 loop traversing the rugged mining trails and flumes of historic Nevada City. The race's slogan, "Run for a good time not a fast time", comes to mind as you struggle up Augustine Hill (approximately 1,450 feet) from mile 15.5 to 18.5. Many top ultra runners use Gold Country to tune up for the famous Western States 100 mile ordeal held four weeks later over neighboring terrain. Unlike Western States, however, you don't have to carry food and drink as aid stations are provided every 2 to 3 miles. While normally drawing less than 50 marathoners, Gold Country also features an accompanying 5K run/walk, 10K and half marathon. Packet pickup and late registration begin at 5:30 a.m. at the race start in Nevada City's Pioneer Park. The marathon starts at 6:30 a.m., and the other races begin at 7:30 a.m. Each participant receives a T-shirt, continental breakfast and full post-race meal. Overall winners receive plaques, and the top three division winners earn medals.

MARATHON DE LA BAIE DES CHALEURS

Contact: Jeannita Caron
Box 8, Site 10
Charlo, NB
Canada E0B 1M0
(506) 684-5133
Date June 1, 1997
June 7, 1998

Taking spousal support to a new level, Jeannita Caron of Charlo, New Brunswick, created Marathon De La Baie Des Chaleurs so her husband could run a marathon in his own, remote village. Though local male runners said the small French-speaking village (6,000 residents) couldn't possibly support a marathon, especially one organized by a woman, the increasingly popular race celebrates its 5th anniversary in 1997. In addition to Caron's husband, about 40 marathoners typically compete, while the accompanying 2-person marathon relay and 6K run attract 100 more participants. Starting and finishing at the Charlo Recreation Center, the moderately difficult out-and-back course runs over rolling terrain beside the Baie des Chaleurs. If you enjoy birdwatching, you'll enjoy the blue herons that frequent the shoreline path. Aid stations are positioned every 2 miles along the course. Pick up your race packet on Saturday from 5:00 p.m. to 7:00 p.m. during the carbo load supper ($8) at La Source Restaurant, 100 Craig Street, or at the Rec Center on race morning from 7:30 a.m. to 8:30 a.m. Every runner receives a T-shirt, and finishers receive medals and participation certificates. Top finishers win cash prizes, while all participants have a chance to win draw prizes. The traditional post-race party, including a delicious hot meal, takes place at La Source Restaurant.

NipMuck Trail Marathon

Contact: **David Raczkowski**
P.O. Box 285
Chaplin, CT 06235
(860) 455-1096
Date: **June 1, 1997**
June 7, 1998

Beginning in 1984 when race director David Raczkowski decided he wanted a trail marathon near his home, the NipMuck Trail Marathon ("Capital M is for Mud") has grown from a sparse inaugural field of 15 to its current average of 135 runners. One of the few marathons with qualification standards (you must have already run a road marathon or a trail half marathon), NipMuck offers directions to the nearest hospital on the course map and a race entry blank commencing with a warning: "It is possible to get a serious injury in this race." To invoke more fear and trepidation, Raczkowski has first-timers read a seemingly fictitious letter from a past participant explaining his distaste for the race and his desire never again to receive an entry blank. Despite Raczkowski's many tongue in cheek race caveats, NipMuck is a very enjoyable race. Featuring a double out-and-back course on a well-maintained, wooded, and narrow trail, NipMuck runners must endure an overall elevation gain of 2,300 feet and an occasional fence scaling. Add an hour or two to your road marathon time to get an idea of your NipMuck journey. However, if the beavers dam one of the streams on the course, as they did a few years ago, traversing through the newly created pond may add a bit more time to your trip. Like most trail events, NipMuck is an informal event. In fact, the winners are awarded apple pies baked by Raczkowski's mom.

God's Country Marathon

Contact: **Jeff & Carol Carts**
R R #3, Box 272A
Coudersport, PA 16915
(814) 274-9109
Date: **June 7, 1997**
June 6, 1998

Taking place in north central Pennsylvania's Potter County (nicknamed God's Country), the God's Country Marathon attracts approximately 130 runners. The paved, point-to-point course starts at Galeton Area High School (1,300 feet) and follows U.S. Route 6 through Pine Creek Valley. Continuing on the left shoulder of the highway, you pass Denton Hill State Park, with its white pine and hemlock trees before reaching Denton Hill at mile 17. The highest point on the course at 2,424 feet, Denton Hill marks the Eastern Continental Divide of the United States. The race finishes in Coudersport Area Recreation Park (CARP) in the Allegheny River Valley at an elevation of 1,700 feet. Major aid stations are located every 5 miles with additional stations scattered along the course. All competitors must preregister and pick up their numbers on race day. Every participant receives a T-shirt, while overall and division winners receive trophies and medals, respectively. The awards ceremony and post-race watermelon party take place on the CARP field. For a small fee, a bus shuttles runners from the finish to the start, and clothing is transported for retrieval at the finish.

RIDGE RUNNER MARATHON

Contact: North Bend State Park
Rt. 1 Box 221
Cairo, WV 26337
(304) 643-2931 or (800) CALL WVA
Date: June 7, 1997
June 6, 1998

Ridge Runner Marathon's figure-8 course, starting and finishing in North Bend State Park in northwestern West Virginia, journeys through the neighboring towns of Cairo and Harrisville. Presenting some difficult hills, the mostly paved course ranges from 500 to 1,300 feet in elevation. Aid stations are present approximately every 2 miles along the route. For those not interested in running the marathon, race day also includes races of 10 miles and 1 mile. All runners receive T-shirts in their race packets, and marathon finishers receive participation awards and certificates. Trophies are awarded to the overall male and female winners. The Ridge Runner Marathon coincides with the North Bend Rail Trail Festival which includes mountain bike rides, sounds of the trail contest and a luminary walk. Dinner and music are provided at the post-race celebration.

HOOSIER MARATHON

Contact: Bob Hockensmith
3732 Thyme Court
New Haven, IN 46774
(219) 749-1237
Date: June 8, 1997
June 14, 1998

Essentially a series of loops, northeastern Indiana's Hoosier Marathon never strays more than four miles from the start. Spectator friendly, the course starts behind a city park golf course, makes a 2-mile loop around it, and then heads to an adjacent city park for three 8-mile loops before finishing 385 yards from the start. Since most of the race runs on a narrow, shaded, asphalt path along a river, the field is limited to 400 runners. Two separate hills occur along the route: the first takes place in the opening two miles and the other on each of the remaining loops. Local youth groups provide aid at four separate stations along each loop, and splits are called each mile. Both the music of local bands and the announcement of your name by a celebrity radio personality welcome you to the finish.

The evening before the race, a pasta dinner is accompanied by authentic German music. Post-race refreshments are provided, and awards are presented in the park, but don't leave at the completion of the ceremony — it's the first day of Fort Wayne's Germanfest!

VALLEY OF THE FLOWERS MARATHON

Contact: Rick Politte
Lompoc Family YMCA
201 W. College Ave.
Lompoc, CA 93436
(805) 736-3483
Date: June 8, 1997
June 14, 1998

In the florally-embroidered Lompoc Valley, the Valley of the Flower's loop course starts at the Lompoc High School stadium and then heads east through the residential streets of suburban Lompoc. At the 3-mile point, the route travels north along Highway 246 to the La Purisima Mission. Here, the course continues on the old, asphalt and dirt-covered El Camino Real Road, climbing about 300 feet from miles 5 to 7. Just before mile 10, the route becomes flat, turning west along the town's edge toward the Lompoc Valley flower fields. You then travel on the flat avenues that wind through the flora. To lessen any influence of the ocean winds, the avenues run north and south from about mile 12 to 21. At mile 21, the course heads back toward Lompoc, finishing at the high school stadium. Race organizers provide 15 aid stations along the course. All finishers receive T-shirts and specially designed medallions. Overall winners are honored with the "Valley Cup," while age-group winners earn plaques.

Race day includes a half marathon run/walk, 3K fun run and 1-mile kids run. Obtain your race packet during the mini-expo at the Lompoc High School Cafetorium, 515 West College Avenue, on Saturday from 1:00 p.m. to 6:00 p.m., or on race day from 6:00 a.m. to 6:45 a.m. Saturday evening from 4:30 p.m. to 7:30 p.m., join other runners and their families at a spaghetti feed held at the La Purisima Church Parish Hall located at 337 South "I" Street. If you have some time after the races, stay around to enjoy some of the local attractions including: La Purisima Mission, Lompoc's large murals and the beaches of nearby Santa Barbara.

PALOS VERDES MARATHON

Contact: Palos Verdes Marathon
Box 2856
Palos Verdes, CA 90274
(310) 601-2968
Date: June 14, 1997
June 13, 1998

As one of the oldest marathons on the west coast, the Palos Verdes Marathon celebrates its 31st annual race in 1997. Featuring a rolling out-and-back course, the race starts and finishes at San Pedro's Point Fermin Park and runs along tree-lined streets of the Palos Verdes Peninsula with breathtaking ocean vistas — if not obscured by the early morning fog. Race day also includes a half marathon, 3-person marathon relay and 5K Run/Walk. Each marathon finisher receives a T-shirt and medal, and the top three finishers in each five-year age group receive special medals. Local bands are on hand to entertain you while you celebrate with post-race refreshments. The Palos Verdes Marathon is a community-supported fundraising event of the Kiwanis Club of Palos Verdes Peninsula.

SUNBURST MARATHON

Contact: Carter Wolf
615 N. Michigan St.
South Bend, IN 46601
Date: June 14, 1997
June 13, 1998

If you love college football and you're a big fan of the Fighting Irish, then the Sunburst Marathon is for you! The race currently draws 450 marathoners and attracts many other participants in the accompanying Elite 5000m, 5K run/walk, 10K and 5K fun walk. Included in the entry fee are a pre-race pasta feed and rooftop party, but don't celebrate too late as the race starts promptly at 6:00 a.m. The point-to-point course begins in downtown South Bend at the College Football Hall of Fame, winds along the beautiful St. Joseph River, on the East Bank Trails, and past the man-made white water rapids of the East Raceway (South Bend's kayak and rafting recreational waterway). After heading toward historic downtown Mishawaka, the route makes its way back to South Bend through the beautiful tree-lined campus of the University of Notre Dame to finish at Cartier Field. With the exception of some hills, the course is mostly flat. Course support comes from approximately 3,000 spectators and 12 aid stations along the way. The finish line festivities include: food, music and an awards ceremony where a $3,500 prize purse is distributed among the top three masters finishers in the marathon.

MARATHON-TO-MARATHON

Contact: Marathon-to-Marathon
216 So. Agora St., Box 289
Marathon, IA 50565
(712) 289-2246
Date: June 14, 1997
June 13, 1998

Created in 1996 to celebrate Iowa's Sesquicentennial, Marathon-to-Marathon stands as the state's only certified marathon. Its flat, point-to-point course begins at the local high school in Storm Lake and finishes at the Marathon Community Center. Along the mostly paved rural route, runners see farmers tilling corn, cattle grazing in green pastures, quaint country churches, and aid stations every 2.5 miles. For those not wanting to run the whole distance, Marathon-to-Marathon features a five-person relay consisting of four 5-mile legs and one 6.2-mile leg. All participants receive T-shirts, and all finishers receive medallions and official race results.

Pick up your race packet on Friday night during the Pasta Party held at Storm Lake High School from 5:30 p.m. to 9:00 p.m. If you anticipate having an appetite after you finish, tickets for a post-race breakfast are also available for purchase. Other activities related to the marathon are a bike ride, kids' games and on-stage entertainment.

NANISIVIK MIDNIGHT SUN MARATHON

Contact: Midnight Sun Marathon
Strathcona Mineral Services Limited, 14th Floor
20 Toronto Street
Toronto, Ontario
Canada M5C 2B8
Date: June 29, 1997
June 28, 1998

Meant for runners seeking a far-flung adventure marathon, the Nanisivik Midnight Sun Marathon runs almost on top of the world on the northern shore of Canada's Baffin Island, about 500 miles north of the Arctic Circle. Starting at sea level in the Inuit village of Arctic Bay, the course winds through the Terry Fox Pass up to an elevation of 1,749 feet at 15.5 miles, then drops 656 feet over the next 3 miles to the mining town of Nanisivik. At this point, the most strenuous part of the marathon begins. Affectionately termed "The Crunch" by the earnest few who have conquered it, the road drops 984 feet over the next 3.1 miles, down to the dock of Nanisivik, and then loops back over the same steep and winding road to the townsite. The entirely gravel course is in various states of repair so watch your footing! Come outfitted for extremes, since the temperatures on race day may vary anywhere from 23° to 50°, and parts of the barren course are quite gusty. The desolation of the region partly makes the course a laborious one; you encounter bare, gray hills and endless expanses of rock. Silence surrounds you all along the course, except for the sounds of the howling wind and your own breathing. Combine all this with the season's endless sun that burns 24 hours a day.

Participants are lodged with local families or placed in single-status accommodations in Nanisivik. Consequently, the number of entrants is limited to 110, and only runners are allowed. Inuit carvings are awarded to race winners, and every finisher receives a commemorative medal, T-shirt, and certificate at the post-race awards dinner.

FRIENDLY MASSEY MARATHON

Contact: Friendly Massey Marathon
c/o Marvin Maahs
505 Aberdeen Street, P.O. Box 706
Massey, Ontario
Canada P0P 1P0
Date: July 13, 1997
July 12, 1998

You can assume by its name that the Friendly Massey Marathon is an inviting little marathon. The Canadian town of Massey, Ontario provides a small-town country setting for the small number of runners. The mostly flat and shady course boasts aid stations every 1.5 miles, while split times are available at mile one and every 5K. Pre-race activities include a cycle tour of the route, fun run, and beer garden with local entertainment. Later that evening, you can attend an all-you-can-eat spaghetti supper. A pancake breakfast is held after the race. All entrants receive T-shirts, and the top 125 finishers receive hand-crafted wooden medallions. And, even if not fond of cows, age-group winners will count the hand-crafted wooden milking stool among their most unique awards. Then, join your fellow competitors for a pint and toast your victory at the beer garden sponsored by the local brewery.

OHIO/MICHIGAN MARATHON

Contact: Ohio/Michigan Run
2338 Laskey Road
Toledo, OH 43613
(419) 474-2649
Date: July 13, 1997
July 12, 1998

The interstate Ohio/Michigan Marathon, which began in 1982, runs on a fairly flat, point-to-point course. Before the race, obtain your race packet at Harris McIntosh Tower, then treat yourself to a pre-race sports injury evaluation and a massage. The race also offers an accompanying 5K and 10K. Prizes and awards are modest at this event; however, male and female overall winners are honored by having their names and finish times engraved on the Chris Falvey Endurance Award, and by receiving a gift certificate donated by a local sports store.

NOVA SCOTIA MARATHON

Contact: Raymond Green
Barrington Municipal Recreation, P.O. Box 100
Barrington, NS
Canada, B0W 1G0
(902) 637-3254
Date: July 27, 1997
July 26, 1998

The Nova Scotia Marathon charms runners with its fresh breezes, hearty post-race chowder, and friendly organization. Since its inaugural running in 1970, the event consistently draws nearly 70 participants between its full and half marathons. Starting at Barrington Municipal High School, the race loops about three miles around Barrington before crossing the causeway to Cape Sable Island. Here you make a figure-8 loop of the island on secondary highways running near the coast most of the way. The race finishes on the Barrington side of the causeway. While open to vehicle traffic, race officials request local dog owners to leash their pets, so you should have a pooch-free course. Rural and moderately rolling, the Nova Scotia Marathon contains three hills of note: a 500-yard moderate climb at mile 14, a 500-yard tough grade at mile 21, and a .75-mile rise at the 24-mile mark. Water stations are available every 3 miles; if you'd like electrolyte replacement drink or other special concoctions, mark your bottles with your name and the aid station where it should be placed. All entrants receive T-shirts, while finishers are awarded completion certificates. After the race, attend the reception where the top three overall and masters winners take home trophies. Also, enjoy the homemade chowder, bread and delicious desserts. Nova Scotia, the lobster capital of the world, offers unique scenery from breathtaking Cape Breton Island, the rocky Atlantic coast, to bustling Halifax for your post-race touring pleasure.

FRANK MAIER MARATHON

Contact: Ben Van Allen
Southeast Road Runners, 6731 Gray Street
Juneau, AK 99801
(907) 586-8322
Date: August 2, 1997
August 1, 1998

Named for a passionate supporter of local running, the Frank Maier Marathon takes advantage of Juneau's incredible setting pinched between the Gastineau Channel and Mt. Juneau. Starting at Savikko Park in Douglas (a community on Douglas Island just across the Gastineau Channel from downtown Juneau), this moderately hilly out-and-back course follows a coastal, two-lane asphalt road north along the Douglas and North Douglas highways where you catch some panoramic views of mountain peaks, glaciers, the Gastineau Channel, Stephens Passage, and southeast Alaska's forested habitat. Just before the turnaround, you attack a formidable hill. Aid stations are at your disposal every 2 to 3 miles, and vehicular traffic is generally negligible. Few spectators come out to observe this small race (about 30 marathoners and 70 half marathoners), so you need to bring your own fan club. A medal is presented to every finisher. Following the race, either enjoy the finish line feast or pig out at the pizza social at downtown Bullwinkle's Pizza Parlor. And, if you're inclined to extend your stay in Juneau, and we suggest you do, look forward to experiencing an endless list of outdoor activities.

CRATER LAKE RIM MARATHON

Contact: Bob & Beverly Freirich
5830 Mack Avenue
Klamath Falls, OR 97603
(541) 884-6939
Date: August 9, 1997
August 8, 1998

One of our top 25 most scenic marathons, the Crater Lake Rim Run & Marathon, which began in 1975, entices runners with breathtaking views of majestic Crater Lake. Don't be deceived by aesthetics; this rugged mountain course at 7,000 feet may overwhelm even the most Herculean individual. Running along the edge of the dazzling, volcano-created waters of Crater Lake National Park, you encounter long, grueling grades of nearly 1,000 feet over 5 miles. Elevation isn't your only obstacle at this mostly-paved race; be prepared for extreme temperatures from the 30s to 90s. To help you along, aid stations are available every two miles beginning at the 3-mile mark. Buses provide transportation to the start line and from the finish line for the marathon, 6.7-mile run, and 13-mile race. You can get a sneak preview of the course at a pre-race video presentation, "The Rim and Its Runners," featured at the Steel Visitor Center. After finishing, join fellow marathoners at the awards ceremony where overall winners receive engraved tankards, while age-group winners receive plaques. All finishers receive T-shirts and certificates.

During this peak tourist season, it may be necessary to seek lodging outside of the Crater Lake area. To receive information about nearby hotels, contact the Klamath Falls Chambers of Commerce (541-884-5193) or Department of Tourism (800-445-6728). If the challenge of the Crater Lake Rim Run & Marathon appeals to you, register early since the field is limited to 500 runners.

SNOW GOOSE MARATHON

Contact: Andrew Ferguson
Anchorage Running Club
P.O. Box 211923
Anchorage, AK 99521
(907) 258-4964
Date: August 17, 1997
August 16, 1998

Typically heading south this time of year, the snow goose lends its name to this Alaskan race created in the early 1980s by the Anchorage Running Club. Starting and finishing at Westchester Lagoon near downtown Anchorage, the race attracts approximately 200 runners (with hundreds more in the accompanying 10K and half marathon). The triple out-and-back course on three separate sections of the extensive Anchorage bike trail system provides spectacular views of the Cook Inlet and a half-dozen mountains, including Mt. McKinley and the Chugach Range. The course layout is also ideal for spectators. The turnarounds occur at approximately miles 3.7, 9, and 18.2, and the only significant hill is encountered at mile 12.5. Mid to late-August Anchorage weather ranges from 50° to 70° with low humidity. A race-packet pickup and pasta party takes place Friday at Humpys Great Alaskan Alehouse, 610 W. 6th Avenue in downtown Anchorage. Race entry includes a long-sleeve T-shirt, food, beverages, random prize drawing, and live music. And, while you may or may not see a moose on the course, you will certainly see a snow goose.

KONA MARATHON

Contact: Jim Lovell
JTL Timing System
P.O. Box 5316
Kailua-Kona, HI 96745
(808) 329-4661
Date: August 23, 1997
August 22, 1998

Why run the Kona Marathon? If you need a reason other than to enjoy the scenery of the beautiful Kona Coast, then you can enter to say you've run on the famous Ironman Triathlon marathon course. Started in 1994 by race director Jim Lovell, the Kona Marathon draws just over 50 participants. The relatively flat, out-and-back race starts at the hosting Keauhou Beach Hotel heading south for 2 miles before proceeding north through shady residential streets until you reach mile 9. This is the beginning of a 10-mile stretch through lava fields before returning along Alii Drive to the finish. Race entry includes a T-shirt and a pre-race Carboload party catered by Bianelli's Pizza. If pasta and salad aren't to your liking, choose from Bianelli's world-famous regular menu. After the race, not only do you receive a pound of Kona coffee, but you are eligible for random drawings for round trip inter-island flights.

EDMONTON FESTIVAL MARATHON

Contact John Stanton
Running Room
8537 109 Street
Edmonton, AB
Canada, T6J 2C4
(403) 433-6062
Date: August 31, 1997
August 30, 1998

Held to coincide with the supposedly-famous Funge Festival, the Edmonton Festival Marathon drew 650 runners in 1995 — its inaugural year. Arrive early at Hotel Macdonald (the host hotel) to attend the pre-race sports clinic, pasta dinner, marathon of movies and the back-of-the-pack beer garden. The relatively fast out-and-back race starts at 7:00 a.m., runs through the university, along a river valley, and through picturesque parks. You also parade past the many spectators at the Funge Festival. Runners encounter a good upgrade at mile 3.75, but it becomes a decent downhill on the way back so it all balances out. Aid is available every 5K, and if you have joined the "back-of-the-pack gang," then an ice-cream stop along the way is essential! After the race, join other festival-goers or wander the humongous West Edmonton Mall with its full-scale replica of Columbus' Santa Maria.

ISLAND MARATHON

Contact: Janet Wood
YMCA of Charlottetown
252 Prince Street
Charlottetown, PEI
Canada, C1A 4S1
(902) 566-3966
Date: September 2, 1997
September 1, 1998

In 1979, the Prince Edward Island (PEI) Roadrunners Association designed a course that revealed the windswept scenery of the island from Cavendish to Charlottetown, the largest city and provincial capital. Now YMCA-run, the race remains a double loop in and around the city of Charlottetown with a few steep grades on the otherwise rolling course. Aid stations are positioned at five points along the course, so runners obtain relief every 2.5 miles. Spotty crowds in this quiet and quaint city encourage you to the finish line at the YMCA.

Each participant receives a T-shirt along with other merchandise donated from local businesses. After completing your island tour, mingle with fellow marathoners at the luncheon, but don't leave after the last course, as a random drawing and awards presentation follow. The marathon coincides with both the Father's of Confederation and Charlottetown Festivals, so come and witness the inspiration of Lucy Maud Montgomery's novel — Anne of Green Gables — which describes the relaxing beauty of PEI. If you can muster up your remaining energy, make certain to visit some of Canada's finest beaches, wind-sculpted sand dunes and salt marshes at PEI National Park — if you're lucky, you might catch a glimpse of the endangered piping plover.

BETHEL MARATHON

Contact: Mary Wilda Warner
P.O. Box 1258
Bethel, AK 99559
(907) 543-2554
Date: September 6, 1997
September 5, 1998

Local legend claims that the Bethel Marathon got its start as a personal challenge between two local runners who were looking for the ultimate showdown. The race hasn't grown much since then, but persists as a result of local volunteer commitment. Located in southwest Alaska near the Kuskokwim River, the Bethel Marathon runs through flat delta lands and tundra. Luckily, the weather is mild this time of the year since the treeless course offers no protection. The flat blacktop and gravel roads are easy on your feet, but you need your own road crew because only three aid stations are available. No roads lead into or out of Bethel — your only access to the town of 4,500 is by air from Anchorage (500 miles away). No need to make hotel reservations though, since the locals open their homes to runners who need a place to crash for the night. And, if crowds make you nervous, don't despair — only six runners typically show up. Our guess is you'll know each of them personally by the time you finish the race.

BISMARCK MARATHON

Contact: Bill Bauman
YMCA, P.O. Box 549
Bismarck, ND 58502
(701) 255-1525
Date: September 6, 1997
September 12, 1998

North Dakota's only marathon, the Bismarck Marathon provides an opportunity to set a personal record on its flat, out-and-back course along the Missouri River bottomlands. The race is well ensconced on the trail of those runners seeking to complete a marathon in each of the 50 U.S. states. Race day also includes a half marathon and 4-person relay. A bargain at $15, race entry includes an official race T-shirt, pre-race pasta party and post-race pizza picnic. Marathon finishers receive special medallions and certificates. An international Pow Wow is held the same weekend, giving children and adults the chance to see the native culture firsthand. The Best Western Doublewood Inn, Exit 159 and I-94 (800-554-7077), is the race motel, offering a special marathon rate.

BEAVERLODGE
TO GRANDE PRAIRIE MARATHON

Contact: Bill Turnbull
6913-97A Street, Grande Prairie, AB
Canada T8V 5E5
(403) 532-7138 e-mail: TurnBL@terranet.ab.ca
Date: September 7, 1997
September 6, 199

The smallest marathon in Alberta, the Beaverlodge to Grande Prairie Marathon attracts a couple of handfuls of runners. An ideal 26 miles from Grand Prairie, Beaverlodge serves as the start of this point-to-point course. Although containing climbs of more than 100 feet, the route drops 200 feet in elevation from start to finish. What's more, no aid stations are available along the course, so you need a support crew to supply your fluids and energy needs. The race can provide you with a support crew if you cannot bring your own. The course rolls through the Alberta countryside, although the first 5 miles contain a total elevation gain of only 20 to 30 feet. Relish the ease of the beginning because miles 5 to 9 are more difficult, rising 113 feet to the highest point of the course. Just beyond, however, you find relief as miles 9 through 12 run downhill. Muster what energy you can during your brief hill holiday as you encounter rolling hills from miles 12 to 17 and a punishing climb to the top of Richmond Hill at 2,465 feet. Here, near mile 18.5, you have a breathtaking view of the agricultural lands as well as a peek at the finish line. From Richmond Hill's summit, it's mainly downhill as you sharply descend some 305 feet over the next two miles. Runners hit a final 50-foot rise, and then the remainder of the course is basically flat past the airport to the finish area. Run on a busy highway, the open course allows for your support crew to follow your progress. The post-race celebration says it all about the small-scale charm of this event: the race director hosts the marathoners at his backyard barbeque.

SASKATCHEWAN MARATHON

Contact: Ray Risling
Saskatoon Road Runners Assoc.
128 Ottawa Avenue S., Saskatoon, Sask.
Canada S7M 3L5
(306) 382-2962
Date: September 7, 1997
September 13, 1998

The handsome valley of the South Saskatchewan River is where the Saskatchewan Marathon, originally the venue of the Western Canada Games trials, takes place. Participation has steadily increased since 1979 on this out-and-back course beginning on the Victoria Bridge in downtown Saskatchewan. Every 2.5 miles you find refreshment at aid stations, and you can track your splits at the 1K, 10K and halfway points. Making your way through a historically rich residential area, you then proceed along Saskatchewan Crescent, through the shady respite of Diefenbaker Park to the halfway point at Spadina Crescent. The generally flat course culminates with a red carpet finish near Broadway Bridge. In recent years, the overall male and female winners have been awarded free airfare, $500, and trophies; their names are also inscribed on permanent display trophies. All participants receive medals and are invited to the post-race pasta reception at the Park Town Hotel.

AMERICAN ODYSSEY MARATHON

Contact: Bruce Iatonni
American Odyssey Marathon
N1260 Center Road
Merrill, WI 54452
Date: September 13, 1997
September 12, 1998

No need traveling to Greece to run from Marathon to Athens, simply head to rural, central Wisconsin's American Odyssey Marathon. Though you won't retrace the steps of the famous messenger who brought news of the Greek victory in the Trojan War, you do run by some pretty cool barns, not to mention (for you geography buffs) mile 19 where you pass the village of Poniatowski — the exact center of the northern part of the Western Hemisphere. It is one of four places on this planet where the 90th meridian of longitude bisects the 45th parallel of latitude. Starting at the Marathon High School parking lot, your Odyssey running voyage heads northwest over mostly paved and challenging, rolling terrain to the finish at the bandstand in downtown Athens. If you have family or friends who would like to participate in a less-grueling event, direct them toward the marathon relay also held on race day. Relay teams consist of two to five runners with hand-offs allowed only at the 5, 10, 15, and/or 20-mile marks. Transportation is provided between the start and finish line both before and after the race, and nine aid stations dot the course. All marathon finishers receive official running shorts, and overall and division winners receive commemorative posters. An all-you-can-eat spaghetti dinner is held the night before the race at the Marathon High School cafeteria.

FORT MCMURRAY OIL SANDS MARATHON

Contact: Ann Locke-Pope
Fort McMurray Running Club, P.O. Box 5792
Fort McMurray, AB. Canada, T9H 4V9
(403) 791-4027
Date: September 14, 1997
September 13, 1998

Titled after the small town that supports the extraction of natural resources from its oil sands, the Fort McMurray Oil Sands Marathon presents a relatively fast course that draws about 70 runners to its start line. An out-and-back route, the race starts and finishes on a local track. A piper calls runners to the start line. The course follows the highway north through the Alberta bush, then returns to the track. Along the course, you approach only one slight acclivity, but locals say it's too insignificant to be considered a hill. You also cross the Athabasco River which flows north — a phenomenon peculiar to most. Known for its amiable atmosphere, the race uses the same shoulder of the highway for its out-and-back, so fellow runners can offer encouragement to one another as they pass each other by. Aid stations are located every 3.1 miles.

A carbo-load dinner is offered to all runners the night before the race, and you are afforded the same hospitality after the race when a hot meal is served at the awards ceremony, together with a random prize drawing.

YELLOWKNIFE MARATHON

Contact: France Benoit
Arctic Runners Club, Box 1841
Yellowknife, Northwest Territories
Canada, X1A 2P4
(403) 920-1019
Date: September 14, 1997
September 13, 1998

One of two marathons in the Northwest Territories, the Yellowknife Marathon hosts a small gathering of runners every fall. Starting at the local pool, this double-loop course heads through Old Town, up Tin Can Hill, then toward Frame Lake South and through the Airport Loop. It's primarily flat except each loop contains a 1K gradual incline. The mostly-paved course offers pleasant scenery, especially along the lakeside. The event typically attracts a sparse crowd, but the volunteers at the eight aid stations are boasted as exceptionally enthusiastic. Not only are the top finishers honored, the last finishers receive trophies as well as honorary titles as King & Queen of the Lake. The odds of winning (or losing) are pretty good, as the race commonly attracts only 10 marathoners. The race is sponsored by NWT Air, so reduced fares are available if you're traveling from afar. Book your flights early and be sure to arrive with enough time to attend the course tour and carbo load.

SUGAR RIVER TRAIL MARATHON

Contact: Chris Roberts
Sugar River Runners Club
601 17th Street
Brodhead, WI 53520
(608) 897-4516
Date: September 20, 1997
September 19, 1998

Named for one of the first rails to trails, the Sugar River Trail Corporation premiered this marathon to increase public awareness of the converted train tracks. On the path of the Sugar River Trail, as the leaves begin to change, the point-to-point course starts in Brodhead, and passes through the communities of Albany and Monticello, crossing the Sugar River 14 times before finishing in New Glarus. Mostly flat, except for two small hills at the 8 and 9-mile marks, the route travels along a combination of city streets and a crushed rock trail. Aid stations are positioned every 2 to 3 miles along the course, and splits are provided about every 3 to 5 miles. All finishers receive commemorative medals.

A packet pickup and pasta party takes place on Friday night. Bus transportation is provided from the finish to the start prior to the race. In even numbered years, celebrate the heritage of the local cheese producers at the Green County Cheese Days.

CLARENCE DEMAR MARATHON

Contact: Clarence DeMar Marathon
P.O. Box 6257
Keene, NH 03431
(603) 357-5891
Date: September 28, 1997
September 27, 1998

Named after this New Hampshire resident and seven-time Boston Marathon champion, the scenic Clarence DeMar Marathon captures the essence of New England in the autumn. The fast, point-to-point course (with a net elevation loss of 420 feet) starts in downtown Gilsum and proceeds toward the community of Surry, heading over the beautiful Stone Arch Bridge. Passing through Surry, the route drops 350 feet by mile 10 just after reaching the Keene town line. After entering Swanzey on Ash Hill Road, you encounter the only major hill on the course just before mile 20. You then proceed through the picturesque Sawyer's Crossing Covered Bridge before making your way to Keene State College for the finish in front of the school library. For 4.5 hours, the course features 15 aid stations (12 water only and three with electrolyte replacement drinks).

Join other participants for pre-race spaghetti at the dining commons of Keene State College. On race morning, buses transport runners from Keene State College to Gilsum, but no transportation is provided after the race so marathoners are encouraged to park at the finish line. If you need clothing transported to the finish, bring your own bag. Plenty of post-race refreshments can be enjoyed while trophies and plaques are presented to the winners at the awards ceremony.

TWIN LAKES MARATHON

Contact: Norm Patenaude
297 Canice Street
Orillia, Ontario
Canada L3V 4J6
(705) 327-2643
Date: October 5, 1997
October 4, 1998

Part of the Celebration City Running Festival, the Twin Lakes Marathon offers a full plate of activities. The evening before the race, satisfy your appetite at the pasta feast, and then stroll over to the Wine & Cheese Social. Top the evening off at the uplifting Gospel Music Festival. The fairly fast out-and-back course starts at Brian Orser Arena. Passing Brewery Bay (the site of the Stephen Leacock Historic Vacation Home), runners travel along the shores of Lake Couchiching, through Couchiching Park, on top of the half-mile long boardwalk, and by Port Orillia before finishing in Wilson Point. En route, aid stations lie every 1.5 miles. Upon completion of the marathon, fill up at the pancake breakfast. Every entrant receives a long-sleeve T-shirt, while finishers also earn certificates and hand-crafted wooded medallions. Age-group winners are honored with hand-crafted wooden milking stools. Race day also features a half marathon.

JOHNSTOWN YMCA MARATHON

Contact: Cliff Kitner
Johnstown YMCA
100 Haynes Street
Johnstown, PA 15901
(814) 535-8381
Date: October 6, 1997
October 5, 1998

Location of the film by Steve Alpert, "Marathon Fever," the Johnstown YMCA Marathon made its first appearance on the running scene in the mid 1970s, attracting an impressive 103 runners. The marathon has certainly met some challenges in its history, including the 1977 flood that wiped out most of the course and the following downpour that drenched participants. On the lighter side, in 1980, 11-year-old Jennifer Amyx won the marathon in a remarkable 3:12:50.

Marathon weekend starts with a small pre-race expo, speaker, and free pasta dinner. The colorful loop course, set in Pennsylvania's autumn scenery, runs through the striking Conemaugh Gap, a 1,000-foot gorge sculpted by the waters of the Conemaugh River. Aid stations sit every 3 miles, then every mile for the last five miles of the race. A $200 savings bond is awarded to the top male and female runners.

ATLANTIC CITY MARATHON

Contact: Barbara Altman
Boardwalk Runners Club
P.O. Box 2181
Ventor, NJ 08406-0181
(609) 646-9009
Date: October 12, 1997
October 11, 1998

Past its heyday, frayed Atlantic City accommodates East Coast runners who want to combine some high-stakes action amongst the geriatrics with some fast-paced running with the fit. Or, if you're not up to the 26.2 miles, perhaps the 10K, 5K or the American Cancer Society 2-mile Healthwalk on the boardwalk will better suit your abilities. Whichever race you choose, arrive early at the race headquarters, Trump Worlds' Fair Casino Hotel at Trump Plaza, to pick up race packets and enjoy the many exhibits at the Sports Expo. The pre-race pasta party features a random prize drawing with all proceeds benefitting the Salvation Army. Soak in the sights of the city, a Las Vegas for senior citizens, including beaches, the Atlantic City Boardwalk, Brighton Park, or one of the many casinos. But, conserve some of your energy for the marathon which starts at 8:30 a.m. This USATF-certified marathon starts and finishes on the boardwalk in front of the Atlantic City Convention Center. It follows a flat route on the boardwalk as well as a 10-mile stretch along the Atlantic coast. Aid stations are abundant; there's one at 17 points along the course. All marathon finishers are awarded medals, and every participant receives a T-shirt. Plenty of post-race activities also take place with refreshments, music, runner expo and an awards presentation on the boardwalk. Overall and masters winners receive cash prizes, and age-group awards are also presented. Also at the awards ceremony, there is a drawing for a trip for two to the Walt Disney World Marathon.

BAYSTATE MARATHON

Contact: Bill Smith
BayState Marathon
6 Proctor Road
Townsend, MA 01469
(508) 597-5204
Date: October 12, 1997
October 11, 1998

Featuring New England's flattest marathon course, BayState's raison d'etre is to help area runners qualify for Boston. The parasitic, two-loop race starts in Tyngsboro at Greater Lowell Regional Vocational High School and runs along the Merrimack River. An annual field of 3,000 runners participates in the marathon and accompanying half marathon, with the vast majority of marathoners hoping to crack the Boston barrier. Kicking off with the Health Fair and Expo on Saturday, race weekend also includes a 5K Walk and pasta dinner. Though spectators are sparse along the route, members of the Greater Lowell Road Runners Club provide good support at the aid stations. All preregistered entrants receive long-sleeve T-shirts. Shower and changing facilities are available at the start/finish.

LAKE TAHOE MARATHON

Contact: Les Wright
Lake Tahoe Marathon
2261 Cold Creek Trail
So. Lake Tahoe, CA 96150
(916) 544-7095
email: 103457.1143@compuserve.com
Date: October 12, 1997
October 11, 1998

One of our top twenty-five most scenic and most difficult races, the one-year-old Lake Tahoe Marathon circles one-third of North America's largest, and arguably most beautiful, mountain lake. Starting at Fanny Bridge in Tahoe City, the pine-lined, point-to-point course journeys alongside the west shore of Lake Tahoe, past the pristine waters of Emerald Bay and Cascade Lake, over the spawning salmon in Taylor Creek, and by historic Valhalla and Camp Richardson in route to the finish at South Lake Tahoe's city limits. Disguised by the beauty of the course is the awesome challenge it presents — especially for those lacking in hill and/or altitude training. Flat to rolling near lake level (6,225 feet) through 14 miles, the route then poses a few long, steep uphills and downhills to 20 miles. The final 10K gradually descend to the finish. All entrants receive long-sleeve T-shirts, and finishers receive certificates. Shuttle bus service is provided to the start, and warmup clothing is transported to the finish. A host of events accompany the marathon including a kids fun run, half marathon, 10K, and 5K; the latter three feature point-to-point courses ending at South Lake Tahoe's city limits.

If you arrive on the eve of the marathon, partake in the pasta party aboard a sunset cruise boat (for a fee) or do some fine dining at one of the surrounding lakeside restaurants. Take in a show or try your luck at one of the casinos.

MOUNT RUSHMORE INTERNATIONAL MARATHON

Contact: Mount Rushmore International Marathon
P.O. Box 9084
Rapid City, SD 57709
(605) 348-7866
Date: October 12, 1997
October 11, 1998

The clean mountain air, lofty pines and fragrant spruce of South Dakota's Black Hills set the stage for the Mount Rushmore International Marathon. Starting just south of the Custer Crossing Campground, the point-to-point course heads southeast on U.S. 385 and continues on S.D. 44 before finishing at Sioux Park in Rapid City. Good downhill runners delight in the route's 2,140-foot elevation loss (from 5,410 feet to 3,270 feet). Except for upgrades at miles 6 and 17, the remainder of the course is rolling or downhill with a steep decline from mile 20 to 22.4. Although spectators are sparse along the way, aid stations appear every 2 miles. Race-packet pickup and runner expo occur Saturday at the Alex Johnson Hotel, 608 Saint Joseph Street, from 9:00 a.m. to 7:00 p.m. In the evening, take the free shuttle bus to Mount Rushmore for the buffet-style pasta dinner followed by the special Mount Rushmore lighting ceremony honoring all marathon competitors. On race day, bus transportation is provided from various locations to the starting line and also from the finish line at Sioux Park, but be aware, no rides back to the start are provided after the race. Each entrant receives a long-sleeve T-shirt, and every finisher earns a medallion. Winners of each age division receive Black Hills gold rings.

PUEBLO RIVER TRAIL MARATHON

Contact: Ben Valdez
Pueblo Family YMCA
700 N. Albany Ave.
Pueblo, CO 81003
(719) 543-5151
Date: October 12, 1997
October 11, 1998

The Pueblo River Trail Marathon began in 1984 with 135 runners, but currently averages about 360. The rolling point-to-point course contains aid stations every 2 to 3 miles. Throughout the course, the Sangre De Cristo Mountains lie in the distance. Starting at 5,173 feet, the course rolls or slightly descends for the first 10.6 miles through the barren subdivision of Pueblo West. At mile 10.6, the route moves onto a bike path which passes the Pueblo Reservoir and follows the cottonwood-lined Arkansas River. The most noticeable uphills take place just after the half marathon point. From there, the route is mostly flat except for the largely ascending final mile. In Pueblo, the wall near 20 miles takes on a new meaning as you reach the longest (4.5 miles) urban art mural in the world painted on the levee wall on the opposite side of the river. Included in the entry fee is an all-you-can-eat pasta dinner at the Gold Dust Saloon (where you can pick up your race packet), a long-sleeve T-shirt, complete race results, and a shuttle from finish to start. Awards are presented to the top five overall and division winners.

RICHMOND TIMES-DISPATCH MARATHON

Contact: Dewayne Davis
Richmond Times-Dispatch Marathon
P.O. Box 85333
Richmond, VA 23293-0001
(804) 649-6738
Date: October 12, 1997
October 11, 1998

Known for getting excellent local press coverage (it helps being sponsored by a newspaper), the Richmond Times-Dispatch Marathon starts its loop course on Broad Street near the 6th Street Marketplace. Making its way through the historic sections of downtown Richmond, the route weaves past Monroe Park and across Manchester Bridge. Runners then continue along the James River, through wooded Forest Hill Park, Willow Oaks Country Club, and James River Park. The course crosses the Huguenot Bridge as it heads toward the finish on Broad Street. Aid stations sit every 2 miles, and split indicators occur frequently along the route. All entrants receive T-shirts, while finishers earn medallions and certificates. The top three overall finishers and top five age-group winners are recognized with awards. Special medals are awarded to those who break personal records, and a marathon key ring is given to the top 100 finishers. Visit the 2-day Sports Expo/Health Fair before the race, while afterward, join your fellow competitors at a live rock and beach music party. If you've brought your family along, take the kids to the children's festival.

VALLEY HARVEST MARATHON

Contact: Steve Moores
RR 1
Wolfville, NS
Canada B0P 1X0
(902) 542-1867
Date: October 12, 1997
October 11, 1998

The Valley Harvest Marathon, named as a tribute to the fall harvest in this primarily agricultural valley, is appropriately held on Canada's Thanksgiving weekend. The gently rolling, out-and-back course ambles through the Annapolis Valley on a lightly-traveled rural road through the golden seasonal brilliance of the region. The marathoners convene on Main Street, just west of the Kentville Fire Hall, loop once around downtown Kentville, cross the Cornwallis River, and proceed to the turnaround in Somerset. At miles 10 and 18, the trees along the course form a tunnel to give you shady respite. What's more, a probable tailwind on the second half of the course pushes you toward the finish line at Centre Square in downtown Kentville. Aid stations are positioned every 2 miles. You find few fans along the course, but you might come upon a grazing cow or two. After the race, a reception and awards ceremony are held to honor all finishers.

GREEN MOUNTAIN MARATHON

Contact: Howie Atherton
6010 Main Road
Huntington, VT 05462
(802) 434-3228
e-mail: NLWC36A@prodigy.com
Date: October 18, 1997
October 17, 1998

For over a decade, the state of Vermont has served as the setting for the Green Mountain Marathon. More than 125 runners typically compete in the marathon, while approximately twice that participate in the accompanying half marathon. The rolling, out-and-back course starts at Folsom School, close to where Clarence DeMar (7-time winner of the Boston Marathon) once lived. It then winds along the west shore of South Hero and Grand Isle, ambling through apple orchards and running past farmland. Strolling along the beautiful shore of Lake Champlain, the route passes quaint summer cottages before returning to the finish lined with the crimson fall leaves of 100-year-old maple trees. Although the course rolls throughout, at mile 24 be aware of a 100-foot hill. Primarily paved, the race does consist of some well-maintained hard-packed dirt roads on this sparsely-populated isle. Cool weather can make the air very dry so be sure to stop at all of the aid stations every 3 miles. Upon completion of the race, certificates are awarded to all finishers, with awards and trophies presented at the post-race ceremony.

WICHITA MARATHON

Contact: Clark Ensz
2451 Winstead Circle
Wichita, KS 67226
(316) 687-1357
Date: October 18, 1997
October 24, 1998

The Wichita Marathon features a flat, double out-and-back course along the scenic Arkansas River. The race attracts approximately 250 participants to its start/finish line at one of the most pleasant sites in the city, Central Riverside Park. From here, the route travels two short loops around the park and then heads to the bike path that parallels the Arkansas River. At the halfway point, the race returns to Central Riverside Park before retracing the route. Aid stations are positioned every 2 miles along the way. Refreshments and massages are provided after the race. All entrants receive long-sleeve T-shirts, and finishers receive completion awards. The top two males and females earn small cash prizes. Age-group winners are also recognized. A companion 5K walk/run takes place one-half hour after the marathon start.

ST. LOUIS MARATHON

Contact: St. Louis Track Club
2385 Hampton Avenue
St. Louis, MO 63139
(314) 781-3926
Date: October 19, 1997
October 18, 1998

Featuring a loop course, the 26-year-old St. Louis Marathon starts on Market at Union Station and travels along gently rolling city streets through downtown St. Louis, Laclede's Landing, and across the spectacular Mississippi Riverfront and Arch Grounds. From there, you venture through pleasant Forest Park, past the neighborhoods of West and South St. Louis, and finish in front of the Soldier's Memorial. Aid stations replenish runners at 13 points along the course, and splits are provided at each mile. Each entrant receives a long-sleeve T-shirt, and finishers receive custom finisher's medallions, personalized certificates, and results booklets. The marathon winners are awarded John Furla Memorial medals and have their names inscribed with past winners on the John Furla Memorial Cup, dedicated to the only St. Louis resident to run the 1904 Olympic Marathon. Prize money, totaling about $17,500, is divided amongst the open, masters, seniors and age-division winners. All this takes place at the awards ceremony at the Hyatt Regency Hotel (west of union Station), site of the Runner's Expo. Although the race expo and awards ceremony take place at the Hyatt, the Drury Downtown Hotel Collection serves as the official marathon hotels: Drury Inn — Gateway Arch (314-231-8100); Hampton Inn — Union Station (314-241-3200); and Drury Inn — Union Station (314-231-3900).

MOHAWK HUDSON RIVER MARATHON

Contact: Lori Christina
Hudson Mohawk Road Runners
P.O. Box 4022
Albany, NY 12204
(518) 273-5452
Date: October 26, 1997 (tentative)
October 25, 1998 (tentative)

Named for the two rivers it parallels, the Mohawk Hudson River Marathon features a point-to-point course through upstate New York's beautiful fall foliage. Typically run under cool, clear skies, the race starts in Schenectady's Central Park and runs along roads and bike paths to the finish at City Square in downtown Albany. Though containing a net elevation loss of 370 feet, the route contains a noteworthy hill between miles 12 and 13. You may pick up your race packet during the mini-sports expo at the downtown Albany Ramada Inn on Saturday from 12:00 p.m. to 6:00 p.m. After the event, enjoy refreshments and an awards ceremony. All preregistered runners receive T-shirts, and finishers earn commemorative medals and certificates. Runners smashing the course records (2:20:59 for men and 2:50:12 for women) leave Albany $500 richer.

ANDREW JACKSON MARATHON

Contact: Les MacDiarmid
Les' Photos
P.O. Box 3832
Jackson, TN 38303
(901) 664-7559
Date: November 1, 1997
November 7, 1998

The 25-year-old Andrew Jackson Marathon starts at Union University (the location of the pre-race spaghetti supper), heads three miles through urban Jackson, and then continues through surrounding farm country for 3.5 miles. Here, you meet expansive fields of cotton and soybean while making a 13-mile loop through seemingly endless agricultural land before you return on the first leg of the course for the last 6.2 miles to the finish. Rolling and completely paved, the course features aid stations every 2 to 3 miles. On the flat portions of the unprotected route, wind direction determines the difficulty of the section.

After receiving your medal, take advantage of the post-race activities which include refreshments and free massages. At the post-race awards ceremony, prizes are presented to the overall and age-division winners in the marathon as well as in the accompanying 10K and 5K. All entrants are eligible for drawings for prizes donated by local businesses. Though the attendance is modest at this event, many enjoy the small-town charm of local attractions, such as the Casey Jones Museum and the many country stores that fill the area. The race headquarters, Garden Plaza Hotel (1-800-3-Garden), offers special group rates to marathon entrants.

ARKANSAS MARATHON

Contact: Bob Waid
Arkansas Marathon
c/o Booneville Chamber of Commerce, #1 The Village
Booneville, AR 72927
(501) 675-2666
Date: November 1, 1997
November 7, 1998

Drawing 150 marathoners, the Arkansas Marathon rolls between 511 and 576 feet on its out-and-back course. Beginning at the A.R. Hedrick Booneville Elementary School, the race runs along scenic Highway 10, giving runners a view of Magazine Mountain (at elevation 2,753 feet, the highest point in Arkansas) from almost every point on the course. As you make your way to the turnaround in Blue Mountain, take in the beauty of the Ozark National Forest to the north and Ouachita National Forest to the south. Appreciate the descent at mile 6, but remember you must ascend this as you head back toward the finish line at Citizen's Bank. Aid stations with water and electrolyte replacement drink are placed every 2 miles, with times recorded every 5 miles and at the turnaround. Every participant receives a T-shirt, while the top four places in each division receive additional awards. But if you don't place in your division, there are several random drawings for prizes donated by local merchants. While you await the awards presentation, check out the Health & Sports Fair, arts and crafts displays and the many food booths.

MORGAN HILL MARATHON

Contact: Dan Barger
California Sports Marketing
P.O. Box 794
Morgan Hill, CA 95038
(408) 776-3035
Date: November 1, 1997
November 7, 1998

The Morgan Hill Marathon, staged 15 miles south of the San Jose area, draws about 150 runners. Almost completely flat, the out-and-back course contains one overpass with an elevation gain of 20 feet. Nine miles of the course guide you along city streets, while the remainder wanders down the Coyote Bike Path. Here, in the absence of vehicle traffic, you wind along a mostly-paved trail past the local golf course, ponds, and softly-rushing waters of area streams. Temperatures average about 65° here. While the course may present little difficulty as far as marathons go, the limited spectator turnout may be an obstacle for those who require lots of encouragement. Most support is limited to the volunteers at the aid stations every 2.5 miles or so along the course.

Post-race activities include refreshments and a prize raffle. Awards are presented to the top five finishers in each age group, and custom trophies are awarded to overall male and female winners. Possible lodging nearby includes: the Executives Choice (408-778-0404); and the Best Western Country Inn (800-528-1234). Need a little kick after the race? Join the rest of the field fifty yards from the finish line at the Morgan Hill Coffee Roasting Company. Or, later, do a bit of antique shopping in downtown Morgan Hill.

OMAHA RIVERFRONT MARATHON

Contact: Omaha Riverfront Marathon
7015 Western Avenue
Omaha, NE 68132
Date: November 2, 1997
November 1, 1998

A loop course with a short out-and-back section, the Omaha Riverfront Marathon starts at Omaha Civic Auditorium. Traveling north on Florence Blvd., the course veers onto Pershing Drive before heading to a crescent around NP Dodge Park. Proceeding back down Pershing, the route loops around Eppley Airport at Lindbergh Plaza, finishing inside Mancusso Convention Hall. All finishers are awarded medallions and also receive much needed massages. The overall winners receive complimentary air transportation to the Boston Marathon. Each athlete who achieves a Boston Marathon qualifying time receives a "Boston Qualifier" running bag.

Included in the reasonable entry fee is a long-sleeve T-shirt, coffee mug, bus tour of the course, and an all-you-can-eat spaghetti feed at Omaha's famous Son's of Italy Hall. Runners can wander through the Omaha Riverfront Health and Fitness Expo held at Peter Kiewet Conference Center. After the race, replenish and rehydrate at the "Survivor's Party." Accommodations can be had at the Red Lion Inn, 16th and Dodge downtown (402-346-7600).

CHICKAMAUGA BATTLEFIELD MARATHON

Contact: **Doug Roselle**
Chattanooga Track Club
3316 Montview
Chattanooga, TN 37411
(423) 493-2760
Date: **November 8, 1997**
November 7, 1998

You've completed the training, are dressed in the appropriate attire, prepared to battle the 26.2 miles of the Chickamauga Battlefield Marathon. Held mostly in Chickamauga Battlefield Park, the rigorous, out-and-back route starts at Gordon Lee High School running over paved roads as it heads for Battlefield Park, site of one of the Civil War's fiercest battles. There, you loop through the park two times before charging toward the finish line. En route you encounter three series of enemy hills at miles 9, 17, and 25 on the otherwise rolling course. Located every 2 to 2.5 miles, aid stations supply water, electrolyte replacement drink, fruit, and petroleum jelly. At the end of your personal skirmish, celebrate your victory with post-race food and refreshments. An awards presentation follows, honoring the overall, masters and age-group winners. There are also special awards for first-timers. Perhaps the most convenient lodging for runners is found at the Best Western Battlefield Inn, Highway 27 just north of Battlefield Parkway in Fort Oglethorpe, GA, 5 miles from the start (706-866-0222). Chattanooga lies about 40 minutes from the race staging area.

HARRISBURG MARATHON

Contact: **HARRC**
c/o Robert T. Daniels
3804 Reichert Road
Harrisburg, PA 17110
(717) 540-5493
Date: **November 9, 1997**
November 8, 1998

Celebrating its 25th Anniversary in 1997, the Harrisburg Marathon features a flat, out-and-back course starting in front of the Pennsylvania State Capitol building and ending at City Island on the Susquehanna River. While blending urban, suburban and rural areas, the race attracts few spectators and provides only eight aid stations along the route. All race-related activities occur at race headquarters, the Ramada Inn, 23 South and 2nd Street. Packet pickup and late registration take place Saturday from 1:00 p.m. to 5:00 p.m. Race-day registration occurs from 6:00 a.m. to 7:30 a.m. A pre-race pasta dinner takes place from 5:00 p.m. to 7:30 p.m. on Saturday night. Every runner receives a T-shirt, certificate of completion, and complete results. The awards ceremony begins at 2:00 p.m. with open, masters and age-group winners receiving awards and others having a chance to win random prizes.

TULSA MARATHON

Contact: Coneil Lafarlette
Glen's Racing Service
263 East 45 Place
Tulsa, OK 74105-4403
(918) 744-0339
Date: November 22, 1997
November 28, 1998

If you're spending the Thanksgiving holiday near Tulsa and crave more than the local town trot to appease you running appetite, then enter the annual Tulsa Marathon. The event draws nearly 400 marathoners and many more runners in the accompanying half marathon and 5K. The completely flat course starts on Riverside Drive and makes a small loop for spectators before heading north to the 10K mark and the finely crushed limestone of the River Parks Trail. The remainder of the race includes three passes along the trail paralleling the Arkansas River. Runners appreciate the brilliant fall colors emanating from the red oaks, white oaks, and hackberry trees surrounding this portion of the route. Aid stations sit every 2 miles. For a slightly larger entry fee, Tulsa allows runners to enter both the half and full marathons and be eligible for awards in each race. All entrants receive long-sleeve T-shirts, and finishers receive race mementos. The top four overall males and females take home prize money — $150, $75, $60, and $40. Age-group awards extend three deep. All finishers enjoy the generous spread of post-race refreshments including Mexican food, pastries, fruit, beer, soda, and barbeque. If you have time before or after the event, see Tulsa's most frequently visited attraction, the 80-foot sculpture of praying hands at Oral Roberts University. You may want to head to the Discoveryland Amphitheatre, 10 miles west of Tulsa, for Rodgers and Hammerstein's "Oklahoma!".

KENTUCKY MARATHON

Contact: Stu McCombs
7004 Beachland Rd.
Prospect, KY 40059
(502) 228-1133
Date: December 6, 1997
December 5, 1998

Paired with the Kentucky 50 Miler in 1997, the Cherokee Road Runners-sponsored Kentucky Marathon offers a flat to rolling route through rural Kentucky landscape. A field of less than 200 runners negotiates an out-and-back route starting and finishing at Sawyer State Park located on the east side of Louisville. The most challenging section of the course occurs around the 7-mile mark where you encounter a half-mile hill. Although few spectators frequent the course, aid stations are positioned every 3 miles. Pick up your race packet and meet with other runners at the Friday night pasta dinner at Breckinridge Inn, the host hotel. After the race, you're invited to a free feast at the park recreation building. If you're a sports enthusiast, you'll find plenty to do in Kentucky. Check out the Kentucky Derby Museum or catch a University of Kentucky or U of Louisville basketball game while you're in town. Or, toast to your marathon victory at one of several distilleries in the region.

SPACE COAST MARATHON

Contact: Bill Dillard
1480 Meadowbrook Road, NE
Palm Bay, FL 32905
(407) 724-2510
Date: December 7, 1997
December 6, 1998

Boasted as the oldest marathon in Florida, the Space Coast Marathon had its inaugural running in December of 1971. The course has been modified a number of times since the early 1970s to accommodate both increased traffic and construction. The current course offers an exceptionally flat loop that starts/finishes in front of the Brevard Community College gymnasium and winds along shady streets through residential areas studded with spectacular new homes. Aid stations are placed strategically along the route, as you can expect warm weather later in the day. Refreshments are available at the finish line, and an awards presentation takes place after the race. The overall male and female winners and top three in each 5-year age group receive trophies. T-shirts are guaranteed to all preregistered runners. A companion half marathon covers the first 10 miles of the marathon course. Afterwards, relax at nearby Cocoa Beach. The Kennedy Space Center, site of the space shuttle launches, is definitely worth a look.

JACKSONVILLE MARATHON

Contact: Doug Alred
1st Place Sports
3853 Baymeadows Rd.
Jacksonville, FL 32217
(904) 739-1917
Date: December 13, 1997
December 12, 1998

The Jacksonville Marathon attracts about 1,700 competitors to its recently-paved, shady, and flat course. Although the main attractions of the race are its Florida location and level route, it does pass through some beautiful mandarin trees. Most support is found in the neighborhoods and at the aid stations available every two miles. Splits are provided every other mile, many by digital clocks. Age-group prizes go three deep. The top three overall finishers receive a small amount of prize money ($300 for first, $200 for second, and $100 for third). Rejuvenate those aching muscles with a free massage, and if you've depleted all your stores from Friday night's carboload, then refuel at the post-race meal. If you can muster the strength, join your fellow competitors for the Saturday night victory party. In recent races, the Holiday Inn, Baymeadows Road and Interstate 95 (904-737-1700), served as the host hotel.

MISSISSIPPI MARATHON

Contact: Mississippi Track Club
P.O. Box 1414
Ridgeland, MS 39157
(601) 856-9884
Date: December 13, 1997
December 12, 1998

Starting and finishing at the Mississippi College Coliseum in the small town of Clinton, the Mississippi Marathon follows an essentially flat, out-and-back course along the Natchez Trace. A 10K run and 5K walk also cover part of the course. Aid stations are available approximately every 3 miles, and splits are called at miles 1, 5, 10, 15, 20, and 25. All marathoners completing the course within 5 hours are awarded commemorative medals, while all preregistered participants receive long-sleeve T-shirts and gloves. After the race, refreshments are provided, and the top male and female overall, masters, grandmasters and age-group winners receive special awards.

Hotel accommodations are conveniently located near the race start/finish, including: the Holiday Inn, 103 Johnston Place (601-924-0064); the Clinton Inn, 400 Highway 80E (601-924-5313); Comfort Inn, 103 Clinton Center Drive (601-924-9364); and the Days Inn, 482 Springridge Road (601-925-5065).

APPENDIX

MARATHON RANKINGS
AND COURSE PROFILES

TOP 100 DESTINATION MARATHONS

Name of Marathon	Crowd	Course Scenery	Race Organization	Overall Rating
1. Big Sur	2	10+	10	100.0
2. Twin Cities	4+	10	10	99.5
3. Marine Corps	3-	10-	10	99.2
4. New York City	5+	8-	10+	97.9
5. Honolulu	3	9+	10	97.5
6. Boston	5+	8	10	97.0
7. San Francisco	3-	10-	9-	95.1
8. Chicago	4+	8	10	94.5
9. Walt Disney World	2	9	10-	94.0
10. Maui	1	10-	9	93.4
11. Los Angeles	5+	6+	10+	92.6
12. Vancouver International	3	8	10-	92.4
13. Humboldt Redwoods	0+	10	9	92.2
14. Vermont City	2+	9	9+	92.2
15. St. George	2	9-	10-	92.1
16. Portland	3	8	10+	92.1
17. Catalina Island	1-	10-	9+	91.9
18. Royal Victoria	2	9	9	91.8
19. Napa Valley	1-	9+	9+	91.6
20. Avenue of the Giants	0+	10	9-	91.3
21. Columbus	4-	9-	10	91.3
22. Cleveland	3-	8-	10	91.0
23. Deseret News	3+	9	9-	90.7
24. Kiawah Island	1	9+	9	90.2
25. Dallas White Rock	3	9	9	90.2
26. Cape Cod	1	9+	8+	88.9
27. Mardi Gras	1+	9-	9	88.8
28. Ocean State	1+	9-	9	88.8
29. Mayor's Midnight Sun	1-	9	9-	88.8
30. Fox Cities	3+	8-	10	88.8
31. Calgary	1+	8	9+	88.4
32. Grandma's	2-	9-	10	88.1
33. National Capital	2-	9	9+	88.1
34. Philadelphia	2+	8+	9-	88.1
35. Montreal	4-	7+	9	88.1
36. San Diego	1	8+	9+	88.0
37. Houston	4+	6+	10+	87.8
38. Pittsburgh	4	7	10	87.7
39. Wineglass	1	9+	9	87.0
40. Kilauea Volcano	0	9+	8	86.4
41. Memphis	2+	7-	10-	86.2
42. Lakefront	2-	8+	9	85.9
43. Madison	2	9-	9	85.4
44. Pikes Peak	0	9	9-	85.4
45. New Hampshire	0	9+	8	85.4
46. Canadian International	2	7	9+	85.4
47. Seattle	1	9-	8+	84.8
48. Shamrock Sportsfest	1	9	9	84.8
49. Austin	2+	7+	10	84.7
50. Marathon By The Sea	2-	7+	9+	84.7
51. San Antonio	2	8-	9-	84.5

TOP 100 DESTINATION MARATHONS

Name of Marathon	Crowd	Course Scenery	Race Organization	Overall Rating
52. Lake County	1+	7+	9	84.3
53. Steamboat	0	9+	8	84.2
54. Toe to Tow	0+	9	8+	83.7
55. Silver State	0+	8+	9-	83.7
56. Capital City	2-	8+	9	83.7
57. Atlanta	1	7+	9+	83.5
58. Lake Geneva	0	9	8	83.2
59. Maine	1	9-	9-	82.9
60. Walker North	0+	9	9-	82.8
61. Smoky Mountain	0	9-	9-	82.6
62. Blue Angel	1	8	9+	82.6
63. Coeur D'Alene	1-	9	8	82.4
64. California International	2+	7+	9+	82.4
65. Leadville Mosquito	0	9	8-	82.3
66. Charlotte	1+	8	9	82.1
67. Equinox	0	8+	8+	82.0
68. Cowtown	2+	8-	9-	81.8
69. Rocket City	2+	7+	9+	81.5
70. Detroit International	1+	8	10-	81.2
71. Las Vegas International	1	6	9-	80.7
72. Dutchess County	1-	8	9-	80.2
73. East Lyme	0+	9-	8	79.6
74. Paavo Nurmi	1	8-	9-	78.8
75. Hartford	2	8-	10-	78.2
76. Trail Breaker	0	8	8	78.2
77. Northern Central Trail	0	8	8-	78.2
78. City of Santa Clarita	1+	7	9+	78.0
79. Manitoba	1+	7+	9-	78.0
80. Monster Trail	0	9	7+	77.8
81. Lincoln	2-	7	10-	77.7
82. Forest City	1	8+	9-	77.5
83. Running Fit	0	9-	8-	77.2
84. Burney	0	9	8	76.9
85. Grandfather Mountain	1	8-	8-	76.6
86. Warwick	1-	8-	9	76.1
87. Marathon of the Roses	1-	8	8-	76.1
88. Sacramento	1-	8	8-	76.1
89. University of Okoboji	0	9	7-	75.9
90. Sugarloaf	0	9-	7+	75.9
91. Taos	0+	8-	8-	75.5
92. Colorado	0	6-	8+	75.0
93. Carolina	1-	8	8+	74.8
94. Ghost Town	1-	8	8	74.8
95. Memorial RoC	0	8	8+	73.7
96. Duke City	1	7-	8-	73.4
97. Med-City	1-	8	8	72.9
98. White Sands	0+	8-	8	72.3
99. Yonkers	0+	6+	8-	70.1
100. Western Hemisphere	1	6+	7+	69.9

THE PR CHASE
TOP 25 FASTEST MARATHONS

Name of Marathon	Crowd	Race Organization	Difficulty	Overall Rating
1. Chicago	4+	10	2	100.0
2. Houston	4+	10+	2+	98.2
3. Twin Cities	4+	10	3-	94.5
4. Austin	2+	10	2	92.1
5. Columbus	4-	10	3-	92.1
6. Pittsburgh	4	10	3+	88.5
7. Cleveland	3-	10	3-	88.1
8. Boston	5+	10	4	88.1
9. New York City	5+	10+	4+	86.4
10. Detroit	1+	10-	2+	85.2
11. California International	2+	9+	3-	85.2
12. Walt Disney World	2	10-	3-	84.8
13. Las Vegas	1	9-	2	84.4
14. Grandma's	2-	10	3-	84.2
15. Philadelphia	2+	9-	3-	84.0
16. Mardi Gras	1+	9	2+	83.8
17. Marine Corps	3-	10	3+	83.4
18. Los Angeles	5+	10+	5-	83.2
19. Rocket City	2+	9+	3	82.8
20. Shamrock	1	9	2+	82.6
21. Fox Cities	3+	10	4-	82.6
22. Lakefront	2-	9	3-	82.2
23. Portland	3	10+	4-	82.0
24. Canadian International	2	9+	3	81.6
25. Seattle	1	8+	2+	81.2

The Raving Beauties

Most Scenic Marathons

1. Big Sur
2. Avenue of the Giants
3. Humboldt Redwoods
4. Twin Cities
5. Maui
6. Catalina Island
7. San Francisco
8. Marine Corps
9. New Hampshire
10. Kiawah Island
11. Cape Cod
12. Steamboat
13. Wineglass
14. Kilauea Volcano
15. Napa Valley
16. Honolulu
17. Crater Lake Rim
18. Lake Tahoe
19. Clarence DeMar
20. Nantucket
21. Deseret News
22. Royal Victoria
23. Vermont City
24. National Capital
25. Dallas White Rock

Get Outta Town

Top Seasonal Destination Marathons

Winter

1. Honolulu (5)
2. Walt Disney World (9)
3. Kiawah Island (24)
4. Dallas White Rock (25)
5. Mardi Gras (27)
6. San Diego (36)
7. Houston (37)
8. Memphis (41)
9. Austin (49)
10. Smoky Mountain (61)

Spring

1. Big Sur (1)
2. Boston (6)
3. Maui (10)
4. Los Angeles (11)
5. Vancouver (12)
6. Vermont City (14)
7. Catalina Island (17)
8. Napa Valley (19)
9. Avenue of the Giants (20)
10. Cleveland (22)

Summer

1. San Francisco (7)
2. Deseret News (23)
3. Mayor's Midnight Sun (29)
4. Calgary (31)
5. Grandma's (32)
6. Kilauea Volcano (40)
7. Pike's Peak (44)
8. Marathon By The Sea (50)
9. Steamboat (53)
10. Silver State (55)

Fall

1. Twin Cities (2)
2. Marine Corps (3)
3. New York City (4)
4. Chicago (8)
5. Humboldt Redwoods (13)
6. St. George (15)
7. Portland (16)
8. Royal Victoria (18)
9. Columbus (21)
10. Cape Cod (26)

In My Own Backyard

Top Destination Marathons by Region

Pacific Region

1. Big Sur (1)
2. Honolulu (5)
3. San Francisco (7)
4. Maui (10)
5. Los Angeles (11)
6. Humboldt Redwoods (13)
7. Portland (16)
8. Catalina Island (17)
9. Napa Valley (19)
10. Avenue of the Giants (20)

Southwest/Mountain Region

1. St. George (15)
2. Deseret News (23)
3. Dallas White Rock (25)
4. Houston (37)
5. Pikes Peak (44)
6. Austin (49)
7. San Antonio (51)
8. Steamboat (53)
9. Silver State (55)
10. Coeur d'Alene (63)

Midwest Region

1. Twin Cities (2)
2. Chicago (8)
3. Columbus (21)
4. Cleveland (22)
5. Fox Cities (30)
6. Grandma's (32)
7. Lakefront (42)
8. Madison (43)
9. Lake County (52)
10. Toe to Tow (54)

South Region

1. Walt Disney World (9)
2. Kiawah Island (24)
3. Mardi Gras (27)
4. Memphis (41)
5. Shamrock Sportsfest (48)
6. Atlanta (57)
7. Smoky Mountain (61)
8. Blue Angel (62)
9. Charlotte (66)
10. Rocket City (69)

Northeast Region

1. Marine Corps (3)
2. New York City (4)
3. Boston (6)
4. Vermont City (14)
5. Cape Cod (26)
6. Ocean State (28)
7. Philadelphia (34)
8. Pittsburgh (38)
9. Wineglass (39)
10. New Hampshire (45)

MARATHON RANKINGS

Canada
1. Vancouver (12)
2. Royal Victoria (18)
3. Calgary (31)
4. National Capital (33)
5. Montreal (35)
6. Canadian International (46)
7. Marathon By The Sea (50)
8. Manitoba (79)
9. Forest City (82)

Looking for a Fast Time?
Fastest Seasonal Marathons

Winter
1. Houston (2)
2. Austin (4)
3. California International (11)
4. Walt Disney (12)
5. Las Vegas (13)
6. Mardi Gras (16)
7. Rocket City (19)
8. Kiawah Island (27)
9. Blue Angel (37)
10. Honolulu (42)

Spring
1. Pittsburgh (6)
2. Cleveland (7)
3. Boston (8)
4. Los Angeles (18)
5. Shamrock (20)
6. Napa Valley (28)
7. Lake County (31)
8. Avenue of the Giants (36)
9. National Capital (38)
10. Forest City (41)

Summer
1. Grandma's (14)
2. Calgary (29)

Fall
1. Chicago (1)
2. Twin Cities (3)
3. Columbus (5)
4. New York City (9)
5. Detroit (10)
6. Philadelphia (15)
7. Marine Corps (17)
8. Fox Cities (21)
9. Lakefront (22)
10. Portland (23)
11. Canadian International (24)
12. Seattle (25)
13. Northern Central Trail (26)
14. Toe to Tow (30)
15. San Antonio (32)
16. Hartford (33)
17. Humboldt (34)
18. Santa Clarita (35)
19. Wineglass (39)
20. Montreal (40)

Looking for a Fast Time in Your Own Backyard?
Fastest Marathons by Region

Pacific Region
1. California International (11)
2. Los Angeles (18)
3. Portland (23)
4. Seattle (25)
5. Napa Valley (28)
6. Humboldt Redwoods (34)
7. Santa Clarita (35)
8. Avenue of the Giants (36)
9. Honolulu (42)
10. Sacramento (43)

Southwest/Mountain Region
1. Houston (2)
2. Austin (4)
3. Las Vegas (13)
4. San Antonio (32)
5. Lincoln (44)
6. Dallas White Rock (51)
7. Cowtown (52)
8. St. George (57)
9. Coeur d'Alene (59)
10. White Sands (67)

Midwest Region
1. Chicago (1)
2. Twin Cities (3)
3. Columbus (5)
4. Cleveland (7)
5. Detroit (10)
6. Grandma's (14)
7. Fox Cities (21)
8. Lakefront (22)
9. Toe to Tow (30)
10. Lake County (31)

South Region
1. Walt Disney World (12)
2. Mardi Gras (16)
3. Rocket City (19)
4. Shamrock (20)
5. Kiawah Island (27)

Northeast Region
1. Pittsburgh (6)
2. Boston (8)
3. New York City (9)
4. Philadelphia (15)
5. Marine Corps (17)
6. Northern Central Trail (26)
7. Hartford (33)
8. Wineglass (39)
9. Dutchess County (48)
10. Vermont City (49)

Canada
1. Canadian International (24)
2. Calgary (29)
3. National Capital (38)
4. Montreal (40)
5. Forest City (41)
6. Royal Victoria (46)
7. Vancouver (48)
8. Manitoba (55)
9. Marathon By The Sea (60)

Easy Riders
Easiest Courses
1. Northern Central Trail
2. Austin
3. Chicago
4. Las Vegas
5. Seattle
6. Houston
7. Mardi Gras
8. Shamrock Sportsfest
9. Detroit

M A R A T H O N   R A N K I N G S

10. Toe to Tow
11. Cleveland
12. Avenue of the Giants
13. Humboldt Redwoods
14. Lakefront
15. Napa Valley
16. Philadelphia
17. Kiawah Island
18. Twin Cities
19. California International
20. Columbus
21. Grandma's
22. Walt Disney World
23. Rocket City
24. Lake County
25. Canadian International

What Was I Thinking?
Most Difficult Marathons

1. Leadville Mosquito
2. Pikes Peak
3. Monster Trail
4. Equinox
5. Nanisivik Midnight Sun
6. Whiskey Row
7. Gold Country
8. Wild Wild West
9. Kilauea Volcano

10. NipMuck Trail
11. Crater Lake Rim
12. Wyoming
13. Catalina Island
14. Lake Tahoe
15. Running Fit Trail

Shower and Shampoo Specials
Top Trail Marathons

1. Catalina Island
2. Kilauea Volcano
3. Pikes Peak
4. Leadville Mosquito
5. Equinox
6. Trail Breaker
7. Monster Trail
8. Running Fit Trail
9. Wild Wild West
10. CBK Walnut Creek Trail

The Well-Oiled Machines
Best Organized Marathons

1. Portland
2. New York City
3. Houston
4. Los Angeles

5. Marine Corps
6. Boston
7. Columbus
8. Twin Cities
9. Chicago
10. Fox Cities
11. Austin
12. Cleveland
13. Grandma's
14. Pittsburgh
15. Big Sur
16. Honolulu
17. Walt Disney World
18. St. George
19. Memphis
20. Hartford
21. Lincoln
22. Vancouver
23. Detroit
24. Vermont City
25. Rocket City

Screamin' Meemies
Marathons With Best Crowd Support

1. New York City
2. Boston
3. Los Angeles
4. Houston
5. Chicago
6. Twin Cities
7. Pittsburgh
8. Columbus
9. Fox Cities
10. Deseret News

Virgin Voyages
Top Marathons For First Timers

1. Marine Corps
2. Walt Disney World
3. Portland
4. Twin Cities
5. Fox Cities
6. Chicago
7. Columbus
8. New York City
9. Vermont City
10. Houston
11. National Capital
12. Austin
13. Pittsburgh
14. Grandma's
15. Mayor's Midnight Sun
16. San Francisco
17. Montreal
18. Los Angeles
19. Cleveland
20. Humboldt Redwoods

The Road Less Traveled
With Plenty of Leg Room (under 500 runners)
Best Small Marathons

1. Humboldt Redwoods
2. Avenue of the Giants
3. Mardi Gras
4. Kilauea Volcano
5. New Hampshire
6. Marathon By The Sea
7. Steamboat
8. Silver State
9. Lake Geneva
10. Walker North
11. Smoky Mountain
12. Leadville Mosquito
13. Equinox
14. Dutchess County
15. East Lyme
16. Paavo Nurmi
17. Northern Central Trail
18. Manitoba
19. Monster Trail
20. Forest City

COURSE PROFILES

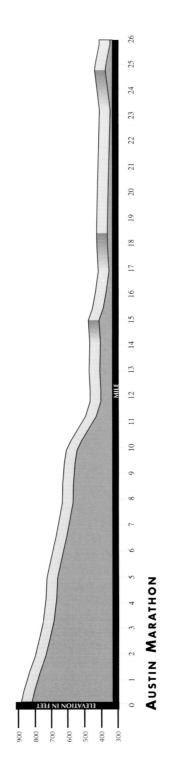

AUSTIN MARATHON

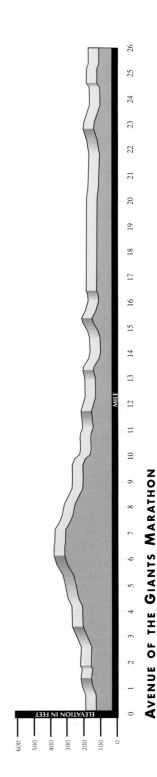

AVENUE OF THE GIANTS MARATHON

311

Course Profiles

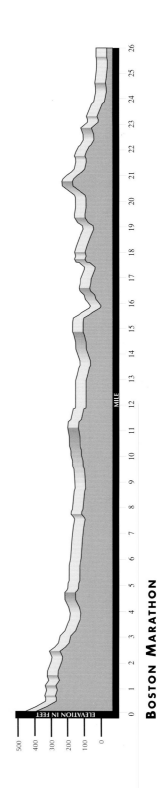

Big Sur Marathon

ELEVATION IN FEET

500 400 300 200 100 0

MILE

0 1 2 3 4 5 6 7 8 9 10 11 12 13 14 15 16 17 18 19 20 21 22 23 24 25 26

Boston Marathon

ELEVATION IN FEET

500 400 300 200 100 0

MILE

0 1 2 3 4 5 6 7 8 9 10 11 12 13 14 15 16 17 18 19 20 21 22 23 24 25 26

COURSE PROFILES

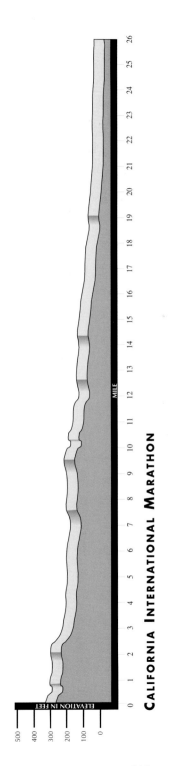

ELEVATION IN FEET

CALIFORNIA INTERNATIONAL MARATHON

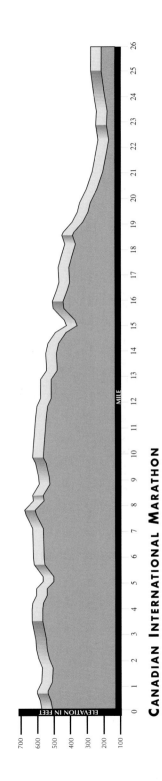

ELEVATION IN FEET

CANADIAN INTERNATIONAL MARATHON

COURSE PROFILES

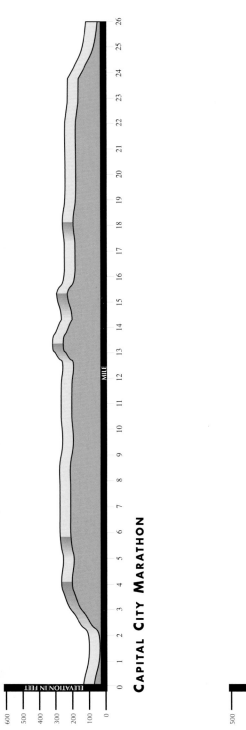

CAPITAL CITY MARATHON

ELEVATION IN FEET

600
500
400
300
200
100
0

MILE

0 1 2 3 4 5 6 7 8 9 10 11 12 13 14 15 16 17 18 19 20 21 22 23 24 25 26

CAROLINA MARATHON

ELEVATION IN FEET

500
400
300
200
100
0

MILE

0 1 2 3 4 5 6 7 8 9 10 11 12 13 14 15 16 17 18 19 20 21 22 23 24 25 26

COURSE PROFILES

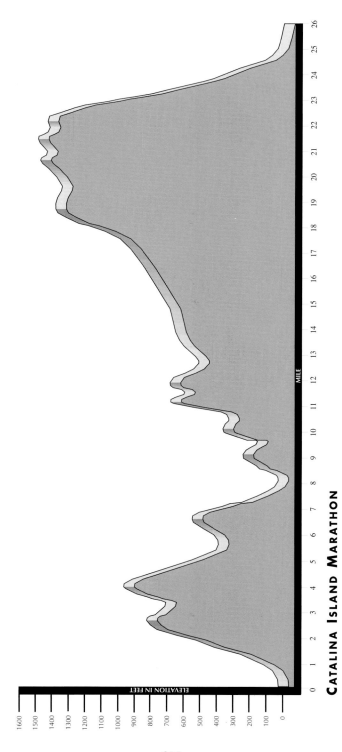

ELEVATION IN FEET

1600 1500 1400 1300 1200 1100 1000 900 800 700 600 500 400 300 200 100 0

MILE

0 1 2 3 4 5 6 7 8 9 10 11 12 13 14 15 16 17 18 19 20 21 22 23 24 25 26

CATALINA ISLAND MARATHON

COURSE PROFILES

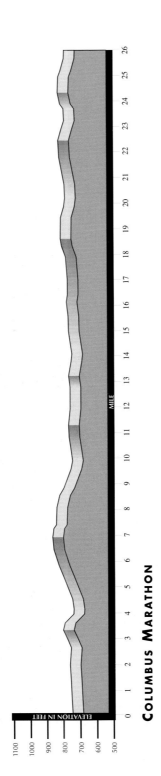

COLUMBUS MARATHON

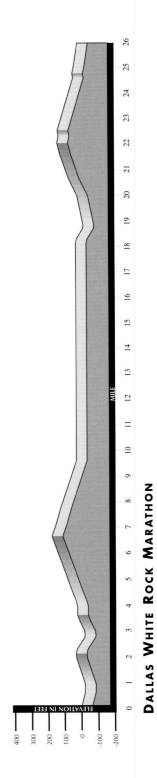

DALLAS WHITE ROCK MARATHON

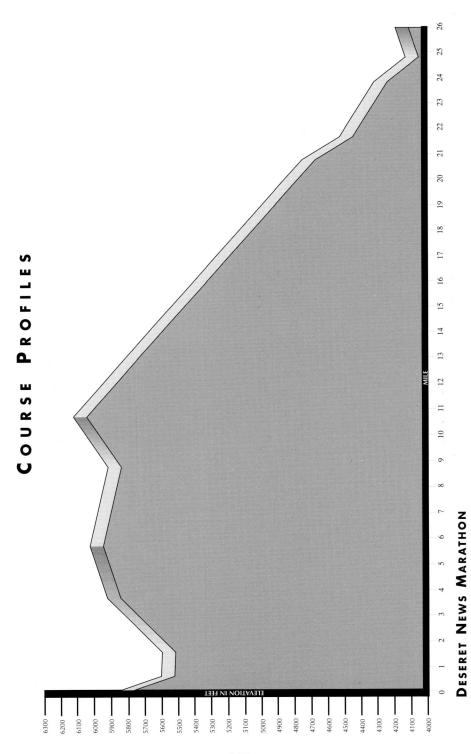

DESERET NEWS MARATHON

ELEVATION IN FEET

6300
6200
6100
6000
5900
5800
5700
5600
5500
5400
5300
5200
5100
5000
4900
4800
4700
4600
4500
4400
4300
4200
4100
4000

0 1 2 3 4 5 6 7 8 9 10 11 12 13 14 15 16 17 18 19 20 21 22 23 24 25 26

MILE

Course Profiles

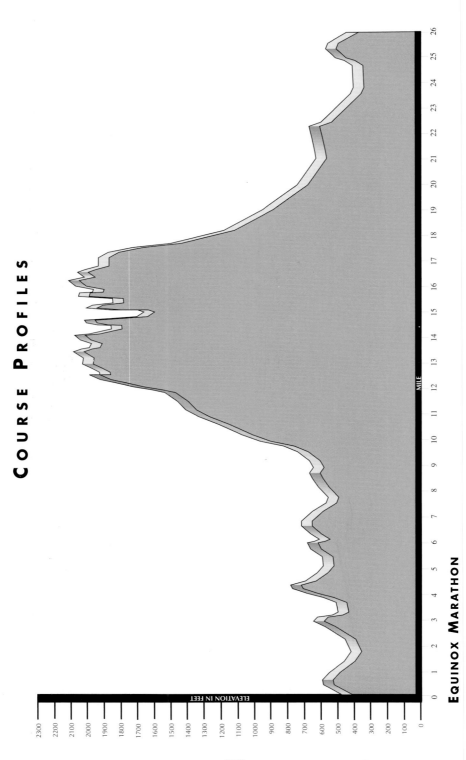

EQUINOX MARATHON

ELEVATION IN FEET

2300 2200 2100 2000 1900 1800 1700 1600 1500 1400 1300 1200 1100 1000 900 800 700 600 500 400 300 200 100 0

MILE

0 1 2 3 4 5 6 7 8 9 10 11 12 13 14 15 16 17 18 19 20 21 22 23 24 25 26

Course Profiles

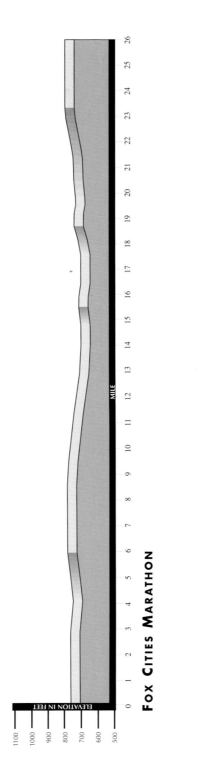

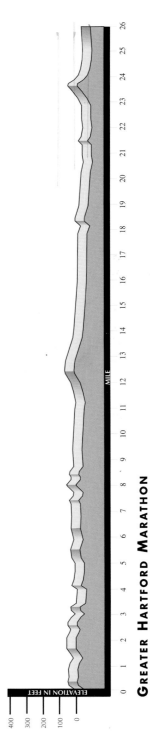

ELEVATION IN FEET

FOX CITIES MARATHON

ELEVATION IN FEET

GREATER HARTFORD MARATHON

319

COURSE PROFILES

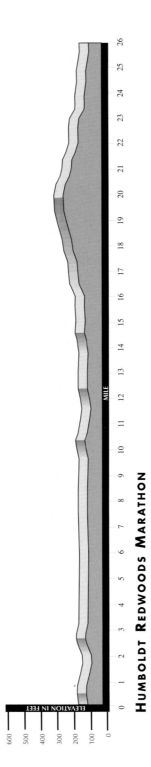

HUMBOLDT REDWOODS MARATHON

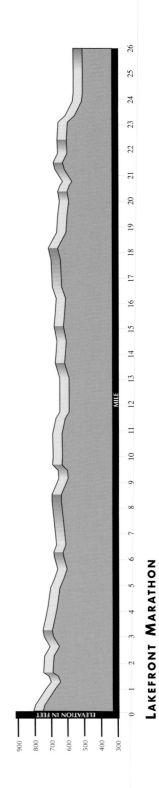

LAKEFRONT MARATHON

Course Profiles

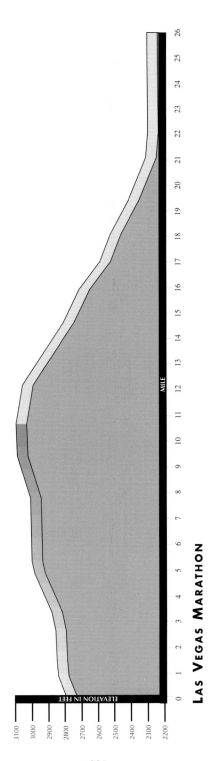

Las Vegas Marathon

ELEVATION IN FEET

3100 3000 2900 2800 2700 2600 2500 2400 2300 2200

MILE

0 1 2 3 4 5 6 7 8 9 10 11 12 13 14 15 16 17 18 19 20 21 22 23 24 25 26

COURSE PROFILES

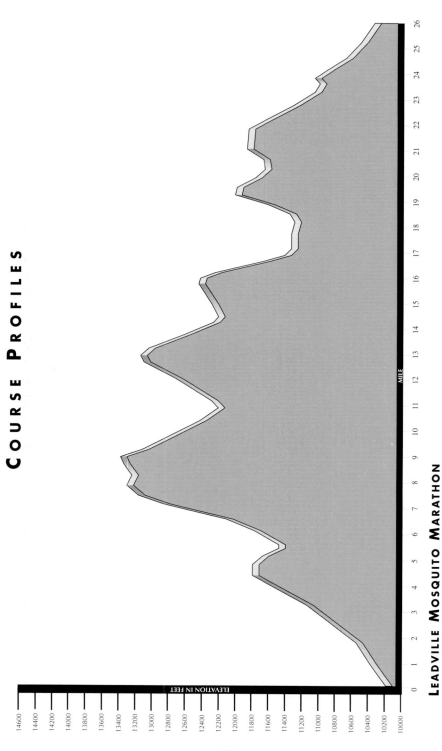

LEADVILLE MOSQUITO MARATHON
NOTE: ACTUAL VERTICAL SCALE IS DOUBLE THAT SHOWN.

ELEVATION IN FEET

14600
14400
14200
14000
13800
13600
13400
13200
13000
12800
12600
12400
12200
12000
11800
11600
11400
11200
11000
10800
10600
10400
10200
10000

MILE

0 1 2 3 4 5 6 7 8 9 10 11 12 13 14 15 16 17 18 19 20 21 22 23 24 25 26

Course Profiles

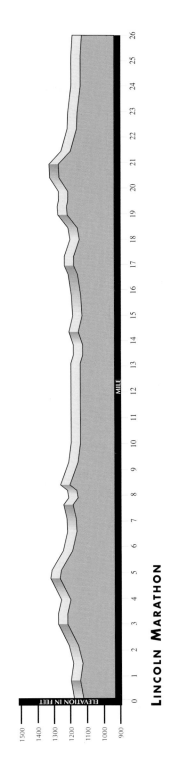

LINCOLN MARATHON

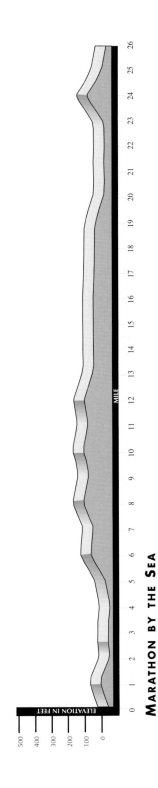

MARATHON BY THE SEA

Course Profiles

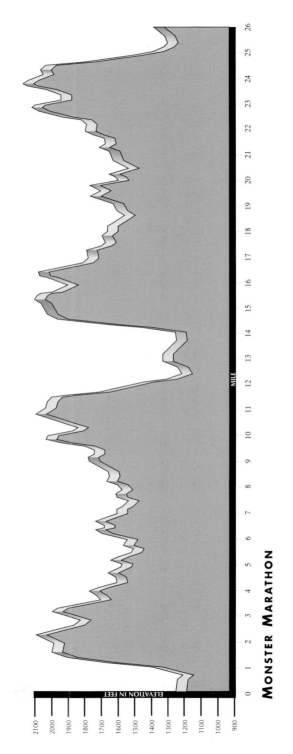

ELEVATION IN FEET

2100 2000 1900 1800 1700 1600 1500 1400 1300 1200 1100 1000 900

MILE

0 1 2 3 4 5 6 7 8 9 10 11 12 13 14 15 16 17 18 19 20 21 22 23 24 25 26

MONSTER MARATHON

Course Profiles

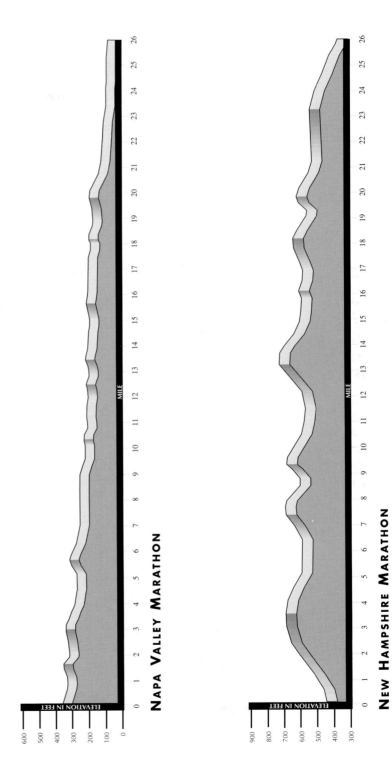

Napa Valley Marathon

ELEVATION IN FEET
600 500 400 300 200 100 0

MILE
0 1 2 3 4 5 6 7 8 9 10 11 12 13 14 15 16 17 18 19 20 21 22 23 24 25 26

New Hampshire Marathon

ELEVATION IN FEET
900 800 700 600 500 400 300

MILE
0 1 2 3 4 5 6 7 8 9 10 11 12 13 14 15 16 17 18 19 20 21 22 23 24 25 26

Course Profiles

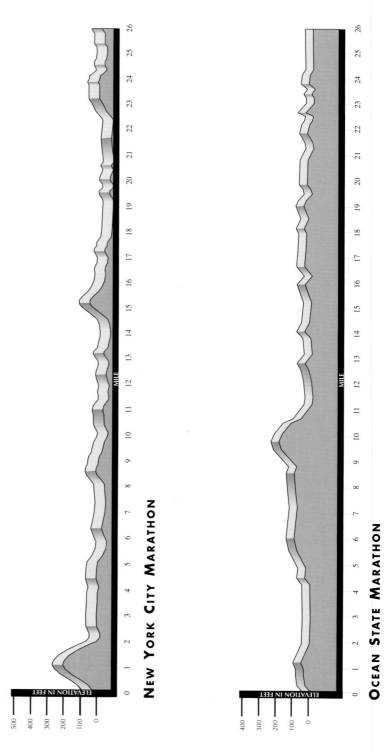

ELEVATION IN FEET

500 400 300 200 100 0

NEW YORK CITY MARATHON

MILE

0 1 2 3 4 5 6 7 8 9 10 11 12 13 14 15 16 17 18 19 20 21 22 23 24 25 26

ELEVATION IN FEET

400 300 200 100 0

OCEAN STATE MARATHON

MILE

0 1 2 3 4 5 6 7 8 9 10 11 12 13 14 15 16 17 18 19 20 21 22 23 24 25 26

COURSE PROFILES

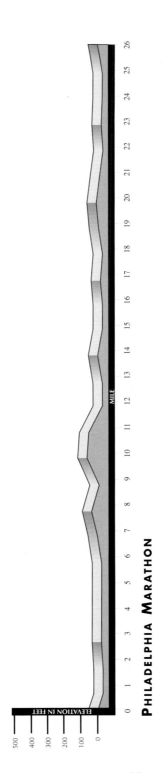

PHILADELPHIA MARATHON

ELEVATION IN FEET

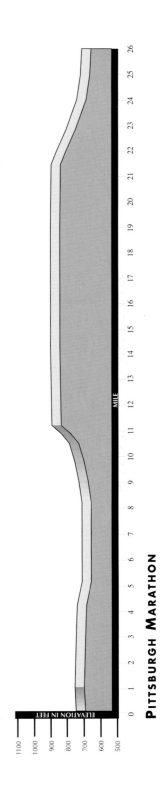

PITTSBURGH MARATHON

ELEVATION IN FEET

COURSE PROFILES

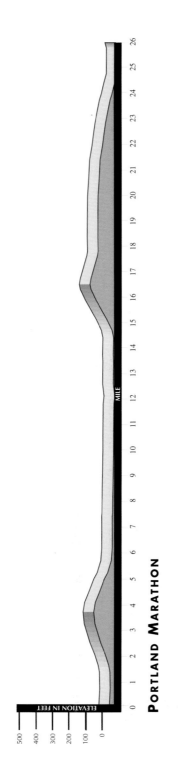

PORTLAND MARATHON

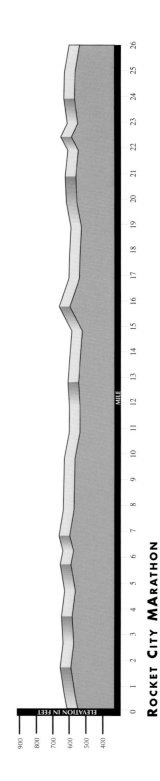

ROCKET CITY MARATHON

COURSE PROFILES

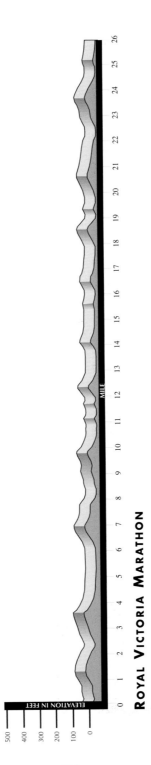

ROYAL VICTORIA MARATHON

COURSE PROFILES
ST. GEORGE MARATHON

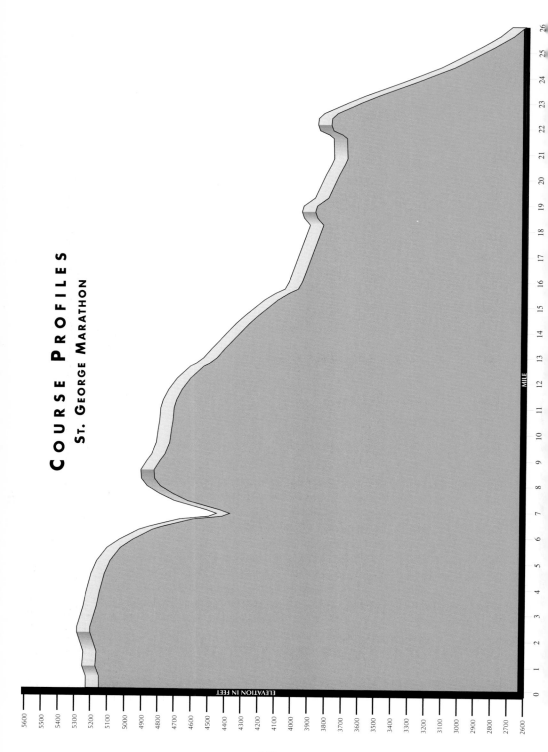

ELEVATION IN FEET

5600 5500 5400 5300 5200 5100 5000 4900 4800 4700 4600 4500 4400 4300 4200 4100 4000 3900 3800 3700 3600 3500 3400 3300 3200 3100 3000 2900 2800 2700 2600

MILE

0 1 2 3 4 5 6 7 8 9 10 11 12 13 14 15 16 17 18 19 20 21 22 23 24 25 26

COURSE PROFILES

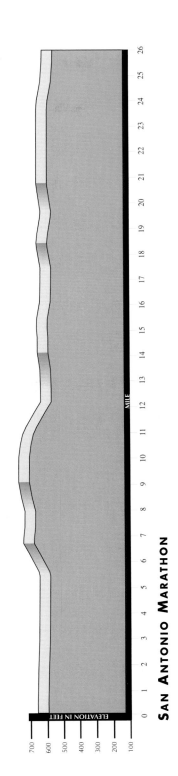

SAN ANTONIO MARATHON

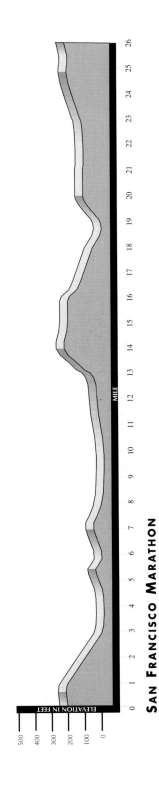

SAN FRANCISCO MARATHON

Course Profiles

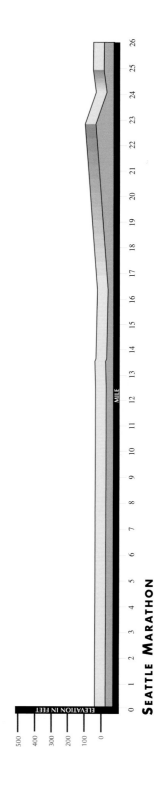

Santa Clarita Marathon

ELEVATION IN FEET

1900 1800 1700 1600 1500 1400 1300 1200 1100 1000 900

0 1 2 3 4 5 6 7 8 9 10 11 12 13 14 15 16 17 18 19 20 21 22 23 24 25 26

MILE

Seattle Marathon

ELEVATION IN FEET

500 400 300 200 100 0

0 1 2 3 4 5 6 7 8 9 10 11 12 13 14 15 16 17 18 19 20 21 22 23 24 25 26

MILE

Course Profiles

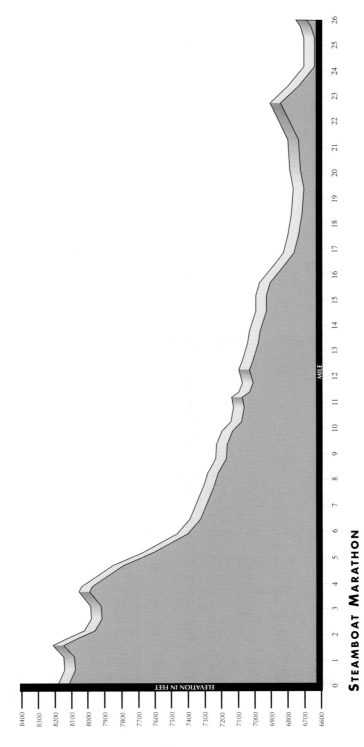

ELEVATION IN FEET

8400
8300
8200
8100
8000
7900
7800
7700
7600
7500
7400
7300
7200
7100
7000
6900
6800
6700
6600

0 1 2 3 4 5 6 7 8 9 10 11 12 13 14 15 16 17 18 19 20 21 22 23 24 25 26

MILE

Steamboat Marathon

Course Profiles

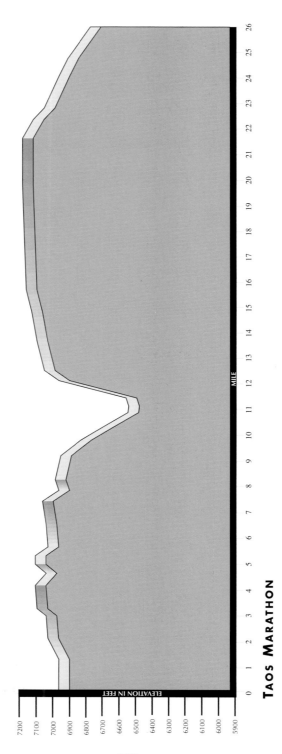

TAOS MARATHON

COURSE PROFILES

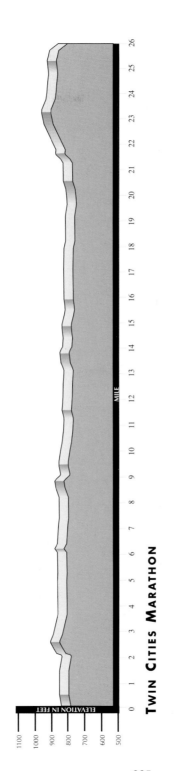

TWIN CITIES MARATHON

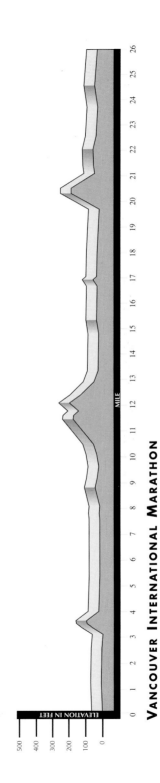

VANCOUVER INTERNATIONAL MARATHON

COURSE PROFILES

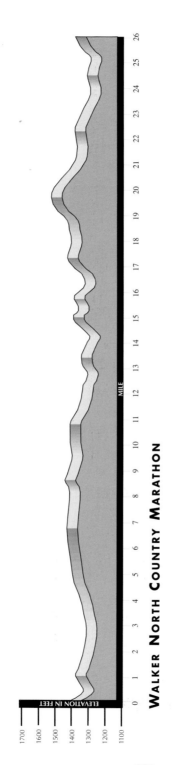

WALKER NORTH COUNTRY MARATHON

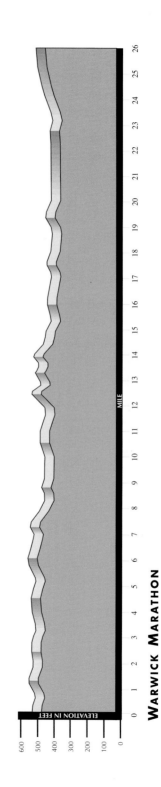

WARWICK MARATHON

Course Profiles

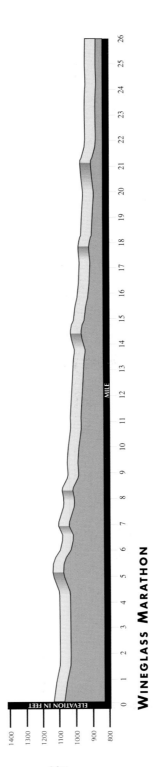

WINEGLASS MARATHON

ELEVATION IN FEET

1400
1300
1200
1100
1000
900
800

MILE

0 1 2 3 4 5 6 7 8 9 10 11 12 13 14 15 16 17 18 19 20 21 22 23 24 25 26

INDEX

BY STATE & PROVINCE

UNITED STATES

MISSISSIPPI
Mississippi Marathon, 301
MISSOURI
Olympiad Memorial Marathon, 263
St. Louis Marathon, 295
MONTANA
Governor's Cup "Ghost Town"
  Marathon, 103
NEBRASKA
Lincoln Marathon, 71
Omaha Riverfront Marathon, 297
NEVADA
Las Vegas International
  Marathon, 27
Silver State Marathon, 140
NEW HAMPSHIRE
Clarence DeMar Marathon, 289
New Hampshire Marathon, 168
NEW JERSEY
Atlantic City Marathon, 290
NEW MEXICO
Duke City Marathon, 163
Marathon de Taos, 110
Shiprock Marathon, 269
White Sands/
  Alamogordo Marathon, 239
NEW YORK
Dutchess County Marathon, 150
Hudson Mohawk Marathon, 262
Long Island Marathon, 270
Mohawk Hudson Marathon, 295
Monster Trail Marathon, 142
New York City Marathon, 218
Warwick Marathon, 222
Wineglass Marathon, 182
Yonkers Marathon, 184
NORTH CAROLINA
Charlotte Observer Marathon, 13
Grandfather Mountain
  Marathon, 120
NORTH DAKOTA
Bismark Marathon, 285
OHIO
Athens Marathon, 265
Cleveland Marathon, 77
Columbus Marathon, 226
Glass City Marathon, 267
Michigan/Ohio Marathon, 281
Toe to Tow Marathon, 193
OKLAHOMA
Andy Payne Marathon, 274
Gage Roadrunner Marathon, 272
Tulsa Marathon, 299

OREGON
Crater Lake Rim Marathon, 282
Portland Marathon, 158
Trail's End Marathon, 264
PENNSYLVANIA
God's Country Marathon, 276
Harrisburg Marathon, 298
Johnstown YMCA Marathon, 290
Marathon of the Roses, 144
Philadelphia Marathon, 231
Pittsburgh Marathon, 74
RHODE ISLAND
Ocean State Marathon, 215
SOUTH CAROLINA
Carolina Marathon, 25
Kiawah Island Marathon, 253
SOUTH DAKOTA
Longest Day Marathon, 266
Mount Rushmore International
  Marathon, 292
TENNESSEE
Andrew Jackson Marathon, 296
Chickamauga Battlefield
  Marathon, 298
Memphis Marathon, 246
Music City Marathon, 265
Smoky Mountain Marathon, 38
TEXAS
Army Medcom Marathon, 268
Austin Marathon, 30
Cowtown Marathon, 36
Dallas White Rock Marathon, 241
Houston Marathon, 18
Lone Star Paper Chase
  Marathon, 273
San Antonio Marathon, 229
UTAH
Deseret News Marathon, 129
St. George Marathon, 170
VERMONT
Green Mountain Marathon, 294
Vermont City Marathon, 98
VIRGINIA
Marine Corps Marathon, 211
Richmond Times/
  Dispatch Marathon, 293
Shamrock Sportsfest Marathon, 54
WASHINGTON
Capital City Marathon, 90
Seattle Marathon, 237
WEST VIRGINIA
Ridge Runner Marathon, 277

WISCONSIN
American Odyssey Marathon, 287
Fox Cities Marathon, 165
Lakefront Marathon, 189
Lake Geneva Marathon, 84
Madison Marathon, 96
Paavo Nurmi Marathon, 133
Pine Line Marathon, 267
Sugar River Trail Marathon, 288
Trail Breaker Marathon, 56
WYOMING
Wyoming Marathon, 274

CANADA

ALBERTA
Beaverlodge to Grand Prairie
  Marathon, 286
Calgary Miracle Marathon, 118
Edmonton Festival Marathon, 284
Fort McMurray Oil Sands
  Marathon, 287
BAFFIN ISLAND
Nanisivik Midnight Sun
  Marathon, 280
BRITISH COLUMBIA
Royal Victoria Marathon, 80
Vancouver International
  Marathon, 80
MANITOBA
Manitoba Marathon, 108
NEW BRUNSWICK
Marathon By The Sea, 135
Marathon De La Baie
  Des Chaleurs, 275
NORTHWEST TERRITORIES
Yellowknife Marathon, 298
NOVA SCOTIA
Johnny Miles Marathon, 271
Nova Scotia Marathon, 281
Valley Harvest Marathon , 293
ONTARIO
Canadian International
  Marathon, 195
Forest City Marathon, 86
Friendly Massey Marathon, 280
National Capital Marathon, 88
Twin Lakes Marathon, 289
PRINCE EDWARD ISLAND
Island Marathon, 284
QUEBEC
Marathon de l'île de Montreal, 152
SASKATCHEWAN
Saskatchewan Marathon, 286

PHOTOGRAPHER CREDITS

Maui Marathon Sweepstakes

(No Purchase Required For Entry)

Maui Marathon and the Valley Isle Road Runners Association congratulate you on your purchase of **The Ultimate Guide to Marathons.** The Guide is a valuable tool in selecting marathons best suited to your interests. In order to encourage participation in the exciting sport of marathon running, Maui Marathon and the Valley Isle Road Runners Association are pleased to provide one lucky winner, subject to the terms and rules indicated below, a trip for two to the 1998 Maui Marathon, one of The Guide's top 10 destination marathons in North America, scheduled for March 29,1998. The trip will consist of the following:

- Complimentary entry for one person and one accompanying person into the 1998 Maui Marathon and all race-related activities, including the pre-race dinner;
- Complimentary, single-room accommodations for one person and one accompanying person at the Headquarters Hotel, the Maui Marriott, for four days and three nights;
- Complimentary rental of one compact car for 4 days during the 1998 Maui Marathon; and
- Complimentary round trip economy airfare for two persons traveling together from any city in the continental United States served by a major airline with service to Honolulu. The Maui Marathon reserves the right to approve the travel route and airline.

No purchase is necessary in order to enter this sweepstakes. Rules and terms are listed below.

How To Enter:

Send the following information on a 3" x 5" postcard to the address indicated below:

Your name, address, phone number, age on December 15, 1997, country of citizenship, signature, where you heard about The Guide, and, if you purchased The Guide, the place of purchase.

Maui Marathon Sweepstakes
c/o Marathon Publishers, Inc.
P.O. Box 19027
Sacramento, CA 95819

Rules & Terms:

Please print or type your entry. Entries must be postmarked by November 1, 1997 to be eligible for the drawing. All entries postmarked after November 1, 1997 will not be entered into the drawing and will be discarded.

The Winner will be randomly chosen in a drawing conducted by the officials of Marathon Publishers on or before December 15, 1997. Only the winner will be notified of the results. By entering the Maui Marathon Sweepstakes, the winner agrees to allow his or her likeness to be used by the Maui Marathon, and/or the Valley Isle Road Runners Association for any promotional purposes.

Winner agrees to hold Maui Marathon, Valley Isle Road Runners Association, Marathon Publishers, Inc. and any of their owners, officers, agents or employees harmless for any injury or damages that result from any portion of the trip or events discussed herein. Winner agrees that if the Maui Marathon is canceled as the result of an Act of God or other unforseen occurrence, the entire trip will be canceled, and Winner shall not be entitled to any compensation whatsoever.

All travel arrangements must be coordinated with and approved by the Maui Marathon and/or the Valley Isle Road Runners Association. You must be at least 18 years of age on or before December 15,1997 to enter the 1998 Maui Marathon Sweepstakes. All entrants must be U.S. or Canadian citizens. This sweepstakes promotion is void where prohibited by law.

ABOUT THE AUTHORS

Dennis Craythorn is president of Marathon Publishers, Inc., a Sacramento-based publisher of running-related books. A runner since junior high school, he has written or co-written several publications on international trade policy and is a published fiction writer. Thirty-years-old, Mr. Craythorn obtained his MSFS from Georgetown University and BA from the University of California — Davis.

Rich Hanna is a veteran of more than 35 marathons and ultramarathons. Mr. Hanna is a two-time U.S. National 100K champion and has represented the United States in several international competitions. He is also a well-known national-class marathoner and has been ranked among the top 25 Americans at that distance. With a personal best 2:17 marathon, Mr. Hanna qualified to run in the 1996 U.S. Olympic Marathon Trials. Executive vice president of Marathon Publishers, Inc., Mr. Hanna contributes his extensive marathon experience as a personal running trainer, radio host, and coach of the Sacramento Chapter of the Leukemia Society's Team in Training program in his spare time. Thirty-two-years-old, Mr. Hanna received his BA from the University of California — Davis.

Both authors live in Sacramento, California.